Malcolm M. MacFarlane
Editor

Family Treatment of Personality Disorders
Advances in Clinical Practice

Pre-publication
REVIEWS,
COMMENTARIES,
EVALUATIONS . . .

"**D**esigned for family therapy practitioners and for clinicians who wish to broaden the scope of their assessment and intervention skills, this book breaks new ground both in its practical use of family therapy modalities in the treatment of personality disorders and in its integration of theory and approaches for matching strategies to the needs of the particular person, disorder, severity level, and family system. Various combinations of personality disorders are examined in a structured chapter format that facilitates careful assessment that may lead to more effective interventions for individuals and their families. Of particular note are the three overview chapters that provide a grounding in the use of family therapy for personality disorders and the chapter by the editor that illustrates an 'integrative approach' in treating persons with borderline personality disorder (BPD). Here, BPD (a

diagnosis that is off-putting to many clinicians) is approached in a respectful and skillful manner that truly integrates theory and practice and includes recognition and use of cultural variables in the treatment setting."

Taylor B. Anderson, MSW, LSW, CPRP
Associate Director,
Division of Behavioral
Healthcare Education,
Department of Psychiatry,
Drexel University College of Medicine

"**I**ntegrating biological, behavioral, and family systems perspectives, this book offers an intelligent overall approach and some unique models for mitigating the effects of personality disorders and making life easier for all concerned."

Harriet P. Lefley, PhD
Professor of Psychiatry
and Behavioral Sciences,
University of Miami
School of Medicine

More pre-publication
REVIEWS, COMMENTARIES, EVALUATIONS . . .

"This book is an excellent compilation devoted to working with families of individuals with personality disorders. The chapters, authored by a cadre of seasoned clinicians, cover the broad range of different personality disorders. An excellent description of each disorder is provided, as well as consideration of the effects of the disorder on the dynamics of family and couple relationships. The book is replete with clinical vignettes, case descriptions, and practical advice for clinicians working with families. A variety of different family therapy models for working with individuals with personality disorders are explicated, with the major emphasis on providing theory driven but practical advice for family work. This book meets a critical and unmet need for therapists working with families and couples, and deserves a place on the shelf of every family therapist."

Kim T. Mueser, PhD
Professor of Psychiatry
and Community
and Family Medicine,
Dartmouth Medical School

"Malcolm MacFarlane has produced a wonderful and important book on the family treatment of personality disorders. Supported by rich and detailed clinical material and in-depth discussions of theoretical perspectives, this is a valuable text for any clinician interested in personality disorders and family treatment. The book

benefits from a thoughtful structure that allows each chapter to closely explore a particular personality disorder. Each chapter presents a mode of family treatment and discusses important considerations, such as cultural and gender issues, the handling of crises and transference issues, and the strengths and limitations of the model. In particular, the opening overview and the chapter on object relations theory should be required reading for all clinicians. This is the first book I have seen that covers so much important clinical ground in such an in-depth and careful manner. This book will usher in a new era of study in the use of family therapy in the treatment of personality disorders."

James A. Marley, PhD
Assistant Professor, Loyola University
Chicago School of Social Work;
Author, *Family Involvement*
in Treating Schizophrenia: Models,
Essential Skills, and Process

"A great step forward for clinicians in understanding the interplay between family dynamics and personality disorders. . . . Offers a sound explication of the major personality disorders."

Craig A. Everett, PhD
Co-author, *Short-Term Family*
Therapy with Borderline Patients
and *Family Therapy*
with Borderline Disorders;
Past President, American Association
for Marriage and Family Therapy;
Editor, *Journal of Divorce and Remarriage*

Family Treatment of Personality Disorders
Advances in Clinical Practice

HAWORTH Marriage and Family Therapy
Terry S. Trepper, PhD
Senior Editor

Family Treatment of Personality Disorders
Advances in Clinical Practice

Malcolm M. MacFarlane
Editor

The Haworth Clinical Practice Press
An Imprint of The Haworth Press, Inc.
New York • London • Oxford

Published by

The Haworth Clinical Practice Press, an imprint of The Haworth Press, Inc., 10 Alice Street, Binghamton, NY 13904-1580.

PUBLISHER'S NOTE
Identities and circumstances of individuals discussed in this book have been changed to protect confidentiality.

Cover design by Jennifer M. Gaska.

Library of Congress Cataloging-in-Publication Data

Family treatment of personality disorders : advances in clinical practice / Malcolm M. MacFarlane, editor.
     p. cm.
Includes bibliographical references and index.
    ISBN 0-7890-1789-X (case : alk. paper)—ISBN 0-7890-1790-3 (soft : alk. paper)
    1. Personality disorders—Treatment. 2. Family psychotherapy. 3. Marital psychotherapy.
I. MacFarlane, Malcolm M.
   RC554.F35 2004
   616.89'156—dc22
                                                           2003014621

CONTENTS

Chapter 3. An Object-Relations Approach to the Treatment of Personality-Disordered Marriages   71

Charles C. McCormack

PART II: SPECIFIC DISORDERS

Chapter 4. Marital and Family Treatment of Borderline Personality Disorder   117

Judith K. Kreisman
Jerold J. Kreisman

Peter D. McLean
Carmen P. McLean

Christine Ann Lawson

ABOUT THE EDITOR

Malcolm M. MacFarlane, MA, is a graduate of the California Family Study Center in Burbank, California (now renamed the Phillips Graduate Institute in Encino, California), with a master of arts in marriage, family, and child therapy. He is a clinical member and an approved supervisor with the American Association for Marriage and Family Therapy (AAMFT), and is a registered marriage and family therapist with the Registry of Marriage and Family Therapists in Canada and the Ontario Association for Marriage and Family Therapy.

Mr. MacFarlane has worked as a frontline mental health clinician for twenty years and is currently employed as a mental health therapist with Ross Memorial Hospital Community Counselling Services in Lindsay, Ontario. He has been a contributor to a number of professional journals as well as editor of the text *Family Therapy and Mental Health: Innovations in Theory and Practice* (Haworth). In addition, he is editor of the "Family Therapy and Mental Health" section of the *Journal of Family Psychotherapy,* and is on the editorial advisory board of *Contemporary Family Therapy.*

Mr. MacFarlane has been a presenter at a number of AAMFT conferences, and presented a workshop titled "Family Therapy and Mental Health: 2000 and Beyond" at the AAMFT Millennium Summit Conference in Denver, Colorado, in 2000. He has qualified as an expert witness in the area of social work practice and family dynamics in family court.

CONTRIBUTORS

Lorna Smith Benjamin, PhD, FDHC, Professor of Psychology and Adjunct Professor of Psychiatry, University of Utah, Salt Lake City.

Jon Carlson, PsyD, EdD, ABPP, Distinguished Professor of Psychology and Counseling, Governors State University, University Park, Illinois, and Psychologist, Wellness Clinic, Lake Geneva, Wisconsin.

Gretta Cushing, MS, Senior Research Associate, Casey Family Services, Shelton, Connecticut.

Marsha J. Harman, PhD, Associate Professor, Department of Psychology and Philosophy, Sam Houston State University, Huntsville, Texas.

Jerold J. Kreisman, MD, FAPA, Associate Clinical Professor, Department of Psychiatry, St. Louis University, St. Louis, Missouri.

Judith K. Kreisman, MSW, LCSW, Adjunct Assistant Professor, Department of Social Service, St. Louis University, St. Louis, Missouri.

Christine Ann Lawson, PhD, LCSW, Independent Practice, Zionsville, Indiana.

Paul S. Links, MD, FRCPC, Professor of Psychiatry and Arthur Sommer Rotenberg Chair in Suicide Studies, University of Toronto, and St. Michael's Hospital, Toronto.

Jeffrey J. Magnavita, PhD, ABPP, Fellow of the American Psychological Association and Diplomate in Professional Psychology; Founder of the Connecticut Center for Short-Term Dynamic Psychotherapy; Adjunct Professor in Clinical Psychology, University of Hartford, West Hartford, Connecticut.

Charles C. McCormack, MA, MSW, LCSW-C, BCD, Independent Practice, Towson, Maryland; Faculty, Residency Training Program, Sheppard and Enoch Pratt Hospital, Towson, Maryland; Visiting Faculty, Couple Psychotherapy Training Program, Washington School of Psychiatry, Washington, DC.

Carmen P. McLean, BA, Research Associate, Fear and Anxiety Laboratory, Department of Psychology, University of British Columbia, Vancouver.

Peter D. McLean, PhD, Professor, Department of Psychiatry, University of British Columbia, and Director of the Anxiety Disorders Unit, UBC Hospital, Vancouver.

Kimberly A. Melton, BSc, Graduate Student, Master of Arts Program in School Psychology, Counseling and Psychology Department, Governors State University, University Park, Illinois.

William C. Nichols, EdD, ABPP, Adjunct Professor of Child and Family Development, University of Georgia, Athens.

Kim Snow, MA, Adjunct Faculty, Counseling and Psychology Department, Governors State University, University Park, Illinois.

Len Sperry, MD, PhD, Professor and Director, Doctoral Program in Counseling at Florida Atlantic University, Boca Raton, Florida, and Clinical Professor of Psychiatry and Behavioral Medicine, Medical College of Wisconsin, Milwaukee.

Michelle Stockwell, MHSc, Nurse Therapist, Independent Practice, and Nurse Therapist, Clinical Behavioural Sciences Program, Faculty of Health Sciences, McMaster University, Hamilton, Ontario, Canada.

Michael Waldo, PhD, Professor, Counseling and Educational Psychology Department, College of Education, New Mexico State University, Las Cruces.

Foreword

Anyone who has treated many cases of personality disorder has encountered patients who worked diligently to change their behavior only to have their attempts to change opposed or even ridiculed by family members. I clearly recall one such patient treated years ago for dysthymic symptoms and major problems with dependency. She was married to a controlling and, at times, abusive husband, and had several children and a large extended family. Many of her difficulties occurred because she could not manage the unrelenting demands of her family to care for sick relatives, baby-sit on demand, help with household routines, and perform numerous other tasks. An inability to say no left her feeling exhausted and harassed from attempts to meet endless expectations, incompetent because she could not cope with the many demands on her time, and despondent because her own needs were rarely meet. In individual therapy, she worked with considerable determination to understand and change this submissive pattern. As she learned more about the pattern and its impact on her mood, she realized that to overcome the dysthymia she had to take more control over her life by being more assertive. However, she could not implement this new learning. Attempts to be more assertive were rejected by her family and met with a barrage of complaints that she was self-centeredly unconcerned about them. Change was only possible when family sessions were successful in getting her husband's support for the changes she wanted to make and his help in dealing with the extended family.

Such cases are important reminders of the influence of situational factors on personality functioning and the extent to which the social world can form a powerful obstacle to change. They also indicate that it is often essential to incorporate family interventions into the change process. Yet many clinicians have been remarkably reluctant to use family therapy to treat personality disorders. Consequently, the publication of a book devoted to family therapy is an important advance and a useful addition to the therapeutic armamentarium for treating this condition. It is also a reminder of the renaissance of interest in personality disorder and an indication of the extent to which ideas about the disorder and its treatment are changing. Since the publication of the *Diagnostic and Statistical Manual of Mental Disorders,* Third Edition (DSM-III) in 1980, new approaches to treatment have appeared and optimism about the benefits of treating personality disorders has begun to replace therapeutic pessimism as evidence emerges that treatment can lead to considerable symptomatic improvement and enhanced quality of life.

Recently, it has become apparent that the study of personality disorders is undergoing a further change. Ideas about classification are changing: Many are coming to realize that the DSM system is not the last word in the classification of personality disorders, but rather a heuristic that brought preliminary order to the field as a prelude to the development of an empirically based system. Shifts are occurring in our understanding of the origins and development of personality pathology: earlier ideas about the psychosocial origins of the various conditions are being supplemented with an understanding of the role of biology and genetics. Similar changes are occurring in ideas about optimal treatment strategies. It is apparent that no single approach is effective in treating all cases or all aspects of psychopathology, and that a combination of strategies and interventions drawn from multiple therapeutic approaches are needed for comprehensive treatment. Ideas about treatment modalities are also changing. Although treatment continues to emphasize individual therapy, it is often more effective to use a combination of individual, group, and family therapy.

In this context, this book makes a valuable contribution. By bringing together descriptions of different approaches to a variety of conditions, it draws attention to the importance of family interventions and, equally important, to the need to understand the effects of the social system on the maladaptive interpersonal behavior that characterize personality disorders.

To this point, treatment has been dominated by individual therapy, often based on treatment models developed to treat other conditions. Little attention has been paid to helping families cope with the impact of having a member with a personality disorder or to changing family systems that contribute to the development and maintenance of maladaptive patterns. This emphasis on individual therapy is not surprising. Most traditional theories explain personality pathology in terms of internal dynamics, and conceptualize change largely in terms of modifying internal structures and processes. The environment is incorporated into these theories mainly as a factor contributing to the development of disorder. Such explanations are not necessarily wrong, but they are incomplete. Context is important, and dysfunctional relationships do not just contribute to the development of pathology—they also initiate and maintain maladaptive patterns throughout life. Under these circumstances, it is unrealistic to expect new patterns of relating to be implemented when the individual continues living in a social situation that instilled and continues to reinforce maladaptive ways.

It seems unlikely that family systems therapy will be the primary treatment modality for most patients. It is, however, an important adjunctive treatment in many cases and essential for some. As part of a comprehensive treatment plan, family therapy may be needed to: (1) enable patients to resolve the more intractable consequences of earlier relationship problems, (2) help families cope with the stresses and difficulties of having a member with severe personality problems, and (3) modulate contemporary family system functioning that reinforces maladaptive patterns or hinders change.

By drawing together a diverse set of approaches for a variety of disorders, Malcolm MacFarlane has performed a valuable service to the field. The array of ideas, concepts, and interventions is characteristic of all contemporary approaches to treating personality disorder. The field is still at an early stage of development and empirical information on the most effective approaches is sparse. The range of concepts and intervention strategies described is a healthy sign: it indicates that the field is active, moving forward, and beginning to define itself. This is a time of innovation prior to systematic empirical evaluation. The presentation of an array of approaches within the same book not only allows the clinician to compare different methods, but also encourages the critical appraisal of concepts and methods needed for the field to advance. At the same time, the text is replete with references to integration and integrative approaches, indicating widespread recognition that an array of interventions is needed that are tailored to the needs of the patient. This emphasis on integration should facilitate the inclusion of family systems therapy into comprehensive treatment plans. Clearly we are moving beyond the use of specific therapies developed by a few charismatic individuals toward more integrated and eclectic approaches that base interventions on evidence of efficacy and a critical analysis of what is needed to manage individual cases rather than the requirements of speculative theoretical models. It seems clear that in the future clinicians who wish to treat personality disorders using an evidence based approach will need to be adept at combining different interventions and in using a combination of individual, family, and group therapy. Personality disorders are not circumscribed conditions. They affect all aspects of the individual's personality, life, and relationships. To bring about lasting change it is necessary to target all components of this system using an array of interventions and modalities.

W. John Livesley, MD, PhD

Preface

As a family therapist working as a frontline clinician in a community mental health center, I have found that individuals with personality disorders are among the most interesting and challenging of the clients I treat. They are interesting, in part, because of the richness of opportunity for exploring internal processes, psychodynamics, and the roots of their disorders in family of origin interactions. This personal exploration, for me, is part of what psychotherapy is all about and one of the reasons I chose psychotherapy as a career. Individuals with personality disorders are particularly challenging because solidly rooted personality characteristics are often difficult to change, especially within the limited time frames that government and private-sector length of service and funding benchmarks provide for working with these clients. Such individuals are also challenging because their personality issues often interfere with routine, effective treatments of the Axis I disorders that are typically their reason for seeking therapy.

I believe that the fascination I have with personality disorders is shared by many other clinicians. Many reasons may account for this fascination. Part of it may be simply the clinical richness mentioned previously. For me, however, and I suspect for many others, the fascination also involves a real curiosity about how we become who we are and how our personalities are formed. A related question, or course, is what goes awry in normal development that results in the emergence of a personality disorder? Perhaps part of the fascination with personality disorders also lies in our recognition of aspects of our own personalities in our clients' disorders. I know that in my own early training, I often read through the DSM with some trepidation, recognizing similarities to myself in many of the diagnostic criteria for the personality disorders; yet never quite seeming to fit the complete profile. I suspect many other clinicians have had similar experiences. Personality disorders represent the often unacknowledged "shadow" parts of ourselves, and in helping our clients to deal with their personality issues, we also work through our own dark issues a little further.

Although they can be fascinating, I also detect a great deal of ambivalence in the field regarding working with individuals with personality disorders. Some part of this ambivalence may lie in the fact that personality disorders are challenging and difficult to treat. Therapists for whom rapid success and a "quick fix" is important to their sense of competence will tend to avoid working with individuals with personality disorders. Another reason therapists may eschew working with personality disorders may involve the challenges of the transference processes and the need to deal with the discomfort of clients' anger and other emotions directed at the therapist or acted out in the therapy session. Finally, many therapists may avoid working with these clients because of the frustration of funding restrictions which limit time available to work through complex personality issues.

I remember talking with a supervisor early in my family therapy training about my desire to do long-term therapy with individuals with personality disorders. She was discouraging of this goal, and told me that training in marriage and family therapy was not sufficient for doing this type of in-depth work. In retrospect, this supervisor was both right and wrong. She was right to the extent that an understanding of individual psychodynamic models and treatment methods is critical to working with personality-disordered individuals. Many marriage and family therapists, with their focus on understanding and treating relationships, are not well versed in individual psychodynamic approaches. She was wrong, however, in failing to recognize the valuable contribution that family therapists and family psychologists have to make to the well-being of personality-disordered individuals and their families.

Although evidence increasingly indicates that genetic and biological factors influence the development and expression of personality disorders, current understanding also emphasizes the role of family of origin dynamics in the development of these disorders. Our personalities are shaped through our interactions with our parents and significant others in our childhood, and are expressed in our day-to-day relationships with our partners, parents, children, co-workers, and friends. Individuals with personality disorders can have a profound impact on the significant others in relationship with them—an impact that often affects the health and well-being of these family members and friends. The ability to understand the complexities of intimate interpersonal relationships and to treat disturbances in these relationships efficiently and effectively is one of the strengths of the family therapy field. If family therapists fail to engage in the treatment of this population, then the many opportunities for family and individual healing and support that family therapists have to offer will be lost to families with a personality-disordered member.

My interest in developing this text began when I was editing my previous book, *Family Therapy and Mental Health: Innovations in Theory and Practice.* The two chapters on family therapy approaches for treating borderline personality disorders in that book piqued my interest in the field, and I was left wondering what family treatment approaches had been used by clinicians for treating other personality disorders. In reviewing the literature on marital and family therapy for personality disorders, I discovered that an emerging literature dealing with family treatment approaches existed. However, many of the significant papers were scattered throughout journals representing different disciplines, and as such were not readily available to family therapists interested in developing their skills in treating personality disorders from a family perspective. It seemed that a book of this type, one that brings together a variety of effective marital and family approaches for treating personality disorders, was needed. I consider myself fortunate to have been able to recruit many of the foremost writers, clinicians, and researchers working with personality-disordered individuals and their families as contributors to this text.

Readers will find that the approaches outlined in this text have a number of elements in common. Most significant, the treatments described are integrative, multidimensional models that incorporate individual treatment modalities and a biological perspective in the context of a family systems approach to understanding the development and impact of personality disorders on significant family and interpersonal relationships. Modern research into the treatment of personality disorders indicates strongly that this type of integrative multimodal approach is what is needed to treat personality disorders effectively. Readers will also find that the treatment models described go beyond a traditional focus on the family as a cause of personality disorders, and attempt to understand the impact of such disorders on the larger family system, and to address this impact therapeutically.

Finally, readers will notice that a number of chapters deal with more than one personality disorder. This is a result of the clinical finding that certain personality disorders tend to cluster. One example is the histrionic/obsessive couple discussed in Chapter 5. Another is the passive aggressive/obsessive-compulsive pairing described in Chapter 2. Individuals often find mates whose issues complement or "fit" with their own personal issues. The interactional patterns of individuals with the disorders listed previously fit together in ways that complement and mutually reinforce one another—a process that will be familiar to systemically trained family therapists. It is the ability to recognize and treat patterns of this type that can make marriage and family therapists excellent treatment providers for personality disorders.

The book is organized into two sections. Part I, Overview, consists of three chapters. In Chapter 1, Jeffrey Magnavita and I provide an overview of the personality disorders field, with special attention to the marriage and family therapy literature. Readers will find this chapter provides a helpful background for understanding later chapters, as well as current issues and controversies. In Chapter 2, Lorna Smith Benjamin and Gretta Cushing describe the Structural Analysis of Social Behavior model and the Interpersonal Reconstructive Therapy approach. Readers should find that this model provides a helpful theoretical and clinical bridge between psychodynamic and family systems approaches. Chapter 3, by Charles McCormack, provides a detailed, yet understandable description of key concepts and treatment approaches needed to work with personality-disordered individuals, couples, and family members from a psychodynamic object-relations perspective. Family therapists who may not be familiar with psychodynamic approaches should find this chapter very useful.

In Part II, Specific Disorders, nine chapters focus on marital and family treatment approaches for specific DSM-IV personality disorders. Specific disorders covered include: borderline personality disorder, histrionic personality disorder, obsessive-compulsive personality disorder, dependent personality disorder, passive-aggressive personality disorder, avoidant personality disorder, narcissistic personality disorder, and paranoid personality disorder. Because borderline personality disorder is so prevalent, and has such a major impact on family relationships, three chapters are devoted to this topic, including one chapter on borderline mothers.

Several personality disorders are not included in this text. For two of these disorders, schizoid personality disorder and schizotypal personality disorder, literature addressing the disorders was sparse. Given that both of these disorders are marked by a pattern of avoidance of close personal relationships, it is likely that individuals with these disorders rarely present for treatment, and even when they do seek treatment, their tendency to eschew close relationships may mean that they are unmarried and disconnected from their families of origin, and therefore not likely to be treated by marital or family therapists.

The other personality disorder not included in this text is antisocial personality disorder. Although a considerable amount of literature deals with antisocial personality disorder, little of it approaches the disorder from a marital or family perspective, except in the case of antisocial youths, who are more appropriately diagnosed as having a conduct disorder. Marriage and family therapists could focus more attention on this area. Even if antisocial personality-disordered individuals are viewed as being unlikely to improve in treatment (a view that was formerly held for borderline personality disorder as well, but is now gradually changing), they can have a profound impact on their spouses, families of origin, and children, and these family members would benefit from the expertise that marriage and family therapists and family psychologists have to offer. This may be an area that warrants further research.

To maintain a consistent "voice" for the book, and to facilitate comparison between treatment models, all chapters from Chapter 3 onward have standard internal headings. The headings for these chapters are: Introduction, Impact on the Family, Setting, Treatment Model, Case Example, Strengths and Limitations, Benefits for the Family, Indications and Contraindications, Management of Transference Issues, Management of Crises and Acting-Out Behavior, Integration with Psychiatric Services and Role of Medication, Cultural and Gender Issues, and Future Directions. The internal headings for Chapter 2 vary from the others only to the extent that the Treatment Model and Case Example sections are integrated, and the benefits for the family are described throughout the chapter. The internal chapter headings used in this book parallel the internal chapter headings from my previous book, *Family Therapy and Mental Health: Innovations in Theory and Practice,* and the two books are intended to complement each other and be used as companion volumes, providing a thorough coverage of a range of mental health problems often encountered by clinicians in their practices.

Although the chapters in this text clearly indicate that an array of useful marital and family treatment approaches exists for treating personality disorders, it is also clear that the field is still in its infancy, and that a need exists for further research into the effectiveness of these models and the development of improved integrated multidimensional models and treatment approaches that incorporate a family systems perspective. Nonetheless, I believe that clinicians who employ a systemic marital and family treatment approach can be encouraged. Effective family therapy approaches for working with personality disordered individuals and their families *do* exist, and there *is* movement toward integrating marital and family therapy approaches with more mainstream individual approaches to treating personality disorders. It is my hope that these chapters will inspire clinicians working with personality-disordered individuals in their practice to consider more consistently the impact of these disorders on family members, and to work to actively involve family members in the treatment process. If this can take place, then both family members and individuals suffering from personality disorders will inevitably benefit from the understanding, support, and improvement that ensues from this more inclusive and integrated approach.

Acknowledgments

This is my second edited book, and the process of bringing it to completion has once again brought home to me the awareness that an edited text is truly a collaborative endeavor. Many people have contributed their time, energy, and expertise to this book. It would be impossible for me to acknowledge by name every individual contribution. I appreciate the efforts of all those who have worked to make this book a reality, and I offer my deepest thanks.

Some individuals and organizations deserve special mention.

First, thanks to The Haworth Press for making this book possible. The contract was signed just weeks after the attack on the World Trade Center, at a time of great political and financial uncertainty. I believe The Haworth Press deserves recognition for its courage in moving forward in that climate with projects such as this book, and for its commitment to furthering our understanding of the complexity of human nature through its publishing efforts.

I have also come to appreciate the dedication and high standards of all those who work behind the scenes at The Haworth Press. The high quality of the final product would not be possible without the attention to detail of the production staff, copy editors, typesetters, graphic artists, marketing staff, and other individuals. Thanks to all those at The Haworth Press who contributed to the final product.

I also thank Haworth Senior Editor Terry Trepper. Terry's guidance, support, and encouragement has been invaluable to me, both in bringing this project to fruition, and in my other editing endeavors.

One of the pleasures of being editor of a text such as this is the opportunity to work closely with colleagues and learn from the process. The contributors to this text represent some of the foremost researchers and clinicians in the field of personality disorders today. I am fortunate to have had the opportunity to work with these creative thinkers, and I thank them for all I have learned from them, and for their willingness to allow me to share their thoughts and ideas in this book.

Special thanks to my mother, Mary MacFarlane, and to my wife, Valerie Cunningham, for proofreading the manuscript, and for their valuable comments. Any errors that remain are my responsibility alone.

Finally, I would like to thank my wife Valerie, and my daughter Rebecca MacFarlane, for their patience and understanding during the time I was working on this book. Having already experienced the loss of many hours of valuable family time during the editing of my first book, they were still supportive and encouraging of my desire to undertake this new project. I look forward to spending many hours of enjoyable time with both of them now that this project is complete.

PART I:
OVERVIEW

Chapter 1

Family Treatment of Personality Disorders: Historical Overview and Current Perspectives

Jeffrey J. Magnavita
Malcolm M. MacFarlane

INTRODUCTION

Since the inclusion of a separate Axis II category for personality disorders in the third edition of the American Psychiatric Association's (1980) *Diagnostic and Statistical Manual of Mental Disorders* (DSM-III), interest has burgeoned in the field of personality disorders, resulting in an explosion of texts and journal articles regarding the etiology and treatment of personality disorders (Magnavita, 1998b). Tremendous development has also occurred in the areas of personality theory and models of treatment, with the result that many personality disorders that were previously regarded as untreatable are now considered amenable to therapeutic intervention (Sperry, 1995).

Many reasons may account for this fascination with personality disorders. Perhaps a part of the fascination is that we all have personalities, and the desire to know and understand what goes awry in individuals who develop personality disorders is central to understanding our own potentials and vulnerabilities. On a more pragmatic level, however, is the reality that personality disorders are extremely pervasive, particularly among clinical populations, and their presence tends to complicate routine treatment for relationship problems and Axis I disorders, such as anxiety, depression, and other clinical syndromes. Most clinicians have had the experience of setting out to treat what seems to be a routine case of depression or a straightforward marital issue, only to find their treatment plan thwarted by entrenched

3

personality characteristics that interfere with the change process. An ability to understand and treat personality disorders effectively is an essential skill for any clinician.

Until recently, individual models for understanding and treating personality disorders have tended to dominate the field. Where family factors have been explored at all, the focus has often been on family variables contributing to the development of psychopathology, rather than on the impact of personality disorders on the family, or on ways the family can aid and enhance effective treatment. This lack of attention to the interpersonal and family impact of personality disorders is strange, since the first three diagnostic criteria for personality disorders outlined in the fourth edition of the DSM (American Psychiatric Association, 1994) clearly target interpersonal aspects. Criterion A includes "interpersonal functioning" as an area in which the personality disorder may be manifested in which criterion B requires that the disorder be pervasive "across a broad range of personal and social situations," and criterion C requires that it lead to distress or impairment in "social, occupational, or other important areas of functioning" (p. 630, reprinted with permission from the *Diagnostic and Statistical Manual of Mental Disorders,* Fourth Edition, copyright 1994 American Psychiatric Association).

Although individually focused psychodynamic and cognitive behavioral models provide useful insights, the lack of a systematic framework for understanding how individual personality traits are enacted in significant interpersonal relationship contexts can leave clinicians floundering. A major need exists for integrative multidimensional models for working with personality disorders that blend individual and family systems treatment approaches. As MacFarlane (2001, p. xxii) states, "It is time for family therapy approaches to be more integrated into the mental health field."

This book attempts to provide mental health clinicians with an integrative framework for understanding personality disorders in a relationship context. The text explores a variety of integrative multidimensional models and approaches for intervening in marital, family, and interpersonal systems to bring about change in the personality-disordered individual, and aid families in coping with the impact of personality-disordered family members. To provide a context for the chapters to come, however, it may be helpful to have a better understanding of historical and current perspectives regarding personality disorders.

WHAT ARE PERSONALITY DISORDERS?

Personality disorders (PDs) are best conceptualized as a dysfunction in the personality system of an individual, their relational matrix, and total ecosystem, that can manifest themselves in a variety of ways, but are most clearly characterized by patterns of relationships and behavior that are repetitive and tend to be maladaptive to the individual's sociocultural setting (Magnavita, in press). The relational matrix broadly includes the internalization of relationships by an individual on an intrapsychic level (e.g., object relations, schematic representations—relational or cognitive schema), dyadic configurations (e.g., couples, parent-child subsystems), triangular relationships (e.g., parent/parent/child triangle, partner/partner/lover triangle), family systems (e.g., dysfunctional personologic systems), and social institutions (e.g., school systems, religious institutions, prisons). The relational matrix also includes the relational components of the therapist and patient, which is the primary foundation on which psychotherapy rests. These are often referred to in the literature as "common factors" (Norcross and Goldfried, 1992).

The maladaptive patterns can include various domains from the biopsychosocial matrix, such as affective regulation, cognitive-perceptual distortion, interpersonal disturbance, behavioral inappropriateness, and impulse control management. The personality "system" of the individual needs to be considered in totality, emphasizing the interrelationships among the components of the biopsychosocial model in the relational field (Magnavita, 2000c).

PERSONALITY DISORDER CLASSIFICATIONS

DSM Definition—Current Categories and Clusters of Personality Disorder Types

The most widely used classification system for personality disorders is the categorical model of the DSM, which has numerous editions (American Psychiatric Association, 1994). The current multiaxial system, whereby five separate axes are used, was an important advance for the study of personality because personality disorders were given their own separate or Axis II classification, differentiating them from the Axis I clinical syndromes (Magnavita, 1998a). This led to an increase in the research and development of new treatments for these disorders, which previously had been considered untreatable, with the exception of long-term psychoanalysis, which itself had questionable results. The DSM classification system gave researchers a criteria-based method for establishing the presence or absence of a personality disorder.

The DSM (APA, 1994, p. 629) defines personality disorders as "an enduring pattern of inner experience and behavior that deviates markedly from the expectations of the individual's culture, is pervasive and inflexible, has an onset in adolescence or early adulthood, is stable over time, and leads to distress or impairment" (reprinted with permission from the *Diagnostic and Statistical Manual of Mental Disorders,* Fourth Edition, copyright 1994 American Psychiatric Association). The DSM divides personality disorders into three clusters:

1. *Cluster A,* characterized by odd or eccentric behavior, includes paranoid, schizoid, and schizotypal personalities. This cluster is considered the most treatment refractory, and is probably the most likely to have strong genetic predisposing factors. Longer-term treatment combined with pharmacotherapy is often required.
2. *Cluster B,* characterized by erratic, emotional and dramatic presentation, includes antisocial, borderline, histrionic, and narcissistic personalities. This cluster includes what are considered the more severe personality disorders with mixed treatment outcome. A number of newer treatment models, primarily psychodynamic (Clarkin, Yeomans, and Kernberg, 1999) and cognitive-behavioral (Linehan, 1993) have been developed.
3. *Cluster C,* characterized by anxiety and fearfulness, includes avoidant, dependent, and obsessive-compulsive personalities. These disorders are considered the most responsive, and have shown good results with short-term dynamic psychotherapy (Winston et al., 1994) and cognitive therapy (Beck, Freeman, and Associates,1990).

Complex and Overlapping Personality Disorders

In addition to the personality disorders and clusters described earlier, the DSM-IV also provides a category called "Personality Disorder Not Otherwise Specified" (NOS). This category is intended to be used for disorders of personality functioning that do not meet criteria for any specific personality disorder, or where the features of several personality disorders do not meet the full criteria for any one category. This category may also be used for specific disorders that are not included in the DSM, such as depressive personality disorder or passive-aggressive personality disorder.

Problems with the DSM Categorical System

Problems with the DSM system of classification should be mentioned. Researchers have found a high incidence of overlap categories, with most patients receiving multiple diagnoses. This problem underscores a lack of precision that may ultimately affect the utility of this categorical system. Another criticism is the system's lack of sensitivity to subsyndromal variations which might have an important bearing on treatment. For example, when a patient does not meet the full criteria for an Axis II diagnosis, provisions are not made for personality attributes that fall below the diagnostic threshold even when they have significant impact on treatment. An individual with major clinical depression, for example, may have strong passive-aggressive or narcissistic traits that make noncompliance with medication and psychotherapy likely.

Some clinicians and researchers have suggested that the difficulty with the DSM categorical systems lies in the descriptive nature of this system and its focus on clinical syndromes. They criticize the system for its lack of a consistent theoretical basis for understanding and accounting for the etiology of these disorders, and its lack of clinical relevance in terms of treatment planning. They also question the basic assumption underlying categorical systems or typologies, which is that personality disorders are discontinuous, or separate and distinct from the normal range of personality development rather than an outgrowth of normal personality characteristics (Livesley et al., 1994; Widiger and Sanderson, 1995).

Other Systems of Classification

Other diagnostic systems of classification offer different and useful perspectives, but also have limitations and disadvantages. Unfortunately, a full exploration of the merits and difficulties of these systems is beyond the focus of this chapter. Four additional systems of classification include: dimensional, prototypical, structural dynamic, and relational classification.

Dimensional Classification

Dimensional classification systems are based on the premise that personality disorders are not discontinuous with normal personality development, but in fact are part of a continuum of normal personality traits. Costa and McCrae (1992), for instance, outline what has come to be called the "five-factor model." This model identifies five core personality dimensions: neuroticism, extraversion, openness, agreeableness, and conscientiousness.

Proponents of dimensional classification systems suggest that personality disorders represent extreme and maladaptive versions of one or more normal personality traits or combinations of traits (Livesley, 1998). Personality pathology is placed on a continuum, and cutoff points are established empirically. This method of classifying personality is useful in that it enables clinicians and researchers to identify threshold and subsyndromal variations of personality disorder, as well as normal traits which, when the individual is under stress, may exacerbate behavior or symptoms.

Prototypical Classification

The prototypical classification system developed by Millon and Davis (1996b) attempts to combine both the qualitative distinctions of the DSM categorical system with the quantitative strengths of the dimensional system. The authors suggest the clinician ask both "how" and "how much" the client resembles the prototypical patient with a particular disorder. One of the advantages of this type of system is that it does not sacrifice sensitivity to the subsyndromal variations mentioned earlier.

Structural Dynamic Classification

This system is based on psychoanalytic character types and arranges personality on a structural continuum: normal, neurotic, borderline, and psychotic (Kernberg, 1984; McWilliams, 1994). Kernberg's structural-characterological system is quite useful for conceptualizing personality organization and structure. Many clinicians find Kernberg's system more clinically useful than the categorical system. In Kernberg's conceptual model, borderline is not a separate category, but refers to the level of ego organization, structural integrity, and ego-adaptive capacity that exists on the continuum from normal to psychotic. Each personality type, such as hysterical, obsessive, depressive, passive-aggressive, and so forth, can be organized at the various levels of the continuum. This diagnostic system informs treatment by allowing the clinician to differentiate, for example, between two obsessive characters, one functioning near the borderline level and the other near the neurotic. The obsessive with borderline organization is going to be more challenging in treatment due to fluctuations in ego-adaptive capacity.

Relational Classification

Relational classification has its roots in the systemic model (Ackerman, 1957, 1958) in that it views personality as existing within a complex biopsychosocial system, not just within the individual. This interpersonal matrix includes both dyadic (Sullivan, 1953) and triadic configurations (Bowen, 1976). Relational diagnosis was advanced by Kaslow (1996) and applied to dysfunctional personologic systems (Magnavita, 2000c). Magnavita's approach attempts to classify the variety of dysfunctional personologic systems that spawn personality disorders, and that often result in multigenerational transmission. One of the advantages of relational classification systems is that they serve to orient the clinician to the impact personality disorders have on significant interpersonal relationships and family members.

A Multisystem Diagnostic Assessment

Perhaps the most useful way to approach diagnosis is to use a multiperspective that eschews a narrowband formulation and classification based on limited clinical data. "Comprehensive assessment utilizes various systems, placing them in the relational matrix to provide a broader perspective" (Magnavita, 2000c, p. 95). In this manner the diagnostician-clinician uses the multiple lenses of the various systems presented earlier without relying exclusively on any one system to construct the clinical holograph of the patient's personality system (Magnavita, in press).

PREVALENCE AND COMORBIDITY

Relatively few studies have documented the prevalence of personality disorders. According to Mattia and Zimmerman (2001), "Due to the relative paucity of national efforts, the epidemiology of personality disorders in the general population is a difficult issue about which to draw firm conclusions" (p. 120). The most widely cited study by Merikangas and Weissman (1986) found that the prevalence of personality disorders in the general population is about one out of ten. More important, they also revealed that about half of those who seek mental health treatment are diagnosed with a personality disorder. Given these findings we can anticipate that those in clinical practice may expect that approximately 50 percent of their patients will suffer from personality disorders, and that the treatment of primary Axis I presenting problems or relationship problems will be complicated by the presence of comorbid or co-occurring disorders. Shea and colleagues (1990) found that this is particularly the case for clients presenting with depression, where up to 74 percent may have comorbid personality disorders.

An understanding of the most common comorbid presentations can assist the clinician in developing a more cohesive treatment plan (Magnavita, 1998c). After a review of the existing literature, Tyrer et al. (1997) reported the following comorbid conditions associated with PDs: borderline PD and depression; depressive PD and depression; avoidant PD and generalized social phobia; cluster B (antisocial, borderline, histrionic, and narcissistic) and psychoactive substance abuse; clusters B and C (avoidant, dependent, and obsessive-compulsive) PDs and eating disorders and somatoform disorders; cluster C PDs and anxiety disorders and hypochondriasis; and cluster A (paranoid, schizoid, and schizotypal) PDs and schizophrenia.

The importance to the clinician of understanding and being able to recognize possible comorbid presentations are as follows (Magnavita, 1998c):

> First, the clinician whose patient is initially assessed with personality pathology of a significant degree should be alert to other common comorbid clinical syndromes. . . . For example, a diagnosis of a Narcissistic Personality Disorder should alert the clinician of the possibility that substance use disorders may coexist, and may be central to conceptualizing the case and formulating appropriate treatment interventions. Similarly, the clinician who is treating a Panic Disorder should be prepared to assess for co-existing Cluster B (Borderline, Histrionic, Antisocial) personality disorder. Second, these findings underscore the necessity for clinicians to be well versed and appropriately trained in the identification and treatment of personality pathology, or treatment effectiveness will be compromised. . . . Third, having an understanding of how personality pathology and Axis I clinical syndromes are interrelated allows us to plan effective short-term interventions that are likely to succeed. (p. 74)

Millon and colleagues (1999) describe this treatment framework as "personality-guided therapy," an integrative approach that underscores the necessity of understanding the interrelationship of personality, maladaptive behavior, and symptom complexes.

HISTORY OF PERSONALITY DISORDERS

Early Theorists and Concept of Character and Temperament

Humankind has been eternally fascinated with personality (Alexander and Selesnick, 1966). The interest in and the study of personality goes back to at least the ancient Egyptians (Stone, 1997). The Greek physician Hippocrates offered the theory of the four humors, relating four basic personality temperaments (choleric, melancholic, sanguine, and phlegmatic) to an excess in certain body fluids such as yellow and black bile, phlegm, and blood. The four-humors model offers a biological model not unlike contemporary neurobiological paradigms, which emphasize the functioning of the various neuro-transmitters (Magnavita, 2002d).

The term *personality* is derived from the Greek word "persona," which refers to the mask that was said to represent the external self of an individual. The Greeks used various masks in their plays to portray the moods and personalities of characters. Terms such as *personality, character,* and *temperament* have changed meanings considerably since the nineteenth century, but personality is now often considered to be a combination of temperament and character. *Temperament,* a term used in Greek medicine to refer to the biological basis of the enduring characteristics that defined a person's character, is now used to refer to the innate, genetic, and constitutional influences on personality. *Character* is used to describe learned psychosocial influences and their resultant effects on behavior and interpersonal style. This distinction between character and temperament, biology and social experience, has led to the development of theories such as that of Cloninger, Svrakic, and Przybeck (1993) who postulate that temperament has four substrates—novelty seeking, reward dependence, persistence, and harm avoidance—and that character is comprised of three factors: self-directedness, self-transcendence, and cooperativeness. They view the development of personality and personality disorders as resulting from a complex interplay between temperament and character.

Lenzenweger and Clarkin (1996) indicate that the modern view of personality as being "disordered" can trace its roots to the nineteenth-century work on "moral insanity." *Moral insanity* was a term used to describe patients who displayed impulsive and self-damaging acts, but who's reasoning abilities were unimpaired, and who were not delusional. Many early personality theorists, such as Kraepelin (1907), tended to believe that personality disturbances were attenuated forms of the major psychoses, and were part of a continuum, or even precursors to major mental disorders (Livesley, 2001). This view was challenged by Kurt Schneider around 1923. Unlike Kraepelin and other early theorists, Schneider did not view personality pathology as a precursor to other mental disorders, but as a separate entity that covaried with them (Millon and Davis, 1995).

Psychoanalytic theorists such as Sigmund Freud and Wilhelm Reich added another dimension to the understanding of personality disorders with their work on character development. Freud's work on psychosexual development led to descriptions of character types associated with each stage. Reich further developed this work, and emphasized that defensive modes acquired in dealing with early experience tend to become stable and transformed into "character armor" or chronic attitudes and automatic modes of reaction (Millon and Davis, 1995; Livesley, 2001). Finally, the interpersonal theory of Harry Stack Sullivan (1953) added another dimension to our understanding of personality disorders with his focus on interpersonal processes and development of a typology of ten personality types or syndromes.

In summary, this early period of interest in personality disorders was characterized largely by clinical description and the gradual emergence of the concept of personality disorders. Although a tremendous amount of clinical richness existed in these formulations and theories of personality disorders, there was also a tremendous amount of confusion regarding terminology, etiology, and treatment options. In part, it was this confusion that gave rise to the decision to classify personality disorders on a separate axis in the DSM distinct from other mental disorders, and to provide precise descriptions of each diagnosis using diagnostic criteria (Livesley, 2001). This decision to incorporate personality disorders under a separate axis ushered in a new phase in our understanding of personality disorders.

The Modern Perspective—Incorporation of Personality Disorders in the DSM

According to Livesley (2001), the incorporation of the personality disorders in the DSM-III under a separate Axis II category may be seen as a turning point in the understanding and treatment of personality disorders, and the beginning of our modern understanding of personality disorders. The development of the Axis II category, distinct from other clinical syndromes, such as anxiety, depression, and so forth, allowed clinicians and researchers to focus more systematically on personality disorders and their relationship to the Axis I clinical syndromes. This decision to give personality disorders their own axis, along with diagnostic criteria that are easy to follow, led to an explosion of interest in these disorders. This increased interest in personality disorders propelled research, leading to the development of a variety of etiological and treatment models, research regarding the validity and effectiveness of these models, as well as epidemiological investigations on their prevalence.

This research and knowledge explosion has led to what Sperry (1995) describes as a "paradigmatic shift" in the field marked by three significant developments: (1) theoretical convergence/technical blending, (2) psychopharmacotherapeutic and psychotherapeutic integration, and (3) multimodal treatment combinations. In addition to these developments, the biopsychosocial model (Engel, 1980) has allowed researchers, clinicians, and theorists to recognize personality disorders as complex multidetermined conditions with origins in neurobiology, family, and environmental experiences. As a result of this paradigmatic shift, many personality disorders that were viewed previously as untreatable are now being seen as amenable to treatment.

THEORIES OF ETIOLOGY

Various proposals are concerned with the etiology of personality disorders, depending on the theoretical model one espouses. These range from neurobiological to sociocultural, although the theory that has held sway for most of the twentieth century has been the psychodynamic model in all its concatenations, including object relations, self psychology, and ego psychology (Magnavita, 2002a,b). We can see how psychoanalytic thinking and what seemed like the opposite, behaviorism, dueled, and out of this matrix emerged humanism, cognitivism, and systemic theory to name but a few. The development of competing models was an important part of the advancing science of psychotherapy, psychopathology, and personality theory during the last century, culminating in the more integrative blend seen in contemporary models. What we now see is a movement toward integrative models and a "unified psychotherapy" approach (Magnavita, in press). A thorough understanding of the individual models that provide the theoretical underpinnings of the current integrative multidimensional approaches to treatment can help clinicians utilize the newer, unified psychotherapy approaches more effectively.

Psychodynamic/Object-Relations Models

The classic view of the psychoanalytic model earmarked the beginning of modern scientific psychotherapy. Many of the pioneering figures of twentieth-century psychoanalysis were interested in understanding character development, which was based on Freud's structural model of the mind. In Freud's conceptualization, the psyche is divided into the id, ego, and superego, and character is shaped by the manner in which the individual's psychosexual development unfolds (Magnavita 2002a,b). Traumatic experience at various stages of development can lead to fixation in that stage and associated character traits. For example, an individual fixated in the anal stage of development will likely develop an anal character, which is manifested by a tendency to be withholding, parsimonious, constricted, and nonexpressive.

Although it is generally believed that the psychosexual stages are not as important as Freud and his followers conceived, the character types that were elaborated, such as phallic, still influence contemporary diagnostic formulations and theory. Freud's theory was basically a conflict theory, the conflict having its origins in the tensions among the intrapsychic agencies of the id, ego, and superego. For example, when a child is treated punitively, he or she may internalize this and develop harsh superego functions that require the person to suffer unnecessarily when they transgress in an attempt to purge the onslaught of guilt. This configuration would be characteristic, for example, of an obsessive character that suffers from harsh superego functions. When the superego is underdeveloped, the result is a lack of guilt over transgressions and an inability to modify one's behavior as a result. If one feels no guilt or shame, it is difficult to learn from experience. This type of configuration may contribute to the development of antisocial personality disorder.

Kohut (1971) expanded upon Freud's conceptualization of narcissism with his origination of self psychology. Kohut's seminal work emphasized the importance of the self-other relationship and the mirroring function of early attachments. In contrast to the conflict theory, this is a deficit theory. Deficits in self-cohesion and structure lead to the overreliance on narcissistic defenses. Without sufficient mirroring of the emergent self, development is often arrested at a narcissistic level—a major departure from Freud's use of drive theory to explain how development goes awry.

Kernberg (1984), a contemporary psychoanalytic innovator, expanded upon object-relations theory, applying this model and developing specialized treatment for the borderline disorders. Object-relations theory was yet another fertile branch of psychoanalysis emphasizing the primacy of early attachments in the development of personality. Those who endure abusive, extremely inconsistent, and neglectful attachments fail to develop a sense of object constancy and mastery of basic ego functions, such as affect regulation, impulse control, and the ability to develop trusting attachments. Instead, they tend to rely on primitive defenses, such as splitting good and bad elements of the self and others, projection, acting out, have a tendency for emotional dysregulation, and have unstable interpersonal relations.

Biological Models

Although the research on the neurobiological basis of personality disorders is in its infancy, increasing evidence suggests that a heritable and biological component to personality traits exists. Lenzenweger and Clarkin (1996) indicate that while the role of genetic influences in the development and stability of normal personality is well established, the picture is less clear with respect to the role of genetic factors in the etiology of personality disorders. Evidence is just beginning to appear that suggests a genetic component for borderline, antisocial, and obsessive-compulsive personality disorders. However even with these disorders, the genetic picture remains mixed, with weak associations and indications that environmental influences play a strong role in the development of personality disorders (Jang and Vernon, 2001).

Some of the most suggestive evidence for a biological basis for personality disorders comes from research into the neuropharmacology of personality disorders and the effects of antidepressants, mood stabilizers, and neuroleptics. Siever and Davis (1991) note that "a preliminary but growing body of evidence supports the existence of genetic and biological substrates of personality" (p. 1647). Coccaro and Siever (1995) found some evidence of familial transmission of borderline-related personality characteristics. Coccaro (1993) also found global improvement in some patients with borderline personality disorder with medication trials. This suggests that at least of some personality disorder traits may be mediated by neurochemical processes, and are not simply a product of environmental factors.

In keeping with these emerging research findings, contemporary theory suggests that various personality types can be understood by the various neurotransmitters and hormonal systems that influence behavior. Cloninger (1986, 1987) developed a "unified biosocial theory of personality" that is rooted in a neurobiological model and based on the premise that three behavioral-brain systems are associated with neurotransmitters and their action. These include (1) novelty-seeking, which is related to high levels of dopamine, (2) harm-avoidance, which is associated with serotonin, and (3) reward dependency, which is associated with the noradrenergic system. In effect, these systems set the constraints for personality, and combining these tendencies allows for the individual differences in personality as well as explaining disorders.

Interpersonal Models

The model of etiology espoused by the interpersonal theorists, the most notable of whom is Sullivan (1953), is that personality is developed through the dyadic relationships that are responsible for establishing our social selves. Personality disorders occur when certain styles of interpersonal adaptation become fixed and repetitive. Leary (1957) and his colleagues at the Kaiser Permanente Foundation constructed a typology of these interpersonal styles based on two dimensions: dominance-submission and hate-love. Leary identified sixteen personality "types" on a circular or "circumplex" model based on the extent to which an individual manifested each of these two dimensions. Personality disorders were based on maladaptive extremes of each "type" of personality. More recently, Benjamin (1993) adapted this circumplex model to provide interpersonal descriptions characteristic of each of the DSM disorders, as well as interpersonal hypotheses regarding the etiology of each disorder (see Chapter 2 for a more detailed outline of Benjamin's interpersonal approach).

Cognitive Models

The cognitive model of understanding personality disorders has been most thoroughly elaborated by Beck, Freeman, and Associates (1990). Their approach is nicely summarized by Pretzer and Beck (1996). The cognitive theory posits that personality is a product of a set of core beliefs and assumptions that consolidate into a schema or cognitive map that guides and shapes all domains of personality functioning and adaptation. These beliefs are thought to be absorbed from parental and environmental influences and become fixed and self-perpetuating. These core beliefs or schemas become problematic when they are marked by various cognitive distortions or errors in thinking that lead to dysfunctional behavioral and emotional responses to environmental stimuli and interpersonal reactions. Millon and Davis (1995) give the example of dependent personality disorder, in which individuals may have a schema that involves a picture of themselves as helpless, needy, weak, and incompetent. This self-view may have originated in childhood interactions with critical or domineering parent figures, and it is maintained by a set of cognitive distortions that perpetuate the individuals' view of themselves as incompetent and needing caretaking. Their interpersonal pattern of dependency and intense emotional fear of abandonment are products of this cognitive schema.

Behavioral Models

The behavioral model emphasizes the importance of learning and social influence in the development of personality and personality disorders. Classical and instrumental conditioning have been used to explain how an individual is shaped by the learning contingencies in his or her environment (Dollard and Miller, 1950). A basic principle of the behavioral model is that behaviors that are reinforced tend to continue, and that behaviors that are ignored or meet with unpleasant or aversive responses tend to decrease or be extinguished. The behavioral model emphasizes that the maladaptive patterns displayed by individuals with personality disorders are learned behaviors that were reinforced in their social and family environment, and that they can be altered in the present by changing the current conditions of reinforcement. The behavioral model is often combined with the cognitive model in planning treatment interventions, and together they make a powerful blend (Sperry, 1999).

Evolutionary Models

Millon (Millon, 1990; Millon and Davis, 1996a) has proposed an evolutionary model for understanding the development of personality disorders that combines elements of both dimensional and categorical models. Millon suggests that there are three biological imperatives: first, each organism must survive; second, it must adapt to its environment; third, it must reproduce. From this, Millon derives three polarities which, in combination, determine personality. To survive, an organism seeks to maximize pleasure and minimize pain. The extent to which an individual focuses on one versus the other influences characteristics such as avoidance. To adapt, an organism either conforms passively to its environment or actively reforms the environment. This polarity has implications for traits such as passivity. Finally, in reproducing, an organism either invests in its offspring or creates many offspring and goes about its own business, leaving the offspring to take care of themselves. This dimension translates into a polarity around a focus on self versus other, which has implications for traits such as narcissism or antisocial characteristics.

Family Dysfunction and Psychosocial Adversity Models

Models that emphasize family dysfunction and psychosocial adversity have suggested that the development of personality disorder is strongly influenced by psychosocial factors, including parental psychopathology, traumatic experiences, such as childhood sexual abuse, physical, or emotional abuse (which is often associated with family psychopathology), or social stressors associated with rapid social change (Magnavita, 2000c). Paris (2001) provides a concise summary of the research on these factors. In terms of family dysfunction, he notes a strong association between antisocial personality disorder, substance abuse, borderline personality disorder, and mood disorders in first degree relatives and the development of borderline personality disorder in offspring. He also notes an association between family breakdown and neglectful parenting practices in the development of personality disorders. Paris's findings are consistent with findings regarding the development of borderline personality disorder (Links, 1990). Although family and social environment clearly play a role in the development of personality disorders, it should be emphasized that contemporary systemic models do not endorse the belief that the family *causes* personality disorders. The current perspective is that personality disorders are multidetermined illnesses that result from complex interactions between the biological, psychological, family, and social domains.

Contemporary Biopsychosocial Model in a Relational Matrix

Most contemporary theorists, researchers, and clinicians would agree that personality disorders are not a single domain or pathway phenomenon, but rather are multiple domains that interact with complicated feedback loops. The best way to conceptualized disorders of personality is with a biopsychosocial model (Engel, 1980; Paris, 1994). This model is strengthened considerably with the addition of a systems model (von Bertalanffy, 1968). Personality is complex, and when it has become dysfunctional it represents a total system response from the microscopic (biological), intrapsychic (cognitive-affective-defense constellation), interpersonal (dyadic configurations), relational (triadic configurations), and the macrosystem (sociocultural influences) (Magnavita, in press). One of the major advantages of using a biopsychosocial model to understand personality disorders is that it can lead to a broad range of effective interventions for promoting personality and relationship change.

THEORIES OF TREATMENT

The treatment of personality disorders is the newest frontier of psychotherapy (Magnavita, 1997b). As with its etiology, multiple perspectives exist on how to conceptualize and approach the treatment of these conditions.

Psychoanalytic/Psychodynamic Approaches

The psychodynamic model of personality and psychopathology offered the first modern approach to treatment of psychological disorders with Freud's development and elaboration of psychoanalysis. Psychoanalysis was the first comprehensive theory of the mind that attempted to understand not only neurosis, but also character development. Almost as soon as Freud presented his theoretical model, new branches of analytic thought began to sprout. Contemporary psychodynamic treatment offers an array of approaches for the treatment of personality disorders, including object-relations, self-psychological, ego-psychology, and structural-drive models, as well as many newly evolved integrative models that blend theoretical components, methods, and technical aspects of various dynamic and nondynamic approaches (Magnavita, 2000b). Some of the essential advances of the psychodynamic model made during the twentieth century include:

1. *Transference.* The concept of transference is one of the cornerstones of modern psychotherapy. Freud observed that we tend to project onto and recreate our early relational experiences. By setting the conditions, psychoanalysis attempted to offer a forum for the patient to understand and rework these patterns.

2. *Countertransference.* Another important paradigm was countertransference, the process by which the therapist reacts to and brings his or her own unconscious and conscious elements to the treatment process. Countertransference continues to be a highly useful construct for understanding the forces generated in the therapist when working with individuals, couples, and families suffering from personality maladaption, particularly the severe personality disorders.

3. *Defense mechanisms.* The elaboration of defensive mechanisms is one of the milestones of twentieth-century psychotherapy and psychopathology. Defense mechanisms are means through which we manage and contain the anxiety from both internal and external sources. An understanding and familiarity with defensive operations is particularly relevant with the personality-disordered individual, couple, and family. A list of many of the common defenses is listed in *Restructuring Personality Disorders: A Short-Term Dynamic Approach* (Magnavita, 1997a), as well in many other psychodynamic and psychiatric texts, such as the DSM-IV (APA, 1994). Readers who are not familiar with these defenses should refer to these sources.

4. *Repression.* Freud underscored the use of repression as a way to avoid the painful effects of unresolved conflict and trauma in our lives. For this we owe him much, as this is another cornerstone of modern "depth" psychotherapy. Repression is an adaptation that is utilized when conflict or trauma become overwhelming to the ego system of an individual. This protective mechanism keeps the ego from being unnecessarily over-

whelmed, but the price for this protection is often increased symptoms and rigid defense mechanisms. These then can be the engine of maladaptive character patterns seen in the personality-disordered patient.

5. *Symptom formation.* Until Freud's work on hysteria, the manner in which symptoms were expressed was murky. Psychoanalysis traced the development of symptoms to unconscious conflict and unbearable affects that were expressed in symptomatic expression. Exposing the conflict and metabolizing the affects led to a resolution of symptoms in many cases.

6. *Character structure.* The development of character structure was another major focus and advance of psychoanalysis. Character or personality was a major interest of many of the psychoanalytic pioneers who developed specialized techniques to treat individuals with disordered personalities.

Overall, contemporary psychodynamics (Magnavita, 2002a) emphasizes the constructs mentioned previously, and uses them in restructuring and modifying personality adaptations. Many of the contemporary models of psychodynamic psychotherapy are strongly integrative in nature, using constructs that have been time tested from psychoanalytic formulations, while including contemporary notions from affective, cognitive, relational, and neurosciences. In general, these models seek to restructure an individual's personality by modifying defenses, processing affect, and enhancing capacity for intimacy and closeness. In doing so, repetitive maladaptive patterns can be altered and substituted with more adaptive ones.

Neurobiological Approaches

As noted earlier, evidence of a biological basis for personality disorders is increasing, and both Cloninger (1987) and Siever and Davis (1991) have provided theoretical frameworks that can act as valuable guides to clinical choices regarding pharmacotherapy. With the increasing recognition of a biological basis for these disorders has come a movement toward the use of pharmacological treatments. A number of excellent papers have reviewed the relevant empirical literature on effectiveness of various psychotropic medications in treating personality disorders (Coccaro, 1993; Coccaro and Siever, 1995).

However, perhaps one of the clearest guides to clinical considerations in pharmacotherapy is one written by Silk (1996).

According to Silk, medications are most effective when used as an adjunct to psychotherapy and a systematic plan for managing the patient's illness and symptoms. Pharmacotherapy is rarely, if ever, indicated as a single-treatment modality. Medications are normally directed toward the management of one of four dimensions of personality psychopathology:

1. the cognitive-perceptual dimension, represented by disorders in the odd cluster, such as schizotypal, schizoid, and paranoid disorders—low-dose neuroleptics may be useful in managing symptoms for these individuals;
2. the impulsivity-aggression dimension, represented by disorders in the dramatic cluster, such as histrionic, narcissistic, borderline, and antisocial personality disorders—selective serotonin reuptake inhibitors (SSRIs) are often helpful with this population;
3. the affective-instability dimension, which is also typical of the dramatic cluster, often responds to mood-stabilizing medications, such as lithium, or to medications that have noradrenergic effects, such as the monoamine oxidase inhibitors (MAOIs); and
4. the anxiety-inhibition dimension represented by disorders in the anxious cluster, such as avoidant, dependent, passive-aggressive, and obsessive-compulsive personality disorders, may respond to a variety of medications that reduce anxiety, including SSRIs, benzodiazepines, and MAOIs.

Many clinicians find that once intense symptoms of anxiety, depression, mood instability, or cognitive-perceptual distortions are more effectively managed, it becomes easier for personality-disordered clients to benefit from psychotherapy and begin making concrete behavioral, interpersonal, and personality changes. More effective containment of these symptoms through use of medication is often helpful in reducing the crises that interfere with the progress of therapy, endanger client's lives, lead to hospitalizations, or place a strain on their close interpersonal relationships, sometimes resulting in family breakdown.

Cognitive and Cognitive/Behavioral Approaches

Cognitive (Beck, Freeman, and Associates, 1990; Young, 1994) and cognitive/behavioral approaches (Sperry, 1999) have also been modified and others, most notably, Linehan's (1993) specially developed for the treatment of personality disorders. The cognitive model seeks to modify underlying beliefs or dysfunctional cognitions that influence perception and emotional response. An individual's personality is expressed in the schema that is maladaptive in the personality disordered patient. This "early maladpative schema" (Young, 1994) is identified and more functional schemata are offered to replace it in a process called "schema reconstruction."

Cognitive-behavioral approaches combine elements of cognitive and behavioral technology to enhance skills and retrain individuals with more adaptive behavior (Sperry, 1999). These behavioral methods include anger management training, assertiveness training, emotional-regulation skills, empathy training, impulse control training, interpersonal skills training, problem-solving skills training, self-management skills, symptom-management training, and thought stopping. These components are offered as part of a comprehensive treatment plan for the personality-disordered patient. When combined in an integrative fashion with the methods of cognitive therapy, such as cognitive restructuring, a powerful amalgam is formed between these two models of treatment.

Dialectic behavior therapy (DBT) is a version of cognitive-behavioral therapy that was developed by Linehan (1993) for treatment of the parasuicidal patient with borderline personality disorder. Linehan's methods combine elements of many treatment approaches, drawing heavily from cognitive, behavioral, and Eastern approaches to the mind. In DBT, patients are treated intensively in group settings using highly structured skills training that prepares the patient for later work on the emotional components of trauma.

Short-Term Therapies

The development and evolution of short-term psychotherapies was one of the main struggles and challenges of twentieth-century psychotherapy. Almost as soon as modern psychotherapy began with the development of psychoanalysis and behaviorism, the search for briefer treatments emerged. In fact, Freud's original work was very short-term oriented often no more than one to six sessions and very eclectic in nature. Ferenczi (Ferenczi and Rank, 1925) began experimenting early with "active therapy," which was much more engaged and affectively arousing than classic analytic treatment. Behaviorism, by its very nature, tended to be symptom oriented and brief (Watson, 1924). Later systemic, Ericksonian, cognitive, and a variety of other models tended to be organized and developed around a brief treatment framework. Interest in short-term models emerged and re-emerged over the last century as various pioneers rediscovered and evolved theoretical and technical elements that allowed for briefer treatment.

One of the most important historical influences on the search for brief treatment was the ascendancy of the managed care movement in the 1980s in North America and the emphasis on cost containment. This led to the labeling of almost every treatment with the preface "short" and development of others that included therapy conducted in a single session. When it came to the personality disorders, little help was available for the therapist looking for briefer models until the 1980s and 1990s, when mainstream treatments were developed for the personality disorders (although by managed care standards these were hardly brief). The disadvantage of ignoring personality disturbance by managed care companies became apparent with the high level of recidivism that was evident, as well as medical overutilization, especially noted in emergency room admission of many PD patients. Also, the rationale for the exclusive focus on symptom disorders or Axis I diagnoses to cut costs became questionable when it seemed that underlying personality pathology interfered with the effectiveness of first-line treatments for depression, anxiety, and interpersonal disturbances. Gabbard (2000) provides an excellent review of the emerging research and literature regarding cost savings in reduced hospitalization, medical utilization, and other cost offsets as a result of treating personality disorders. Gabbard (2000) concludes that:

> Despite frequent statements from insurance and managed care companies that personality disorders are not treatable, there is substantial evidence that they respond to psychotherapy. Extended therapy appears to be necessary for the full effect of treatment. . . . Moreover, although intensive and extended psychotherapy may be expensive, in the long run it is highly cost-

effective because it reduces inpatient stays and other costs. (p. 5)

The Importance of Assessment

The assessment phase of therapy is immensely important in utilizing a brief treatment model. Not all patients with symptom disturbances or personality disorders can benefit from a brief treatment model. In particular those with attachment disorders who are unable to form a trusting relationship with the therapist will have difficulty with the level of collaboration required for a brief treatment. Better suited are patients with intimacy and closeness issues who have not suffered from profound or chronic abuse, severe neglect, or other experiences that interfere with the ability to trust and make attachment bonds. In order to conduct short-term treatment, the clinician must be on solid ground with his or her formulation, making sure a determination of adequate or above ego-adaptive capacity is evident (Magnavita, 1997a). Although the potential benefits can be great if the patient can tolerate the intensity, brief treatment puts a greater strain on the resources of the patient, and can be detrimental to those who are fragile or borderline.

The Length of Treatment for Personality Disorders

Personality disorders are not a homogeneous group, so the length of treatment is going to be dictated by the level of severity and adaptive functioning. Patients who fall within the spectrum of the severe personality disorders that are usually organized at the borderline level will inevitably require longer treatment. Using the DSM criteria, the cluster A disorders are the most refractory and require the longest treatment and possibly some maintenance treatment over the life span. Cluster B has mixed results with a brief treatment model, and cluster C has the best results with brief treatment. The latter group is generally going to do better with affect-arousing treatments aimed at rapidly undoing repression and internalization, as opposed to patients from cluster B, who tend to act out and need more structure and containment. With the right patient at the right time, when the patient is in a transition or a crisis has occurred, brief treatment can result in some profound personal transformations. Although many factors determine the length of treatment for the personality-disordered patient, sufficient restructuring can occur with about forty sessions (forty-five to fifty minutes) for the patient with higher ego-adaptive capacity, and with the moderate up to eighty sessions. Those with more severe personality disorders generally require years of treatment and many need lifetime maintenance treatment.

Relational Approaches

As can be seen from the discussion so far, individually focused treatment approaches have historically dominated the field of personality disorders. Although these individual approaches make some attempts to address the way personality dynamics are developed and expressed in interpersonal relationships, a consistent focus on relational approaches to understanding personality disorders has been lacking. A notable exception to this is the work of Magnavita (2000c, 2001a,b, 2002c), which develops a relational approach to understanding and treating personality disorders. Magnavita outlines a number of reasons for incorporating a relational perspective, including the following:

- Personality is formed by the relationships present from the earliest interpersonal experience and attachments, and an understanding of these experiences and attachments is critical to understanding the disorder.
- Personality-disordered individuals consistently demonstrate disturbances in the relational matrix, which may include spouse abuse, parent-child problems, marital disturbances, and so forth. The impact of these disturbances in the relational matrix needs to be understood and addressed to promote healthier functioning.
- Personality-disordered individuals have major defenses against intimacy and closeness that interfere with the healing possibilities of human connectedness. Personality-disordered individuals need to be helped to make healthier and more intimate interpersonal connections.
- The benefits of enhanced relational capacities and family support are evident in almost every current line of research. Families are valuable sources of healing and support, and it is often a mistake to neglect their healing resources.
- Personality disorders are reinforced and often exaggerated by cultural and family systems. The family may play a role in main-

taining personality dysfunction, and the role of family members should be explored and addressed through treatment.

MARITAL AND FAMILY TREATMENT APPROACHES

Although we are beginning to see the emergence of interpersonal and relational approaches in the treatment of personality disorders, the literature on marital and family interventions for personality disorders remains sparse, and many marriage and family therapists remain underinvolved in the treatment of personality disorders. An indication of this under involvement may be seen in the results of Doherty and Simmons' (1996) practice patterns survey of 526 marriage and family therapists from fifteen states. They found that although 72.9 percent of these therapists viewed themselves as competent to treat personality disorders, these therapists listed only 5.1 percent of their client's presenting problems as being personality disorders, despite being free to list multiple presenting problems. Given the estimates noted earlier in this chapter that approximetely 50 percent of clients in clinical settings are diagnosed with personality disorders, either personality disorders are underrepresented in these therapists' caseloads, or they are not identifying personality disorders when they are present.

It could be argued that the development of marital and family treatment approaches for personality disorders is in its infancy. However, the literature on marital and family treatment of personality disorders is emerging, and a number of excellent works address the treatment of personality disorders from a systemic marital and family treatment perspective. One of the earliest works dealing with family therapy for personality disorders is by Harbin (1981). Harbin takes a fairly broad-based approach, commenting on family therapy approaches and considerations for several personality disorders, including antisocial, dependent, histrionic, paranoid, and obsessive-compulsive. Most authors writing about family treatment approaches, however, have chosen to focus more narrowly on one disorder, or in some cases on significant pairings of personality disorders that are often found in conjunction with one another in married partners. The existing literature on marital and family treatments is reviewed in the following paragraphs.

DSM-IV Cluster B—Dramatic, Erratic Group

It is perhaps not a surprise that most of the marriage and family literature on personality disorders addresses the dramatic-erratic group, which includes the borderline, narcissistic, histrionic, and antisocial personality disorders. Borderline personality disorder in particular has been a source of fascination for clinicians for some time because of the dramatic impact individuals with borderline personality disorder have on both the treatment system and their significant interpersonal relationships. A hallmark characteristic of the disorder is unstable relationships, and afflicted individuals are noted for their tendency toward crises during treatment and their transference issues with therapists. Of all of the personality disorders, borderline personality disorder has perhaps the most profound impact on significant marital and family interpersonal relationships, as well as the greatest amount of research implicating family of origin factors in its etiology.

One of the earliest works examining borderline personality disorder from a family systems perspective is that of Everett et al. (1989), whose comprehensive clinical model of the borderline family also integrates psychodynamic concepts, such as splitting and projective identification. Their treatment approach addresses such issues as family triangles, intergenerational boundaries, and family structure. Other authors who have taken a fairly broad-based family systems approach include Glick et al. (1995), Glick and Loraas (2001), and Gunderson and colleagues, who employ a family psychoeducational approach to work with both borderline patients and their families (Gunderson, Berkowitz, and Ruiz-Sancho, 1997; Ruiz-Sancho, Smith, and Gunderson, 2001).

Although Everett and colleague's (1989) model takes a broad family systems approach, this has been somewhat unusual in the literature. Much of the current literature focuses on marital interventions and couple therapy, and many of the models attempt to blend psychodynamic or object-relations approaches with a family systems perspective. Many of these papers also address more than one personality disorder, due to reports that common pairings of personality disorders have been found in married couples presenting for treatment. Lachkar (1992, 1998) outlines a psychodynamic conjoint treatment approach to working with narcissistic/borderline couples. Other writers who employ a similar approach include Koch and Ingram

(1985), Slipp (1995), Doherty (1997), Solomon (1996, 1998), who also focuses on borderline/narcissistic pairings, and Kalogjera et al. (1998). Although an integration of psychodynamic and systemic models is common, other approaches exist, notably the relationship-enhancement model (Waldo and Harman, 1993; Harman and Waldo, 2001; Snyder, 1994). The relationship-enhancement approach is strongly focused on improving dysfunctional patterns of communication.

One of the personality disorders included in the dramatic, erratic group is antisocial personality disorder. Relatively little literature has focused on marital and family treatment of this disorder, perhaps because it was thought to be largely untreatable. However, Nichols (1996) has written on antisocial/histrionic pairings, and increasing evidence indicates that this disorder may also be amenable to treatment. Even if the individual with antisocial personality disorder is not a suitable candidate for treatment, providing treatment and support to families who have members suffering from antisocial personality disorder may have many benefits.

Cluster C—Anxious, Fearful Group

This group, which includes the dependent, avoidant, obsessive-compulsive, and passive-aggressive personality disorders, seems to have generated considerably less marital and family literature than the dramatic, erratic group discussed earlier. Perhaps part of this rests in the tendency of these individuals, with the exception of dependent personality disorder, to avoid interpersonal relationships. When disordered individuals do enter into significant interpersonal relationships, these relationships may be short-lived due to the difficulties their symptoms cause. Also, these individuals, because of their fears and anxieties, may be less willing to seek or follow through with treatment, especially marital or family treatment where exploration of interpersonal conflicts may provoke intense anxiety.

Despite the relative lack of literature on these cluster C personality disorders, a few papers are significant, several of which again focus on significant pairings. Nurse (1998) outlines a treatment approach for dependent/narcissistic couples which draws heavily on Millon's (1990) evolutionary model described earlier. Sperry and Maniacci (1998) employ an integrative model which draws on cognitive, Adlerian, and structural family therapy techniques to work with histrionic/obsessive-compulsive couples. Finally, Slavik, Carlson, and Sperry (1998) outline an Adlerian approach to marital therapy with passive-aggressive personality disorder.

Cluster A—Odd, Eccentric Group

The odd, eccentric group, which includes the paranoid, schizoid, and schizotypal personality disorders, has little in the way of marital and family literature of significance, again, likely due to the tendency on the part of these individuals to avoid significant close interpersonal relationships. A notable exception in the literature is a paper by McCormack (1989), which focuses on the borderline/schizoid marriage. McCormack's approach incorporates a combination of individual and couple work in the context of a "holding environment" created by the therapist where clients can safely work through their issues while the therapist helps to contain their conflict and anxiety.

IMPACT OF PERSONALITY DISORDER ON FAMILIES

Although we have begun to see the emergence of a variety of marital and family treatment models for intervening with personality disordered individuals and their families, relatively little research has focused on the impact of personality-disordered individuals on their family members. As Mitton and Links (1996) write, "Little attention has been paid to assisting the parents, siblings, spouses, children, and other family members of patients with personality disorders in managing their close relationships with the patient, or to considering the family's involvement in the ongoing treatment plan" (p. 196). This is an unfortunate situation, since the literature has increasingly indicated that knowledge about mental illness and supportive family intervention can improve family interaction, reduce family burden, and have a positive impact on the prognosis of the mentally ill family member.

The number of emerging self-help books that are aimed at helping family members to cope with the impact of personality-disordered individuals is an indication of the current need in this area. Kreisman and Straus (1989) and Mason and Kreger (1998) have both produced excellent books describing the impact of living with a relative with borderline personality disorder, and these books are well worth reading for clinicians. Kreisman and Straus focus on helping family members in dealing with borderline rage, living with borderline mood swings, and handling impulsivity. Mason and Kreger discuss feelings of grief experienced by partners of borderline personality-disordered individuals, as well as common reactions and coping mechanisms, such as feelings of bewilderment, loss of self-esteem, feelings of guilt and shame, isolation, depression, withdrawal, and physical illnesses.

It is clear from these works that family members of personality-disordered individuals experience a variety of negative effects, and would benefit from supportive interventions aimed at strengthening family coping skills. Unfortunately, few programs address the needs of family members, and family members often feel blamed by both the ill family member and by helping professionals for their loved one's illness. Fortunately, some creative family intervention programs are beginning to evolve, including the family psychoeducational program at McLean Hospital in Belmont, Massachusetts, described by Gunderson and colleagues (1997); the program run by Jerold Kreisman and colleagues at St. John's Mercy Medical Center in Bethesda, Maryland; and the program described by Mitton and Links (1996) at Whitby Mental Health Centre's Psychotherapy Treatment Unit in Whitby, Ontario. These programs offer a variety of interventions to families of personality-disordered individuals, including information, psychoeducation, support, validation, crisis management skills, stress management, risk management (regarding the ill relatives self-injurious or aggressive behavior), and other services.

TOWARD AN INTEGRATED
FAMILY-FOCUSED APPROACH

From this literature review, it should be clear that personality disorders are complex, multidetermined illnesses for which a variety of neurobiological, developmental, familial, and social factors must be taken into consideration in treatment planning. Although personality disorders were once considered difficult or impossible to treat, a variety of effective integrative treatment approaches are evolving that have solid research support for their effectiveness. These multidimensional treatment approaches draw typically on biological/pharmacological, psychodynamic, cognitive-behavioral, and psychosocial interventions.

What remains lacking in this approach are treatment models that incorporate a family systems perspective, focus on interventions designed to help support the families of personality-disordered individuals, and assist individuals with personality disorders in their efforts to develop healthier interactions with their spouses and families. A trend is beginning toward the development of these needed multidimensional marital and family treatment models, but family-focused treatment of personality disorders treatment remains in its infancy (Magnavita, 2000a). This book addresses the gap in the existing literature by bringing together descriptions of a number of promising multidimensional family treatment approaches. Hopefully, the information and ideas contained in this work will help clinicians and families work more closely together to facilitate change in personality-disordered individuals, and develop healthier and more fulfilling relationships for all family members.

REFERENCES

Ackerman, N. W. (1957). The emergence of family diagnosis and treatment: A personal view. *Psychotherapy: Theory, Research, and Practice, 4*(3), 125-129.

Ackerman, N. W. (1958). *The psychodynamics of family life: Diagnostic and treatment of family relationships.* New York: Basic Books.

Alexander, F. G. and Selesnick, S. T. (1966). *The history of psychiatry.* New York: Harper Row.

American Psychiatric Association (1980). *Diagnostic and statistical manual of mental disorders* (Third edition). Washington, DC: Author.

American Psychiatric Association (1994). *Diagnostic and statistical manual of mental disorders* (Fourth edition). Washington, DC: Author.

Beck, A. T., Freeman, A., and Associates (1990). *Cognitive therapy of personality disorders.* New York: Guilford Press.

Benjamin, L. S. (1993). *Interpersonal diagnosis and treatment of personality disorders.* New York: Guilford Press.

Bowen, M. (1976). Theory and practice of family therapy. In P. J. Guerin Jr. (Ed.), *Family therapy: Theory and practice* (pp. 42-90). New York: Gardner Press.

Clarkin, J. F., Yeomans, F. E., and Kernberg, O. F. (1999). *Psychotherapy for borderline personality.* New York: John Wiley and Sons.

Cloninger, C. R. (1986). A unified biosocial theory of personality and its role in the development of anxiety states. *Psychiatric Developments,* 3, 167-226.

Cloninger, C. R. (1987). A systematic method for clinical description and classification of personality variants: A proposal. *Archives of General Psychiatry,* 44, 573-588.

Cloninger, C. R., Svrakic, D., and Przybeck, R. (1993). A psychobiological model of temperment and character. *Archives of General Psychiatry,* 50, 975-990.

Coccaro, E. F. (1993). Psychopharmacologic studies in patients with personality disorders: Review and perspective. *Journal of Personality Disorders,* 7(suppl.), 181-192.

Coccaro, E. F. and Siever, L. J. (1995). The neuropsychopharmacology of personality disorders. In F. E. Bloom and D. J. Kupfer (Eds.), *Psychopharmacology: The fourth generation of progress* (pp. 1567-1580). New York: Raven.

Costa, P. T. and McCrae, R. R. (1992). The five-factor model of personality and its relevance to personality disorders. *Journal of Personality Disorders,* 6, 343-359.

Doherty, N. (1997). For better, for worse: Marital and family therapy and the personality disorders. *Journal of Analytic Social Work,* 4(1), 43-59.

Doherty, W. J. and Simmons, D. S. (1996). Clinical practice patterns of marriage and family therapists: A national survey of therapists and their clients. *Journal of Marital and Family Therapy,* 22(1), 9-25.

Dollard, J. and Miller, N. E. (1950). *Personality and psychotherapy: An analysis in terms of learning, thinking, and culture.* New York: McGraw-Hill.

Engel, G. L. (1980). The clinical application of the biopsychosocial model. *American Journal of Psychiatry,* 137(5), 535-544.

Everett, C., Halperin, S., Volgy, S., and Wissler, A. (1989). *Treating the borderline family: A systematic approach.* San Diego: The Psychological Corporation.

Ferenczi, S. and Rank, O. (1925). *The development of psychoanalysis.* New York: Nervous and Mental Disease Publishing Co.

Gabbard, G. O. (2000). Psychotherapy of personality disorders. *Journal of Psychotherapy Practice and Research,* 9(1), 1-6.

Glick, I. D., Dulit, R. A., Wachter, E., and Clarkin, J. F. (1995). The family, family therapy, and borderline personality disorder. *Journal of Psychotherapy Practice and Research,* 4(3), 237-245.

Glick, I. D. and Loraas, E. L. (2001). Family treatment of borderline personality disorder. In M. M. MacFarlane (Ed.), *Family therapy and mental health: Innovations in theory and practice* (pp. 135-154). Binghamton, NY: The Haworth Press.

Gunderson, J. G., Berkowitz, C., and Ruiz-Sancho, A. (1997). Families of borderline patients: A psychoeducational approach. *Bulletin of the Menninger Clinic,* 61(4), 446-457.

Harbin, H. (1981). Family therapy with personality disorders. In J. Lion (Ed.), *Personality disorders: Diagnosis and management* (Second editon) (pp. 472-497). Baltimore: Williams and Wilkins.

Harman, M. J. and Waldo, M. (2001). Family treatment of borderline personality disorder through relationship enhancement therapy. In M. M. MacFarlane (Ed.), *Family therapy and mental health: Innovations in theory and practice* (pp. 215-235). Binghamton, NY: The Haworth Press.

Jang, K. L. and Vernon, P. A. (2001). Genetics. In W. J. Livesley (Ed.), *Handbook of personality disorders: Theory, research, and treatment* (pp. 177-195). New York: Guilford Press.

Kalogjera, I. J., Jacobson, G. R., Hoffman. G. K., Hoffman, P., Raffe, I. H., White, H. C., and Leonard-White, A. (1998). The narcissistic couple. In J. Carlson and L. Sperry (Eds.), *The disordered couple* (pp. 207-237). Bristol, PA: Brunner/Mazel.

Kaslow, F. W. (Ed.) (1996). *Handbook of relational diagnosis and dysfunctional family patterns*. New York: John Wiley and Sons.

Kernberg, O. (1984). *Severe personality disorders: Psychotherapeutic strategies*. New Haven: Yale University Press.

Koch, A. and Ingram, T. (1985). The treatment of borderline personality disorder within a distressed relationship. *Journal of Marital and Family Therapy*, 11(4), 373-380.

Kohut, H. (1971). *The analysis of the self*. New York: International Universities Press.

Kraepelin, E. (1907). *Clinical psychiatry* (A. R. Diefendorf, Trans.). New York: Macmillan.

Kreisman, J. J. and Straus, H. (1989). *I hate you—don't leave me: Understanding the borderline personality*. New York: Avon Books.

Lachkar, J. (1992). *The narcissistic/borderline couple: A psychoanalytic perspective to marital conflict*. New York: Brunner/Mazel.

Lachkar, J. (1998). Narcissistic/borderline couples: A psychodynamic approach to conjoint treatment. In J. Carlson and L. Sperry (Eds.), *The disordered couple* (pp. 259-283). Briston, PA: Brunner/Mazel.

Leary, T. (1957). *Interpersonal diagnosis of personality*. New York: Ronald Press.

Lenzenweger, M. F. and Clarkin, J. F. (1996). The personality disorders: History, classification, and research issues. In J. F. Clarkin and M. F. Lenzenweger (Eds.), *Major theories of personality disorder* (pp. 1-35). New York: Guilford Press.

Linehan, M. M. (1993). *Cognitive-behavioral treatment of borderline personality disorder*. New York: Guilford Press.

Links, P. (Ed.) (1990). *Family environment and borderline personality disorder*. Washington, DC: American Psychiatric Press.

Livesley, W. J. (1998). Suggestions for a framework for an empirically based classification of personality disorder. *Canadian Journal of Psychiatry*, 43, 137-147.

Livesley, W. J. (2001). Conceptual and taxonomic issues. In W. J. Livesley (Ed.), *Handbook of personality disorders: Theory, research, and treatment* (pp. 3-38). New York: Guilford Press.

Livesley, W. J., Schroeder, M. L., Jackson, D. N., and Jang, K. L. (1994). Categorical distinctions in the study of personality disorder: Implications for classification. *Journal of Abnormal Psychology*, 103, 6-17.

MacFarlane, M. M. (2001). Preface. In M. M. MacFarlane (Ed.), *Family therapy and mental health: Innovations in theory and practice* (pp. xxi-xxv). Binghamton, NY: The Haworth Press.

Magnavita, J. J. (1997a). *Restructuring personality disorders: A short-term dynamic approach.* New York: Guilford Press.

Magnavita, J. J. (1997b). Treating personality disorders: Psychotherapy's frontier. *Psychotherapy Bulletin*, 32(1), 23-28.

Magnavita, J. J. (1998a). Challenges in the treatment of personality disorders: When the disorder demands comprehensive treatment. *In Session: Psychotherapy in Practice*, 4(4), 5-17.

Magnavita, J. J. (1998b). Advancements in the treatment of personality disorders: Introduction. Special edition. *In Session: Psychotherapy in Practice*, 4(4), 1-4.

Magnavita, J. J. (1998c). Methods of restructuring personality disorders with comorbid syndromes. *In Session: Psychotherapy in Practice*, 4(4), 73-89.

Magnavita, J. J. (2000a). Integrative relational therapy for complex clinical syndromes: Ending the multigenerational transmission process. *Journal of Clinical Psychology/In Session: Psychotherapy in Practice*, 56(8), 1051-1064.

Magnavita, J. J. (2000b). The growth of relational therapy: Introduction. *Journal of Clinical Psychology/In Session: Psychotherapy in Practice*, 56(8), 999-1004.

Magnavita, J. J. (2000c). *Relational therapy for personality disorders.* New York: John Wiley and Sons.

Magnavita, J. J. (2001a). Affirmation and active defense restructuring: Accelerating access to the unconscious. *Quaderni di Psichiatria*, 6(17/18), 77-79.

Magnavita, J. J. (2001b). Restructuring personality disorders to metabolize affect associated with trauma. *Quaderni di Psichiatria*, 6(17/18), 149-156.

Magnavita, J. J. (2002a). Contemporary psychodynamics: Major issues, challenges, and future trends. In F. W. Kaslow (Editor in Chief) and J. J. Magnavita (Vol. Ed.), *Comprehensive handbook of psychotherapy, Volume 1: Psychodynamic/object relations* (pp. 587-604). New York: John Wiley and Sons.

Magnavita, J. J. (2002b). Psychodynamic approaches to psychotherapy: A century of innovations. In F. W. Kaslow (Editor in Chief) and J. J. Magnavita (Vol. Ed.). *Comprehensive handbook of psychotherapy, Volume 1: Psychodynamic/object relations* (pp. 1-12). New York: John Wiley and Sons.

Magnavita, J. J. (2002c). Relational psychodynamics for complex clinical syndromes. In F. W. Kaslow (Editor in Chief) and J. J. Magnavita (Vol. Ed.), *Comprehensive handbook of psychotherapy, Volume 1: Psychodynamic/object relations* (pp. 435-453). New York: John Wiley and Sons.

Magnavita, J. J. (2002d). *Theories of personality: Contemporary approaches to the science of personality.* New York: John Wiley and Sons.

Magnavita, J. J. (in press). *Personality-guided relational psychotherapy: A component systems model.* Washington, DC: American Psychological Association.

Mason, P. T. and Kreger, R. (1998). *Stop walking on eggshells: Taking your life back when someone you care about has borderline personality disorder.* Oakland, CA: New Harbinger Publications.

Mattia, J. I. and Zimmerman, M. (2001). Epidemiology. In W. J. Livesley (Ed.). *Handbook of personality disorders: Theory, research, and treatment* (pp. 107-123). New York: Guilford Press.

McCormack, C. C. (1989). The borderline/schizoid marriage: The holding environment as an essential treatment construct. *Journal of Marital and Family Therapy,* 15(3), 299-309.

McWilliams, N. (1994). *Psychoanalytic diagnosis: Understanding personality structure in clinical practice.* New York: Guilford Press.

Merikangas, K.R. and Weissman, M. M. (1986). Epidemiology of DSM-III Axis II personality disorders. In A. J. Francis and R. E. Hales (Eds.). *Psychiatry update: The American Psychiatric Association annual review* (Volume 5) (pp. 258-278). Washington, DC: American Psychiatric Press.

Millon, T. (1990). *Toward a new personology: An evolutionary model.* New York: Wiley-Interscience.

Millon, T. and Davis, R. D. (1995). Conceptions of personality disorders: Historical perspectives, the DSMs, and future directions. In W. J. Livesley (Ed.), *The DSM-IV personality disorders* (pp. 3-27). New York: Guilford Press.

Millon, T. and Davis, R. D. (1996a). An evolutionary theory of personality disorders. In J. F. Clarkin and M. F. Lenzenweger (Eds.), *Major theories of personality disorder* (pp. 221-346). New York: Guilford Press.

Millon, T. and Davis, R. D. (1996b). *Disorders of personality: DSM-IV and beyond.* New York: John Wiley and Sons.

Millon, T., Grossman, S., Meagher, S., Millon, C., and Everly, G. (1999). *Personality-guided therapy.* New York: John Wiley and Sons.

Mitton, M. J. E. and Links, P. S. (1996). Helping the family: A framework for intervention. In P. S. Links (Ed.), *Clinical assessment and management of severe personality disorders* (pp. 195-218). Washington, DC: American Psychiatric Press.

Nichols, W. C. (1996). Persons with antisocial and histrionic personality disorders. In F. W. Kaslow (Ed.), *Handbook of relational diagnosis and dysfunctional family patterns* (pp. 287-299). New York: John Wiley and Sons.

Norcross, J. C. and Goldfried, M. R. (Eds.) (1992). *Handbook of psychotherapy integration.* New York: Basic Books.

Nurse, A. R. (1998). The dependent/narcissistic couple. In J. Carlson and L. Sperry (Eds.), *The disordered couple* (pp. 315-331). Bristol, PA: Brunner/Mazel.

Paris, J. (1994). The etiology of borderline personality disorder: A biopsychosocial approach. *Psychiatry: Interpersonal and biological processes,* 57(4), 316-325.

Paris, J. (2001). Psychosocial adversity. In W. J. Livesley (Ed.), *Handbook of personality disorders: Theory, research, and treatment* (pp. 231-241). New York: Guilford Press.

Pretzer, J. L. and Beck, A. T. (1996). A cognitive theory of personality disorders. In J. F. Clarkin and M. F. Lenzenweger (Eds.), *Major theories of personality disorder* (pp. 36-105). New York: Guilford Press.

Ruiz-Sancho, A. M., Smith, G. W., and Gunderson, J. G. (2001). Psychoeducational approaches. In W. J. Livesley (Ed.), *Handbook of personality disorders: Theory, research, and treatment* (pp. 460-474). New York: Guilford Press.

Shea, M. T., Pilkonis, P. A., Beckham, E., Collins, J. F., Elkin, I., Sotsky, S. M., and Docherty, J. P. (1990). Personality disorders and treatment outcome in the NIMH Treatment of Depression Collaborative Research Program. *American Journal of Psychiatry*, 147, 711-718.

Siever, L. J. and Davis, K. L. (1991). A psychobiological perspective on personality disorders. *American Journal of Psychiatry*, 148, 1647-1658.

Silk, K. R. (1996). Rational pharmacotherapy for patients with personality disorders. In P. S. Links (Ed.), *Clinical assessment and management of severe personality disorders* (pp. 109-142). Washington, DC: American Psychiatric Press.

Slavik, S., Carlson, J., and Sperry, L. (1998). The passive-aggressive couple. In J. Carlson and L. Sperry (Eds.), *The disordered couple* (pp. 299-313). Bristol, PA: Brunner/Mazel.

Slipp, S. (1995). Object relations marital therapy of personality disorders. In N. S. Jacobson and A. S. Gurman (Eds.), *Clinical handbook of couple therapy* (pp. 458-470). New York: Guilford Press.

Snyder, M. (1994). Couple therapy with narcissistically vulnerable clients: Using the relationship enhancement model. *The Family Journal: Counselling and Therapy for Couples and Families*, 2, 27-35.

Solomon, M. F. (1996). Understanding and treating couples with borderline disorders. In F. W. Kaslow (Ed.), *Handbook of relational diagnosis and dysfunctional family patterns* (pp. 251-269). New York: John Wiley and Sons.

Solomon, M. F. (1998). Treating narcissistic and borderline couples. In J. Carlson and L. Sperry (Eds.), *The disordered couple* (pp. 239-257). Bristol, PA: Brunner/Mazel.

Sperry, L. (1995). *Handbook of diagnosis and treatment of the DSM-IV personality disorders*. New York: Brunner/Mazel.

Sperry, L. (1999). *Cognitive behavior therapy of DSM-IV personality disorders: Highly effective interventions for the most common personality disorders*. Philadelphia, PA: Brunner/Mazel.

Sperry, L. and Maniacci, M. P. (1998). The histrionic-obsessive couple. In J. Carlson and L. Sperry (Eds.), *The disordered couple* (pp. 187-205). Bristol, PA: Brunner/Mazel.

Stone, M. H. (1997). *Healing the mind: A history of psychiatry from antiquity to the present*. New York: W. W. Norton and Company.

Sullivan, H. S. (1953). *The interpersonal theory of psychiatry*. New York: Norton.

Tyrer, P., Gunderson, J., Lyons, M., and Tohen, M. (1997). Special feature: Extent of comorbidity between mental state and personality disorders. *Journal of Personality Disorders*, 11(3), 242-259.

von Bertalanffy, L. (1968). *General systems theory: Foundations, development, and applications.* New York: Braziller.

Waldo, M. and Harman, J. (1993). Relationship enhancement therapy with borderline personality. *The Family Journal, 1,* 25-30.

Watson, J. B. (1924). *Behaviorism.* Chicago: University of Chicago Press.

Widiger, T. A. and Sanderson, C. J. (1995). Toward a dimensional model of personality disorders. In W. J. Livesley (Ed.), *The DSM-IV personality disorders* (pp. 433-458). New York: Guilford Press.

Winston, A., Laikin, M., Pollack, J., Samstag, I. W., McCullough, L., and Muran, C. (1994). Short-term psychotherapy of personality disorders. *American Journal of Psychiatry, 15(2),* 190-194.

Young, J. (1994). *Cognitive therapy for personality disorders: A schema-focused approach* (Revised edition). Sarasota, FL: Professional Resource Exchange.

Chapter 2

An Interpersonal Family-Oriented Approach to Personality Disorder

Lorna Smith Benjamin
Gretta Cushing

INTRODUCTION

Having a personality-disordered family member can offer special challenges to the identified patient (IP), family, and health care providers. According to the *Diagnostic and Statistical Manual of Mental Disorders,* Fourth Edition (DSM-IV, American Psychiatric Association, 1994, p. 628), a personality disorder is "an enduring pattern of inner experience and behavior that deviates markedly from the expectations of the individual's culture, is pervasive and inflexible, has an onset in adolescence or early adulthood, is stable over time, and leads to distress or impairment" (reprinted with permission from the *Diagnostic and Statistical Manual of Mental Disorders,* Fourth Edition, copyright 1994 American Psychiatric Association). The DSM-IV describes ten different personality disorders, and substantial debate continues about their reliability and validity (e.g., O'Connor and Dyce, 1998; Perry and Perry, 1996). Much of the debate centers on (1) whether personality disorders are better described in terms of underlying dimensions instead of the categories described by the DSM, and (2) whether and where a boundary exists between normal and abnormal personality traits. An illustrative discussion of these questions concerning categorical diagnosis and definitions of normality appeared in Widiger and Costa (1994).

This chapter begins with a brief review of Benjamin's (1979, 1987) Structural Analysis of Social Behavior (SASB), followed by Benjamin's (1996) interpersonal descriptions of personality disorder, based on the SASB-directed dimensional descriptions of the DSM categories. Passive-aggressive personality disorder is used to illustrate how the SASB system describes personality disorder (PAG is used in this chapter to refer to either the category passive-aggressive personality disorder or to an individual with the disorder). Next is a brief summary of Benjamin's (2003) Interpersonal Reconstructive Therapy (IRT), which was developed as an effective treatment of the so-called nonresponder population, and frequently includes personality disordered individuals. Finally,the chapter focuses on the use of conjoint family therapy within IRT to treat PAG.

The SASB Dimensional Model of Interpersonal and Intrapsychic Interactions

In 1996 Benjamin applied a dimensional model called the structural analysis of social behavior to the DSM-IV items that describe personality disorder (Benjamin, 1996). The model, presented in Figure 2.1, classifies interactional events, whether they are interpersonal or intrapsychic, according to two underlying dimensions: affiliation

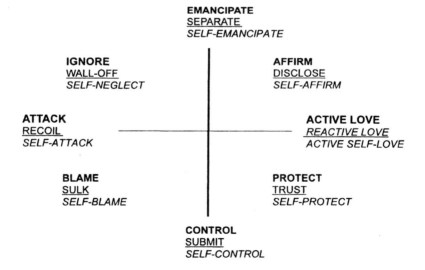

FIGURE 2.1. Simplified Cluster version of the SASB model. (*Source:* Benjamin, L. S. [1996]. *Interpersonal Diagnosis and Treatment of Personality Disorder, Second Edition.* New York: Guilford Press.)

and interdependence. Guttman (1966) first described for social scientists the mathematical advantages and disadvantages of such a model, which is called a *circumplex*.

Benjamin's version of a circumplex assumes three forms, or variations, that differ in terms of attentional focus. These are represented by the three types of print in Figure 2.1. The first variation is focus on other, a transitive action that has to do with what is being done to, for, or about another person (e.g., "You are wrong about that," SASB coded **BLAME**). Transitive behaviors are prototypically parentlike. A glance at Figure 2.1 shows that parentlike behaviors include far more than the stereotyped restriction of parenting to exertion of **CONTROL**.

A second variation is focus on self, an intransitive reaction to another that has to do with what is being done to, for, about, or with the self (e.g., "I resentfully give in to your perspective," SASB coded *SULK*). Focus on self is prototypically childlike. However, as will be shown in the examples to follow, focus on self can be manifest by parents. In an ideal adult relationship, focus on self and other is shared equally by each partner.

The last type of focus is introject, which represents transitive action directed inward toward the self (e.g., "I am wrong about that," SASB coded *SELF-BLAME*). Introjective focus was clearly described by Sullivan (1953) in his discussion of the development of the self.

The horizontal dimension of the SASB model, affiliation, is represented on the horizontal axis and ranges from love to hate (e.g., **ATTACK** to **ACTIVE LOVE** when the focus is on other, RECOIL to REACTIVE LOVE when focus is on self, and *SELF-ATTACK* to *SELF-LOVE* when focus is introjected).

The vertical dimension of the SASB model is called interdependence, and ranges from enmeshment to differentiation. Maximal enmeshment is shown by the lowermost points on the vertical axis of Figure 2.1: **CONTROL**, SUBMIT, and *SELF-CONTROL*. Differentiation is depicted by the uppermost poles on the vertical axis, **EMANCIPATE**, SEPARATE, and *SELF-EMANCIPATE*.

Any interactional event can be dissected into these underlying dimensions (focus, affiliation, and interdependence) and placed in categories with expanding or diminishing boundaries, depending on the complexity of the situation and the preferences of the SASB clinician or research user. For example, consider a father scolding an adolescent during a family conference for breaking curfew last week. This would be described on Figure 2.1, which presents the simplified cluster model, in terms of the category **BLAME**. Given that he is focusing on his son in a hostile and controlling manner, this category lies between the underlying dimensions of **CONTROL** and **ATTACK** on Figure 2.1. The two-word cluster model (Benjamin, 1996) would name this event **Belittling and Blaming.** The full SASB model (Benjamin, 1979) offers several possibilities within this same region of hostile, controlling focus on other, depending on the relative degrees of **ATTACK** and **CONTROL** that comprise the event. If the father's words, tone, and the overall context suggested more emphasis on hostility than on control, the full model point chosen to represent the event might be the most hostile point within this cluster, **Punish, take revenge.** If less fury was in the delivery and more emphasis was on control, the father's behavior might better be described by the most controlling point within this cluster, **Put down, act superior.**

By allowing the user to draw on continuous underlying dimensions to define categories, and by allowing combinations of categories to apply to a single event, the SASB model provides an unlimited number of ways to describe an event. The most complex example published to date appeared in Humphrey and Benjamin (1986), in which the classic Bateson "double bind" was dissected into three process components (informally described here as affection, coercion, and miscuing) that were directed toward (content codes of) self-definition and attachment.

Several predictive principles accompany the SASB model, including complementarity and introjection. Complementarity predicts likely matches within dyadic interactions. They are shown in Figure 2.1 as adjacent **BOLD** and UNDERLINED points. To illustrate: **BLAME** by the parent is likely to yield SULK by the child. As suggested earlier, the SASB model is indifferent as to who can be classified on the parentlike surface and who reacts on the childlike surface. In fact, by the time families engaged in hostile enmeshment arrive in the clinic, it is frequently the child who **BLAME**s and the parent who SULKs.

A number of circumplex models have been proposed for use in describing social interactions. The best known is the Interpersonal circle, proposed by Leary (1957). A comparison of SASB with the Leary circle has appeared elsewhere (Benjamin, 1996). Olson (1986, 1991) used circumplex theory to describe family functions. His circular model characterizes families according to levels of cohesion on one axis and adaptability on the other. At extreme levels of cohesion, families are said to be "enmeshed" (too close) or "disengaged" (too separate). Adaptability refers to the presence or absence of structure in the family. At extremely high levels, families are characterized as rigid or too controlled, and at extremely low levels, chaotic. A number of areas of similarity exist between Olson's circumplex model, and Benjamin's SASB model, but there are also major and significant theoretical differences regarding their theoretical underpinnings and how the dimensions of each model are conceptualized. A full discussion of the similarities and differences between these models is beyond the scope of this chapter.

Application of the SASB Model to the DSM Definitions of Personality Disorder

Benjamin's (1996) application of the SASB model to the DSM descriptions of personality disorder yielded (1) interpersonal descriptions ("translations") of each disorder; (2) testable and refutable hypotheses about likely interpersonal antecedents to the interactional patterns characteristic of the respective DSM disorders; and (3) testable and refutable hypotheses about DSM descriptors that should be considered "necessary" and "exclusionary" for the DSM to define interpersonally coherent patterns of interaction. For PAG, results were:

> There is a tendency to see any form of power as inconsiderate and neglectful, together with a belief that caregivers are incompetent, unfair and cruel. The PAG agrees to comply with perceived demands or suggestions, but fails to perform. He or she often complains of unfair treatment and envies and resents others who fare better. His or her suffering indicts the allegedly negligent caregivers or authorities. The PAG fears control in any form and wishes for nurturant restitution. (Benjamin, 1996, p. 269)

Using the SASB predictive principles and clinical experience, Benjamin suggested that a typical person with PAG would have had (1) a nurturant infancy followed by (2) abrupt loss of that nurturance with unfair demands for performance, and (3) harsh punishments for anger, autonomy, or failure to perform tasks at the standard expected. As a result of these interpersonal lessons, the PAG expects and feels entitled to nurturance, is extremely sensitive to being coerced, and sees caregivers as inconsiderate, incompetent, and neglectful. He or she feels deprived, complains of unfairness, and is resentful and envious.

Necessary conditions for this disorder are a pattern of punitive neediness and a tendency to seem to comply while actually resisting demands to perform. It is believed that self-harm indicts authorities and caregivers. Exclusionary conditions include uncomplicated deference more characteristic of individuals with dependent personality disorder, or excessive devotion to productivity, usually seen in individuals with obsessive-compulsive personality disorder.

Passive aggressive personality disorder was moved from Axis II in the DSM-III-R to the appendix of the DSM-IV. The main reason was that diagnoses of PAG had been markedly unreliable in field tests. In the DSM-IV, PAG is called "personality disorder, not otherwise specified, passive-aggressive type." The diagnosis may have disappeared from the main body of the DSM, but the pattern has not disappeared from the clinic. In Benjamin's practice for nonresponder cases, a very large percentage of unremittingly depressed, anxious, and suicidal patients that have had repeated hospitalizations qualify for the PAG label.

Several reasons may account for the unreliability of the PAG diagnosis. One is that the DSM's description of this pattern needs to be improved. Another is the disorder's comorbidity with borderline personality disorder (BPD) on Axis II, and the fact that these two personality disorders share comorbid Axis I patterns as well. For example, both PAG and BPD patients are highly comorbid with depression, show chronic suicidality, and are irritable and angry around the subject of having their needs met. Axis II comorbidity is well documented in the research literature (e.g., Morey, 1988; Becker et al., 2001). Benjamin (1996) compared these two disorders in terms of their interpersonal dimensionality as described by SASB.

> [T]hese two share the baseline labels of **BLAME** and *SELF-ATTACK*, as well as the wish for **PROTECT.** There are very important differences in their fears: the BPD dreads receiving **IGNORE,** while the PAG, who is quite capable of autonomy, is exquisitely sensitive to **CONTROL.** The BPD behaves in a colorful way and shifts from position to position. The PAG shows complex combinations of submission and autonomy, friendli-

ness and hostility. Both will blame the therapist and engage in self-sabotage through suicidal and other self-destructive acts. But the goals and the styles are different. The BPD is chaotic and passionate, trying to coerce caregiving; the PAG is surly and convoluted, resisting control and punishing defaulting care-givers. (pp. 401-402)

These differences suggest that a treatment approach that is highly structured, such as Linehan's dialectical behavior therapy (Linehan, 1993), will be well received by BPD individuals because warm struc-ture is the opposite (see Figure 2.1) of abandonment, which is dreaded by BPDs because of their history of traumatic abandonment. By con-trast, PAGs are more likely to feel injured and abused by any demands to follow rules and comply with structure. These individuals are ready to react to structure with self-destruction, which suggests the caregiver is incompetent and cruel. They often respond better to what Benjamin calls "cat therapy," meaning any structure offered is simply placed "outside the door" in case the PAG might be interested. It is extremely important that such structure be offered, albeit in an indi-rect way. The reason is that individuals with PAG are highly ambiva-lent. Even as they resent any demands, they are also vulnerable to feeling neglected and not cared about if they are not included!

The salience of ambivalence and contradiction are possible addi-tional reasons for the unreliability of the PAG diagnosis, which does not presently include that feature as a formal descriptor. Further dis-cussion of PAG and its relation to BPD and other personality disor-ders is beyond the present scope of this chapter.

Interpersonal Reconstructive Therapy (IRT)

Benjamin (2003) described a psychotherapy that addresses the needs of the so-called nonresponder population. The basic idea is that people who have been unable to respond to treatment as usual (TAU), including medications and psychotherapy, have more reasons to stay as they are than to change. According to IRT, such reasons are likely to be derivatives of the fact that problem patterns are linked to learn-ing with important early loved ones via one or more of three copy processes. These are: (1) be like him or her, (2) act as if he or she is still there and in control, and (3) treat yourself as he or she treated you. For example, if a child has a relentlessly critical parent, the child is very likely to become critical of and displeased with himself or herself. The copying is maintained by fantasies that an Important Person and his or her Internalized Representation (IPIR) ultimately will provide the desired love if the patient's living testimony to the IPIR's rules and values is good enough. Patients who criticize and disapprove of themselves morbidly are probably treating themselves as important loved ones treated them. Applying that old view to themselves represents incorporation of the perceived parental rules and values. Such intense devotion to relentless self-criticism suggests a continuing wish to please that parent. When patients fully recognize the role of copy processes and the underlying wishes that support them, they have insight as defined in IRT.

Since the relationship with the internalization is immensely powerful, treatment must focus sharply on grieving and letting go of these fantasy residues of early attachments. In IRT, flow charts guide the clinician in using the theory to develop the individual case formulation and choose optimal treatment interventions on a moment to moment basis. The core algorithm details the required domains of focus. IRT has five steps, each requiring activities that facilitate self-discovery (psychodynamic) and self-management (cognitive-behavioral). All steps address a basic conflict between the Regressive Loyalist (red: the part that seeks the approval of the IPIRs) and the Growth Collaborator (green: the part that comes to therapy for constructive change). The five steps are:

1. Collaboration (the therapy relationship);
2. Learning about patterns, where they are from, and what they are for (insight);
3. Blocking problem patterns (crisis and stalemate management);
4. Enabling the will to change (in steps that compare to Prochaska, DiClements, and Norcross's [1992] transtheoretical stages of change); and
5. Learning new patterns (via standard behavioral technology [Benjamin, 2003]).

IRT uses any and all therapy approaches so long as they are consistent with the core algorithm.

The emphasis on differentiating from problem wishes, fears, and problem patterns associated with IPIRs is similar to Bowen's (1978) focus on self differentiation in transgenerational family systems theory. In Bowen's approach, differentiation of self from one's family of origin was the central therapeutic goal and considered a precondition for one's psychological health and ability to form healthy marital and family relationships. As in IRT, Bowen's conceptualization of differentiation was both intrapsychic and interpersonal. He described intrapsychic differentiation as the ability to separate thought from feeling, and posited that interpersonal differentiation occurs in concert with intrapsychic differentiation. Undifferentiated people are governed by emotional reactions, have little autonomous identity, and tend to either conform or assume pseudoindependence through counterconformity, responding reactively in patterned behaviors learned within their families of origin. In contrast, individuals with a higher level of differentiation typically are more proactive and goal directed, maintain a balance between thought and feeling and a clear sense of self. Bowen worked toward assisting patients in achieving higher levels of differentiation by mapping out their family relationship patterns in genograms, coaching them in recognizing relational triangles, and learning to relate in ways that promote differentiation.

IMPACT ON THE FAMILY

Personality Disorder in Family Dynamics and Family Burden

The suffering of an individual with PAG is immense. To resist perceived coercion and punish the perceived coercers, the PAG develops the strategy of winning by losing. This causes endless despair and pain and, too frequently, ultimate self-destruction through suicide. Necessarily, this pattern inflicts comparable degrees of pain upon the family. Having been quite focused on the PAG individual, whom the parent had tried to force into having a much better life, the PAG's "in-your-face" failure to perform is devastating. Parent ultimatums to conform and perform, and patient accusations of inadequate and cruel parenting frequently dominate family sessions. Patients express or suppress tremendous feelings of despair, hurt, and rage over perceived abuse and broken promises. Parents are highly likely to have been told by health care providers to stop trying to control the PAG. Honoring that injunction as best they can, parents struggle with frustration and worry over how to avoid control and yet provide the requested and needed support to prevent suicide and encourage recovery.

This dilemma reflects the ambivalence on both sides: the PAG wants to be taken care of but does not want to be controlled. The SASB model makes it clear that nurturance (**PROTECT** on Figure 2.1) has a strong component of control. Hence, the PAG's wish is also his or her fear. Because the investment in compliance with standards of comportment and performance usually is great, parental nurturance is likely to arrive in the form of pure **CONTROL.** In their zeal, parents are likely to fail to be responsive to the PAG's developmental needs, and hence also would be described by the SASB category **IGNORE.** If the pressure to comply increases, aggression is added to the control, and the patterns settle in at **BLAME:SULK,** with children engaging in BLAME as often as SULK. Here lies the domain of hostile enmeshment that is so apparent in therapy with families displaying PAG patterns. Working with such high ambivalence and passion within the family is a challenge that frequently exhausts and deeply wounds nearly everyone. According to the SASB model, **BLAME** from health care providers is the last thing such families need. It only rubs more of the same toxin into an open wound. Better alternatives are discussed at length in Benjamin (2003).

Personality Disorder and Marriage

A PAG is highly likely to marry an individual with obsessive compulsive personality disorder (OCPD), a perfectionist who performs at a high level and is likely to take control to assure that all is in good order. During courtship, the PAG typically is initially attracted to the familiar pattern of control and the associated competently managed environment. But of course, those same features are also dreaded and compulsively resisted. Soon tension escalates over PAG messiness and OCPD excessive neatness. Everything from bill paying, child management, housekeeping, and more becomes an undeclared power struggle. The PAG soon wears a badge of martyrdom and the OCPD carries the label of cruel oppressor. Both suffer intensely. The PAG eschews taking responsibility for his or her feelings or actions (thereby avoiding **BLAME,** a most feared but familiar position). The OCPD likely will exhaust himself or herself in pursuit of mastery of the problem, and so the painful deadlock can drag through the years. Along the way, an inexperienced marital therapist might observe the OCPD is "too controlling," and fail to detect the oppositionalism, the demoralizing insincerity (e.g., compliant—indicting defiance) that contaminates the PAG's "agreeability." A more overt and clear example would be the PAG spouse who decides, after six months of procrastination that he or she must complete a cleaning project on the very Saturday night that an exciting new play is opening in town, and for which the OCPD spouse had managed to get tickets. If the therapist is not aware of the complicated meanings in such exchanges, problem patterns in the dyad will not be effectively addressed and the war will go on and on—everyone trying to win, and everyone actually losing.

Effect of Parent's Personality Disorder on Children

A child with a PAG parent will be confronted with a confusing mixture of **CONTROL** and <u>WALL OFF</u>. The PAG parent likely delivers what he or she saw modeled and becomes quite controlling of children, even as he or she will resist to the death any **CONTROL** from others. The natural complement to these parenting behaviors are <u>SUBMIT</u> and **IGNORE.** In more familiar language, the child with a PAG parent will face many rules, strictly enforced, not accompanied by parental disclosures that facilitate understanding about who the parent is as a person. The complementary results are that the child learns to defer to rules without much understanding or affectionate connection, and learns to be inattentive to what others are doing, feeling, and thinking. In extreme form, combined with other features, this pattern begins to resemble schizophreniclike social withdrawal and an utterly undefined sense of self.

Effect of a Child's Personality Disorder on a Parent

Having a child with well-developed PAG patterns is supremely frustrating, particularly to a parent highly invested in control of the child. Just as in the case of an OCPD married to a PAG, the unde-clared power war festers under a thin veil of affability. Seeming to comply, the PAG manages not to succeed, even if—as is often the case—what the parent wants is obviously for the child's own good. A trivial example is that the parent gets very upset if the teen does not put on socks for school, and the teen has a great day as he or she "for-gets" to put on his or her socks after gym class. A more serious exam-ple is the parent who carefully monitors and tries to maintain control over the teen's caloric intake. Although compliant at family meal-time, the teen finds many ways to binge in private and becomes mor-bidly obese.

SETTING

IRT centers on the so-called identified patient (IP). It draws freely on any and all approaches that can contribute to the five steps and be delivered within the core algorithm. Uses of conjoint family therapy to implement the therapy process and achieve the goals of IRT are discussed in this section. The model may be applied in a variety of in-patient and outpatient settings, including private practice. Examples used in this chapter are drawn from Benjamin's private practice and supervision of trainees in university-based inpatient and outpatient settings.

TREATMENT MODEL AND CASE EXAMPLES

The Underlying Theory of Psychopathology

The IRT theory of psychopathology holds that presenting problem patterns are residuals of wishes to adhere to rules and values of inter-nalized figures, who more often than not are family members. A PAG, for example, suppresses anger and other overt forms of asser-tion because he or she has learned that these behaviors bring strong disapproval from loved ones. A high level of performance is ex-pected, but instead of delivering as expected, the PAG is devoted to winning by losing. For example, the PAG will become hopelessly im-mersed in misery if the parent is seen as highly invested in his or her happiness. On the other hand, if the parent cares greatly about achievement, the PAG will fail miserably. As mentioned earlier, the PAG is both compliant and oppositional. He or she works hard toward an agreed-upon goal, such as earning a college degree. Despite apparent compliance with expectations, something untoward always happens so that the goal is never reached. Perhaps the PAG misses the final examination in a required course because of some relatively minor problem, such as a flat tire on his or her bicycle. The professor is deemed "unreasonable and unfair," because she failed the PAG, claiming there already had been too many missed assignments and exercises. The pattern repeats over and over. The contradiction between apparent compliance and functional failure vexes not only people who live with PAGs, but also, as mentioned above, diagnosticians who attempt to define the disorder reliably.

The IRT theory of psychopathology hypothesizes that the PAG is strongly attached to family, but also strives to self-define in ill-advised ways. The compliant aspects of his or her patterns represent an effort to please. The defiant side represents the effort to self-define. When the defiance becomes seriously self-destructive, as it frequently does (relentless failure, impulsive suicidality), IRT theory nonetheless maintains that attachment to early figures and wishes for love from them drive the pattern. The idea usually is that if the PAG suffers overtly, while not being "responsible," the (internalizations of) family figures will recognize the degree of suffering and their alleged role in it. They will stop withholding the desired goods and services, stop making unreasonable demands, confess that they have defaulted and been unfair, and they will make amends. Then, love and happiness will prevail. Every psychopathology is a gift of love (Benjamin, 1993).

The IRT Goal

The SASB model presumes to define normal behaviors, which are the therapy goal. Goal behaviors are basically friendly, moderately enmeshed, and moderately differentiated. Focus on self and focus on other is equally balanced. Note that in Figure 2.1, the friendly and moderate therapy goal behaviors are shown on the right-hand side of the model. Pathological behaviors are marked by hostile behaviors on the left-hand side of the model, and by the extremes of enmeshment and differentiation located at the poles of the vertical dimension.

Models of affective and cognitive behaviors that parallel the SASB model suggest that the therapy goal behaviors are accompanied by pleasant affects and effective cognitive styles (Benjamin, 2003). If an individual has internalized representations of persons who modeled normative behaviors, he or she will exhibit normal behaviors and affects. If an individual has internalized representations of persons who had hostile or excessively enmeshed or differentiated behaviors, he or she will show pathological behaviors via the mechanism of copy processes. In other words, a major difference between the development of a normal person and a disordered person is in what was copied. A common example of problem family interactive rules is: "win, lose, or leave." People whose interpersonal vocabulary is limited to these positions are trapped in unsatisfying relational systems, and are at high risk for feelings of omnipotence (win), defeat (lose), or loneliness (leave). The therapy challenge for these and other nonresponders is to transform or replace the internalized representations that are being honored by these limited views of relationship.

Problem Goals That Must Be Addressed by the Therapy

Change in the internalizations associated with hostile and unmodulated enmeshment or differentiation is not so easy. Insight will not suffice. Instead of genuine, friendly mutuality, families with a PAG member (or two or three) more likely are caught up in the win/lose/leave, right/wrong/resign standards of exchange. When those values predominate, the norm of noncontrolling, attentive affection is overshadowed. The PAG adaptation to such a milieu is to win by losing. By annihilating oneself, the PAG "proves" he or she has been egregiously harmed, neglected, and unfairly treated. On the other hand, if the PAG thrives, that means the neglectful commanders have been "let off the hook," and, according to the internal logic, this is worse than death. For one thing, performing and living normally means there never can be the fantasied reconciliation on terms that would leave the PAG friendly and whole (shown in the upper right hand side of Figure 2.1). So long as the old wishes prevail, it is unlikely that any treatment can be effective. IRT therefore focuses as often as possible on these underlying, angry motivators, and attempts to help the patient let go of them. Once the patient gives up the dream of rewriting history and understands that what never was never will be, he or she is free to learn more adaptive ways of being in his or her adult world. In IRT, the normative goals are, as mentioned previously, to be friendly with moderate degrees of enmeshment and moderate degrees of differentiation.

Early Family Sessions in IRT

Given the centrality of internalized loved ones in IRT's interpretation of the presenting problems, it follows that family can have a major effect on the success or failure of therapy. For example, an important family figure's vociferous antitherapy stance severely interferes with steps one (collaboration) and four (enable the will to change) in IRT.

If the simple act of keeping a therapy appointment is opposed by an important loved one, the odds for collaboration in treatment are diminished. Families frequently assume, perhaps on the basis of previous experience, that assessment of blame is what will happen in therapy. In reality, the IRT therapist will not support or model nonnormative behaviors such as confrontation, winning, or taking sides. Nonetheless, because families with a PAG member are so entrenched in the win/lose or right/wrong ethic, they may feel confronted when they are not. To enlist the collaboration of as many family members as possible, the IRT therapist makes every effort to have a family conference early in the treatment process. The earliest agenda is to hear the family views and wishes regarding the IP *in the presence of the IP*, and, of course, vice versa. The hope is that views of the IP and key family members will be shared openly, and that all will be able and willing to understand and support the treatment plan. Clearly defining the goal in terms of friendly differentiation and freedom to become more peaceful and effective helps everyone become more comfortable with the therapy process.

For example, one repeatedly suicidal woman with PAG entered therapy with a promise of support from her parents. She got a job commensurate with her training, showed up at work on time, and completed all assignments from her supervisor. After little more than a month, her parents withdrew their support for therapy on the grounds that she could pay for it herself now that she had a job. However, her level of income was not great enough to support having an apartment, car, food, and therapy as well. She had not been extravagant, and considered her expenses to be basic. Her conclusion was that she would have to terminate therapy. With respect to her marked improvement in the workplace, it seemed that "no good deed goes unpunished."

There was every reason to expect that if therapy was discontinued, her problem patterns, including a vulnerability to impulsive suicidal action, would remain unchanged at best. A family conference revealed that her parents were nonplussed about questions having to do with her dependence and independence. They supported independence in principle, but, were inclined to think in all or nothing terms. Hence, they felt that either they would support her completely or not at all. By now, they knew that it would not work to try to control her, but they were also frightened by the idea of letting go because of her demonstrated capacity for lethal actions. A highly collaborative family conference reviewed PAG patterns as they applied to this person, and enlisted their understanding and support so that IRT could proceed. The way out of this patient's "win by losing" dilemma was not at all easy, but parental blessings and support were of enormous help.

The potential benefit of using family meetings to enlist family members in support of the treatment plan was recognized by Anderson, Reiss, and Hogarty (1986). They developed psychoeducational family groups in their work with schizophrenics, having recognized that family members often felt alienated or blamed for the patient's illness. This group emphasized fostering collaboration with family members and informing them of treatment issues, such as specific sources of stress that should be reduced (e.g., conflict, boundary confusion), because they would likely exacerbate the schizophrenic illness.

Later Family Sessions in IRT

Addressing internalized representations of important others is central to IRT. If it is possible to have a family conference with important persons related to the presenting problems, changes in their internalized representations sometimes are facilitated.

Changes in Family Patterns and Changes in Internalizations

The first and most straightforward potential use of occasional family conferences for changing internalizations would be to try to change family ways of relating, and hence change internalizations associated with them. Unfortunately, early internalizations can be far more powerful than current realities, and so this method for changing internalizations rarely is successful. Ongoing family therapy is a procedure that more likely can change internalizations. An IRT version of ongoing family therapy as the primary mode of treatment has not yet been attempted.

Listening to a Tape of an Occasional
Family Conference

A second use of occasional family conferences later in therapy is to continue efforts to improve patterns of relating within the family, and provide in vivo tape-recorded samples of interactions that can be reviewed and contemplated in later individual sessions. Patients are prepared for this conference by discussing its goals. It is very important that the goals be realistic, and not support fantasies that the conference will fulfill long-standing wishes for restitution or uncomplicated reconciliation. The PAG IP is helped to understand that although the conference will invite and pursue to the extent possible the goal of immediate improvement in ways of relating, the more likely outcome is that the conference will do no more or less than facilitate the patient's IRT learning process. That learning will be enhanced in subsequent individual sessions that involve reviewing the tape of the conference.

The family meeting itself is introduced by explaining that the immediate goal is to increase understanding among family members and perhaps develop better ways of relating. Family members are told they are very important to the patient. It will be helpful to hear their views about him and her and review those later in individual sessions. The process of making the recording is conspicuous.

Study of the family tapes is a wonderful way for patients to discover their own patterns and relate them to interactions with loved ones. In some cases, this experience can help them develop more compassion for themselves and begin to let go of old dreams about how the family should be. This, in turn, can help them make the decision to relate to the family in ways more consistent with the therapy goals (described earlier), whether or not the family will subscribe to those goals. In more technical terms, the IP is encouraged to move toward the therapy goal of friendly differentiation. This goal is to be achieved on the basis of internal directedness chosen and practiced by the patient. IRT theory does not hold that changing the family is required for the patient to change. This vision of the therapy process as a matter of the IP's self-directed personal development using family as a helpful adjunct (if they are willing), eliminates, for example, the need to confront and fix blame. Blaming is appropriate to the "justice model" of treatment, but is not an IRT goal behavior. In general, IRT is not "justice" oriented (Benjamin, 2003).

For example, one PAG listened to a tape of a family conference and was astonished to hear the degree of blame that was centered on her. With the support of the therapist, she was able to see that she was not guilty as charged and that the assessment of blame did not even make sense. Her choice of friends as an adolescent was not, in fact, responsible for her father's first heart attack. She "got it," and resolved to try neither to absorb nor return the blame. This view from a safe distance helped her decide to work hard not to participate further in the "courtroom style of family relatedness." She chose instead to practice friendliness and balance in her relationship with her supportive husband and friends.

Another example of useful learning that comes from review of such a sampling of family patterns is the study of elusive logic. Slippery logic is by no means rare. One version is to imply A is true because B is true, even if B does not always imply A. This version unfolded for a PAG as follows:

PARENT: I don't believe you when you say you don't use drugs.

PAG ADOLESCENT: But I don't.

PARENT: How about that time when you went to a friend's house after school and told me you stayed for choir practice?

The patient understood this meant that if the child lied about going to the friend's house (statement B), he *therefore* was lying when he said he does not use drugs (statement A). To argue that lying once about a small, onetime matter "proves" he is lying about a large, ongoing matter is to violate both logic and common sense. "A proposition P(p,q, . . .) is said to *logically imply* a proposition Q(p,q, . . .) if Q(p,q, . . .) is true whenever P(p,q, . . .) is true" (Lipschutz, 1966, p. 28).

Listening to such exchanges on a tape can help a PAG (and people with other problem patterns) learn to recognize such questionable logic and appreciate the reasons for it. In this case, the PAG felt a bit saner and less unsteady when his sense that something was amiss in this exchange was confirmed by a well-established principle of logic. He then was able to press on to the question of what pattern was inherent in the exchange, and realized quickly that an expected consequence of the argument was that he should better comply with parental directions. The analysis can help him reclaim his own judgment about his self-concept (he is not a generic liar), and more clearly understand the underlying issues (not that parents try to crush his judgment, but rather that they desperately want him to do what they think is best).

As illustrated earlier, family sessions in IRT can provide a patient with the opportunity to reevaluate how family members relate, and compare a current sample with their preexisting perceptions that are often based both on history as well as fantasy and some distortion. Framo (1976, 1981) recognized the benefit of family-of-origin sessions in his work with couples. He believed that marital conflicts were usually due to unconscious attempts to deal with and master family-of-origin issues using current partners as stand-ins. Based on the object-relations conceptualizations of Fairbairn (1954) and Dicks (1967), Framo (1981) argued that frustrating aspects of the relational world during infancy were introjected and then became part of the structure of one's personality. As an adult, one's mate or children are seen in terms of the individual's own needs (e.g., mates might select each other on the basis of rediscovering lost aspects of their primary object relations). Framo audiotaped sessions so that each family member and spouse could listen to the session. He reported that as a result of a family of origin session, the grip of the introjects would become loosened, and perceptions of current spouses and family members would became more realistic due to a diminished influence of family-of-origin-based transference distortions. He also found that these sessions helped him to point out patterns from the family of origin that were being inappropriately played out in the current family.

Couples Therapy

SASB-based complementarity theory predicts, usually correctly, that the patient will have selected a partner who matches and enables his or her own problem patterns. The expected marital destiny of a PAG was discussed in the section Personality Disorder and Marriage. Given that a marital partner likely is supporting problem patterns in the IP (and that the IP is supporting the partner's own problem patterns), it follows that changes in marital interactions could facilitate changes in the IP's personality disorder. Such change in the partner is not required in IRT, but sexual relationships usually have extraordinary impact on internalizations and can often facilitate change in either partner.

In the case of a PAG married to a person with obsessive compulsive personality disorder, for example, the marital therapy will necessarily involve discussions of **CONTROL**/SUBMIT/**BLAME**/SULK/WALL-OFF/SEPARATE/ as problems. Because of these salient patterns, the PAG/OCD marital dyad is highly likely to be labeled by marital therapists as a demand/withdraw couple (Heavey, Layne, and Christensen, 1993).

IRT includes two recommended approaches to couples therapy. The preferred method is for each partner to be in individual therapy with a different IRT therapist, where he or she works on recognizing and transforming internalizations and intrapsychic gifts of love. Periodic joint sessions are held with each partner and his or her therapist. At the beginning, both participants agree on the mutual therapy goal of IRT, namely to relate with basic friendliness, moderate differentiation, moderate enmeshment, and an equal balance of focus. Again, the affects and cognitions that accompany these patterns are highly desirable (Benjamin, 2003).

When participants are hoping the IRT marital therapy will hand down indictments and final judgments of who is the bad guy, who is wrong, and who has to change, they will be very disappointed. One strategy for dealing with these problem expectations and hopes is for the therapist to blame everyone equally, or to note that the whole system is at fault. That approach can be effective, especially if the family or couple can speak no language other than the language of blame. Nonetheless, IRT therapists do not often engage in behaviors that are

SASB coded in the region of **BLAME** because, as indicated in the discussion of therapy goals, that in itself is a problem pattern.

Although the IRT therapy goals of basic friendliness and moderation usually sound desirable to couples, the implications are not always fully appreciated. For example, if one agrees to be moderately enmeshed, one has to give up "making sure" things turn out as desired. In controversial matters, the most that can be done is to express any preferences to the other. Under the model of moderate enmeshment, TRUST is central. If partners are faithful, that is because they wish to honor the relationship in this way, and not because they are forced to do so (to SUBMIT to **CONTROL** by partner or institution). On the other hand, under the moderate model, a person is not forced to remain partnered with someone who is unfaithful. They have the choice to leave if the relationship is not so honored. The unfaithful partner would then also have to suffer the consequences of loss, if the relationship matters.

The point is that a decision to be faithful is based on the desire to avoid damage to or loss of something valuable. In a strong partnership, the decision to take good care of the relationship is not based on coercion. This strategy of being collaborative because you want to be and not because you are forced to be keeps the marriage centered directly on its own inherent value. Moreover, change is based on each person's willingness to take responsibility for his or her own growth, and not on a perceived need to change the partner. Once each partner agrees to the IRT therapy goal, the conjoint couples sessions can provide a wonderfully powerful place for learning to practice therapy goal behaviors.

An alternative approach to couples therapy with the IRT model can be used if the partner of the IP is relatively stable, and does not need much focus on his or her own problem patterns and motivations. In this situation, the same IRT therapist can see the IP intensively in individual therapy, and see the couple on occasion. At the joint sessions, the IP can practice his or her new patterns. Assertiveness, for example, is an oft-needed new response. According to the SASB model, ASSERT is nothing like **CONTROL** (see Figure 2.1), and learning about the differences is likely to make a dramatic difference in the nature of couple interactions. For example, the depressed PAG IP with a nurturant partner may build considerable strength by learning to express preferences directly. A partner who already has mastered the therapy goal behaviors will hear these preferences and be appropriately responsive. The PAG will have the new experience of learning that his or her view does matter and there is, in fact, little need to continue to suppress the self and suffer.

STRENGTHS AND LIMITATIONS

Strengths of the IRT model include its specificity and its ability to provide clear guidance for how to draw from any and all treatment modalities. For example, the core algorithm and five steps explicitly draw upon wisdom from psychodynamic therapy, behavior therapy, client centered, and existential-humanistic therapies. Its principles can be applied in many modes including individual, couples, family, and group therapies. The IRT model therefore does not require the clinician to develop allegiance to any particular school or approach to therapy. Rather, it invites clinicians to master them all and perhaps to find IRT useful in indicating when and how to draw from each with optimal effectiveness.

The use of the SASB model aids the clinician in implementing IRT. It helps identify patterns and develop hypotheses about links between current patterns and early relationships. It defines an absolute goal for therapy. The clinician does not have to imagine he or she should or could treat all comers with a given constellation of symptoms regardless of their values or agendas. Moreover, the SASB model provides a reliable, objective method to test *and refute* hypotheses basic to IRT. Its associated technology can provide valid assessments of current relationships and internalized relationships. This feature also makes it possible to directly test the question of whether greater adherence to the IRT model improves therapy outcome.

One obvious limitation of IRT is that the theory of psychopathology and the model for treatment interventions is not simple. Clinicians must invest considerable time and effort in mastering the concepts of IRT and in learning how to implement them. Wider clinical practice of IRT and completion of research studies will tell whether developing expertise in IRT is worth the trouble.

INDICATIONS AND CONTRAINDICATIONS

IRT is not offered to, or may have to be discontinued for individuals whose potential for benefiting from the use of a learning model has become compromised either by lack of motivation or by compromised learning ability. Compromised motivation is implemented by too much loyalty to the Red and not enough access to the Green. Some patients are simply unable or unwilling to respond to therapists' efforts to help them give up the driving wishes. Examples of more general factors that can contribute to inability to engage the Green include disagreement with the treatment model, adherence to incompatible cultural values, chronic undermining of the treatment goals by important family members that also refuse to participate, and excessive, chronic use of alcohol or drugs as a method of coping. Ability to learn can be compromised by limited intelligence and by a damaged central nervous system (CNS). Examples of such sources of damage include: inherited defects of the CNS, trauma, chronic exposure to harmful chemicals, and so forth. IRT can be used with psychotic patients, although not in the acute phases and not if the interpersonal habits of alienation and dysfunction are deeply entrenched for motivational or structural reasons.

MANAGEMENT OF TRANSFERENCE ISSUES

An IRT therapist is quite active. Hence, family reactions to the therapist may not necessarily reflect distortion as they would if the therapist is a "blank screen." In IRT, the term *transference* simply refers to patients' views of the therapy relationship, whether distorted or not. *Transference distortion* specifically refers to a patient's view of the therapist that is distorted in a way that relates to the case formulation (Benjamin, 2003). When conjoint family therapy is included in IRT, the definition of transference distortion is broadened to include distortions of the therapist according to the norms of the family group.

For example, if a family rule is "you are for us or against us," then any deviation by the therapist from family preferences is seen as grounds for alienation from the therapy. If the IP is a PAG, then the therapist may be expected by the family to develop effective plans to make the PAG perform better. At the same time, the PAG will expect the therapist to support him or her in confronting the family and making them confess to and provide restitution for harm done. With the "for us or against us" ultimatum from everyone, the therapist is at risk to displease all.

In IRT, this dilemma is addressed directly as the therapist actively tries to discuss these expectations, and talk about the dilemmas from the various perspectives. He or she will express empathy for the parents' sense of disappointment in and worry about the IP. The IRT therapist also will show understanding of the IP's pain from loneliness, punishment, and compromise of self. Once everyone's perspective is clearly on the table, the IRT therapist proposes constructive alternatives consistent with the IRT therapy-goal model. Examples provided are specific and realistic, and the family is asked whether it wants to work toward those ways of relating.

Suppose, for example, a male PAG IP is not studying for his college courses, and is wasting tuition money as well as time. The PAG clearly has a record of never finishing what he starts. His parents are frightened he will never make it, and the PAG is too depressed to care. The IRT therapist might encourage sharing of the IP's perspective that if he successfully finishes these classes and this major, then the parents will have "won" the battle. The IP is encouraged to acknowledge his expectation that parents will crow about their success in childrearing when, in fact, he feels they have not supported what he has done or what he really wants to do. Helping the family see that the PAG will be in charge of his own success or failure, and that it must belong to him, is a mighty challenge. It is hard for the parents to let go of their dreams for this grown child. It is equally hard for the PAG to take responsibility for himself. He both hates and craves parental support.

The IRT therapist proposes that at least for the short term, the PAG be supported in his or her wish to pursue his own sense of identity, while still maintaining cordial, if not compliant, relations with family (shown in the upper right-hand side of Figure 2.1). The parents are invited to accept the risk in this plan, and to resolve to allow the PAG to enjoy or suffer the consequences of his choices. The PAG is encouraged to define his plans and to be responsible for the process and outcomes that follow.

In sum, transference distortion is expected and obtained often in IRT family sessions. The IRT therapist is not deterred by anger about his or her failure to conform to family expectations. He or she acknowledges the different perspectives, whether negative or positive, and continues steadily to try to facilitate understanding, communication, and collaborative support for IPs as they pursue the agreed upon therapy goals.

MANAGEMENT OF CRISES
AND ACTING-OUT BEHAVIOR

In IRT, acting-out and crisis behavior is contained quickly in most instances (Benjamin, 2003). If the usual mechanisms for eliminating crisis behavior fail, one alternative is to call a family conference to help deal with the crisis. In the family conference, the threat is openly discussed. Suggestions for monitoring and safekeeping are elicited and consolidated. Such a conference sometimes can serve to provide an alternative to hospitalization. If a reasonable plan does not emerge from such a conference, IRT moves directly to the hospitalization option.

Some individuals in IRT are severely addicted to crisis, and there is significant risk of enabling their problem patterns by holding such a family conference. Risk is assessed in relation to the IRT case formulation. For example, if a PAG is threatening suicide and won't contract for safekeeping, the therapist might observe that enlisting the help of family in providing safekeeping would be to go right back into the lion's den. It would ask family to do what they previously have been asked not to do, namely to let the PAG be responsible for himself or herself. It might therefore compel the PAG to self-destruction just to make the "point" that family cannot "control" him or her.

Discussing the possibility of (distinct from actually having) a crisis-based family conference can challenge a transference fantasy that the therapist will now be the one to take responsibility for the PAG. The proposal for a family conference puts the focus back on the perceived sources of the problem internalizations. Most PAGs have enough Green to realize that asking family to monitor them is to rub salt in their wounds. They see the reasons for the proposal, given the challenge they have just posed to the therapist. On collaborative reflection, the PAG usually will decide not to ask family to watch over them this time, and instead agree to a short-term safekeeping contract. Then, in postcrisis sessions, IRT can turn to the more relevant underlying reasons for the crisis behavior that are specified by the case formulation.

This particular example of family role in crisis management is one of a much larger set of possibilities. Variations on this theme are united by the simple idea that (1) sometimes family can help with safekeeping, but (2) the plan must be understood and acted upon with explicit reference to the IRT case formulation. As always, the choice of any intervention in IRT ultimately needs to be directed by its likely success in transforming the internalizations that are driving the problem behaviors. If all else fails, the IRT therapist takes required ethical and legal steps to commit patients. However, involuntary commitment is not considered to be a part of treatment, and there is explicit acknowledgment by the therapist that it represents a severe breakdown of collaboration with the Green and results in de facto suspension of IRT (Benjamin, 2003).

INTEGRATION WITH PSYCHIATRIC SERVICES AND ROLE OF MEDICATION

IRT therapists regularly refer patients for prescription and monitoring of medications whenever indicated by conventional standards, however, since the nonresponder population, by definition, already has failed to respond adequately to medications or psychotherapy, this step usually is an adjunct to IRT. By contrast, use of medications, other somatic treatments, and hospitalization is absolutely vital when the IRT flow diagrams lead the clinician to the procedure called *switching to symptom management.* The *switch* usually occurs during crisis, when the patient and the IRT therapist are unable to manage threatening symptoms by mobilizing Green and minimizing Red. As mentioned in the section on crisis management, if collaboration cannot be elicited during a crisis, IRT ceases temporarily (if not permanently). Talk about social history, wishes, relations with important others stops, while medical and legal management techniques prevail. Interestingly, discussion of an impending need to switch to symptom management usually reduces acting out and the need for repeated hospitalizations. Patients almost always prefer to continue working collaboratively with the IRT therapist and to avoid being "medically managed," albeit in an empathic way.

CULTURAL AND GENDER ISSUES

The goals of IRT are not culture free. As noted earlier, IRT seeks to facilitate the development of interpersonal behaviors that are friendly, moderately enmeshed, and moderately differentiated, with equally distributed focus on self and other. Behaviors toward the self are expected to be predominantly friendly and balanced in degrees of self-control and self-acceptance. These interpersonal rules and values guide the treatment plan regardless of the reasons individuals may have had for behaving in a personality-disordered manner. For example, a person might have developed PAG patterns because cultural or gender-related forces suggested the PAG style was an adaptive way of coping. Internalizations can be affected by cultural, religious, political, and other values as they have been transmitted by caregivers, teachers, and other important figures. Nonetheless, the IRT therapy goal remains constant. If a person belongs to a culture or subculture that eschews the IRT goals, then IRT is not appropriate. For example, if a culture supports the idea that one gender or ethnic or other group should be dominated by another, IRT should not be offered to individuals from that culture—whether they be dominators or submitters. At the beginning of therapy, patients are fully informed of the goals offered by IRT. This gives them an opportunity to decline or discontinue IRT treatment that might violate their cultural values or perceived gender-appropriate roles.

FUTURE DIRECTIONS

Pilot data on small samples clearly suggest that the IRT model is effective with nonresponder cases (Benjamin, 2003). A larger research protocol is in place in the IRT clinic for nonresponders at the University of Utah's Neuropsychiatric Institute. To date, no data exist specific to the use of family conferences in IRT.

Other future directions include plans to train more clinicians in IRT, and to complete the present research protocol at more than one site. Stricter protocols that involve randomized assignment of nonresponders to IRT and comparison treatments need to follow. More training opportunities and materials are also needed. Research questions with respect to the role of family therapy as described in this paper are untouched. Pursuit of them will be important. In addition, it would be fascinating to explore the degree to which primary treatments with family therapy can change internalizations and their associated problem behaviors.

REFERENCES

American Psychiatric Association (1994). *Diagnostic and statistical manual of mental disorders* (Fourth edition). Washington, DC: Author.

Anderson, C.M., Reiss. D.J., and Hogarty, G.E. (1986). *Schizophrenia and the family: A practitioner's guide to psychoeducation and management.* New York: Guilford Press.

Becker, D.F., Grillo, C.M., Edell, W.S., and McGlashan, T.H. (2001). Comorbidity of borderline personality disorder with other personality disorders in hospitalized adolescents and adults. *American Journal of Psychiatry, 157,* 2011-2016.

Benjamin, L.S. (1979). Structural analysis of differentiation failure. *Psychiatry, Journal for the Study of Interpersonal Process, 42.* 1-23.

Benjamin, L.S. (1987) Use of the SASB dimensional model to develop treatment plans for personality disorders, I: Narcissism. *Journal of Personality Disorders, 1,* 43-70.

Benjamin, L.S. (1993). Every psychopathology is a gift of love. *Psychotherapy Research, 3,* 1-24.

Benjamin, L.S. (1996). *Interpersonal diagnosis and treatment of personality disorders* (Second edition). New York: Guilford Press.

Benjamin, L.S. (2003). *Interpersonal reconstructive therapy: Promoting change in nonresponders.* New York: Guilford Press.

Bowen, M. (1978). *Family therapy in clinical practice.* New Jersey: Jason Aronson.

Dicks, H.V. (1967). *Material tensions.* New York: Basic Books.

Fairbairn, W.R.D. (1954). *An object relations theory of personality.* New York: Basic Books.

Framo, J.L. (1976). Family of origin as a therapeutic resource for adults in marital and family therapy: You can and should go home again. *Family Process, 15,* 193-210.

Framo, J.L. (1981). The integration of marital therapy with sessions with family of origin. In A.S. Gurman and D.P. Kniskern (Eds.), *Handbook of family therapy* (pp. 133-158). New York: Brunner Mazel.

Heavey, C.L., Layne, C., and Christensen, A. (1993). Gender and conflict structure in marital interaction: A replication and extension. *Journal of Consulting and Clinical Psychology, 61,* 16-27.

Humphrey, L.L. and Benjamin, L.S. (1986) Using structural analysis of social behavior to assess critical but elusive family processes: A new solution to an old problem. *American Psychologist, 41,* 979-989.

Guttman, L. (1966). Order analysis of correlation matrixes. In R.B. Cattell (Ed.), *Handbook of multivariate experimental psychology*. Chicago: Rand McNally.

Leary, T. (1957). *Interpersonal diagnosis of personality: A functional theory and methodology for personality evaluation*. New York: Ronald Press.

Linehan, M. (1993). *Cognitive-behavioral treatment of borderline personality disorder*. New York: Guilford Press.

Lipschutz, S. (1966). *Theory and problems of finite mathematics. Logic, set theory, vectors and matrices, probability and markov chains, linear programming, game theory*. New York: McGraw-Hill.

Morey, L.C. (1988). Personality disorders in DSM-III and DSM-IIIR: Convergence, coverage, and internal consistency. *American Journal of Psychiatry, 145,* 573-577.

O'Connor, B.P. and Dyce, J.A. (1998). A test of models of personality disorder configuration. *Journal of Abnormal Psychology, 107,* 3-16.

Olson, D.H. (1986). Circumplex model VII: Validation studies and FACES III. *Family Process, 25,* 337-351.

Olson, D.H. (1991). Commentary: Three-dimensional (3-D) circumplex model and revised scoring of FACES III. *Family Process, 30,* 74-79.

Perry, J.D. and Perry, J.C. (1996). Reliability and convergence of three concepts of narcissistic personality. *Psychiatry: Interpersonal and Biological Processes, 59,* 4-19.

Prochaska, J.O., DiClements, C.C., and Norcross, J.C. (1992). In search of how people change: Applications to addictive behaviors. *American Psychologist, 47,* 1102-1114.

Sullivan, H.S. (1953). *The interpersonal theory of psychiatry*. New York: Norton.

Widiger, T.A. and Costa, P.T. (1994). Personality and personality disorders. *Journal of Abnormal Psychology, 103,* 78-91.

Chapter 3

An Object-Relations
Approach to the Treatment
of Personality-Disordered Marriages

Charles C. McCormack

INTRODUCTION

According to Kernberg (1967, 1975), to understand personality disorders, one must understand the "borderline state" that is the essence of personality disorder. The "borderline state" is characterized by four elements: identity diffusion, an idiosyncratic interpretation of reality, a devotion to the internal world of pathological object relationships, and an excessive reliance on primitive defenses.

Identity diffusion refers to a blurring of boundaries between self and other, between what is "me" or "mine," and what is "not me" or "not mine," leading to confusion in areas of responsibility and accountability in relationships.

An *idiosyncratic relationship to reality* refers to the interpretation of events in ways that are unique and unusual—events and perceptions are filtered through an internal world of pathological relationships.

The *internal world of pathological object relationships* (Fairbairn, [1944] 1952, [1946] 1952) is peopled by various unconscious self and object relationships that were excessively need-frustrating or need-rejecting in early childhood. These object relationships were repressed to allow the child to maintain an idealization of the parents, and to ameliorate unbearable anxiety and psychic pain (Fairbairn, [1940] 1952). The internal world created is part of a universal psychic process, in that all children experience need-frustration or need-rejection, at least some of the time. Personality disorder differs from normal/neurotic functioning in that the level and degree of repression is extensive and has impeded development, resulting in the hardening and relative intransigence of the internal world to modification by new experience. The internal world is formed as the child represses experiences of excessive need-rejection or need-frustration. Unable to physically escape the painful situation, the child escapes psychologically by repressing the "bad" experience. This allows the child, who is *absolutely dependent,* to remain in conscious relationship to an idealized caregiver, thereby ameliorating unbearable insecurity and anxiety (Fairbairn, [1940] 1952).

What the child represses is the totality of the rejecting experience: both the need for attachment *(libidinal yearning)* that made the child vulnerable to rejection, and the feelings of rage, humiliation, or shame *(antilibidinal feelings)* that followed in the wake of rejection. The ego is the organ of perception (Fairbairn, [1944] 1952). The parts of the ego that experienced libidinal yearnings (part-self representations) form the *libidinal ego,* which, buried alive, remains yearning for relationship with the *exciting object:* the perception of the primary caregiver as promising need fulfillment (part-object representation) that remains to be delivered. This enthrallment with the exciting object is evident in the state of infatuation.

Simultaneously, the part of the ego that experienced feelings of humiliation, hate, and shame that followed on the heels of rejection forms the *antilibidinal ego.* The antilibidinal ego also remains in singular relationship to its object: the *rejecting object,* the perception of the primary caregiver as totally rejecting or invasive. The libidinal and antilibidinal egos are in a split-off relationship to each other (secondary splitting) for the same reason each was split-off and repressed from consciousness (primary splitting): the infantile psyche is not capable of tolerating the anxiety and insecurity entailed in recognizing the paradox that the need-exciting object and the need-rejecting object are one and the same. Thus, instead of an integrated relationship, the libidinal and antilibidinal egos are in a split-off and polar-opposite relationship to each other. As the object of the libidinal-ego promises only fulfillment, the object of the antilibidinal ego promises only pain. Together, they form the *dynamic unconscious:* the source of intra-psychic conflict and the universal fear of intimacy (Fairbairn, [1944] 1952).

The more extreme and chronic the experience of rejection, the more powerful the internal world and its influence in shaping the subsequent way of perceiving and relating. For example, the assumption that "If you meet my needs, you are loving and I am lovable, and if you don't, you are sadistically rejecting and I am rejectable" will inevitably create havoc in adult relationships. Adult relationships become characterized by the *dominant affect* that links the internal world part-self and part-object representations that derived from childhood. The fact that the affect can be toxic and even painful does not take away from its organizing power or from the unconscious, even if spurious, comfort of the familiar and the familial. Hate is as powerfully connecting as love and provides a form of attachment, even if perverse, that guards against the nihilistic anxiety of no attachment at all. In other words, the basic assumption is: "Better a toxic relationship than no relationship."

The fourth element of the borderline state is *an excessive reliance upon primitive defenses.* Founded in splitting and denial, primitive defenses separate the *endangered* (the "good") from the *endangering* (the "bad"), providing the illusion of security and leading to all-or-nothing ways of perceiving and relating. In this psychological situation, the experience of self and other is idealized when needs are satisfied, and devalued when needs are frustrated. It is the experience of the moment with its associated affect, not the history of the relationship, reason, or cognition that defines the relationship of self and other. Consequently, there is no affective (meaningful and soothing) understanding that the frustration of the moment may be temporary and arise not from sadism or rejection, but from the separate and equally valid needs of the other.

Integration of the self results from and culminates in integrity: an acknowledgment of separateness and of both the need-satisfying and need-disappointing aspects of self and other. Integration allows for all the parts of the self to dialogue and enter a modifying relationship to one another. This provides the capacity for self-soothing, context, and perspective. Conversely, *dis-integration* (splitting and denial) of the self arises from and results in *dis-integrity* as the divergent part-self experiences are split off and isolated from consciousness (denial). Acts of integration (abiding with, observing, and reflecting on self-experience) lead to an initial increase in anxiety as conflicts are confronted, and a subsequent decrease in overall underlying anxiety as *dis-integrated* parts are acknowledged, understood, accepted, and reintegrated, allowing for a whole, rather than part, relationship to self and other.

The defense of *primitive projective identification* (Ogden, 1989; Sandler, 1987) extends splitting and denial into interpersonal relationships. To ameliorate intrapsychic conflict, the projector splits off and projects onto or into the other in the external world either the internal part-self or part-object representation that is currently in conflict. This defuses the intrapsychic conflict (anxiety) by replacing it with interpersonal conflict. Now, the problem is no longer one of "me" or "mine," but one of "not-me" and "not-mine," i.e., the problem is "you." "I'm not miserable because of conflicts or dissatisfaction within myself, but because *you* are making me miserable! I don't need to change me, I need to change *you*.

The projected part-self or part-object representation can be of either the libidinal or antilibidinal egos. For example, libidinally infused projections may result in the projector perceiving and identifying with the internal needy and yearning self-representation and relating to the other as the exciting object: a wonderful and incredible person who can fulfill all of the projector's needs and protect him or her from the terrors of separateness. Conversely, the projector may project the internal needy and yearning self-representation onto the other, and identify with the internal exciting-object representation. The projector would thereby feel empowered by the needs and desire of the other. This process also supports an idealized sense of self (narcissism), which reduces the vulnerability entailed in needing an other and in recognizing one's own human foibles and insecurities. Similarly, from an antilibidinal ego perspective, the projector can either identify with the victimized, enraged or humiliated self-representation, relating to the other as sadistically rejecting or invasive, thereby fending off any personal responsibility for the state of his or her own life and relationships, or the projector can identify with the power of the aggressor (the rejecting object) and treat the partner as totally worthless, thereby defending against the experience of fear, inadequacy, and vulnerability.

It is important to remember that what is projected always communicates something important about the projector's intrapsychic conflicts. Simultaneously, the projectee's introjective identification with that which is projected says something important about the projectee's level of differentiation and readiness (familiarity) to be involved in a particular kind of part-self and part-object relationship. The end result is that the projector, observing the projectee's reactions to be congruent with that which is projected, feels confirmed in the validity of his or her perceptions (projection). In this way, the internal world of each spouse is re-created in the external reality of the marriage.

No one is immune from regression. Most of us intermittently visit borderline states, manifested in those occasional fight-or-flight interactions characterized by screaming and yelling or withdrawal that occur behind closed doors with a parent, mate, or child. In contrast, personality-disordered individuals dwell in the borderline state. As noted, this results from a deficit in development. To understand personality disorders one must understand the nature of the development deficit.

In object-relations theory the development of the self involves three *modes of organization,* which evolve more or less sequentially during the first three years of life. Subsequently (in health) they continue to function together throughout the rest of life in mutually enriching, dialectic relationship to one another. These modes are the *autistic-contiguous,* the *paranoid-schizoid,* and the *depressive* (Ogden, 1986).

The *autistic-contiguous mode* is a sensory mode that dominates in infancy. Sensation is the basis of all perception and forms the platform of the *sense* of self. It is from this platform that all subsequent, more elaborate *senses* of self arise. The autistic-contiguous mode has no self-structure: no sense of self, self-awareness, or self-concept. Rather, the self is unformed and in the process of *becoming* as it begins to coalesce around sensory experience. In this sense there is no *infant* that *feels* wet; there is only *wetness.* The *early emerging self* forms and reforms around the sensations of the moment. The normally devoted parent intuits this and spends the vast majority of care regulating the infant's sensory state: from empty to full, wet to dry, cold to warm, agitated to calm, and so on (Stern, 1985).

With continuing physical and psychological development, the child begins to differentiate between variant and invariant sensations (Stern, 1985), leading to a rudimentary sense of "me" (relatively invariant sensation) and "not me" (relatively variant sensation). The capacity for language is emergent and along with it comes the ability to translate sensory experience into ego needs (feelings, thoughts). Rather than crying in hunger, the child is now able to say "hungry." This first formal structuring of the self heralds the emergence of the *paranoid-schizoid mode* of development. Here a rudimentary sense of self exists but one that is reactively shaped by the experience of the moment: sensations, thoughts, and feelings of the "me." It is important to recognize that in this mode, sensations, thoughts, and feelings have no symbolic (representational) meaning. They do not refer to experience (symbolism proper), but are felt as the experience itself (symbolic equivalence) (Segal, 1957). In other words, thoughts and feelings and the words used to describe them, are felt like actions, concretely as "the thing in itself"—sticks and stones that *do* break bones, or at least the fragile skeleton of the psyche. For example, at this level, the individual doesn't *feel* "good" or "bad," afraid or happy, rather he or she *is* "good" or "bad," afraid or happy. This results from the fact that, although a rudimentary sense of "me" and "not-me" exists, as yet there is no over-arching sense of self or self-concept: no "I" that can observe the experience of the "me" in order to reflect upon it (self-relationship).

This deficit results in the absence of the yet-to-be-developed capacity for *thinking through.* Consequently, *acting out* (discharge: crying, yelling, screaming, withdrawal) is the only existent means of processing (dealing with) experience. Accordingly, the individual does not feel self-governing and self-directed (a subject): the architect of his or her existence and the interpreter of his or her own meaning. Rather, the individual feels much like an inanimate object to which things (sensations, thoughts, and feelings experienced as actions) just happen and to which no alternative exists but reaction. In this psychological situation the locus of control of the sense of self is felt to be external rather than internal. Consequently, the individual holds his or her others (children, parents, or mate) responsible for his or her experience. Thus, if I feel "good," I am "good" and you are "good." If I feel "bad," I am "bad," and you are making me "bad." "You are either the pill for my ill, or the cause of it." In other words, the personality-disordered individual relates to primary others as primitive self-objects: commodities or resources the relative value of which is to regulate the sense of self (Stolorow, Brandchaft, and Atwood, 1987).

The development of an over-arching self-concept and the associated capacity for self-direction is attained with the developmental achievement of the *depressive mode* of organization. It is important to know that although the word *depressive* often leads to associations with the clinical state of depression, it is actually meant to refer to the capacity for empathy (genuine concern) and for guilt when one's actions, real or imagined, have done harm to those we care about. I prefer to use the term *depressive-subjective* to highlight the capacity for guilt and concern, and the emergent experience of self as a *subject* rather than simply an object: an "I" that is capable of observing and reflecting on the experience of the "me," in service of learning and growing from experience.

With ongoing biological, emotional, and psychological development, the individual (with caregiver help) is increasingly able to tolerate the psychic tensions associated with recognizing the paradox that the need-satisfying "good" object and the need-frustrating "bad" object are one and the same. This awareness leads to the recognition that attacks on the "bad" object also risk injury to the "good" object. The capacity for empathy and compassion emerge as an alternative to ruthless aggression, and aggression is moderated in order to preserve and protect the "good" part of the loved and hated object. Acts of reparation follow acts of aggression (even if only fantasized) to preserve the good object. The *malignant circle* of love, hate, and aggression of the paranoid-schizoid mode (and of personality disorder) becomes the *benign circle* of love, hate, and reparation of the depressive-subjective mode (Klein and Riviere, 1937, Winnicott, [1954] 1975).

In health, the three modes of organization are inextricably intertwined. The sensory experience of the autistic-contiguous mode is the basis of all perception. The thoughts and feelings of the paranoid-schizoid mode (the "me") translate sensation into thoughts and feelings. The secondary process thinking of the depressive-subjective mode allows for learning from experience and the recognition of self and other as subjects rather than objects.

Psychiatric illness occurs whenever there is a collapse in the direction of one or two modes of organization to the exclusion of the other(s). In personality disorders there is a truncation in the development of the depressive-subjective mode so that afflicted individuals remain in a reactive relationship to, and defined by, perceptions, rather than reflection and ongoing development. According to the DSM-IV (American Psychiatric Association, 1994, p. 633), the result is

> an enduring pattern of inner experience and behavior that deviates markedly from the expectations of the individual's culture and is manifested in at least two of the following areas: cognition, affectivity, interpersonal functioning, or impulse control (Criterion A). This enduring pattern is inflexible and pervasive across a broad range of personal and social situations (Criterion B) and leads to clinically significant distress or impairment in social, occupational, or other important areas of functioning (Criterion C). The pattern is stable and of long duration, and its onset can be traced back at least to adolescence or early adulthood (Criterion D). (reprinted with permission from the *Diagnostic and Statistical Manual of Mental Disorders,* Fourth Edition, copyright 1994 American Psychiatric Association)

IMPACT ON THE FAMILY

The primary mission of the family is to foster the development of *each* of its members. Growth naturally occurs given a good-enough *holding environment* (Winnicott, 1958) that is designed to protect the tender and early emerging roots of the self from impingement. Impingement forces the child to *react* at the expense of *being*. As the child *goes on being,* actions are initiated from within, leading to an internally derived infrastructure and the development of a personally meaningful sense of self. If the child is forced to react to "too much, too much" (abuse) or to "too little, too little" (neglect) (Shengold, 1989) the child's *sense of self* becomes reactively shaped to the mold of the environmental impingements, creating an exoskeleton self: a *false or pseudoself* and associated sense of emptiness or hollowness (Winnicott, [1960] 1965).

The parents are the managers of the holding environment of the family. The personality-disordered parent desperately uses others as primitive self-objects to regulate the sense of self. The personality-disordered parent(s) perceives the family as a single psychic entity, relating to each family member through an internal part-self or part-object representation. Mate and children are treated as "good" when need satisfying and as "bad" when need frustrating, and as repositories for disavowed aspects of the self. Thus, one child may be perceived as "good" (kind, loving, smart) and the other as "bad" (mean, selfish, dumb), regardless of their respective characteristics. Or, the parent may vary the roles of the children, but always require someone in the role of "bad" object and another in the role of "good" object. Consequently, rather than providing a stable and secure holding environment attuned and responsive to the needs of the children, the personality-disordered parent creates a chaotic, abusive, or neglectful environment, reflective of his or her own conflicted and precarious sense of self.

If both parents are personality disordered, the children are at high risk of becoming personality disordered. If one parent is normal/neurotic and able to provide a modicum of stability and responsiveness to the children, protect them from the mate's excessive abuse or neglect, and lend his or her own depressive-subjective mode capacities in helping the children to understand their experience, the children's tendency to internalize the "badness" of the situation can be ameliorated and development will be sustained.

Although the parents are the managers of the holding environment, the children contribute to its nature. The requirements of some children (genetic influences, constitution) can exceed the capacities of a normally devoted parent. The parents' understandable difficulty and ensuing frustration, exhaustion, anger, and guilt associated with dealing with the child further complicates the child's development. A personality-disordered child has a devastating effect upon the family. The child becomes the center of the family's focus, consuming an inordinate share of time, attention, and emotional energy, depleting the family's resources. The parents may come to feel that they are "bad" parents given their inability to please or correct the child's behavior. The siblings may feel "bad" in expressing their own needs, which they fear may injure the already overburdened parents, or because of their hateful feelings toward the personality-disordered sibling. As the needs of family members go unmet, aggression, anxiety, and depression rise. A survival mode of functioning takes hold. Family life is no longer oriented around the pursuit of happiness, but rather the avoidance of conflict, a strategy that exacerbates the problem in that it fails to provide the firm and compassionate limit setting that the personality-disordered child so desperately needs in order to internalize it. Deprived of real relationship and the limits it entails, the child feels unbounded and increasingly isolated and alienated. Under continued stress the other members of the family regress to *borderline states* of functioning, appearing personality disordered themselves.

SETTING

This model is used in inpatient and outpatient settings, including private practice. It may be used as a primary treatment modality or as an adjunct to individual therapy. The clients described in the following case example were seen in the author's private practice, which is located on the grounds of the Sheppard and Enoch Pratt psychiatric hospital in Baltimore.

TREATMENT MODEL

The personality-disordered marriage is an undifferentiated, polarized, and complementary part-self and part-object relationship. Since personality disorder is a pre-Oedipal condition, the individual has not negotiated the *"twoness"* of the *mother and child* dyad to arrive at the *"threeness"* of the *mother and father and child* triad in which the father is experienced as a viable alternative to the mother. Without the lived experience of alternatives, the child, now adult, continues to relate in a binary, "my way" (internal world) or "not-my-way" (external reality), fashion. In this circumstance, no space exists for other possibilities, no intermediate area of experience that bridges the intrapsyche and external reality. Such a space is necessary to secondary process thinking, metaphor, curiosity, spontaneity, play, creativity, poetry, spirituality, and *genuine relationship*. This *potential space* (Winnicott, 1971) both separates and connects the internal world and external reality, which is exactly how a genuine relationship both separates and relates two individuals: Self and Other. Given this space, a mutually enriching relationship to reality is possible. Without it the intrapsyche (Self) and external reality (Other) can only exist in competitive relationship: "my way" or "not my way," along an axis of dominance and submission. In this psychological situation the individual either superimposes the internal world upon external reality or feels swallowed up by it, which leads to nihilistic anxiety: not dead but nonexistent. It is with the development of the capacity for thirdness that a "my way," a "not my way" or "your way," *and* an "our way" (thirdness) are possible.

Given the totality of the personality-disordered individual's psychological situation, the primary motivation of a relationship is the pursuit of survival of the precarious sense of self, *not* fulfillment. The Other is related to in primitive self-object fashion: (1) as a resource to fill deficiencies in the sense of self (trophy partner, sugar daddy, teddy bear), and (2) as a repository for disavowed aspects of the self (part-self or part-object representations), so that intrapsychic conflict is ameliorated by evacuating one or the other pole of the resident internal conflict and attributing that role to the Other. This ameliorates intrapsychic conflict, as the "cause" of the problem is now perceived to be located outside the self where it can be controlled.

When the spouses first enter the consulting room a "couple" only exists in the mind of the therapist (McCormack, 2000). It is only the therapist who can imagine *threeness* (his, hers, theirs) and the intermediate area in which a genuine relationship exists. The therapist's task is to renew the developmental journey of each spouse to attain depressive-subjective mode capacities: an "I" that can abide with, observe, and reflect upon the experience of the "me." Development inevitably involves the recurrent process of separation, individuation, and differentiation across time and changing circumstances. It is only by making the unconscious conscious, both cognitively and affectively, that the timeless internal world can be brought into the time awareness of consciousness, and that past can be differentiated from present. Personality-disordered spouses are resistant to this effort for two unconscious reasons. First, a "normal" relationship requires that they eschew the fantasy of merger and oneness with the all-fulfilling exciting object that promises deliverance from the terrors and dreads of life and mortality in favor of the less tantalizing but far more substantial and realizable satisfactions to be found in reality. Second, it requires that they give up their omnipotent defenses against impingement, neglect, and the return of the repressed, exposing them to the possibility of further primary narcissistic wounding.

For renewal of development, the self requires a *holding environment* that fosters space for abiding with experience and a *containing environment* that processes experience in service of understanding. In general, the spouses have come to therapy because each perceives the other as a defective self-object. From the first moment of the first meeting, the therapist understands that direct spouse-to-spouse interactions will soon lead to intense transference interactions, a loss of observing ego, and spiraling regression. Communication in service of understanding will give way to *communication by impact* (Casement, 1985), which is intended to coerce the Other into functioning as a "good" primitive self-object, or to use the Other as a repository for disavowed aspects of the self. Words are used as projectiles, which damage the fragile structures of the Self of the Other. Communication is only in service of attempting to superimpose internal world upon external reality: the Other.

Acting-out behavior signals that the spouse(s) is experiencing a threat to the sense of self and a loss of observing ego. No possibility exists of learning from experience. The holding environment of therapy has been breached and the containing environment is nonexistent. The therapist must intervene to establish a holding environment that allows time and space for each spouse to *be with* his or her experience as opposed to discharging it via acting out. This is accomplished by the therapist's entering *alternating separate dyadic interactions* (McCormack 1989, 2000) with each spouse. The therapist interrupts the direct spouse-to-spouse interaction by engaging each spouse in separate, sequential, and dyadic therapist-and-spouse interactions. The focus of the therapist-and-spouse dyadic interaction is to (1) identify and process with each spouse what his or her experience was that threatened the self, and/or (2) to clarify and deepen the therapist's understanding of what each spouse is trying to communicate.

The technique of alternating separate dyadic interactions has the following effects:

1. It immediately interrupts acting out, diverting the focus of the acting-out spouse from the mate to the therapist, who is intent on protecting the mate and creating time and space for experience for the acting-out spouse.
2. It allows the therapist to *freeze frame* the spouse-to-spouse interaction, impeding the discharge of experience and creating the opportunity for *thinking through.*
3. It creates time and space for *abiding with* experience in service of observation and reflection as an alternative to discharge of experience.

4. It replaces the transferentially laden spouse-to-spouse inter-action with the typically less intense therapist-to-spouse inter-action, reducing the sense of threat, increasing the sense of safety, and facilitating the return of observing ego capacities.

5. It affords each spouse the opportunity to engage with an other (the therapist) who is genuinely interested in identifying with (versus counter-identifying with) and understanding (validating versus invalidating) his or her experience.

6. It allows the therapist to engage each spouse in a dyadic form of interaction that is more attuned to their developmental capacity.

7. It re-creates aspects of the Oedipal conflict, which the spouses have yet to developmentally negotiate: each spouse experiences being both a part of and apart from a relationship to the therapist and provides each with the experience of the therapist as both "mine" (affiliation) and "not-mine" (separation).

8. It fosters the development of empathetic identification in relationship to the therapist as each spouse struggles to be understood by the therapist and experiences the therapist as struggling to understand.

9. It fosters empathetic identification between the spouses as each spouse observes the other in similar, yet different struggles with the therapist.

10. It promotes "I-ness" as it cultivates *abiding with* experience, self-observation, and self-reflection.

11. It promotes differentiation as the *observing spouse* becomes privy to the similar, yet different ways of perceiving and relating of the therapist and of the mate.

12. It makes the therapist's depressive-subjective capacities available for internalization, since these are repeatedly manifested by the therapist in an effort to create room for and learn from experience.

The process of therapy is characterized by a fluid shifting between an interpersonal focus of spouse-to-spouse relatedness, which tends to generate grist for the therapeutic mill in the form of transference relating, and an intrapsychic (intrapersonal) focus via the use of separate therapist-and-spouse dyadic interactions that allow for the processing of each spouse's transference as it becomes manifest in the interpersonal dynamics of the spouse-to-spouse interaction. In terms of each spouse, the therapist's goal is to weave the disparate strands of the self and internal object representations into a coherent whole by bringing them to consciousness, where they can be thought about and where past can be differentiated from present. As self-understanding increases, so does the capacity to relate. In terms of the couple, the focus is to help the spouses communicate their experiences to each another without blame, shame, or attack, and without demands for change. The goal becomes one of *coming to know and to be known* by the other, rather than one of getting the other to change. This process fosters separation, individuation, and differentiation on the road to autonomy: separate and related.

The individual work in the therapist-and-spouse dyad is crucial to fostering each spouse's relationship to his or her own self-experience (sensations, thoughts, feelings) that arises from the field of the relationship, but is also filtered and organized through the prism of past experience—the internal world of pathological object relationships. Often, an almost a one-for-one relationship exists between the spouses' perceptions of each other and their respective internal part-self and part-object relationship configurations. The case of Jenny and John is illustrative. Jenny had a history of emotional neglect in relationship to her parents. She subsequently perceived John as not desiring or needing her. She typically had to initiate time together. Yet his great efforts at helping around the house and with the kids went unrecognized. John grew up in relationship to overburdened parents. He remembers consciously trying to ensure that his parents would never perceive him as a burden or problem. In other words, he never expressed his needs (desires). In his relationship with Jenny, he worked diligently to perform the tasks she requested. However, he could not be himself with her because he was in an antagonistic relationship to his needs and desires. Jenny's perception that John didn't "need or desire her" was understandable, but not necessarily valid. In turn, John's frustration of "never being able to get anything right" with Jenny was also understandable because he was trying to be loved by her through the crafting of an image of himself, rather than fully investing himself in the relationship.

It is through separate dyadic relationships that the therapist begins the arduous process of building a *real* (whole-object) relationship with each spouse. A real relationship is founded in the ability of two people to identify personally and accurately with each other's experience (joys, heartaches, fears). It is exactly this capacity for empathetic identification that is missing in personality-disordered marriages. Due to the reliance on primitive defenses, each spouse disintegrates, rather than integrates, various aspects of experience (parts of self and object). Accordingly, the spouses are often in a counter-identifying (invalidating) relationship rather than an identifying (validating) relationship to each other. When therapists intervene via separate dyadic interactions with each spouse, they are offering what neither spouse is providing the other: an Other who is actively interested in providing validation by identifying with and understanding his or her experience. Therapists, having the ego strength to identify with an Other *without superimposing their experience upon the other or becoming swallowed up by the experience of the other,* become the living embodiment of potential space. They are separate and relating. Identifying with each, they separate and relate the spouses, bridging the intrapsyche and external reality (of which the Other is a part). In this sense, the spouses meet in the mind and through the person of the therapist.

The therapist's empathetic identification with each spouse is achieved through a process of *successive approximations.* Through the use of *clarifying questions, trial identifications,* and *rejectable interpretations,* the therapist repeatedly explores, tries on for size, and struggles to understand what each spouse is communicating of his or her experience. The therapist recurrently returns these tentative understandings or trial identifications to the field of the relationship with the explicit expectation that each spouse will modify and correct the therapist's understanding until such time that the spouse feels truly heard and understood. Each spouse is regarded as the final interpreter of his or her experience. In this light, the therapist's communications are intended not so much to tell the spouses what he or she "knows," but to inform them of what he or she does "not know."

In the face of the therapist's genuine interest, without any agenda other than deepening his or her understanding of each spouse and their relationship, the spouses gradually feel safe from impingement or invasion, and begin to relax their defenses in the effort of educating the therapist about their experience. The spouses soon find that it is difficult to adequately explain their acting-out behavior because of their excessive reliance on primitive defenses. Instead, they respond in concrete and literal-minded fashion, without subtext or context. Accordingly, as they struggle to identify and explain their respective perceptions to enlighten the therapist, they also illuminate themselves.

Early in treatment, due to the therapist's focus on acting-out behavior, the inconsistencies, gaps, and incongruities between words, thoughts, feelings, and actions are brought to the awareness of each spouse. The spouse is faced with a personal experience that he or she is unable to explain: the "not known." This moment of potential embarrassment or shame is soon converted into one of achievement and curiosity, as the therapist highlights the importance of discovering the "not known." The "not known" is the only place anything new can be discovered or learned. The therapist emphasizes that mental health entails the capacity to feel all of one's feeling and to acknowledge all of one's thoughts, even though at first glance they may seem contradictory, unimportant, or even "bad."

Every feeling and every thought is associated with a part of the self (ego), which is the organ of perception. Consequently, movement toward mental health involves not getting rid of the universal human experiences of sadism, masochism, love, hate, lust, jealousy, envy, shame, etc., but their inclusion toward the development of a whole relationship to self and other (Klein and Riviere, 1937). Only when all the parts are acknowledged can a dialogue be held between the parts that leads to the development of perspective and the capacity for moderation, modulation, and deepening of understanding. Conversely, when parts are excluded (splitting and denial) perception is distorted, and that which is isolated and denied gains intensity. When excluded parts do come to the fore, it is at the expense, due to the same process of splitting and denial that isolated them, of the other parts, which are now pushed aside along with their potentially modifying and moderating perceptions. Only with full freedom of thought and of feeling can all parts of the self be available for *thinking through* and the "not yet understood" become understandable.

Upon entering the realm of the "not known," the therapist shifts from a reliance on *linear thinking* (cause and effect, reason and logic) to *associative thinking* and *psycho-logic*. Perceptions that seem *illogical* in respect to present-day relationships are understood to be profoundly *psycho-logical* in subjective reality. Thus, each area of the "not known" serves as a window into the subterranean world of the *dynamic unconscious:* the prism through which the personality-disordered individual's perceptions are organized and filtered. It is the prism of this internal world that permeates personality-disordered ways of perceiving and relating. In this sense, the unconscious hides in plain sight in the way people perceive and relate to one another. It is the therapist's task in collaboration with each spouse to make the unconscious conscious. This does not ensure change, only a freedom of choice that otherwise would not exist.

Although surface incongruities frustrate efforts to understand through linear thinking, the therapist's reliance on the psychological and his or her own subterranean connections (associative thinking, countertransference, reveries, and intuitive leaps) in conjunction with the capacity for thinking through yield partial or trial identifications that, in addition to the spouses' willingness to reject or modify these identifications, further illuminates the therapist's understanding of the needs and fears of relationship of each spouse and the interlocking psychodynamics of the marital relationship.

This process entails the therapist's modeling of self-observation and reflection, sharing thoughts, feelings, impressions, and confusions via clarifying questions, trial identifications, and rejectable interpretations. The therapist struggles and is seen to struggle to ensure accurate identifications, aware that his or her perceptions of the spouses are influenced by his or her own psychological matrix. In addition, the therapist is cognizant that words may lack shared meanings and can lead to the illusion of a shared understanding that is in fact nonexistent. To guard against this possibility, the therapist repeatedly returns his or her thought-through perceptions to the field of the relationship with each spouse and the couple in descriptive fashion, using tones, rhythms, facial expressions, body language, and words in the complex effort to communicate his or her perceptions in ways that encompass the full range of verbal and nonverbal communication.

For example, in response to a wife describing the ending of a previous relationship, the therapist might share a partial identification with such an experience. "If I'm hearing you correctly, and I'm not sure I am, I think I might have mixed feelings in that situation, both sad and relieved. Sad that this person who is important to me is no longer there, relieved that this person who was so frustrating of my need for recognition is now gone." The wife might confirm the therapist's interpretation of her experience: "That's exactly what I felt." Or, she might modify it by responding, "That's close to what I felt," giving the therapist an opportunity to explore what was different. Or, the wife might totally reject the therapist's identification, saying, "No. I wasn't sad and I wasn't relieved. I was just angry," and helping the therapist to recognize that she has done little to think through and learn from that relationship as suggested by her never having gotten beyond her anger. The wife's understanding of the therapist's identification might have been different if the therapist simply said, "You must have been sad and relieved," as if the wife would know to what he or she was referring.

The overriding objective of the therapist is to identify with the experience of *each* spouse, forming and reforming identifications into increasingly finer attunement with what the spouse experiences. An effect of the therapist's *thinking out loud* is that his or her developmental capacity for self and other observation and reflection, for taking in (receptivity, introjective identification) without being taken over, for flexibility without loss of the self, becomes experientially available to the spouses and therefore available for internalization.

Over time, the story of each spouse evolves, like a puzzle taking shape. More and more pieces are added as present (the contemporary relationship) is associated to past (history of conscious and unconscious experience in early relationship), and past is associated to present, gradually clarifying the interlocking relationship of the internal world of each spouse to the present-day difficulties of the marriage. Often, before they know it, the spouses come to better observe and think about their own experiences, as these are held, identified, thought about, and clarified in a continuing relationship with the therapist. As *cognitive-affective* understanding of self increases, integration of bits and pieces of the self increases, and the self is strengthened so that previously disavowed parts become less endangering and thereby more easily reintegrated. It is impossible to say what comes first because these processes are inextricably interwoven. Like a snowball being pushed downhill, gathering mass until it eventually continues to roll under its own weight, so the development of the self is a painfully slow and difficult process that can last for years, but once underway takes on a momentum of its own.

This is a labyrinthine, confusing, and painful journey, often more so for the therapist than the spouses, given their reliance on primitive defenses that anesthetize feelings. Nonetheless, the spouses' defensive needs must be respected, signaling as they do the fear of the dissolution of the self. Consequently, one of the functions of the holding environment is to expose the spouses to realities at a pace that does not overwhelm them. For the most part, the spouses must set the pace of therapy. If the therapist's thoughts are rejected, alternative explanations are explored. If alternatives are not forthcoming, the issue is put on hold until it comes up again, as it inevitably will.

Useful work along the interpersonal dimension becomes increasingly feasible as each spouse develops a more differentiated, autonomous, and consequently less defensive sense of self. As this occurs, acting out decreases in favor of thinking through. Such gains are won, lost, and won again, but over time the spouses become increasingly capable of working toward resolution of issues in direct spouse-to-spouse interactions. In response, the therapist's use of separate dyadic interactions decreases as the couples therapy takes on more normal/neurotic form.

CASE EXAMPLE

As Judy and Ralph first entered the consulting room, Judy appeared tense, seemingly absorbed in somber thoughts, while Ralph strained to appear affable and worry free. His anxiety was conveyed in his exaggerated efforts to monitor Judy's reactions as he interacted with me.

When asked what brought them my way, Judy dove right in, presenting in organized businesslike fashion the following information. She and Ralph had dated for eight months, lived together six, and were planning to marry. Now, she was troubled. Ralph rarely initiated conversations or sexual relations, and didn't seem glad to see her when she came home at night. She was alarmed that he repeatedly "forgot" to do chores or did them poorly, and absented himself during important couples' occasions, such as leaving her just before the stroke of midnight on New Year's Eve to have a cigarette, and in spending their anniversary weekend at the beach chain-smoking and watching TV.

Judy was also concerned by Ralph's attributing needs to her, such as saying she needed to go for a ride in the country or to see a movie. She also felt unprotected by Ralph, noting an occasion when he didn't stop a drunken acquaintance from grinding up against her in a parody of having sex, and his stepping back when a homeless man approached them for money, effectively leaving her in the forefront. When asked, she reported feeling "played with" and that Ralph was "settling for" her rather than really wanting to be with her.

How individuals present the details of their life and relationship situation provides important clues about their particular ways of perceiving and relating—the prism of the internal world of pathological object relationships. Judy is describing several relationships to several different primary Others (Ralph). One is her relationship to Ralph as unfortunately childlike, ineffectual, passive-aggressive, and dependent. In this particular relationship configuration, she is in the role of a good, competent mother who is organizing and directing the child, but is also pained and disappointed by the child's resistance to becoming more responsible. Judy also describes another relationship, that of a woman to a man in which she perceives Ralph as a devaluing, rejecting, and neglecting Other, who sadistically "plays with" and withholds from her, all the while claiming that he loves her.

The therapist begins by reflecting his initial impression of what Judy is saying back to her (trial identification).

THERAPIST: I gather—and please correct me if I'm misperceiving—that you perceive Ralph as unavailable and uninterested, that he goes through the motions of relationship, but isn't really caring or invested. As if that isn't hard enough to bear, you also feel that he enjoys "playing you," taking some pleasure in driving you crazy with his behavior. What once you thought was "love" you now fear is "settling for." You fear that he is with you because it's easier to be with you than not. Is that what you experience?

JUDY: I don't think it's that bad, but I don't think he really wants to be with me. I don't feel very important to him.

Judy modifies my perception of her experience. However, her response is in headline fashion, without elaborations that would increase my understanding of her experience and clarify why it isn't "that bad."

THERAPIST: I appreciate your correcting my impression. As you'll see, I do a lot of thinking out loud, to let you know what I don't know so you can help me better understand. Still, given what you've described, I'm not clear how things aren't that bad?

JUDY: There are times that we get along really well. Ralph can be very playful and will hold me when I'm upset. There used to be lots of times when we were dating. Now, all of that has dropped away. I feel the love is gone but I still hope we can get it back. [Ralph reaches over and gently touches Judy's shoulder.]

Judy demonstrates whole-object relatedness: remembering the "good" as well as the "bad" of the relationship. Yet, she also readily reverts to a paranoid-schizoid way of perceiving, equating a feeling with reality: the fear of "love being gone" becomes the reality of "love is gone." Ralph's spontaneous empathic touch is incongruous with Ralph as sadistic and withholding.

THERAPIST: [Clarifying] Ralph doesn't play or hold you any more?

JUDY: [Despairing] No, he does. It just doesn't mean the same. I guess he cares but he doesn't change.

Judy elaborates and modifies her perception, noting that it isn't that Ralph is completely different, but that the meaning *she* attributes to his actions is different given the continuing frustration of her needs. Always follow affect.

THERAPIST: [Speaking softly] I have the impression that your world feels pretty dark right now (portrayed in her tone of voice). I imagine that you maintain hope but that it is dwindling, and that you expect and fear the worst [paraphrase of what Judy has been saying]: that Ralph doesn't love you and, perhaps that you'll never find anyone that will [therapist's intuitive leap].

JUDY: [Tearful] That's exactly how I feel.

Judy's cognitive-affective response completes a cycle of interaction leading to a moment of mutual understanding. The therapist's verbal and nonverbal reflections and empathy help to create a healing interaction in which Judy no longer feels alone and alienated in her experience.

THERAPIST: When people feel what you're feeling it's very painful and frightening. It's a terrible thing to feel that the "love is gone," not knowing why, or what to do about it, or whether or not you'll ever have it again. [Judy cries softly.]

This comment further validates the humanness and poignancy of Judy's experience, showing that others, such as the therapist, can compassionately identify with it. Please note that no effort has been made to change anything or to assess the reality of Judy's perceptions regarding Ralph or the relationship. The sole focus has been on the therapist working to identify with Judy's *perception* of reality and how it affects her. Time and space have been created for Judy's experience—an experience that she may only have been able to fully feel or acknowledge after it was recognized and acknowledged by another. Still, I wonder about Judy's fear of being unloved and unlovable, and her perception of the Other as sadistic. This is not to say that Ralph might not be sadistic, only that other possible interpretations exist and yet she naturally perceives him in this way. I wonder why? Judy breaks into my reverie.

JUDY: I hadn't found the words for it but that's right. I want it with Ralph, but my worse fear is that I'll never be able to have it.

Given the quiet and thoughtful atmosphere of the moment a response does not seem required. Although I have more questions, I am acutely aware that I need to attend to Ralph. He seemed attentive and okay with the focus being upon Judy, but it is time to engage him as a full participant in the session.

THERAPIST: I'm sorry to have left you sitting there all this time. What's been on your mind as Judy and I've been talking?

I ask a nondirective question to avoid superimposing my own ambitions (areas of interest) on Ralph or to suggest that he should organize himself around what Judy has been saying, rather than what has been in his own mind or heart.

RALPH: (Looking confused) I'm not sure what you would like to know.

Ralph's response is passive-dependent. He wants to organize himself around me. As yet, it is not clear whether this reflects a resistance to participation, lack of interiority (absence of thoughts and feelings), passive-aggressiveness (making the therapist "pull teeth"), or avoidance of any possibility of conflict that might arise from saying the proverbial "wrong thing." This last possibility came to mind given his monitoring of Judy's facial reactions and Judy's childlike depiction of him. Whatever the case, fostering the emergence of the self of each spouse is the goal of this therapy. Accordingly, I resist the impulse to decide for Ralph what is or isn't important to talk about.

THERAPIST: All I'm really interested in is *whatever* is on *your* mind.
RALPH: [After a pause] All the things Judy says happened are true. But, that doesn't mean I don't love her. Sometimes I'm really not thinking.
JUDY: [Judy angrily interrupts, displaying an intense reactivity not evident when interacting with me.] How can you say that? How can you not get it? I think you're full of shit. You make excuse after excuse. You're pathetic.

Her tone of voice is contemptuous and her words are attacking. At best she accuses Ralph of being stupid, and at worst an outright liar. This is a *communication by impact:* a blaming and shaming personal assault on who Ralph is. Judy is in the role of aggressor. Ralph can counterattack or withdraw. In any event, the holding environment of therapy will collapse. Note that Judy's acting-out behavior signals that her internal world is now alive in the room: past is present, the intrapsyche is interpersonalized. If Judy was more differentiated she would not have internalized the "badness" of the situation with the resultant need to attack Ralph to regulate her sense of self. I intervene immediately via beginning the use of separate dyadic interactions.

THERAPIST: Judy. Judy. [Gradually Judy shifts her enraged focus from Ralph to me.]

JUDY: Yes?

THERAPIST: I bet you've had many of these kinds of fights at home and that they haven't been very useful.

JUDY: That's true; nothing changes.

THERAPIST: When we human beings can't make sense of why our needs aren't being met in relationship it drives us crazy. [I normalize Judy's experience.] Your pain and anger are understandable, but I'm not clear as to what just upset you.

JUDY: I'm not sure. Maybe it was the feeling that he was just making more excuses, that he's playing you and me. He keeps saying he loves me, but he doesn't act like it.

THERAPIST: I see what you mean. From what you've said, Ralph keeps doing things that would upset any woman that aspired to relationship with him. But still, and maybe it's just me, your sensitivity to this issue suggests that Ralph is not the first important person in your life to say one thing and do another. I have the impression that Ralph's behavior triggers a landmine within you that is buried just below the surface and that it existed far before Ralph was in the picture. [Judy considers for a moment.]

JUDY: You mean like in my family?

THERAPIST: That's often where it starts; the familiar is most often familial. I think for most of us childhood sensitizes us to certain things, which are re-evoked in our adult relationships, particularly marriage. Suspend your judgment about your thoughts or feelings for a moment and see what comes up. [Encouragement of associative thinking.]

JUDY: I know I wasn't a happy child. My mother drank too much and still is verbally abusive. She's always screaming and yelling. She doesn't drink now, but she still slaps me when she gets angry. I didn't know what made her so mad. She just says that I'm selfish and that no matter how hard I try I can't do anything about it; that it's just who I am.

Judy describes a volatile, physically, emotionally, and verbally abusive mother who projectively identified Judy as an irredeemably defective and selfish person.

THERAPIST: Do you believe her?

JUDY: Not really. I can't stand the idea of it, but sometimes I'm not sure.

THERAPIST: Do you ever feel that you're selfish in relationship to Ralph?

JUDY: Sometimes, when my needs aren't being met I think that maybe I'm too needy, and that it's selfish of me and I shouldn't say anything. I feel like I always want something from Ralph, while he never wants anything from me. That makes me feel selfish.

THERAPIST: So when your needs are frustrated you're sometimes not sure whether it's because you're asking for too much?

JUDY: Right.

Judy is tearful as she sits with her experience. An important anxiety has been identified and acknowledged. But, I am still not clear about her need to attack.

THERAPIST: You mentioned that your mother screams and yells, and you just did that with Ralph. I wonder whether there is a connection. What do you think?

JUDY: Just thinking that I might be like my mother gets my blood boiling. I can't stand it. I think I act like my mom because I don't know what else to do when I get angry?

Judy describes seeing no alternative to behaving like her mother when she gets angry. She also delineates Ralph as irredeemably flawed (stupid or a liar) similar to the way her mother had delineated her. In Judy's internal world there is only one way to express upset (via attack) and someone must be irredeemably flawed: better the Other than the Self.

THERAPIST: That makes sense if that was the only way emotions were expressed in your family. Reverting to old ways of relating that existed between your mom and you suggests the possibility that when you're upset you might confuse your relationship with Ralph with your relationship with your mother [A tentative interpretation; Judy makes no response]. What were you feeling when you got furious with Ralph a short while ago?

JUDY: I felt very frustrated. I also felt helpless and afraid. If he continues to deny his part in all this it won't work out.

THERAPIST: Did you feel anything else? What I mean is how did you see Ralph in particular at that moment in time?

JUDY: I felt like he had to be lying and was playing you like he plays me. He's a smart man. He can't believe what he is saying.

THERAPIST: Does that feeling about Ralph relate in any way to the way you felt in relationship to your mother?

JUDY: Oh, yeah. No matter how I tried I just couldn't get it right. I often felt that something was wrong with me, that I was bad or stupid. I just couldn't get it right.

THERAPIST: So, in relationship to Ralph you sometimes wonder what is wrong with you that you can't get him to love you, that you can't get it right. At other times you think something is wrong with Ralph, that he is lying or just plain stupid, because no matter how much he says he loves you, he doesn't change?

JUDY: Yes. I feel both those things. I get furious with myself and then I get furious with Ralph.

THERAPIST: And, then sometimes, you treat Ralph the way your mom treated you.

JUDY: [Stridently] Well, they're not the same. I'm not my mother and I would never tell anyone they couldn't change.

THERAPIST: You're right. That is a huge difference, although I'm not sure someone on the receiving end of your anger could make that distinction. Thinking about things is like trying things on for size to see whether they fit. Only you can decide what fits for you and what doesn't.

I immediately desist from exploring Judy's identifications with her mother because Judy's tone of voice signals that she feels threatened. Nothing is lost in doing this. If this association is valid it will return again and again for further exploration.

THERAPIST: What was your relationship like with your dad?

JUDY: My dad doesn't criticize me, but he doesn't defend me. He never stopped my mother, but sometimes he would let me know he cared about me, like with a touch, but he never said anything. [I'm reminded of Ralph's earlier touch.]

THERAPIST: He's a quiet presence, somewhat like Ralph?

JUDY: Now that I think about it, he's a lot like Ralph.

THERAPIST: In what ways?

JUDY: My dad never fought and wasn't very protective. Ralph never fights and isn't very protective.

THERAPIST: So both your father and Ralph are conflict avoiders?

JUDY: Yes. I hadn't thought about it that way. They avoid conflict.

THERAPIST: So, do you realize that Ralph and your dad's avoidance of conflict at any cost doesn't say anything about you, but something about them?

JUDY: I think I can see what you're saying. It doesn't mean that they don't care about me?

THERAPIST: Yes. That's what I'm thinking. It means that they both can love you even though they may be too afraid to protect you. [Judy wells up with feeling.]

JUDY: I don't like that they don't protect me, but I can see how it doesn't mean that they don't love me.

THERAPIST: What about the rest of your family? What are they like?

JUDY: My brother, sister, and mother tell jokes and tease at other peoples' expense. Even today, I'm targeted because I get upset. Then they tell me that I think I'm better than everybody else. I get so confused. Now, I avoid getting together with them, but I also worry about losing them completely.

I am sickened by the pain and destructiveness of the sadistic forms of relating that Judy describes that leads her to highly value something as small as a touch because it is the only expression of caring that she gets.

THERAPIST: [Incredulous] They accuse you of thinking you're better than anyone else if you get upset about being the brunt of their teasing?

I am only partially aware of the incredulousness and anger growing within me at these perverse and destructive forms of relating, and only then because I hear it in the sound of my own voice (countertransference).

JUDY: Yes.

I resist the impulse to attack Judy's family, now more clearly recognizing the anger I feel toward them. I wonder where Judy keeps her anger.

THERAPIST: No wonder you feel confused, you're damned if you do and damned if you don't. What do you do with your own anger?

JUDY: I don't know. At least with Ralph I can express it. He doesn't change, but he also doesn't attack me or make me feel crazy for being angry. With my family I generally learned to swallow it. I didn't have any other alternative. It would just create more problems for me. But, I do feel angry, like right now, after you said that about "damned if I do or damned if I don't." I never thought of it that way. But, that's right. With them there was just no winning.

I have lost my focus due to the impact of the countertransference feelings generated within me by what Judy has described. I pause to regroup. I think about what has happened so far. Judy's focus has moved away from Ralph and onto herself. She is no longer acting out, but exploring the prism of early relationship experiences: of feeling stupid and flawed, her fear that her needs are excessive or unrealistic, her early history in relationships characterized by sadistic teasing and attack, of feeling isolated and alienated from the rest of her family, except for small indications of affection from her father.

THERAPIST: Judy, I appreciate your giving me a glimpse into your family life. I think I understand better how you would be inclined to interpret Ralph's behaviors as "playing you," and how you could feel not very loved or important to him. On a basic level the brain tends to equate similar as same, even when there can be a huge difference between the two. Maybe Ralph is being sadistic and withholding, but that's only one possibility and it hasn't been clearly established. Anyway, thanks for letting me in on what at least some of your life has been like.

JUDY: You're welcome.

THERAPIST: Unless there is something else you would like to say, I would like to talk to Ralph for awhile.

JUDY: No. I can't think of anything else right now.

Much is yet to be discovered, but given that Judy is now sitting quietly and clearly feeling drained, I turn once again to the effort of creating time and space for Ralph.

THERAPIST: So, what's been on your mind while Judy and I've been talking?

RALPH: I feel terrible that I've hurt Judy in this way. I don't know what goes on with me. All I know is that I do love her. I know I have to try harder to be available when she needs me.

Ralph has empathy. His words seem sincere, yet there is an incongruity between his feelings and his actions. Where Judy is worried about being selfish, Ralph presents as selfless. How can a "hollow man" (selfless) speak in ways that don't sound hollow? He doesn't speak of his disappointments, frustrations, or needs in the relationship. He relates as if Judy's reactions are all that are of value, minimizing his needs and desires.

THERAPIST: I don't know about that; that's up to you to decide. I'm sure there are good reasons why it is so hard for you to make these changes. What kind of frustrations or disappointments do you have in this relationship?

RALPH: I don't have any. Judy's great.

Interestingly, in Judy's family she could never get it right. With Ralph she can never get it wrong. Ralph's idealization of Judy suggests that he relates to his primary others as "all good," which would then leave him totally responsible for any problems in the relationship, i.e., inadequate or "bad." Judy interjects.

JUDY: How about when I come home at night and all you want to do is watch TV instead of talk to me?

RALPH: You're right. I should turn it off right away and be there for you.

Ralph holds the naïve conviction that he should always attend to Judy's needs, regardless of his own.

THERAPIST: Aren't there times that you would rather finish a program before talking or sometimes not feel like talking at all?

I'm trying to delineate some seed of separateness and individuality.

RALPH: Sure. But, I can videotape the program and it's not hard to talk for a few minutes.

Ralph again minimizes his wishes and desires and never considers the possibility that Judy could wait, at least some of the time, until the show was over. Such extensive self-suppression generates underlying frustration, resentment, and aggression. I wonder whether Ralph acts out these feelings and the need to retain some sense of self apart from Judy by "forgetting" to do chores, doing them poorly, in not initiating conversations or sexual relations, and in his absenting himself at important moments when he would naturally be expected to be there.

THERAPIST: I'm confused. Let me walk through this with you. You feel bad when something you do upsets Judy. Judy's clear about what those things are and so they're not a mystery to you. Indeed, you agree with her. Yet, you persist in this pattern of not doing them. I'm missing something here.

I continue to highlight the incongruities between Ralph's thoughts, feelings, and behaviors.

RALPH: I know. It doesn't make sense. I don't understand it.

Ralph acknowledges the incongruity and joins with the therapist in feeling confused, demarcating an area of the "not known." It is now the collaborative task of the therapist and spouse to come to understand the "not yet understood"; to discover the missing pieces of information that will make sense of this nonsense.

THERAPIST: It's puzzling. It's a good example of how our brains work on autopilot, programmed by our history of experience. This saves us from having to learn the same thing over and over again, yet, at the same time some of the things we learn don't apply as adults because we learned them in a different time, a different place, and a different relationship. This is how we end up saying we want one thing and yet continue to do another. To change this we have to figure out what the old lessons were and how we may be applying them outside of our awareness in the present.

I begin educating Ralph to some of the tools I use for thinking about things (a theoretical framework) so he'll understand where I am coming from and therefore be a more effective collaborator in the treatment effort. In this process, I am also suggesting to Ralph the possibility of looking at his experience and his reactions as apart from himself, beginning the fostering of "I" that can abide with, observe, and reflect upon the experience of the "me." This approach helps take the blame out of things and challenges the equating of one's thoughts, feelings, and reactions with who one is.

THERAPIST: Your situation is difficult because you're not aware of all of your reactions. I can say this because you're not aware of even momentary frustrations or disappointments in relationship. I've never encountered nor can I conceive of a relationship that is perfectly satisfying most of the time, much less one that is perfectly satisfying all the time. It's even more difficult to imagine a loving relationship that is perfectly satisfying to one partner, while incredibly frustrating to the other. Still, you say you aren't aware of any dissatisfaction. That suggests that part of what you learned earlier in your life is that you should suppress any negativity you experience in relationship. Typically, this is accomplished by repressing needs. Still, that's what you feel and that's all you've got to work with. You feel perfectly satisfied in the relationship. That suggests that you have needs and desires that are being perfectly met. But I'm still not clear as to what they are. Judy says you never express any of this to her.

RALPH: I guess I don't have many and that Judy naturally meets the ones I have.

THERAPIST: Well. That could explain it. What exactly are the needs you do have?

RALPH: I love her just being there.

Ralph describes the need of the soothing presence of the other, a primitive self-object need that is part of loving relationships. What is noteworthy is the absence of other more elaborate desires.

JUDY: [Judy interjects.] You don't act that way. You don't seem glad to see me when I get home at night.

The need of a soothing presence doesn't necessarily entail interaction, only presence. It is the very presence of the other that is calming. Nonetheless, Judy offers a reality-testing observation. Turning to me she explains:

JUDY: I'm glad to see him but he'd rather watch TV or work on the computer, and I think it's been worse since I started my new job four or five months ago. We had a routine before, but now I never know when I'll be home.

Judy observes, reflects, and speculates: important capacities for thinking through experience. I wonder whether the uncertainty associated with Judy's new job has rendered her an unreliable object in Ralph's eyes, perhaps reevoking experiences of a rejecting object in Ralph's internal world, fanning the flames of insecurity and needfulness that result in his feeling excessively vulnerable to the return of the repressed. If this is the case, one defense would be to actively attack the need and defend against such vulnerability via withdrawal and indifference.

THERAPIST: Ralph, what do you make of Judy's observation?

RALPH: I don't know. All I know is that I miss her.

As I think about the firmness of tone and absoluteness of Ralph's response I realize that missing her represents the frustration of a wish or need. Given Ralph's antagonistic relationship to his needs and desires, I wonder how he knows he misses her.

THERAPIST: How do you know you miss her?

RALPH: That's easy. I think about her all the time.

I am surprised by the clarity and spontaneity of his response.

THERAPIST: What do you mean?

RALPH: Since Judy took this new job she's been working very hard. So, I think about what I can do that will make her happy, like cleaning the bathroom or emptying the litter box, and I do that. Then I think about her look of happiness when she comes through the door.

Again, I'm surprised. This time by the richness of Ralph's response, which conveys the intensity of his investment in the experience he is describing: the wish for relationship to a well-pleased Other (exciting object). This suggests something that we already know, that Ralph has an other-validated sense of self. Ralph is not self-validating, therefore he needs a well-pleased Other (exciting object) to maintain a positive and secure sense of self (libidinal self-representation). Conversely, if the Other isn't pleased (rejecting object) then Ralph would secure a disappointing sense of self (antilibidinal self-representation). One thing is clear: in this area of experience Ralph is acutely self-aware.

THERAPIST: Wow! You sure know what you're experiencing in the times you describe. It's clear that at those times you really are looking forward to her coming home. I guess we could say that you need or desire her to come home. Yet, when she gets home you meet her with seeming indifference. Think carefully. Try to remember. Suspend your judgment about the relative merits of your thoughts or feelings. Just see what comes up. How is it you get from the aliveness of anticipation, to the deadness of indifference?

RALPH: I know. I'll be caught up in a TV show or with the computer and then it's hard to tear myself away.

Ralph returns to the less-than-illuminating explanation of being overly invested in the TV or the computer, which belies the excited sense of anticipation he clearly conveyed just moments ago. As I continue to press my nose to the grindstone of the work, I wonder whether I can say the same about Ralph.

THERAPIST: Well, if it's interesting it's hard to stop in the middle of a program.

Just when I thought that Ralph and I might be making some progress, he retreats. I question whether I am going to be of help here. I then wonder whether my growing feeling of ineffectuality might be an effect of Ralph's unconscious (both to him and to me) use of projective identification to give me the direct experience of what he is feeling: inadequate, ineffectual, helpless, hopeless.

RALPH: [Halfheartedly] I could videotape it and watch later.

My feelings of frustration grow. Every seeming movement forward is soon undone by Ralph's return to a passive-dependent position without aliveness. Moments ago we were both engaged as he richly conveyed his experience of excited anticipation of Judy coming home. Now we are both relatively lifeless, with little emotional energy or investment. In becoming aware of what I am feeling, I am able to separate myself from the feeling. I find renewed energy and interest in sorting through this conundrum. I still do not know where to go from here. I need more time to allow my mind to both wonder and wander. Where is here? Ralph treats his own wishes as of secondary importance. He seems to assume that if his needs carry the potential of conflict, then his needs, and he himself, are wrong or "bad." I can empathize with Judy's frustration, of having an experience of real connection with Ralph repeatedly offset by the experience of disconnection, of aliveness followed by apathy. Why does Ralph shut down? Why is his sense of self so threatened? Is Judy excessive in her demands? Is he defending against engulfment? What about this job change? Something seems to have been amplified with it. Why is he so intent on "putting a smile on her face" to the extent of doing chores? How does he get from the anticipatory excitement associated with Judy coming home, to the aloofness he conveys upon her arrival? Of these various thoughts, the last congeals most strongly in my mind, perhaps because to answer it Ralph must rely on his own experience.

THERAPIST: Ralph, you describe investing considerable interest and energy in figuring out what you can do around your home that will put a smile on Judy's face when she comes home. It occurs to me you don't know when she's going to come through the door and sometimes she can be really late. My question is, once you've completed a chore, what happens then?

RALPH: After a while I think of something else that would please her and do that.

Ralph describes a pattern of engaging in an activity to please Judy in anticipation of her coming home, followed by another cycle of activity and anticipation. Why wasn't one gift enough? Also, something is missing: Ralph describes moving from anticipatory activity to anticipatory activity, without anything to demark one cycle from another. I would think some disappointment or frustration would punctuate the end of one cycle and the beginning of the next. Again, it appears that Ralph literally avoids acknowledgment of *any* negative feelings associated with Judy. This thought is not new; what is new is my growing appreciation for the depth of his repression.

THERAPIST: Something seems to be missing. I get the part about looking forward to surprising Judy, what I don't get is that you don't describe any sense of letdown, impatience, frustration, or disappointment when Judy doesn't come home when you had hoped.

RALPH: Yeah. I guess that's right. That does sound strange, doesn't it?

THERAPIST: Well, it wouldn't match how I would feel, but no one's elected me the arbiter of reality. (Ralph and Judy laugh.) What's especially puzzling is that despite your not being aware of any sense of disappointment that that is exactly what Judy recurrently feels when she arrives home to find you indifferent.

RALPH: [Looking troubled] Yes. I see that. What does it mean?

THERAPIST: I don't really know. What we do know is that you anticipate her return with excitement, that you repress any negative feelings about her being delayed, and that when Judy gets home you seem preoccupied with the TV or computer, and that Judy, rather than feeling warmly welcomed, feels indifference to her arrival.

RALPH: I'm confused. None of it makes sense.

THERAPIST: So am I, but be patient with yourself. The only thing I'm sure of is that it does make sense [normalizing rather than pathologizing], we just haven't discovered how yet. Take a moment . . . remember . . . what do you recall about that time between your completion of one chore for Judy and the beginning of the next? Remembering may be in the form of thoughts, feelings, or sensations that you might have thought were unimportant at the time and pushed them away.

RALPH: [Long silence] The feeling that comes to mind is tired [sensation]. I keep expecting Judy to come home but she doesn't. To tell you the truth I think I get a little frustrated [aggressive feeling]. I know she can't help it [rationalizing thought], but it doesn't feel fair [experience in relationship to rejecting object]. I know it's ridiculous [attack on an unacceptable feeling], but I feel like I'm expecting too much [self-attack or reality testing] and that Judy doesn't care [rejecting object], even though I know that isn't true [cognition versus feeling].

Ralph finally grants access to Judy and me (and perhaps even to himself for the first time) to the reactive experience of the "me."

THERAPIST: I don't think it sounds ridiculous at all. What I'm thinking—see if it fits with your experience—is that you begin to feel needful of Judy, looking forward to her coming home [libidinal feelings], but not knowing when that will be. You want to please her and she to be pleased with you. To this end, you do various chores, but each results in the frustration of your wish when she does not come home. On some level, each disappointment might feel something like rejection; again the law of the unconscious that similar equals same. The disappointments mount and the feeling of rejection gradually takes over, along with the fear that Judy will not be responsive to you when she arrives. You feel that what you're going through isn't fair, as if Judy's doing something to you. This feeling signals that something from the past has been re-evoked. Another feeling from the past then comes over you: the feeling that you are being ridiculous; that you shouldn't be having these feelings and that they're not acceptable. Feeling conflicted and vulnerable you withdraw into yourself where you feel safest. So, when Judy gets home, all she sees is your pretended indifference, as if you don't have a need in the world. In actuality, your defensive need is to avoid Judy to protect yourself from the fear or expectation of rejection. In essence, in expectation that Judy will reject your needs, you reject them before she can. Anyway, that's my fantasy for the day, Ralph. What, if anything, resonates for you?

RALPH: As you were talking I remember having the thought on New Year's Eve that I wished Judy would look for me. I'm more comfortable when Judy shows she needs me.

Ralph's associative memory provides partial support for my fantasy (tentative interpretation). Ralph's memory indicates that he was aware of not being with Judy at an important time and also of a wish that she would seek him out. His absence was designed to test or evoke a need, perhaps to see whether he is as much in her mind as she is in his.

THERAPIST: What a wonderful memory. Emotionally, it's certainly safer to be wanted than to want. You seem to be a person who has a hard time knowing and feeling okay about what he wants. That's not genetic, that's a learned experience. The problem is that it's far more difficult to have your needs met if you don't know what they are and if you're afraid to express them. In addition, Judy's left carrying all the needs in the relationship. Indeed, she's left feeling exactly what you fear: alone, unneeded, undesired, frustrated, and not of much value. What are your thoughts?

Ralph went on to describe his family life. He felt himself inadequate and a disappointment to his unpredictable father, a bad-tempered gambler and alcoholic who often disappeared for days. His father brushed Ralph's need for attachment aside, always promising time together, but never delivering. Ralph remembers one Christmas when his father gave him a package comprised of boxes within boxes, his excitement growing until he reached the last box. Within was a piece of paper, IOU written upon it. Ralph's mood plummeted, another false promise. Ralph's mother was a constant worrier, relying on Ralph as a confidant. Her anxieties were such that he couldn't share his feelings with her because she would either minimize their importance or amplify them as they added to her burden of worries. His brother, a heavy drug user, was incarcerated several times and is currently in prison. His sister, an alcoholic, constantly created scenes while bemoaning the wretched state of her existence. In this constellation of tumultuous and endangering family relationships, Ralph could relax only when he was alone. Otherwise, he was always performing, trying to avoid conflict by modeling himself as the "good boy" who rarely troubled his parents. He experienced his needs and desires only as endangering vulnerabilities, never as part of an internal compass for the pursuit of fulfillment.

The problem with needs is that they are *needs*. They do not go away. Under the repressive weight of the defenses aligned against them, they arise in displaced and substitute form. Ralph's needs of Judy were manageable, satisfied by Judy's own pursuit of relationship needs, until she changed jobs and started coming home at unpredictable hours. This change made her an unreliable object, perhaps triggering in Ralph unconscious associations to his father's unpredictable comings and goings, as well as promises of eventual fulfillment that went unmet. In this heightened state of insecurity, Ralph engaged in behaviors designed to control the situation, that is, to "put a smile" on Judy's face so that she would be pleased with him instead of disappointed as his father had been, thereby soothing his separation anxiety with nurturing attachment. However, if she came home later than expected, his needs and associated insecurities intensified until the internal world of pathological object relationships predominated, i.e., past became present. At this juncture, enveloped in the internal world, Ralph would defend against his endangering vulnerability by becoming aloof and withdrawn, preferring the relative safety of the nonhuman environment of TV or computer.

At other times, if his needs were more personal and less relationally dependent, he would attribute his needs to Judy in displaced form: "I think a ride in the country would be good for you." At still other times, when feeling relationally needful, he would function in ways to evoke Judy's own needfulness and hurt, such as disappearing at grossly inappropriate times. Such actions are reminiscent of Ralph's memories of his father, who disappeared for days on end and also promised time together but never delivered. The result is that Ralph re-created his internal world of relationships in his interpersonal relationship with Judy. Judy ends up feeling like Ralph felt in childhood: needful of attention and spurned in its pursuit. She comes to feel tolerated, but unloved.

Judy also re-created part of her internal world in the external reality of the relationship. In her object choice (Ralph) she picked someone who was conflict avoidant, passive, and relatively unavailable like her father and who was just the opposite of her mother (volatile, attacking). This provided the security of being in a relationship free from an endangering Other and, indeed, one in which Ralph reassured her she could do no wrong. This was a distinct improvement over the familial relationships in which she could do no right.

The problem here is that the pursuit of excessive security comes at the expense of the pursuit of fulfillment. This relationship configuration could only remain in existence as long as Ralph remained passive and conflict avoidant, placing his security needs over his needs of fulfillment. Yet it was exactly these features, Ralph's antagonistic relationship to his needs, that left Judy feeling alone, unneeded, unprotected, and undesired, much as she had felt in childhood.

As therapy continued, progress was made in terms of both cognitive and emotional insight, but movement was slow in terms of deep and enduring change. Eighteen months into treatment, Ralph and Judy reported an intense argument, precipitated by Ralph's failure to plan for a weekend that took his own needs into account. In response, he opted for a trip to Georgetown, which Judy refused, declaring: "Why should I go? So I can do all the talking while you just react to whatever I say?" Uncharacteristically, Ralph was furious, saying, "Fuck it, I don't care." Subsequently, he began thinking about his failure to make plans as promised, recognizing that he was continuing the defensive use of passivity and avoidance, rather than asserting himself. Judy's rejection of his halfhearted effort made him realize that his defensiveness was close to bringing about the very thing he defended against: the loss of Judy. He apologized to Judy and they went to Georgetown. She reported having a great time. He reported that he had enjoyed himself, but that for him it had been a lot of work involving the effort to stay aware of and communicate his own thoughts and feelings, whatever they were. Ralph reported an eye-opening discovery: "I discovered that it's just as hard not saying anything as it is to say what's on my mind. And, not saying anything is destroying our relationship and me. I'm just not willing to do that anymore. What stuns me is how much courage it takes to just say what's on my mind. But, I'm determined to *be* me. I realize that Judy will either love me or not, but I know trying to be what I think Judy wants me to be isn't working for either of us."

After eighteen months of therapy Judy and Ralph were married. Five months later, with the process that is relationship securely established, they terminated therapy.

STRENGTHS AND LIMITATIONS

This model addresses the keystone of personality disorder: the developmental deficit (depressive-subjective) of an "I" that can abide with, observe, and reflect upon the experience of the "me." Constructing a holding environment in therapy, it uses the spouses' acting-out behavior, the very feature that contributes to the infamous personality-disordered intransigence to treatment efforts, as a primary vehicle for renewing the development of the self. The power of this approach is not in the therapist, but in the use of the spouses' own experiences as the point of reference from which relationship to Self and Other derives. As befitting subjects, rather than objects, each spouse is held firmly as the final arbiter of the meaning of his or her experience. The use of separate dyadic interactions, trial identifications, successive approximations, and rejectable interpretations allows the therapist's own depressive-subjective capacities to be directly experienced in the relationship by each spouse. That which is experienced is available for internalization. The use of these techniques also creates a forum that reiterates the developmental challenges of the Oedipal period, which must be navigated for development to proceed.

As with any model, treatment failures exist. The therapist may suffer a loss of differentiation under the projective bombardment of the spouses that leads to countertransference acting out. The spouses may be so severely personality disordered in conjunction with a high index of sociopathy that they are unwilling or unable to forego their win-or-lose, dominance-or-submission world of pathological object relationships. Others may be so dysfunctional that progress is extremely slow and lifelong, marked by gradual strengthening that impacts positively on one or both spouses, but not in terms that are easily measured or valued by those who have not been nearly as damaged in their lives. Finally, some view longer-term therapy as a weakness in itself. I am not among them. Indeed, I view short-term treatment approaches as selling a bill of goods. Personality disorder entails core problems embedded on the level of cellular memory that profoundly effects ways of perceiving and relating that are impervious to long-lasting modification without in-depth treatment. This is not to say that short-term treatment cannot be helpful; it can. However, the work is far from complete and these patients often engage in a revolving door of treatment.

BENEFITS FOR THE FAMILY

The therapist's use of separate dyadic interactions impedes acting-out behavior and turns it into a vehicle for understanding and change. Family members become better able to relate to and differentiate themselves from the personality-disordered member's behaviors and idiosyncratic interpretations of reality. This allows for an enhanced ability for putting the personality-disordered person's behaviors into perspective, and to confront, limit, and process the experience. The chaos of the family is reduced as parents learn to set limits and protective boundaries in service of a real relationship with personality-disordered children. Children with a personality-disordered parent also benefit when the parent's acting-out behavior is interrupted, processed, understood, and gradually modified. Even in extreme circumstances in which the personality-disordered parent remains totally intransigent to treatment efforts, the children benefit from witnessing the therapist's interpretations and explicit confrontations of the parent's acting-out behavior and its destructiveness, which squarely frame the problem as the parent's, not the children's. Given an alternative explanation, the children become less likely to internalize the "badness" of the situation as their own. This is particularly true if the other parent is more normal/neurotic and available as a viable alternative to the personality-disordered parent. The personality-disordered individual benefits because his or her behavior is normalized rather than pathologized, and because understanding increases along with the capacity to learn from experience.

INDICATIONS AND CONTRAINDICATIONS

Conjoint therapy (couples form) is indicated anytime: (1) one spouse is interested in working on the relationship, even if the other is reluctant; (2) whenever the relationship is a significant complaint, particularly if an individual therapy is stuck; or if (3) the personality-disordered individual denies having a problem, and the presence of a family member is necessary to confront the denial.

Conjoint therapy (family form without patient present) is indicated for families with a chronically acting-out adolescent, while the adolescent is referred for individual therapy. Family therapy with the parents, but without the adolescent, provides a venue for educating the parents and addressing parental resistances to providing both appropriate nurturing and firm limit setting. Parental resistance becomes apparent as the parents encounter difficulty in the ongoing implementation of agreed-upon interventions.

Parental resistance is typically rooted in each parent's history of relationships to their own parents. As the parents' self-understanding concerning their difficulties in nurturing and limiting their adolescent deepens, their ability to set and maintain appropriate limits increases.

Initially, the adolescent's behavior intensifies, testing the parents' genuineness, and then deintensifies and stabilizes as the parents' resolve is understood and structures are internalized. In the long term, what the child or adolescent experiences are protective boundaries and genuine caring. The absence of the adolescent from the session creates time and space for the parents to work through their respective issues without constantly having to contend with the adolescent's acting-out behavior. It also protects the therapist from undermining the parents in the eyes of the adolescent as the therapist confronts the parents with their own issues.

MANAGEMENT OF TRANSFERENCE ISSUES

Transference and transference acting-out behaviors are managed by the use of the technique of separate dyadic interactions, which is employed whenever acting-out behaviors arise or when the therapist recognizes the need for an individual exploration of a spouse's projective identification system (a form of transference). This technique allows the focus to shift seamlessly from the interpersonal to the intrapsyche and back again as transference issues arise. The therapist recognizes that countertransference reflects his or her own history of experience in relationships. The therapist also recognizes that countertransference is often evoked by the spouse's reliance upon projective identification processes. As such, they are understood as a communication from the unconscious of the clients to the unconscious of the therapist. Accordingly, the therapist spends much time and effort observing and reflecting upon his or her own experience and abiding with this experience rather than engaging in acting out countertransference reactions. It is hoped that this process of abiding allows the therapist to achieve a deeper understanding of the projector's internal world on an experiential feeling level, rather than the more surface level of words and verbal labels. The therapist, presumably normal/neurotic and relatively more differentiated than the spouses, is better able to have an experience without acting out, particularly when the therapist's focus includes his or her internal experience. A defining difference exists between a countertransference experience and countertransference acting-out behavior. Although the former can be extremely informative, the latter is often destructive.

MANAGEMENT OF CRISES
AND ACTING-OUT BEHAVIOR

A crisis exists anytime there is a serious threat of suicidal or homicidal behavior. In this circumstance the therapist must insist on psychiatric hospitalization. Situations in which a danger to self or other exists must be distinguished from suicidal or homicidal feelings or ideation without intent, communications by impact, and from self-mutilation without serious permanent consequences. Many personality-disordered individuals use self-cutting and other forms of pain induction to help organize and regulate the sense of self. This form of self-regulation is better than none at all, which can lead to psychotic breakdown or serious homicidal or suicidal risk. Whether the patient is a child or an adult is also an important consideration. If the patient is a child, hospitalization for self-mutilating behavior is indicated. Physically assaultive behavior in an older adolescent or adult requires a call to protective services and/or the police.

INTEGRATION WITH PSYCHIATRIC SERVICES
AND ROLE OF MEDICATION

This approach was developed at a long-term psychiatric inpatient unit. Accordingly, it fits with and appreciates the important role of medications in treatment. The use of antidepressant, anxiolytic, and antipsychotic medications is often essential in helping patients to manage what otherwise would be chronically overwhelming affects and thoughts that make it impossible to gain the perspective necessary for self-observation and self-reflection. Medications do not eliminate thoughts and feelings—they make them less intense and thereby easier to experience. As the manager of the holding environment, the therapist must try to protect the patient from impingement, internal as well as external. Medications help manage internal impingement. This said, as the patient develops an increasingly integrated sense of self and corresponding capacities for self-management and self-direction, it is not uncommon that the patient's need for medication decreases, and in some cases is eliminated.

CULTURAL AND GENDER ISSUES

Two values underlie this model. The first is the value of individual development. Implied in this is a value for autonomy, separation, individuation, and differentiation from one's family of origin and one's current significant others. Interventions described here and the entire process of sequential dyadic interaction in a triadic context are designed to promote individual development, leading to two maturing individuals in empathic affiliation with each other. Members of cultures that value commitment to the "group," as culturally defined, over and above individual development, may find this treatment approach anathematic to normative desired outcomes. Indeed, interventions promoting individuation and differentiation may be experienced as promoting deviance from cultural norms. Some Asian and African cultures and most Islamic societies consider individual submission to group norms a greater value than individual expression. Members of such cultures may experience cultural dislocation and its concomitant psychosocial distress resulting from involvement in such treatment. Cross-cultural pairs may wish to consider this underlying value before proceeding with therapy as described here.

Second, this model values a democratic relationship between partners, regardless of gender, sexual identity, or ethnicity. The equal right of individuals "to be," and to be in mutual empathic affiliation with one another is prized. Cultures that value and proscribe relationships along the continuum of dominance-submission may clash with some of the ultimate and prized aims of this treatment model. Values of individuality and democracy imbue this model and would not be a good fit for members of cultures that do not hold these values dear (Zuskin, personal communication, 2002).

FUTURE DIRECTIONS

Psychoanalytic object-relations approaches to family and marital therapy tend to be underrepresented in the family therapy field and are opposed by managed care companies. Behaviorally oriented approaches are far more straightforward and easier to learn than psychoanalytically informed approaches that require a relatively complex understanding of intrapsychic and interpersonal dynamics. My own formal training of three and a half years was in structural/strategic family therapy. One nationally known instructor (whose identity will not be disclosed here) commented, "Please stop bringing in these kinds of cases. They are not good training cases. I hate these kinds of cases." My problem and that of many of my colleagues was that these "cases" were the people I treated. It was the experience of trying and failing in these behaviorally oriented structural/strategic approaches that drove me, and others, to study psychoanalytic teachings in the effort to better understand what we were dealing with.

Although they are more complex, these studies were far more satisfying, and provided greater understandings of not only personality-disordered people, but of the human condition. The advocated approach emphasizes the importance of recognizing reality, internal and external, not superimposing managed care fantasies (wishing and hoping) on it. This is not to oppose short-term treatment, because the advocated approach has resulted in rapid benefit to some people. However, it staunchly opposes the ill-founded and destructive idea that short-term treatments are for everybody or even for most people. This said, when a short-term treatment effort is all that is available, I work carefully with patients to diagnose various aspects of the problem and to clarify what can be addressed on a short-term basis and what takes longer-term work for modifications to occur. I also explore strategies for helping patients to get the treatment they need within the resources available.

A final comment relates to the resistance of health insurance companies to cover couples and family therapy. These companies continue to subscribe to DSM coding that recognizes only individual psychopathology, without taking into account systemic influences that can create or amplify psychiatric problems. Insurance support of individual therapy to the relative exclusion of couples and family therapy is ignorant and ineffective. Many times I have encountered spouses, one or both of whom have been in ongoing individual therapy and on medication for years, that were able to end their individual therapies and eventually wean themselves from the need of medication as their underlying anxiety and depression, largely arising from their unhappiness in relationship, was alleviated through relationship therapy. Clearly, improvements need to be made in funding formulas to allow clinicians to address the complex systemic and interpersonal processes that are intertwined with individual personality-disorder pathology.

REFERENCES

American Psychiatric Association (1994). *Diagnostic and Statistical Manual of Mental Disorders* (Fourth edition). Washington, DC: American Psychiatric Association.

Casement, P. (1985). *On Learning from the Patient.* London: Tavistock Publications.

Fairbairn, W. R. D. ([1940] 1952). Schizoid factors in the personality. In W. R. D. Fairbairn (Ed.), *Psychoanalytic Studies of the Personality* (pp. 3-27). New York: Routledge.

Fairbairn, W. R. D. ([1944] 1952). Endopsychic structure considered in terms of object-relationships. In W. R. D. Fairbairn (Ed.), *Psychoanalytic Studies of the Personality* (pp. 82-136). New York: Routledge.

Fairbairn, W. R. D. ([1946] 1952). Object-relationships and dynamic structure. In W. R. D. Fairbairn (Ed.), *Psychoanalytic Studies of the Personality* (pp. 137-151). New York: Routledge.

Kernberg, O. (1967). Borderline personality organization. *Journal of the American Psychoanalytic Association, 15,* 641-685.

Kernberg, O. (1975). *Borderline Conditions and Pathological Narcissism.* New York: Jason Aronson.

Klein, M. and Riviere, J. (1937). *Love, Hate, and Reparation.* London: Hogarth Press.

McCormack, C. C. (1989). The borderline/schizoid marriage: The holding environment as an essential treatment construct. *Journal of Marital and Family Therapy, 15*(3), 299-309.

McCormack, C. C. (2000). *Treating Borderline States in Marriage: Dealing with Oppositionalism, Ruthless Aggression, and Severe Resistance.* Northvale, NJ: Jason Aronson.

Ogden, T. H. (1986). *The Matrix of the Mind: Object Relations and the Psychoanalytic Dialogue.* Northvale, NJ: Jason Aronson.

Ogden, T. (1989). *The Primitive Edge of Experience.* Northvale, NJ: Jason Aronson.

Sandler, J. (1987). Internalization and externalization. In J. Sandler (Ed.), *Projection, Identification, Projective Identification* (pp. 1-11). Madison, CT: International Universities Press.

Segal, H. (1957). Notes on symbol formation. *International Journal of Psycho-Analysis, 38,* 391-397.

Shengold, L. (1989). *Soul Murder: The Effects of Childhood Abuse and Deprivation.* New York: Fawcett Columbine.

Stern, D. N. (1985). *The Interpersonal World of the Infant: A View from Psychoanalysis and Developmental Psychology.* New York: Basic Books.

Stolorow, R.D., Brandchaft, B., and Atwood, G. E. (1987). *Psychoanalytic Treatment: An Intersubjective Approach.* Hillsdale, NJ: The Analytic Press.

Winnicott, D. W. ([1954] 1975). The depressive position in normal development. In D. W. Winnicott (Ed.), *Through Paediatrics to Psycho-Analysis* (pp. 262-277). New York: Basic Books.

Winnicott, D. W. (1958). *Collected Papers.* London: Tavistock.

Winnicott, D. W. (1960/1965). Ego distortion in terms of true and false self. In D. W. Winnicott (Ed.), *The Maturational Process and the Facilitating Environment* (pp. 140-152). New York: International Universities Press.

Winnicott, D. W. (1971). *Playing and Reality.* New York: Basic Books.

PART II:
SPECIFIC DISORDERS

Chapter 4

Marital and Family Treatment of Borderline Personality Disorder

Judith K. Kreisman
Jerold J. Kreisman

INTRODUCTION

Borderline personality disorder (BPD) is a clinical psychiatric disorder defined by specific characterological and behavioral components. Approximately 2 percent of the general population fulfill criteria for this diagnosis. Ten percent of psychiatric outpatients and 20 percent of inpatients fulfill criteria for BPD (American Psychiatric Association, 2000).

According to the DSM-IV-TR (American Psychiatric Association, 2000, p. 654), borderline individuals experience

a pervasive pattern of instability of interpersonal relationships, self-image, and affects, and marked impulsivity, beginning by early adulthood and present in a variety of contexts, as indicated by five (or more) of the following:

(1) frantic efforts to avoid real or imagined abandonment
   Note: Do not include suicidal or self-mutilating behavior covered in Criterion 5.
(2) a pattern of unstable and intense interpersonal relationships characterized by alternating between extremes of idealization and devaluation
(3) identity disturbance: markedly and persistently unstable self-image or sense of self

(4) impulsivity in at least two areas that are potentially self-damaging (e.g., spending, sex, substance abuse, reckless driving, binge eating) **Note:** Do not include suicidal or self-mutilating behavior covered in Criterion 5.
(5) recurrent suicidal behavior, gestures, or threats, or self-mutilating behavior
(6) affective instability due to a marked reactivity of mood (e.g., intense episodic dysphoria, irritability, or anxiety usually lasting a few hours and only rarely more than a few days)
(7) chronic feelings of emptiness
(8) inappropriate, intense anger or difficulty controlling anger (e.g., frequent displays of temper, constant anger, recurrent physical fights)
(9) transient, stress-related paranoid ideation or severe dissociative symptoms (reprinted with permission from the *Diagnostic and Statistical Manual of Mental Disorder,* Fourth Edition, Text Revision, copyright 2000 American Psychiatric Association)

THE DEVELOPMENT OF THE BPD CONCEPT

The evolution of the current definition of BPD resulted from the work of many theorists, beginning with psychoanalytical writers nearly a century ago. Freud's descriptions of the unconscious offered explanations of the psychopathology that existed between the primitive, unconscious impulses and the conscious desire to keep those horrific thoughts at bay. Other psychoanalysts, such as Wilhelm Reich and Melanie Klein, published articles in the 1920s and 1930s, describing patients whose symptoms were less responsive to psychoanalysis (Kreisman and Straus, 1991).

Adolph Stern (1938) first used the term *borderline* to describe patients who were characterized somewhere between neurotic and psychotic. During the 1940s and 1950s, it was becoming evident that some patient populations were not conforming to the current definitions of psychopathology. Depending on the focus of therapy, the extent of hospitalizations, and the variations in moods and interactions with others, some patients were noted to behave differently from others with similar diagnoses. Robert Knight (1953) published a work that referred to these *borderline states*. He described patients with differing symptoms and different diagnoses who, nevertheless, seemed to exhibit common psychopathology. Grinker, Werble, and Drye (1968) defined four subtypes of the borderline patient, which described a spectrum of severity.

This group of difficult, changeable patients eventually came to be recognized with certain consistent features. In the 1970s two prominent psychiatrists, John Gunderson and Otto Kernberg, defined more concrete conceptualizations of this disorder. Gunderson viewed the borderline personality in more structured, descriptive terms. His model was eventually incorporated into the official definitions of BPD described in the most recent editions of the American Psychiatric Association's *Diagnostic and Statistical Manual* (DSM). Kernberg's taxonomy emphasizes intrapsychic processes, particularly primitive defense mechanisms, such as splitting. Kernberg (1975) terms this classification *borderline personality organization* (BPO). BPO encompasses a much larger patient population, including not only patients classified as BPD, but those with other Axis I and Axis II disorders.

The borderline individual wanders through a vast wasteland, unsure of an identity or role in relationships. The emptiness and loneliness he or she feels trigger defense mechanisms used to soothe distorted thoughts. Splitting is black or white thinking, which divides the world into extremes of good or evil, right or wrong. Through this lens, borderlines desperately try to maintain control of their universe by banishing ambivalence and ambiguity. Paradoxically, it only keeps them farther away from the closeness they crave. Splitting is the primary mechanism that underlies most borderline behavior.

The defense mechanisms of projection and projective identification lead to the devaluation of the other person, by disclaiming and projecting the very qualities borderlines cannot tolerate in themselves. This results in a tenuous bind that is used to manipulate relationships and to avoid personal responsibility.

Borderline rage is another significant coping characteristic, which reflects intrinsic contradictions. The wide and sometimes violent mood swings and distorted and contradictory expectations of others contribute to the turbulence within borderline relationships. The recipient of a borderline's affections may be riddled with angst and confusion.

BPD and the Family

To fully understand and treat the borderline individual, the therapist must be cognizant of the social context of the BPD patient: the family. "The task for clinicians who work with borderline patients is to evaluate the varying conditions of their family environments, past and present" (Shachnow et al., 1997, p. 179). This does not insinuate that the family of a BPD patient is responsible for this disorder, or, for that matter, any other mental illness. Rather, the family, as the initial primary social group, has great influence. The foundation embedded in the family system establishes profound patterns of interactions throughout life. The family represents the first laboratory in which relationships are created and tested. It becomes the training ground for present and future interpersonal connections. It is the family that provides the critical structure of our humanity, and it is the relationships between its members that breathe life into it. Understanding these family interactions within the context of our changing society broadens our conceptualization of the development of this disorder.

Significant changes in traditional family structure have been made over the past fifty years. Dual career families are prominent. More single-parent families, divorced families, remarried families, and same-sex couple families exist today. The loss of societal structures and familiar customs has altered our perspective of the role of the family. Mobility, with less availability of extended family, may create a chasm that lessens support from others during times of stress. Boris M. Segal (1996) suggested that these changes have "enabled an increased incidence of the borderline personality organization, first of all among the most vulnerable groups with familial and (or) organic predispositions" (p. 233).

Early models of family therapy evolved from a psychoanalytic conceptualization of hospitalized schizophrenic patients and encounters with their relatives. Many theorists today view the nuclear family system as a set of smaller subsystems, such as the marital subsystem, parent-child subsystem, and the sibling subsystem. In addition, grandparents and in-laws generate a multigenerational mix that also impacts the family. In the ideal family situation, a constant flow of exchanges exists between these multiple relationships, resulting in healthy disagreements and adjustments. The borderline individual is encumbered with much personal turmoil, instability, and intense feelings that disrupt and distort productive communications.

One of the most tumultuous and conflictual relationships in the family often involves the adolescent relationship. The adolescent's developmental quest for identity mimics the borderline individual's struggle. It is a constant mix of reaching for intimate connections and retreating from them. The crucial distinction is that the normal adolescent will eventually evolve into a more mature adult, whereas the borderline individual does not approach adulthood with a clearly defined sense of self.

The marriage of a borderline patient can be riddled with conflict and unease. A borderline woman is often attracted to a narcissistic male, since her neediness and search for identity "fit" the self-absorbed, controlling man (Paris and Braverman, 1995). This relationship is often fraught with emotional reactivity and difficulty in establishing a mature interpersonal bond. Ultimately, attractions may turn into repellants: the self-confidence and protectiveness that first attracted the borderline individual transforms into control and engulfment; the dependency and worshipful admiration that may have attracted the spouse mutates into demands and insatiable insecurities.

IMPACT ON THE FAMILY

The relevance and impact on the family members of a borderline patient cannot be overstated. In the family system, all members experience family events within a context peculiar to their roles. Each family member is impacted by the actions and behaviors of the others. Every family unit embodies a unique developmental history that evolves as family members grow and change. A new marriage, the birth of a child, adolescent turbulence, separating offspring, death of a spouse, or other external events, such as illness or job loss, can produce conflict and difficulty in adapting. The healthiest families are those that can withstand and adapt to these stresses. If discordant behaviors persist past an age-appropriate transition time, the diagnosis of BPD may be considered (Glick et al., 2000). When one or more members exhibit borderline pathology, the reverberations are experienced throughout the family unit.

Impact on the Child

In addition to possible biological contributions, most theories on the etiology of BPD focus on interaction/relationship experiences. One study that evaluated mother-child interactions concluded that maternal inconsistency in parenting practices and maternal over involvement contributed to the later development of BPD (Bezirganian, Cohen, and Brook, 1993). Successful transition into adolescence first requires the child to master separation-individuation tasks, wherein differentiation and an inchoate identity are formed. Appropriate relationships, first inside, then outside the family, can develop as object constancy is attained. The individual, family, and impacting others are perceived as consistent and stable with reciprocal attachments.

The development of BPD has often been associated with physical or sexual abuse or child neglect (Kemp, 1998). An individual with a documented history of childhood mistreatment is four times more likely to develop a personality disorder during adulthood (Johnson, Cohen, Brown, et al., 1999). Adolescents with BPD are twice as likely to experience suicidal ideations and develop major psychopathology in early adulthood (Johnson, Cohen, Skodol, et al., 1999). Defective communication patterns may follow the individual, infecting future relationships even after he has departed from the nuclear family (Allen and Farmer, 1996).

Impact on Siblings and Others

When stressors attack the borderline family system, any of the members may regress. For children, this may take the form of conduct disorders, depression, eating disorders, drug or alcohol abuse, sexual acting-out behaviors, and suicidal behavior. Families tend to organize themselves around the presenting problems of the borderline member, thereby bypassing other significant family dynamics. Consequently, the siblings of a borderline individual may be neglected, since the parents are distracted by the more tumultuous behaviors of the difficult child. Siblings may then develop their own, distinct acting-out styles or function as the family hero, fulfilling a role as peacemaker, adviser, or "good child." Similarly, extended family, friends, or neighbors may intercede in attempts to rescue the family from chaos.

Impact of Borderline Parents

One study of families of borderlines distinguished several patterns. Both parents frequently exhibited significant psychopathology. Neglectfulness toward the children and malignant dependency on the spouse by the borderline parent were often evident. Overinvolvement with the child was seen less often in this study. Denial of blatant acting-out behaviors and projection of blame were also common characteristics (Gunderson, Kerr, and Englund, 1980).

Healthy separation proceeds smoothly when parents are unambivalent about their own identities and present coherent expectations to their offspring (von Broembsen, 1986). Parents with borderline psychopathology (whose own parents may have exhibited borderline traits) may lack healthy role models from which they can derive favorable parenting skills. In such a family, it becomes difficult for children to trust and form close attachments with parents, who themselves are struggling with issues of identity, autonomy, and impulsivity. Single parents with borderline characteristics are even more handicapped, because they may lack many social supports. In addition, they are deprived of a parenting partner who can assist in childrearing and dilute the intensity of the child-parent relationship (Glick et al., 2000, p. 497).

SETTING

The marital and family therapy with borderline patients discussed in this chapter emphasizes an outpatient setting. In the current climate of managed care, hospital stays are now severely limited. Long-term treatment for the borderline patient is usually not covered by insurance and is financially exclusive. Time-limited outpatient care is viewed more favorably by insurance companies as cost effective. However, some insurance plans allow for individual therapy only, thereby eliminating the advantages to be gained from including marital and family therapies.

Those patients who exhibit threatening behaviors to themselves or others may qualify for brief hospitalization. Unfortunately, many psychiatric hospital programs are not tailored to specific disorders. The psychiatric hospital is used more for crisis intervention, than as an organized, directed-treatment facility. Nevertheless, crises do erupt frequently for the borderline patient and must be addressed. Hospitalization is often invoked to treat these critical emergencies. Hospitalization may do more than derail the current upheaval for the borderline patient and his or her family. It can allow initiation of marital or family therapy. Some families who may normally be reluctant to begin therapy, may seem more agreeable as they rally around the identified patient during a hospitalization.

Treatment is dependent on the severity of the symptoms and the psychological limitations of the borderline patient and his or her relationships. Because of the depth and complexity of BPD, therapy may need to occur over the course of several years, utilizing multiple modalities and therapists. It is helpful for the borderline patient's providers to function as a team, seeking supportive consultation with one another.

Trained individuals from the disciplines of medicine, psychology, social work, counseling, and recreational and occupational therapies can actively contribute to the treatment team. A psychiatrist, who can hospitalize the patient during a crisis and initiate pharmacotherapy, is a necessary part of the treatment team. A family therapist, who is available to assess the living situation and align support systems is also essential. Individual and group therapists evaluate and provide psychotherapy. Expressive therapies, such as music, art, movement, and psychodrama therapy, can be helpful for borderline patients, who often have difficulty in communicating (Kreisman and Straus, 1991). Even insurance company case workers can serve as an important part of the team, since they can collaborate with the other treaters to fashion and support a consistent approach to the patient's needs, especially when there are manipulative threats. Clear, consistent treatment goals among all of the providers, in collaboration with the patient, will minimize splitting.

TREATMENT MODEL

Since no consensus has been reached regarding a treatment approach to BPD, the specific needs of the patient will determine the direction of therapy. Although a borderline patient may first be seen in individual therapy, severe disturbances in personal relationships are usually prominent. Family members, friends, and co-workers experience the impulsive and erratic behaviors that define borderline relationships. For every individual complaint, a complementary family/marital disturbance often looms. Family or marital therapy can therefore be valuable.

Confronting the Crisis

Therapy is often precipitated by a crisis situation. A spouse or parent(s) may hospitalize a family member who is unmanageable or threatening to self-harm. It is often the first contact the therapist has with the borderline patient and the family. This event can be used to draw support and input from all of the borderline patient's social systems. Although past traumas may have contributed to the patient's volatile feelings, it is first necessary to curtail the current destructive impulses, usually in individual therapy (American Psychiatric Association, 2001). After the crisis has been addressed, continued contacts with the family can provide much-needed family history and insights.

Family therapy, especially in borderline families, should not be passive. Without active intervention, patterns of blame, anger, frustration, projection, guilt, rigidity, and lack of conflict resolution may persist (Jones, 1987). Repetitious behaviors that promulgate unhealthy interactions create disturbed transactional patterns (Minuchin, 1974). Actively identifying these transactions and redirecting their outcome can teach the family more effective ways of interacting.

Couples Therapy

Although several models have been proposed for the treatment of borderline couples, no strategy has consistently demonstrated superiority. One report described intensive, twice-weekly therapy with a couple, both diagnosed with BPD. After three months, the female cotherapists concluded that traditional marital therapy was unsuccessful, because assessment of each partner was impaired by the presence of the other. Eventually, individual therapy for both was recommended (Seeman and Edwardes-Evans, 1979).

Often, the borderline patient is too fragile and unable to listen and participate in marital therapy, whereas the nonborderline spouse's anger may constrain the effectiveness of conjoint therapy. Nevertheless, it is important to garner the support of the borderline patient's partner. A common scenario involves the spouse of a borderline patient seeking individual treatment for an unhappy marriage. The partner is often faced with self-doubt in the ability to function within the marriage. This can be further complicated when children are included, because the spouse may assume the role of their protector. Therapy that is supportive and psychoeducational will help the spouse gain a better understanding of BPD and devise coping strategies (Weddige, 1986).

Despite the lack of consensus for treating BPD couples, some areas of concern alert the therapist to the potential sabotage of treatment. Gunderson and Kolb (1978) identified certain characteristics of borderline individuals that derail the progress of therapy. These include devaluation, manipulation, dependency, and masochism. Transference and countertransference issues must also be managed.

BPD in Children

The utilization of family therapy with borderline patients is particularly applicable to financially dependent adolescents or young adults living at home. With a recalcitrant youth, an alliance must be made with the parents to ensure continued treatment. In such a situation, focusing on the family system as a whole, rather than on the individual child, allows the adolescent to participate and feel less threatened (Rockland, 1992). Ideally, however, a solid therapeutic alliance with the borderline adolescent is helpful before initiating family therapy, to offset splitting and triangulation. Some therapists believe that these obstacles are minimized by mandating separate therapists for the individual and the family, with occasional conjoint meetings with all. However, practical time and cost factors may limit this approach. In contrast, Meissner (1988) finds that the issues of transference coming from both settings can be handled more effectively and efficiently with one therapist, if that professional feels competent to handle both assignments. Since borderlines are experts at creating angst and self-doubt in the therapist, consultation with other colleagues throughout treatment provides much-needed support for the treating therapist.

Although the adolescent's primary task is to manage separation-individuation, other family members may resist change. Issues of dependency and autonomy compete with the family's need to maintain homeostasis. The inevitable transference issues arising from these conflicts can threaten the continuation of therapy. Sometimes parents are overly involved with their children and other times they may appear neglectful. With overinvolvement, the child may feel compelled to assert himself or herself in destructive ways in an attempt to separate from the family. This may create much conflict and power struggles. Children who are neglected often find that they are unable to connect in intimate relationships with others. Neglectful parents need to be respectfully engaged in treatment. Estrangement will occur if parents feel blamed.

Meissner (1988) emphasizes the importance of transgenerational factors in family relationships. Parents often interact in ways that mimic their upbringing. Problematic, developmental issues in relationships are often repeated in future generations. Familial patterns of alcoholism, child abuse, and other psychiatric disturbances may recur. Children may be scapegoated. The therapist must carefully navigate the family relationships, as he or she helps them understand and then interrupt these repeating patterns.

Psychoeducational Approaches

Gunderson (2001) has advocated a psychoeducational strategy in working with borderline families. This approach is based on informing the borderline patient and his or her family about the specifics of the diagnosis and its impact. It is a technique based on support and understanding, rather than culpability. Assigned reading about BPD can be illuminating. Family therapy can begin in earnest when there is acceptance of the diagnosis, acknowledgement that treatment will take time, and a willingness to learn new ways of interacting (see Gunderson, 2001, Chapter 9). The goals of the family center on improved communication and ways to defuse conflictual situations. Initially, the therapist is active and instructional, guiding the family in new interactional patterns. If, over time, the family is able to monitor impulses and communicate more meaningfully, a more psychodynamic, insight-oriented family therapy may be instituted.

Cognitive-Behavioral Approaches

Another useful approach in treating borderline families emphasizes cognitive-behavioral concepts. The active, task-oriented dimension of this therapy fits well with the matter-of-fact, instructional elements that the therapist models. Clear direction and coaching can help parents diminish emotional overreaction and allow them to reinforce more acceptable behaviors. Utilizing positive and negative reinforcers helps shape dysfunctional behavior. Dialectical behavior therapy (DBT), developed by Marsha Linehan (1993), is a prescribed treatment package that incorporates weekly individual therapy, a weekly social skills group, telephone consultations with a therapist, and regular meetings among the involved therapists. This approach is highly structured, with accompanying manuals that provide clear directives in managing a toxic borderline environment. The underlying concept of DBT embraces the borderline patient's struggle with the opposing forces (the dialectic) of need for self-acceptance and desire for change. One of the main tenets of DBT is to address the borderline dysfunction in behavioral, nonemotional terms. Cognitive therapies focus on the borderline's thought processes and distortions. How those thought patterns are formulated into fears of abandonment, loss, dependence, lack of identity, and poor self-discipline is what defines the borderline patient's maladaptive behaviors. Therapy is designed to refashion these patterns into healthier behaviors.

The SET Model

With all treatment interventions, communication with the borderline patient is critical. In the borderline world, turmoil is standard procedure. *How* a communication is conveyed has an impact on borderline individuals, who often discount and challenge their exchanges with others because of their fears of abandonment and of being misunderstood. A communication strategy developed by Jerold Kreisman (Kreisman and Straus, 1991) attempts to develop better interactive patterns with the borderline patient, while helping the therapist (and family members) maintain objectivity. It is referred to as SET, an acronym for support, empathy, and truth. During extreme emotional interactions with a borderline patient, it is helpful to use statements that convey all three sentiments during each engagement. The support statement conveys a personal "I" statement of concern for the borderline patient's dilemma, such as, "I want to try to help you." The empathy communication, a "you" statement, acknowledges the stresses the borderline is experiencing: "This must be very difficult for you, right now." Support and empathy convey *feelings*—the therapist's concern for the patient and the acknowledgment of his or her pain. The truth statement is about *reality*. It refers to the borderline patient's own ultimate responsibility in managing the situation. The problem is recognized, appreciated, then addressed in a way that emphasizes practical problem solving. All three statements are presented in a neutral, nonjudgmental way.

All three facets of SET communication should be applied in interactions with the borderline patient. However, they are not often absorbed quickly. The truth part of this communication pattern is the most uncomfortable for the patient because it directly challenges his or her capacity to be responsible for the difficulty. The SET principles are best expressed in a caring, yet matter-of-fact way. It is the nature of BPD to challenge these elements, insisting that the therapist does not care or understand. As in Linehan's DBT, the goal of the therapist is to remain calm and consistent, and to discourage the patient's overreacting to problems. In all of these therapeutic approaches, the ultimate responsibility for change rests with the patient.

The Course of Treatment

The length of therapy with a borderline patient requires time and stamina. However, it is not unusual for treatment to have many beginnings and endings. Sometimes treatment termination occurs because certain initial treatment goals are met. Often, however, the patient exits therapy prematurely, when they feel misunderstood or rejected. Borderlines frequently move from therapist to therapist, repeating the separation-individuation issues that parallel their lives. Conflict can arise from the borderline's anger at confrontation or the dependency of the therapeutic relationship. Crises are frequently handled through multiple hospitalizations. A veritable "push-you-away" and "pull-you-back-in" dynamic may emerge. The drain on financial resources may also require curtailing therapy. Managed care companies limit lengths of hospitalizations and the number of therapy contacts, which can undermine treatment. The intensity of therapy sometimes requires a respite to allow the patient time to practice changes and to appreciate the progress made thus far. Family therapy may only extend for as long as the adolescent or young adult remains at home. Marital therapy will continue only as long as both spouses maintain their commitments to withstand and work to improve their tumultuous relationship.

The borderline individual's lack of a solid core identity interferes with the development of healthy intimacy. Relationships may vacillate between extreme polarities. Anxiety about the lack of closeness with others, and simultaneous fear of engulfment and loss of identity may exist. Yet with proper intervention, family members can develop a repertoire of new interactions that can then be extended to others.

In the consideration of various treatment models for BPD, the intricate relationship between the borderline patient and the therapist is most vital. The therapist must recognize the significance of a strong therapeutic relationship and the impact it has upon the treatment. The patient may create obstacles that challenge the therapy. This mimics the dilemmas they face in other relationships. Remaining resolute yet caring in the face of borderline rage sends a powerful message. The therapist may become discouraged and question the value of therapy. However, often just logging the hours and maintaining the connection is the most therapeutic part of the treatment. Indeed, this relationship may be the most consistent ever experienced by the patient.

CASE EXAMPLES

Marital

Doris is thirty-nine years old and has been married for nineteen years. She has three children, a son who is fourteen years old and two daughters, ten and eight. When she initiated therapy, Doris had been employed for six years as an administrative assistant for a large company. She entered outpatient therapy after a hospitalization for a drug overdose with a tranquilizer and alcohol. She attributed this serious depression to stress at work and at home. Her husband, Alex, traveled often with his job and could be away from home three to five days each week. Doris felt overwhelmed managing her home, family, and work.

Doris was a perfectionist who placed many demands on herself. Alex also placed a high premium on neatness in the house, which was especially difficult to maintain because of their three young, active children. Doris would drink after the children were put to bed, while she feverishly housecleaned to keep her home in immaculate order. When her husband was home, he constantly berated her and the children for their noise and messiness. Doris was unable to tolerate Alex's berating, and tried constantly to gain his approval. It was easier to assume the responsibilities for home and family silently, than to approach her husband with her frustrations.

In the early years of their marriage, Doris and her husband enjoyed partying and heavy drinking. They rarely discussed problems and preferred to lubricate their frictions with alcohol. As Doris started to have children, she felt empty. Her marriage was not fulfilling, she had assumed more responsibility as a parent, and she and her husband spent little time together as a couple. She saw Alex as controlling and demanding. He expected Doris to micromanage the family while he devoted his attention to work.

Doris was the oldest of three daughters. Her mother worked in the home and was rather passive. Her father was an angry, controlling man. As the eldest child, she assumed many of the caretaking roles. She learned that by "being good," there would be some degree of harmony in the family. As a teenager, Doris was molested by a church pastor, the cousin of a good friend. Due to her deep religious convictions, Doris was fearful of telling anyone about the abuse, and was convinced that if it were discovered, she would be blamed. Throughout her life, she experienced flashbacks. As an adult, Doris distrusted her own judgment and memory. She felt she should subjugate her own desires to maintain the status quo in her household.

The night Doris overdosed, Alex was home and took her to the emergency room. At that time he was confronted with Doris's drinking problem and was duly concerned for her and the children's safety. In the hospital she began to confront many issues she had been trying to hide for years: her past sexual molestation, alcohol abuse, and depression.

In the hospital crisis situation, she participated in a "dual diagnosis" unit with other patients experiencing psychiatric and substance abuse problems. Group and individual therapies emphasized behavioral controls and skills development. Assertiveness training classes were valuable. Her psychiatrist initiated antidepressant medication, which immediately relieved her sleep and appetite disturbances, and began to improve her mood. The hospital social worker contacted her husband to obtain more background information and to arrange a conjoint meeting. At that meeting, underlying issues of alcohol misuse, reciprocal demands on roles in the home, and relationship expectations were explicated. Educational information was supplied to both, discussing the diagnoses of depression, substance abuse, and BPD. Recommendations were made for Doris to pursue individual psychotherapy and involvement with Alcoholics Anonymous (AA). Alex was also encouraged to attend AA, and both were urged to participate in Al-Anon. Conjoint therapy was also promoted, with consideration of having the children engaged at a later date.

Although Alex participated in treatment while Doris was hospitalized, he refused involvement in her outpatient therapy, blaming his travel schedule. Doris did not push this issue because she did not want to antagonize him. He was supportive of her attending therapy and AA meetings, but refused involvement in AA or Al-Anon.

In her individual therapy, Doris and her therapist initially focused on behavioral issues, especially concerning her self-destructive activities when depressed. She also utilized recommended references to better understand her impulsiveness and mood changes, and how they interacted with her past alcohol use. She expressed relief that her feelings and behaviors constituted understandable and treatable diagnoses, such as BPD, and that change was possible.

After stabilizing her mood, maintaining her sobriety, and minimizing dangerous behaviors, the therapy evolved into psychodynamic realms, exploring past relationships and traumas, and connecting them to current situations. Doris recognized her husband's alcoholism and the personality changes that occurred when he was intoxicated. She became less self-blaming and more aware of Alex's contributions to their struggles. The more she gained in psychological health, the more Alex would drink and become more demanding. The children were reacting to the tension at home and were misbehaving at school. Although Doris developed better understanding of family problems, she was reticent to confront them, fearing her husband would leave.

Doris regularly attended AA meetings. She found the all-women's meetings to be the most helpful, because she felt more open and trusting with women. In one of her mixed AA groups, Doris formed a relationship with one of the other male members. She perceived him as attentive and sympathetic to her struggles. The relationship had been continuing for six months before she brought it up in therapy. She feared her therapist would criticize and reject her, but the guilt and deception were causing anxiety.

During therapy Doris realized that this new connection was turning exploitive, as this man began to make more demands on her. She was able to terminate the relationship, and, shortly after, told her husband about it. She then affirmed her need to have Alex join in her marital therapy. Intrigued and, perhaps, threatened by her newfound assertiveness, he finally assented. In the marital therapy, Doris became more direct in explaining her needs, since she recognized that she and her husband had recapitulated the relationship of her parents. She also confronted their use of alcohol to avoid addressing intimacy issues. They agreed that the responsibility for dealing with the children should be shared, and her husband agreed to be more engaged in childrearing.

Family

Kate M is a sixteen-year-old tenth grader who was brought into therapy because of volatile outbursts at home with her parents. Kate is an only child. Her mother had two miscarriages before she carried Kate to term. A much-wanted child, Kate was adored by her parents. They shared family outings and up until the past two years enjoyed a relaxed, open communication. Two years ago, Mr. M was let go from his managerial position at a pharmaceutical company when the company downsized. It took him nearly a year to secure full-time employment. Mr. M enjoyed his new job managing contracts at a construction company, but it involved long hours and sometimes weeks away from home. The past year had been difficult for Mrs. M, since she had returned to work after her husband lost his job and was unable to be home as much. Although Kate worried about the family's financial insecurity, she enjoyed the respite from all the parental attention. She developed more peer friendships and preferred to spend time with her friends. She began to resent being supervised by her parents and yearned for more personal freedom. Kate's need to assert herself was in direct opposition to her parents' need to cling to her and maintain the old ways.

Kate started lying to her parents about where she was after school and began shoplifting with some of her friends. Her grades dropped, and she began skipping classes. At one point, she was caught with marijuana at school and expelled. Mr. and Mrs. M were perplexed at the precipitous transformation of their sweet little girl and began quarreling about how they should manage her provocative behavior. Mr. M was a more lenient parent, whereas Mrs. M felt she needed to guide Kate more strictly. Kate used this discrepancy to maneuver each parent to her advantage. This family turmoil was further complicated by the emergence of Mrs. M's diabetes. She made major life changes regarding diet and exercise and lost forty pounds. Kate had always been overweight. In the past, she and her mother had enjoyed lunching together and savoring rich desserts. On her new diet, Mrs. M could no longer indulge this activity, which disappointed Kate. As Mrs. M lost weight, Kate put on more. Power struggles over food emerged, as Kate defied her mother's exhortations for a healthier lifestyle.

Mrs. M was the youngest child with two older brothers. Her mother was distant. Her father was involved with her brothers' sports activities, but showed little interest in her accomplishments. Growing up, she had always yearned to be a mother for a little girl. Becoming pregnant had been risky for her, and when she eventually carried her third pregnancy to term she was ecstatic. She craved affection and wanted her baby to love her.

Mr. M was the oldest son of five boys. He idealized his parents and felt the family was close. However, since he had never grown up among girls, he felt uncomfortable dealing with his wife and daughter.

The more Mr. and Mrs. M argued about how to deal with their daughter, the more Mrs. M turned to Kate for comfort. This triangulation caused Kate to pull back from her mother and move closer to her circle of friends. The close relationship that Kate and her mother once enjoyed was disintegrating rapidly. Mrs. M was becoming depressed and self-incriminating about her abilities as an effective parent. The separation-individuation process for Kate was being sabotaged by her parents, particularly her mother. At this point, Mrs. M sought counseling for the family.

The few instances in which Mr. M agreed to come to therapy revealed his unwillingness to take an authoritative stand with his daughter. Mr. M felt ineffectual in parenting a daughter and withdrew. In essence, he maintained a childlike position in the family by removing himself from the hierarchal position as a parent. Kate's manipulation of the parental inconsistencies kept the family in constant turmoil. During one particularly difficult altercation with her mother, Kate threatened to hit her. The next day, Kate cut her wrists and was hospitalized.

The hospitalization brought a measure of relief for Mrs. M, but Mr. M could not understand why his daughter was in the hospital "with those people." Mr. M blamed his wife, because he did not have the problems getting along with Kate that she experienced. In the hospital, Kate was initially angry and resistant. She refused to see her mother and blamed her for forcing her into the "nut house," colluding with her father's denial. Kate refused to talk with staff and begged her father to release her from the hospital, threatening to run away if she remained.

In confronting Kate, the staff utilized SET techniques, providing acceptance and acknowledging her frustration, but gently reminding her that her self-destructive gesture, not her parents, precipitated her hospitalization. Although initially hostile to the other adolescents in the unit, Kate became more open and accepted their encouragement to participate in programming. Consistent behavioral approaches by staff reinforced that Kate would not gain privileges or be allowed to leave the hospital until she was more cooperative with the evaluation. A physical exam revealed scars from previous self-mutilation. Kate acknowledged that she had low self-esteem and depression, and agreed to a trial of antidepressant medication.

A social worker met with Mr. and Mrs. M. He reassured them that hospitalization was appropriate to intervene in Kate's deteriorating behavior, and that it was providing much-needed structure for Kate and the family. He offered support and psychoeducational materials to reinforce their decision. He explained how Kate's splitting resulted in her allying with one parent against the other, thus deconstructing their own relationship and undermining parental authority. Mr. M acknowledged his withdrawal from the joint parenting responsibility and pledged to participate more in family therapy.

The social worker arranged several family meetings before Kate's discharge. A behavioral contract was initiated, outlining expectations for the family members. The contract included commitment to treatment, Kate's responsibilities around the house, and her parents' consensual agreement for privileges.

With the contract as a starting point, outpatient family therapy centered on restructuring the intrafamily relationships. Mrs. M was encouraged to diminish the pressures on Kate, especially regarding issues of food. Mr. M was empowered to interact more with his daughter. The parents were commissioned to find compromise in their joint handling of Kate's discipline and to maintain closer collaboration. Kate was able to articulate her fears that she did not live up to her parents' expectations. She acknowledged her reliance on food to avoid her anxieties about growing up and becoming more responsible. Ultimately, as the family members felt closer, they were able to separate more easily and pursue healthy individuation without feeling that they were abandoning the family unit.

STRENGTHS AND LIMITATIONS

The advantage of including marital or family therapy in the treatment plan for the borderline patient is the added dimension of acquiring other family members' perspectives. Family relationships, such as sibling affiliations and the marital dyad, may be impacted by the borderline furor. The assessment of the problem can be made clearer when the other family systems can be evaluated. Although family counseling can be an important component of the treatment plan, because of the severe character pathology in these patients, other modalities, especially individual psychotherapy and pharmacotherapy, are usually also necessary.

The severity of the family dysfunction and the degree of borderline pathology should determine when these adjunct therapies should be initiated. Identifying the range of symptoms in order of their severity can help determine when a particular therapy should be applied. Assessments of potential suicide risk, the possibility of physical or sexual abuse, and the contribution of substance abuse must be made. If any of these factors exist, getting the borderline patient to a place of safety is critical. Hospitalization can have a mobilizing effect on family members. Families who have experienced multiple hospitalizations of the borderline member may be more reluctant to get involved with therapy, feeling that it has not been useful (Gunderson, 2001). It can be more difficult, however, to engage family members in an outpatient setting when an immediate crisis is lacking. The degree of frustration and the commitment to change will determine whether the family stays the course of treatment.

The therapist has a monumental task in establishing a therapeutic alliance with the borderline patient and his or her family members. The therapist will be tested in much the same way as the borderline patient's family. Depression, mood swings, alcoholism, schizophrenia, antisocial behavior, drug abuse, mental retardation, and attempted/ committed suicide are often reported in first-degree relatives of borderline individuals (Soloff and Millward, 1983). This propensity for psychiatric disorders within the family can make it more difficult for them to accept and participate in meaningful therapy.

The question often arises whether the same therapist should work with both the borderline patient and the family. Such an arrangement can be precarious and exhausting. Maintaining alliances with all family members is the crucial issue. The primary disadvantage of multiple therapists is the potential for splitting among them. For example, the psychopharmacologist and the primary psychotherapist may receive competing and contradictory messages from the patient, who may devalue or idealize one approach over the other. One treatment provider should maintain the role of primary clinician (Gunderson, 2001).

Another limitation of initiating family or marital therapy is insurance reimbursement. Many managed care companies do not cover these therapies. Even if only individual therapy is approved, the number of visits may be limited. The therapist who works with managed care programs must learn how to traverse the system in ways that will allow maximum benefit for the patient.

Working with borderline patients and their families can be exhausting and demanding. Part of the borderline pathology involves challenging therapeutic interventions and testing therapeutic alliances, which inexperienced therapists can find unsettling. The therapist who is willing to work with these patients will benefit from support from his or her colleagues.

BENEFITS FOR THE FAMILY

The significance of the family in any psychiatric disorder cannot be overemphasized. This is especially vital for the borderline patient, whose interpersonal relationships are intensely difficult. Conflictual parent-child interactions can foster some borderline behavior. Including the family in the therapy helps guide them through difficult interactions. The family's history and patterns of interacting enable the therapist to see the family operation in its entire context and to offer appropriate interventions.

The benefits of the psychoeducational approach in treating BPD are found in the collaborative efforts of the therapist, patient, and family in teaching and learning about the illness. The borderline individual and family that display intellectual curiosity, motivation to collaborate for change, and insight into their contribution to unhealthy communication will benefit from this model. By focusing on BPD as a psychiatric illness, rather than simply bad behavior, the patient and family members can work collaboratively to define the problems and solutions needed to improve interpersonal relationships and lessen the burden of guilt.

Cognitive/behavioral therapy focuses on adjusting family members' distorted beliefs about themselves and their world. Homework assignments foster collaboration and a "we're all in this together" sentiment. DBT offers an organized, concrete method to interrupt the borderline's maladaptive behaviors. It is a very directive and matter-of-fact method of intervention. DBT is complementary to utilization of SET principles.

The SET method directly addresses communications with the borderline patient. It prepares family members for predictable dilemmas and helps them maintain in their mind a simple approach for interaction. SET is the application of clear, matter-of-fact statements that show concern for the borderline individual's predicament without becoming entangled in their reactive behavior.

Treating the families of borderline individuals is the most direct approach to understanding the root of borderline disturbance. Reaching out to the families and marital partners of borderline individuals provides support and hope for those dealing with this frustrating illness.

INDICATIONS AND CONTRAINDICATIONS

The first assessment to be done in considering the role of family therapy in an overall treatment plan is to understand the relationship between the identified patient and his or her family. How influential is the family in the patient's life? How pathological are the other family members? How willing are the patient and other family members to work together? Should separation or integration be a major consideration? Answers to these questions help determine which family members to include in the treatment and the timing of their introduction.

For example, an older borderline teenager may be expressing rage at a family perceived (correctly) to be pathologically suffocating. In preparation for college, aiding separation from the family may be a primary goal. In such a case, family therapy might be limited. More emphasis would be placed on individual therapy geared toward helping the adolescent deal with guilt over abandoning the family. Family therapy would focus on educating family members about the adolescent's need to separate. Much younger siblings would probably not be involved, but those closer in age, who are more significantly affected by their sibling's impending departure from the family, probably would be included at some point.

Alternatively, a couple containing a BPD partner that is enmeshed in a strained but committed relationship will benefit from conjoint therapy, in which education and behavioral techniques can be combined with developing insight to treat the relationship. Paris and Braverman (1995) demonstrate that such couples achieve a better outcome when they are able to emphasize problem-solving objectives in therapy.

In general, family therapy is indicated as an adjunctive tool. It is usually introduced after a crisis has resolved. When pathological behavior affects particular family members, their presence in the treatment can be helpful. When emotional or financial dependence is significant, family therapy may be indicated. Motivation and cooperation among all participating members is necessary.

Family therapy is contraindicated when a crisis remains unresolved or when family relationships remain volatile. If continued physical or sexual abuse of a child or an ongoing threat of violence exists, family therapy could stimulate unmanageable affects. If both spouses in marital therapy are severely impaired, treatment may fail. Similarly, if several family members are disruptive and uncooperative, they may sabotage therapy. In such cases, individual treatment may be preferable.

MANAGEMENT OF TRANSFERENCE ISSUES

Transference is one of the crucial issues in working with borderline patients. It occurs with much intensity and fury, escalating within the therapeutic relationship when frustrations rage out of control. The borderline patient will test the parameters of therapy, challenging the staying power and commitment of the therapist. The patient's transference will reflect regressive projections of previous flawed relationships onto the therapeutic relationship. This sets the stage for distortions to emerge within the therapeutic alliance. The borderline patient may look to the therapist to fulfill the needs that may have previously gone unmet, demanding to be considered more "special" than any other client. Increasingly frequent phone calls, rebellion against the time constraints of the session, and demands for a more intimate relationship with the therapist are some of the features of borderline dependency. When the therapist, as in all previous relationships, ultimately disappoints, a hostile transference frequently emerges. The seductive need to please is replaced with accusations that the therapist is uncaring and insensitive. Sometimes, litigation is threatened. Often, this anger is turned against the self, and suicidal threats and regression to previous self-destructive behaviors, such as drug abuse, bulimia, self-mutilation, and other increased risk taking actions, may emerge (Meissner, 1988).

Countertransference must also be closely monitored. Some therapists may be charmed by the patient's idolizing and deferential behavior. They may succumb to flattery and accept the implications that both the therapist and the patient are special. In the most egregious extension of this collaboration, a sexual or other exploitive relationship may ensue, thus destroying therapeutic boundaries. More common, the therapist eventually suffers the borderline patient's disappointment at failing to satisfy needs. Frustration and rage at the patient may replace the previous empathy. Indeed, the very diagnosis of BPD is sometimes considered a diagnosis of countertransference, a label accorded to a patient who frustrates the therapist (Reiser and Levenson, 1984). Because of the intensity of transference/countertransference feelings and the inherent danger in enmeshment, supervision and consultation are important components in treating borderline patients. Indeed, most organized approaches to the treatment of BPD, such as DBT, emphasize a team approach, with mandated peer consultation an essential part of the therapy strategy.

Managing transference and countertransference issues in a borderline patient is like jockeying a powerful racehorse—controlling a dynamic force, sometimes lightly, sometimes forcefully, but all the while trying to stay within the boundaried lanes of the track. Maintaining consistent and reliable boundaries is essential to managing these issues. Variations from routine may reinforce transference expectations. Responding with similar equanimity to praise and accusation preserves the consistent relationship. When transference is positive, the therapist's main job is to guard his or her own countertransference. However, clarification of persistent negative transference may be necessary to sustain the therapy.

A major advantage of family therapy with the borderline patient is that the primal transference figures may actually be present in the treatment. Unrealistic projections are minimized because the original cast is present. Transference is diffused among all the participants in the therapy. With the presence of more "witnesses," acting-out behavior is less viable, since distortions can be confirmed by other participants. Parallels between feelings toward the counselor and a family member are more readily apparent. Furthermore, since all members are willing to work on problems, less blaming and defensiveness exists.

MANAGEMENT OF CRISES
AND ACTING-OUT BEHAVIOR

Marital Example

Mrs. C, a woman with a history of BPD, has been married twelve years and has three children. Mr. and Mrs. C argue constantly, particularly when Mrs. C accuses her husband of having multiple affairs. Mrs. C feels very ineffective as a parent and her mood swings interfere with her communications with her husband and her parenting abilities. After a particularly nasty argument, Mrs. C left the house with her three children and moved in with her divorced mother. In a rage, she obtained a restraining order against her husband. Mr. C was a passive man who loved his wife, but felt helpless in dealing with her outbursts. The more she raged, the more he retreated. Usually, after a few days of living with her mother, Mrs. C would return home and the couple would make attempts to reconcile. These opportunities were short-lived, however, and every time Mr. C suggested she seek treatment, she would become incensed and threaten to leave again. Mrs. C had a strained relationship with her mother, yet would seek her mother's help whenever she had troubles with her marriage.

Mrs. C had been molested by her alcoholic father, which precipitated her parents' divorce. Her mother, too, was distrustful of men, and would reinforce her daughter's suspicions about her husband. As an only child, Mrs. C was reluctant to leave home. After her parents' divorce, she and her mother developed an impenetrable bond. Only when Mrs. C became pregnant did she agree to marry her husband. Her mother was furious that her daughter was leaving her. Mrs. C alternated between neediness and hostility toward her husband. Mr. C did not seem to understand his wife's needs and was unable to verbalize his own. The restraining order placed on Mr. C encapsulated the turbulence of their marriage.

Desperate to reunite his family, Mr. C contacted his wife's previous therapist, whom she had not seen in several years, and asked for guidance. To avoid alienating Mrs. C, the therapist recommended that Mr. C engage in individual therapy with a colleague. In therapy, Mr. C explored his own need for control, and began to back away from pressuring both his wife and himself to immediately resolve their separation. As he appeared less demanding, Mrs. C became less defensive and decided to return to her previous therapist. In the past, Mr. C had pressured her to return to therapy, but now recognized that she was much more open when he was less insistent.

In her individual therapy, Mrs. C examined the intergenerational factors affecting her marriage. She conceded that she was acting out some of her mother's disappointments with men. She recognized that by aligning with her mother she was avoiding confronting her insecurities with her husband directly. After several weeks, she and her husband agreed to engage in marital therapy. Although they might have chosen another counselor, they both felt comfortable continuing with Mrs. C's therapist.

Although Mrs. C initially attempted to ally with the therapist by referring to discussions in their individual therapy, the practitioner was careful to remain balanced in addressing the couple. The practitioner attempted to maintain Mrs. C's positive transference without alienating her husband. Nevertheless, because the therapist was aware of Mrs. C's greater defensiveness, treatment initially focused on her husband's issues. Mr. C modeled for his wife thoughtful, nondefensive consideration of painful issues, so that she was later more open to confrontation. In the beginning, the therapist employed a psychoeducational approach, helping the couple enumerate their obstacles and set goals for the therapy. The role of the children in their lives was emphasized. The couple felt united in accepting the necessity of considering the children's welfare as primary. Reading materials about relationships, families, and BPD were recommended and discussed. SET principles were offered to help Mr. and Mrs. C communicate more openly and with more patience.

Family Example

"I hate you! You can't tell me what to do! I want to live somewhere else!" These are the volatile outbursts of an out-of-control borderline adolescent. Sara is a fourteen-year-old teenager, who has struggled for the past year with bulimia, drugs, and self-mutilating behavior. Sara is the youngest of five children, with her older siblings married and out of the house. Sara's parents are struggling with her spiraling depression and impulsive behavior. They never experienced these difficulties with their older children, and are exhausted from trying to keep order in their house.

Sara's mother had returned to work when Sara was six years old. Because her other siblings were so much older, Sara often felt alone and alienated from the family. Her father traveled frequently, and Sara's mother was exhausted from working and raising the children. Sara was aware that she resulted from an unexpected pregnancy and essentially felt unwanted. By the time Sara entered adolescence, she was struggling with her independence and identity but desperately sought acceptance from her family. These two opposing forces provided constant internal conflict. By acting out and trying provocative roles, she could finally get her parents' attention. They felt intimidated by her anger and tended to accede to her threatening demands or ignore her outbursts, which only made Sara angrier.

Sara reluctantly agreed to see a therapist. The initial goal was to establish a trusting relationship, help Sara ventilate her frustrations, anchor her feelings, and channel her impulsivity in a more acceptable way. After establishing their relationship in individual therapy, Sara and her therapist agreed to include her parents in the treatment. In family therapy, Sara's frustrations with her parents were legitimized, and her parents' roles were clarified. All agreed that Sara retained too much power in the family system. Her parents were given permission to regain control of the family.

Psychoeducational materials that were provided reminded the family of the realities of raising a teenager again. Behavioral contracting with Sara and her parents was utilized to define family rules and expectations. Phone and computer privileges, allowance, and, later, curfews and car privileges were useful elements of a contract, which also outlined *specific* expectations. Supporting the parents as they solidified boundaries was essential. They were prepared to expect challenge to their authority. Support from others, such as teachers, counselors, and friends was utilized. If behavior became dangerously uncontrollable, the parents were advised that hospitalization could be employed. They were also informed about child protective services and temporary placement options, in case these became necessary.

Discussion of these issues angered Sara. Utilizing SET techniques, the therapist explained that although Sara was understandably stressed, the counselor, family, and others were available to help her. However, threats of harm or dangerous behavior toward oneself or others could not be ignored, for that would surely convey a message of not caring. Instead, all would understand that potential harm could not be allowed, and predictable, protective procedures would naturally result in such situations. By walking the family through several potential scenarios, the therapist prepared the family to respond to crises in preordained ways. In addition, however, the therapist prepared the family for more positive outcomes as well, and recommended reinforcement for these situations. The clear, nonthreatening communication to Sara that she is loved, but that destructive behaviors are not tolerable, was the consistent, underlying message of therapy.

INTEGRATION WITH PSYCHIATRIC SERVICES AND ROLE OF MEDICATION

Often, psychiatric intervention into the life of a borderline individual begins with a crisis. Such a crisis frequently involves the potential for harm, following a suicidal gesture or an outburst of violence. Hospitalization then becomes the first therapeutic contact with the patient and his or her family. In today's medical climate, hospitalizations are usually acute, temporary maneuvers, serving to diminish the risk of danger and to initiate stabilizing treatment.

Family therapy is ideally begun while the patient is in the hospital. In this acute setting, the family may be the most cooperative and available. Denial and minimalization are at their nadir. Important history-gathering can be achieved. Finally, a rudimentary therapeutic alliance can be inaugurated, which can endure after the acute event has resolved. Throughout treatment, the family therapist should be an important part of the therapy team, exchanging information and coordinating services with other treaters (including the physician, individual psychotherapist, etc.) and support groups (Alcoholics Anonymous, etc.).

Medication is frequently an important adjunct in the treatment plan. According to the practice guidelines published by the American Psychiatric Association (2001), "The primary treatment for borderline personality disorder is psychotherapy, complemented by symptom-targeted pharmacotherapy" (p. 4).

These guidelines, which are summarized below, divide BPD symptoms into three behavioral dimensions, which suggest specific pharmacological approaches. These categories are affective dysregulation, impulsive-behavioral dyscontrol, and cognitive-perceptual distortions.

Most research has endorsed the use of selective serotonin reuptake inhibitors (SSRIs), a class of antidepressants, in treating symptoms of the first two categories. SSRIs (such as Prozac [fluoxetine], Zoloft [sertraline], Paxil [paroxetine], and Celexa [citalopram]) are particularly efficacious in addressing depressed mood, anger, and aggressive, destructive impulsivity, including self-mutilation. Other antidepressants, such as tricyclic antidepressants (TCA) and monoamine oxidase inhibitors (MAOI), can improve mood, however these medicines have more side effects and are more dangerous if overdosed.

Lithium carbonate and anticonvulsant mood stabilizers (including Tegretol [carbamazepine], Depakote [valproic acid], and others) can ameliorate symptoms of mood changes and behavioral dyscontrol. Usually, these medications are used in combination with SRIs or other medicines.

The most studied class of medicines for the treatment of BPD are the neuroleptics (antipsychotics). These medicines reduce paranoid and other psychotic distortions. They also decrease anxiety, anger, and impulsivity. These medications may also help control mood swings and improve depressive symptoms. Most research has involved the older neuroleptics (Thorazine [chlorpromazine], Stelazine [trifluoperazine], Mellaril [thioridazine], Haldol [haloperidol], Navane [thiothixene], etc.) Newer (so-called "atypical") neuoleptics (including Clozaril [clozapine], Risperdal [risperidone], Zyprexa [olanzapine], Seroquel [quetiapine], and Geodon [ziprasidone]) appear to be similarly effective, but are safer and have less side effects.

Antianxiety (anxiolytic) medicines may help diminish anxiety symptoms. However, they may also disinhibit the borderline patient, causing an increase in impulsivity. Longer-acting anxiolytics (such as Klonopin [clonazepam]) may be safer, but must be used judiciously. Opiate antagonists (ReVia [naltrexone]) have been used to diminish self-mutilating behavior, but efficacy has not yet been firmly established. Electroconvulsive treatment has been employed for severely depressed borderline patients with mixed results.

CULTURAL AND GENDER ISSUES

BPD has been observed in many cultures throughout the world. Research from Japan, Denmark, and other countries illustrate borderline symptoms identical to those observed in this hemisphere (Ikuta et al., 1994; Mors, 1988).

Women are diagnosed with BPD three times as often as men (American Psychiatric Association, 2000). Surely, the changing roles of women in society contribute to this imbalance. Women typically experience more role changes (wife, worker, mother) than men, and often assume more responsibilities within the family. The phrase "single parent" usually refers to a woman. Gender role socialization may follow stereotypical paths, in which male children are valued more than females (Atwood, 2001). These stereotypes may be perpetuated in diagnostic biases (Simmons, 1992). Whereas competitiveness in men may be valued, in women it may be criticized and viewed as pathological. Mood swings, destructive impulsivity, and outbursts of anger in a man may be construed as features of antisocial personality. In a woman, these symptoms are more likely to be diagnosed as BPD. Some have argued that BPD is a diagnosis of counter-transference, invoked primarily by male clinicians toward female patients who are frustrating and difficult to treat (Kreisman and Straus, 1991).

Since the standardization of the BPD diagnosis more than twenty years ago, some have speculated that the prevalence of the disorder has been increasing in our society. This may be related to many changes in our culture that influence family structure and parent-child interactions (Kreisman and Straus, 1991). Divorce rates are at their highest level, and marriage and/or parenthood is delayed or postponed entirely. Climbing divorce rates have resulted in the creation of more stepfamilies and single-parent families. Ethnic intermarriages expand diversity, but sometimes at the cost of diluting family traditions. Family and job mobility require frequent moves away from stabilizing anchors, such as extended family, neighborhoods, churches, and other systems that sustain traditions and customs. For the borderline individual, who is constantly struggling for consistency, all of these remarkable changes confound their capacity to adapt. What is lacking in the microsociety of the family will have an enormous impact on the borderline individual in the macrosociety. Society's reconfiguration has added to the turmoil and confusion of how we define ourselves separately and collectively. Family structure has adapted to these societal changes, but at the cost of family continuity.

We live in a "fast-food" society. Not only do the managed care companies desire a quick therapy outcome, but the patient too wishes to get the problem fixed *now*. Some problems can be addressed quickly and do not require in-depth treatment. However, with BPD, the quick fix is usually not enduring. The family cannot be thoughtlessly dispatched through the therapy process. Understanding, commitment, nurturance, and time are required to successfully guide a family through its journey to self-understanding.

FUTURE DIRECTIONS

The diagnosis of BPD has been established and continuously refined over the past twenty years. It is a diagnosis that is now both accepted and often feared by clinicians. This disorder commands attention because of its prevalence in society and its significance within the family. Its frequent comorbidity with other diagnoses requires thorough knowledge of various treatment approaches. Discoveries of biochemical, genetic, and environmental risk factors will continue to provide enormous understanding for future treatments. Yet much remains to be done to adequately understand BPD.

Gunderson (2001) supports the development of a spectrum of services available for borderline patients. This treatment approach utilizes different modalities (including individual, group, and family therapies) in specialty centers, which can offer services with varying degrees of confinement. Treatment can be conducted in outpatient, partial-hospital, and inpatient facilities. Supervised living quarters and support groups can also be part of a total treatment approach. Developing a clinical standard of care specific to BPD could provide uniformity for treatment and specialized tr.ining for clinicians dedicated to working with borderline patients.

Treatment of BPD is an arduous process. Multiple interventions are usually necessary. In years past, the prognosis has generally been reported to be poor. However, as new techniques and scientific discoveries continue, and as these individuals are followed over time, we are beginning to appreciate the resilience of the borderline patient. Prognostic estimates are much more hopeful today than in the past (American Psychiatric Association, 2000). The future holds promise for our patients and for those who are willing to assume the rigors of their treatment.

REFERENCES

Allen, D. M. and Farmer, R. G. (1996). Family relationships of adults with borderline personality disorder. *Comprehensive Psychiatry, 37,* 43-51.

American Psychiatric Association (2000). *Diagnostic and statistical manual of mental disorders* (Fourth edition, Text revision). Washington, DC.

American Psychiatric Association (2001). Practice guideline for the treatment of patients with borderline personality disorder. *The American Journal of Psychiatry, 158* (Supplement).

Atwood, N. C. (2001). Gender bias in families and its clinical implications for women. *Social Work, 46,* 23-35.

Bezirganian, S., Cohen, P., and Brook, J. (1993). The impact of mother-child on the development of borderline personality disorder. *American Journal of Psychiatry, 150,* 1836-1842.

Glick, I., Berman, E. M., Clarkin, J. F., and Rait, D. S. (2000). *Marital and family therapy* (Fourth edition). Washington, DC: American Psychiatric Press.

Grinker, R., Werble, B., and Drye, R. C. (1968). *The borderline syndrome.* New York: Basic Books.

Gunderson, J. G. (2001). *Borderline personality disorder: A clinical guide.* Washington, DC: American Psychiatric Press.

Gunderson, J. G., Kerr, J., and Englund, D. W. (1980). The families of borderlines. *Archives of General Psychiatry, 37,* 27-33.

Gunderson, J. G. and Kolb, J. E. (1978). Discriminating features of borderline patients. *American Journal of Psychiatry, 135,* 792-796.

Ikuta, N., Zanarini, M. C., Minakawa, K., Miyake, Y., Moriya, N., and Nishizono-Maher, A. (1994). Comparison of American and Japanese outpatients with borderline personality disorder. *Comprehensive Psychiatry, 35,* 382-385.

Johnson, J. G., Cohen, P., Brown, J., Smailes, E. M., and Bernstein, D. P. (1999). Childhood maltreatment increases risk for personality disorders during early adulthood. *Archives of General Psychiatry, 56,* 600-606.

Johnson, J. G., Cohen, P., Skodol, A. E., Oldham, J. M., Kasen, S., and Brook, J. (1999). Personality disorders in adolescence and risk of major mental disorders and suicidality during adulthood. *Archives of General Psychiatry, 56,* 805-811.

Jones, S. A. (1987). Family therapy with borderline and narcissistic patients. *Bulletin of the Menninger Clinic, 51,* 285-295.

Kemp, Alan (1998). *Abuse in the family: An introduction.* Pacific Grove, CA: Brooks/Cole Publishing Co.

Kernberg, O. F. (1975). *Borderline conditions and pathological narcissism.* New York: Jason Aronson.

Knight, R. (1953). Borderline states. *Bulletin of the Menninger Clinic, 17,* 1-12.

Kreisman, J. J. and Straus, H. (1991). *I hate you—Don't leave me: Understanding the borderline personality.* New York: Avon Books.

Linehan, M. M. (1993). *Skills training manual for treating borderline personality disorder.* New York: The Guilford Press.

Meissner, W. W. (1988). *Treatment of patients in the borderline spectrum.* Northvale, NJ: Jason Aronson.

Minuchin, S. (1974). *Families and family therapy.* Cambridge, MA: Harvard University Press.

Mors, O. (1988). Increasing incidence of borderline states in Denmark from 1970-1985. *Acta Psychiatrica Scandinavica, 77,* 575-583.

Paris, J. and Braverman, S. (1995). Successful and unsuccessful marriages in borderline patients. *Journal of the American Academy of Psychoanalysis, 23*(1), 153-166.

Reiser, D. E. and Levenson, H. (1984). Abuses of the borderline diagnosis: A clinical problem with teaching opportunities. *American Journal of Psychiatry, 141,* 1528-1532.

Rockland, L. H. (1992). *Supportive therapy for borderline patients: A psychodynamic approach.* New York: The Guilford Press.

Seeman, M. V. and Edwardes-Evans, B. (1979). Marital therapy with borderline patients: Is it beneficial? *Journal of Clinical Psychiatry, 40,* 308-312.

Segal, B. (1996). A borderline style of functioning—the role of family, society and hereditary: An overview. *Child Psychiatry and Human Development, 18,* 219-238.

Shachnow, J., Clarkin, J., DiPalma, C. S., Thurston, F., Hull, J., and Shearin, E. (1997). Biparental psychopathology and borderline disorder. *Psychiatry, 60* (Summer) 171-181.

Simmons, D. (1992). Gender issues and borderline personality disorder: Why do females dominate the diagnosis? *Archives of Psychiatric Nursing, VI,* 219-223.

Soloff, P. H. and Millward, J. W. (1983). Psychiatric disorders in the families of borderline patients. *Archives of General Psychiatry, 40,* 37-44.

Stern, A. (1938). Psychoanalytic investigation of and therapy in the border line group of neuroses. *The Psychoanalytic Quarterly, 7,* 467-489.

von Broembsen, F. (1986). Separation crisis in a family with a borderline adolescent. *American Journal of Psychoanalysis, 46,* 62-75.

Weddige, R. L. (1986). The hidden psychotherapeutic dilemma: Spouse of the borderline. *American Journal of Psychotherapy, XL,* 53-61.

Chapter 5

Family Therapy with a Histrionic-Obsessive Couple

Len Sperry

INTRODUCTION

Until recently, an unspoken assumption has been that systemic family therapy approaches are sufficiently potent and focused to effect major changes in the individual subsystem as well as the couples subsystem, even when one or both partners met criteria for a major psychiatric disorder. Unfortunately, the author's clinical experience has not supported this assumption. Instead, when psychopathology is present, particularly psychopathology involving personality-disorder dynamics in both partners, systemic interventions have had limited impact, resulting in undertreatment of such couples. Until recently few published reports offered viable treatment options for effectively dealing with personality disorders within a couples and family context (Carlson and Sperry,1998). Similarly, efforts to utilize psychodynamic approaches in treating partners with personality disorders individually have also been unsatisfactory (Sperry and Maniacci, 1998).

This chapter describes an integrative psychodynamic-systemic approach that has been effective in treating a relatively common relational pattern of psychopathology in couples. The pattern, known as the histrionic-obsessive couple, involves histrionic personality disorder in one partner and obsessive-compulsive personality disorder in the other. Following a detailed description of the systemic and individual dynamics of this relational pattern, an integrative treatment approach is described and illustrated with an extended case example.

Furthermore, a number of related therapeutic issues are discussed, including indications and contraindications, and use of medication.

The Histrionic-Obsessive Couple in Treatment

At one time relational conflict between an obsessional partner and a histrionic partner was the prototypic presentation in couples and marital therapy. Until the middle 1980s, the histrionic-obsessive pattern was the most common couple relational pattern presenting in a private practice setting for couples therapy (Sperry and Maniacci, 1998). Today, it is the second or third most common relational pattern encountered in clinical practice (Sperry and Maniacci, 1998). Since it remains a significant treatment challenge for most therapists, this chapter proposes a potent clinical approach that combines both systemic and dynamic intervention strategies.

To provide a background for understanding the histrionic-obsessive couple, this section briefly describes two perspectives for understanding histrionic and obsessive personalities: the DSM-IV-TR (*Diagnostic and Statistical Manual of Mental Disorders*, Fourth Edition, Text Revision) (American Psychiatric Association, 2000) view and the psychodynamic view. Although both perspectives are useful in understanding an individual's behavior, they are of limited value in understanding the interactions of partners with each of these personality disorders in a committed couples relationship. The integrative psychodynamic-systemic perspective—discussed in a subsequent section—offers a much fuller understanding of such relational dynamics.

DSM-IV-TR and Histrionic and Obsessive-Compulsive Personality Disorders

Because of the pervasive influence of the DSM-IV-TR on clinical training and practice, it may be helpful to begin with the distinction the DSM makes between personality traits and personality disorders. Personality traits are enduring patterns of perceiving, thinking, and relating. Personality disorders are enduring patterns of perceiving, thinking, and relating that are inflexible and maladaptive, and which cause significant functional impairment or subjective distress, or both (American Psychiatric Association, 2000).

The obsessive-compulsive personality-disorder pattern is characterized by perfectionism, orderliness, and mental and interpersonal control. Typically, a preoccupation with work at the expense of leisure and interpersonal relationships exists. Although individuals with this disorder may fantasize about relaxation, pleasure, and intimacy, they tend to postpone such rewards and focus instead on work. Decision making is difficult and harsh judgments of oneself and others are common (Sperry, 1978, 1995a).

By contrast, the histrionic personality disorder pattern is characterized by excessive emotionality and attention seeking. Individuals with this disorder tend to draw attention to themselves by their enthusiasm, apparent openness, or flirtatious behavior. When they cannot be the center of attention they may engage in dramatic behavior (i.e., make a scene) to focus attention on themselves. In other words, they need others to attend to and have a high regard for them. The quality of their emotional and sexual relationships is typically shallow or immature (Sperry, 1995a). Although this personality disorder is believed to be more common in women than men, research does not support this characterization. For instance, "some studies using structured assessments report similar prevalence rates among males and females" (American Psychiatric Association, 2000, p. 712, reprinted with permission from the *Diagnostic and Statistical Manual of Mental Disorders*, Fourth Edition, Text Revision, copyright 2000 American Psychiatric Association).

Psychodynamic View of the Histrionic and Obsessive Personalities

Early descriptions of the histrionic and obsessive personalities emphasized core features of personality structure and dynamics rather than the behavioral features emphasized in DSM-IV-TR. Thus, the histrionic—previously called the "hysterical" personality—was typically profiled as the only girl, only child, or youngest child in a family constellation in which her mother was cold, masochistic, and resentful of being a mother and woman, and so overindulged her daughter as a compensation for not being able to love and nurture her. Her father was described as charming, indulgent, and seductive at times, while controlling and rejecting at other times. The end result was that the histrionic-in-training came to believe her father loved her more than he loved his wife. Thus, she learned to get her own way by playing each parent against the other, by being coy, seductive, pretending she was ill, or having temper tantrums. In this case, adulthood for the histrionic female became a search for a strong, idealized father-husband who would take care of her (Horowitz, 1991).

The obsessive personality, on the other hand, is believed to arise from feelings of not being sufficiently loved and valued by parents. Accordingly, they seek perfection and avoid making mistakes, believing that if they can be perfect and flawless they can regain the parental approval and love they missed as children. Similarly, intimacy is often avoided by these individuals out of a fear of being overwhelmed by powerful wishes to be taken care of. At the same time, these individuals are frustrated by these wishes for nurturance not being met, resulting in feelings of hatred and resentment toward others for failing to meet their needs. Intimate relations are threatening since they fear being "out of control," and so they tend to overcontrol others and situations. This need to control others originates from their belief that nurturance is tenuous and unpredictable (Sperry, 1995a).

IMPACT ON THE FAMILY

Couples in which one partner exhibits the histrionic pattern and the other the obsessive pattern impact their families in a unique and predictable manner. This section describes this pattern and its impact in terms of the integrative dynamic-systemic perspective.

An Integrative Psychodynamic-Systemic Perspective

From this perspective, relational conflict is viewed as a function of both personality structure and interactional patterns. A dynamic-systemic view of the histrionic-obsessive couple is a relational perspective that incorporates both sets of personality dynamics (Sperry and Maniacci, 1998). The discussion that follows emphasizes the role of conflict in the relationship.

Although initially attracted to the strong, capable, organized presentation of the obsessive partner, the histrionic partner comes to recognize that a great deal of ambivalence underlies this strong outward presentation. As the histrionic partner begins to realize the obsessive partner's underlying ambivalence, he or she feels insecure, and begin to test his or her partner's commitment by doing things the obsessive partner finds provocative and objectionable. Yet seldom does the obsessive partner protest or react emotionally. Rather than voicing any strong personal wants or desires, the obsessive insists that "anything is fine." In time this predictable response leads the histrionic to draw a number of conclusions. The histrionic comes to view the obsessive partner as indecisive, ineffectual, and impotent. The histrionic thinks that the obsessive must be angry or have some objections to the histrionic's behavior, but since the obsessive says nothing the histrionic concludes the obsessive partner must be dishonest and untrustworthy in his or her dealings. The histrionic wonders whether the obsessive's failure to show anger means he or she no longer cares. The histrionic feels increasingly unloved, emotionally abandoned, and unable to make intimate contact with his or her mate. Furthermore, the histrionic partner experiences an increasing sense of rage.

The realization that the obsessive partner can only superficially respond to his or her needs is devastating for the histrionic. Although the obsessive partner displays an endless willingness to listen to the histrionic's troubles, to provide reassurance, and to present logical solutions to his or her difficulties, the obsessive offers little else. Consequently, the histrionic feels overburdened and overwhelmed. This state of affairs provides even more reason for the histrionic partner to experience an increasing sense of abandonment and rage as the months and years go by. In their anger and desire to gain revenge, the histrionic partner resorts to predictable behaviors.

Initially, the histrionic attacks the obsessive partner verbally. Rather than being informative and potentially constructive, these attacks are often marked by scathing, global indictments of the partner's character. The histrionic assaults his or her partner simultaneously on numerous fronts. Next, the histrionic becomes provocative: they overspend, have affairs, or resort to hypochondriacal preoccupations. When the partner seems substantially unmoved by this behavior, the histrionic may pull out his or her ultimate weapon—the suicidal gesture. All too frequently, the histrionic is left with the painful notion that his or her partner is really a "great person" who deserves better, that the histrionic is the helpless victim of overpowering and irrational emotions and actions, and that he or she is doomed by external forces to be a "dysfunctional person."

As with the histrionic partner, the obsessive initially believes he or she has made the ideal mate choice, choosing a partner who makes him or her feel capable, confident, and sure, without requiring him or her to be authentic and assertive—both of which the obsessive finds difficult. Nevertheless, the enormous emotional consequences of this choice soon become increasingly evident. The obsessive begins to realize that they are being exploited, that their relationship is a one-way street in which the obsessive's partner does all the taking and he or she does all the giving. The histrionic partner's wants and desires always seem to take priority in the relationship. Furthermore, the obsessive has great difficulty expressing the growing anger he or she feels toward his or her partner or taking a stand against his or her behavior. On those rare occasions when the obsessive was forthright, their assertiveness is met with dire consequences. Predictably, the histrionic becomes rageful. The obsessive ultimately concludes that it is not worth fighting or taking a stand. Instead, the obsessive settles into other ways of expressing his or her anger and preserving a sense of autonomy. Typically, the obsessive employs passive-aggressive tactics learned in his or her family of origin. The obsessive withdraws more and more from his or her partner, often into his or her job, citing as his or her justification the requirements of the job and the increasing expenses of the family. The obsessive makes greater use of the tactic of "stonewalling" or emotional detachment. Finally, the obsessive gets even by abdicating his or her relational responsibilities outside those of breadwinner, resulting in the partner becoming overburdened with responsibilities and enormously harried in his or her attempts to fulfill them.

As the relationship progressively deteriorates, and the histrionic partner engages in more extreme behavior, the obsessive becomes ever angrier. The obsessive becomes furious at the histrionic's seemingly unprovoked verbal attacks, overspending, affairs, hypochondriasis, and suicidal threats and gestures. At the height of the relational crisis, the obsessive feels thoroughly exploited. Even more devastating is the mounting conviction that the obsessive is neither loved nor respected, and is kept around only for his or her income, and because the histrionic is afraid to leave (Sperry and Maniacci, 1998).

SETTING

The histrionic-obsessive couple is seen frequently in private practice and clinic settings, and private practice was the context for the case example in this chapter. An informal survey of colleagues involved in couples therapy suggests that the histrionic-obsessive pattern is the second or third most common relational pattern encountered following the narcissistic-dependent and narcissistic-histrionic patterns. Typically, this relational pattern is reasonably functional and intact, and is less likely to require treatment teams, case managers, or heightened security measures than other couple relational patterns. These clients are generally not seen in inpatient settings except briefly when the interactional pattern escalates to the point of suicidal threats or behaviors, most often by the histrionic partner.

Typically, the couples are seen in conjoint sessions for assessment of systemic dynamics and working through systemic issues, i.e., rebalancing the couple subsystem. Assessment of individual partner styles, particularly psychodynamics, and modifying personality dynamics takes place in individual sessions with the same therapist that works conjointly with the couple.

TREATMENT MODEL

Five treatment phases, with specific treatment goals, are used to treat the histrionic-obsessive couple in couples therapy. The phases are: (1) engagement (i.e., establishing a working therapeutic alliance); (2) assessment and formulation; (3) rebalancing the couple relationship; (4) modifying individual dynamics; and (5) maintenance and termination. Sometimes, an additional phase of skill training may be necessary. If so, skill-training interventions are utilized concurrent with or following the third phase.

Engagement

The first phase of treatment involves establishing and maintaining a therapeutic alliance as well as establishing a contract for treatment. Initial contact with the therapist frequently occurs during a period of extreme emotionality and behavior and severe marital maladjustment. These couples can be helped to a state of greater calm, order, and optimism about their relationship. It is particularly valuable for the couple and the therapist to share certain assumptions. The first is that neither partner is "crazy" or "mentally ill," but rather that each is an individual whose behavior makes sense and who is responsible for this behavior. The second is that neither partner is "the problem," but rather that each is in therapy in the role of client because the behavior of each contributes to the shared marital difficulties. The third is that each partner's family-of-origin pattern can powerfully influence the couple's relationship (Sperry and Maniacci, 1998).

These assumptions short-circuit some destructive and distressing conceptions typically held by the histrionic-obsessive couple at the outset of the treatment. Initially, the couple believes that the histrionic partner is insane, because of the histrionic's extreme behavior and emotionality in the apparent absence of any adequate reasons for such behavior. The therapist's treatment of the histrionic partner as an individual whose behavior has rational antecedents, who is responsible for his or her behavior, and who is sane, has a multiple impact. First, it reduces the distressing fear the other partner will abandon him or her. Second, it deprives the histrionic of his or her excuse for being irresponsible. Third, it deprives the obsessive of an excuse for not confronting the histrionic about his or her behavior.

Similarly, each partner tends to believe that he or she alone is completely at fault for the relationship's problems. This phenomenon is most easily observed in the histrionic partner, and accounts for vacillations in each between rage at the partner and severe self-condemnation. A consistent stance on the part of the therapist in which they repeatedly insist, demonstrate, and act in accord with the view that each partner is contributing to the marital difficulties provides each with a more livable, realistic general view and, in the bargain, a better basis for responsible self-scrutiny and action. The achievement of such a therapeutic alliance usually results in a rapid and dramatic diminution of intense emotionality and extreme behavior. The end result is that the couple becomes amenable to viewing themselves and their relationship in a calmer and more orderly fashion.

Assessment and Formulation

An adequate assessment of this relational pattern involves an evaluation of both the couple subsystem and the individual styles of each partner. The evaluation of the couple subsystem should include, at the minimum, the stage of the relationship, related boundary, power and intimacy issues, relational skills, family-of-origin issues, and commitment to and expectations for the couple relationship. Similarly, the assessment of individual styles should include both their personality styles, i.e., psychodynamic themes, such as loss or abandonment issues, and ego functions, such as the ability to maintain attachments without splitting, as well as the capacity for self-soothing and self-mastery. It would also include identification of the couple's dominant cognitive style (e.g., global, thematic, reflective; see Sperry and Carlson [1991] for a more detailed explanation of these styles). Needless to say, the couple's readiness for change and commitment to remaining in and strengthening their relationship are important prognostic indicators.

Based on this assessment, the clinician develops diagnostic, clinical, and treatment formulations. Diagnostic formulations tend to be couched in DSM-IV-TR terms, and may include a full five-axis diagnosis. Whether the partners meet Axis II criteria for a personality disorder or psychodynamics criteria is immaterial in establishing a clinical formulation. The purpose of the clinical formulation is to provide a reasonable explanation for the couple's conflicts, distress, and concerns. Ideally, such a formulation integrates both systemic dynamics and individual psychodynamics. For example, the couple's conflict might be explained as an attempt to sustain a relationship when the obsessive partner is greatly stressed and emotionally unavailable to the histrionic partner. A more detailed example of such a clinical formulation will be given in the case example section. The treatment formulation establishes an intervention strategy based on the clinical formulation. In general, this intervention strategy involves both a systemic strategy (e.g., rebalancing the couple subsystem) and an individual strategy (e.g., modifying individual psychodynamics).

Rebalancing the Couple Subsystem

After the couple is sufficiently engaged and an assessment and formulation of couple dynamics has been accomplished, the focus of treatment shifts to intervention. The third phase of treatment consists of establishing or restoring *balance* in the couple's relationship. Rebalancing is typically needed in the areas of boundaries, power, and intimacy, and represents the main systemic focus of change in couples therapy with histrionic-obsessive partners. Structural family techniques (Minuchin and Fishman, 1981), as well as strategic family therapy methods and techniques (Haley, 1963), have been quite effective in accomplishing this rebalancing of boundaries and power. Rebalancing intimacy issues in the relationship can be effectively addressed with communication or family-of-origin interventions. Discussion of the family-of-origin patterns and their impact on the couple's relationship can be quite useful to the couple by helping them understand the specific learned patterns they have acquired. This is often beyond each partner's conscious awareness and helps them realize how much their relational problem is not of their making, although they can still take responsibility for it.

Modifying Individual Psychodynamics

The fourth phase of treatment involves modification of personality features in individual partners. This phase represents psychodynamic change in couples therapy. This phase of treatment occurs typically in individual sessions with each partner, often weekly, with conjoint sessions every three to four weeks.

The primary individual goals for both the histrionic and his or her partner are relatively similar, though their starting points differ. There are two goals: first, that each partner adopts more direct, honest, and fair modes of influence and assertion, and second, that each comes to cooperate and communicate honestly in the face of control efforts on the part of the other partner.

As noted previously, both the histrionic and the obsessive are often dishonest in their attempts to control each other. The histrionic misrepresents facts, dishonestly seduces, and exaggerates his or her feelings, whereas the obsessive pretends to have no personal needs or desires, or is not bothered by the histrionic's behavior. In addition, the histrionic pretends utter helplessness, feigns illness, threatens suicide, and finds other unfair means of exerting enormous pressure on the obsessive. The obsessive may resort to passive-aggressive tactics, such as physical and emotional withdrawal, feeling avoidance, procrastination, and indecisiveness. Through all of this, both partners remain remarkably uninfluenced by the rather extreme means taken by the other. By their actions each is saying to the other that they will not be controlled.

The goal of this phase of treatment is to get each partner to abandon such tactics and to employ more honest, forthright, and fair measures in relating to each other. This goal is central in the treatment of this relationship, and may be pursued therapeutically in any number of different ways. Cognitive therapy (Sperry, 1999) that is directed at modifying maladaptive schemes, i.e., core personality themes, can be a particularly effective treatment strategy to deal with these problems simultaneously.

Maintenance and Termination

Efforts to rebalance the couple subsystem typically reduce conflict and distress in the relationship. To the extent that this rebalancing occurs early in the course of treatment, symptom relief is achieved. The challenge then is to shift the focus to individual psychodynamics while keeping both partners in treatment. This second treatment focus occupies much of the middle and maintenance phases of treatment. Many histrionic-obsessive couples can complete such treatment in the range of ten to fifteen couples sessions and twenty to thirty individual sessions. Markers that anticipate a planned termination are a reasonable degree of stability, insight, and behavior change. Because relapse is not uncommon, relapse prevention is an essential aspect of this phase of treatment. After termination, follow-up sessions at six to eight weeks and then four to six months later are not uncommon.

CASE EXAMPLE

Alex and Elizabeth were married for close to twenty years when couples therapy began. Elizabeth was an elementary school teacher in her middle forties. She was an attractive woman who seemed constantly tense and strained. She wore excessive makeup, forced smiles that seemed insincere, gesticulated with her hands, and made facial expressions that seemed exaggerated in the context of whatever was being discussed. Elizabeth gave the impression of a little girl playing the part of a grown up. It appeared as if she had gotten into her mother's clothes and makeup and played dress up for an admiring but unseen audience.

She had been in long-term treatment with a therapist for chronic, recurrent bouts of depression from which she seemed to have only temporary relief. Antidepressant medications proved relatively ineffective. She still reported intense periods of dysphoria, fleeting thoughts of suicide, and chronic dissatisfaction with her life. Her individual therapist provided supportive psychotherapy for her, and claimed that "adjustment" to her "condition" was the best she could attain.

Well into her third year of supportive therapy, she began reporting that her husband's health had become an issue. After seeing numerous physicians, the consensus opinion was that he was experiencing "stress-related" disorders, and should consider some form of counseling himself. Elizabeth's psychotherapist referred him to the author.

Alex was a large man in his late forties, moderately overweight, and balding. He had an MBA from a state university, worked as a logistics consultant for a local firm, and reported that in his duties he flew more than 100,000 miles per year. He and Elizabeth had one son who was in his mid-twenties, who had recently graduated from a well-known university with an advanced degree and had moved back home with his parents. The son's educational career had been paid for by his parents.

Alex insisted initially that he did not need any counseling. Yet he did admit that his physician had referred him because of problems with anxiety and insomnia. Insomnia was his greater concern. When he traveled and stayed in hotels, he had trouble sleeping, barely getting more than two or three hours per night. Since he was often on the road more than four nights per week, this was becoming a serious issue for him, yet despite this chronic insomnia, he never missed a meeting or failed to report to work. He believed that sooner or later this fast pace would catch up to him and more seriously affect his health. Finally, he reported a third problem: fear of heights. Flying was a nightmare for him. He couldn't cross bridges, take escalators, or ride in glass elevators without experiencing severe anxiety. Given his extensive travel schedule, this was problematic, yet he felt confident he could manage it himself. He had been prescribed Valium by his family physician, and while he rarely used it, he knew he had the tranquilizer in his pocket should it be necessary.

Alex was reluctant to talk much about himself. He was an excellent, methodical reporter of the various details of his life, but he seemed to lack any ability to discuss the personal impact of the assorted irritations and frustrations he experienced. In other words, he talked about the events that happened to him, but in an impersonal way, so that he himself rarely seemed to be present in any of his descriptions. He was polite and even cordial, yet he gave the impression of a man discussing brake problems with an auto mechanic when he discussed the serious emotional problems in his life.

Assessment and Case Formulation

Both partners manifested significant personality-disorder dynamics, which had complicated both their marital relationship and Elizabeth's previous therapeutic work. The interlocking of Elizabeth's histrionic personality dynamics with Alex's obsessive-compulsive dynamics would likely neutralize a systemic couples therapy approach. Accordingly, a combined individual and couples approach that focused on these interlocking personality dynamics was indicated.

A two-pronged treatment approach was recommended. First, individual therapy was suggested to help Alex understand the nature of his problems. Second, couples therapy was recommended. Alex had reported numerous stresses and strains in his marriage. His wife was moody and unpredictable and given to outbursts, which frustrated him. At one point during the initial interview, he sheepishly admitted that he had secretly looked forward to his trips away from home to "get some space." If he could not sleep on the road, and he found no peace at home, he feared he might lose his mind. He choked up as he said this, clearly the most visible show of emotion in that session.

The therapist suggested to Alex that by working on the relationship, he might experience some "relief," both at home and on the road. Such an approach, he was told, would be the most efficient way of working. He liked that concept, and agreed to it. He would be seen twice a month individually, and twice a month in couple therapy.

It was explained to the couple that neither of them were "sick" and that each was simply expressing in his or her characteristic style what neither had "permission" or ability to say with words. Both partners were intrigued with this notion. Alex was fascinated with the thought that communication could occur beyond someone's control. He knew it happened, he had seen it at work many times, but he never thought such a process would be going on within himself without his knowledge. Elizabeth was amused by his comment and pointed out that if Alex knew he was doing such things, he would not be able to do them. She beamed at the therapist, as if waiting for a reward or praise.

Rebalancing the Couple Subsystem

Rebalancing the relationship was challenging. Power was fairly well distributed between the partners: Alex was distant, didactic, decisive, and in charge, at least until Elizabeth became upset, emotional, and hysterical. She typically got her way at that point. Alex would calm the situation by arranging things the way she wanted, and in the process, he would take charge, organize, and structure the necessary changes, and therefore, be in power again. She would allow this until she felt he cared more about his work schedule than he did about her, then she would grow impatient, become upset, and the cycle would repeat itself. This cyclic relational dynamic had worked rather well for them for some years before becoming unduly problematic.

This cyclic dynamic, which in their sessions became known as their "map," was pointed out to them. Alex readily grasped it and examined it in all its ramifications. Elizabeth had a harder time comprehending it. The therapist realized that two processes were at work: First, although the verbal-analytic presentation suited Alex's style well, it did not meet Elizabeth's more global and visual cognitive style, and second, the very cycle that the couple engaged in at home was repeating in session. Alex, in best parental mode, began teaching and lecturing her, and she, in her childlike manner, tried to follow but could not. Graph paper was used to map out the relational transactions that were taking place, including those occurring in session. Elizabeth readily grasped the relational transaction pattern once it was represented graphically by the map, and wanted to post copies of it all over their house.

Unfortunately, boundaries and intimacy issues were not as easily addressed. A triangle existed, with their son vacillating between being a husband-surrogate for his mother when Alex was on the road, and acting as a close friend and loyal student-child to his father when Alex was home. Their son's presence kept the negative relational dynamics intact and perpetuated the very problems which, without his presence, might lead to some kind of resolution. The next several weeks of couple treatment struggled with these issues. Although it was tempting to bring in the son and switch to family therapy, the therapist was concerned that bringing him into a couple therapy format would replicate the very issue the therapist was attempting to address: the son's intrusion upon the couple's relationship. It was decided to keep the son out of the treatment process and work to strengthen the couple's bonds without the son in the session. A therapeutic ritual was established: after every session, the couple was to go out on a date. This helped. In addition, the map was expanded—both verbally and pictorially—to show how their son fit in the pattern, and how he could be removed.

For Alex, the boundary setting regarding his son was presented in terms of his son needing to "stand on his own," and Alex needing to expand his own social network. For Elizabeth, the rationale for boundary setting was framed that, by encouraging her son to individuate, she would be strengthening not only her marriage, but her son's future as well. She agreed, but the weaning process was difficult for all of them. Eventually, the couple were able to remove the son's involvement from the "map" of their couple relationship.

Modifying Individual Dynamics

Alex was being seen individually twice a month by the couple therapist. Elizabeth was being seen by her individual therapist on a weekly basis. Communication between the therapists became crucial. Although skeptical at first, Elizabeth's therapist agreed to engage her in more exploratory treatment. The following dynamics slowly emerged for each of them.

Elizabeth had been the youngest of four siblings and the prized girl of the family. She was especially cute and received considerable attention for her brightness and vivaciousness. Shortly after her fifth birthday, her mother became ill with what was diagnosed as "involutional melancholia." This "illness" was very difficult for the family. Elizabeth's father did his best to function as both mother and father. He worked two jobs, and did what he could to take care of the children when he was at home, but he was gone much of the time, and when he was home he seemed preoccupied. The result was that he withheld much of his attention from Elizabeth.

Although Elizabeth was still the favorite grandchild of her grandparents, she secretly envied her mother's privileged position. Mother gained considerable sympathy and seemed to be excused from much of the burden around the house. Everyone accommodated her every whim, and a common family motto was, "Don't upset your mother!" Elizabeth's first episode of depression manifested in middle adolescence after being heartbroken with the breakup of her first serious relationship with a young man three years older than her. He left her to go away to a major university and she felt devastated. She eventually decided to pursue elementary school teaching and specialized in drama.

Elizabeth's earliest memory was of her birthday party at age four. She was sitting around the table, with everyone looking at her. She felt special, loved, and amazed by all the gifts and the "huge cake" that was placed before her. Her next memory was from her first day of school, at age six. She remembers walking into class, feeling pretty in her new dress. A female teacher told her she needed to take a seat near the back of the room, since her name was at the "back" of the alphabet, and Elizabeth felt offended. She believed the teacher did not like her. Her first reaction was to object, but then she thought: "Maybe I'm not dressed nicely enough to be sitting up front where everyone could see me." She felt sad.

Alex was the oldest of three children and the only boy. His father was a marijuana user with occasional, unpredictable mood swings. His mother was a depressive woman who used Alex as her sole support. His sister had been disabled following a car accident at age four, and Alex remembers the many times she was hospitalized and went for medical appointments. He recalls his guilt that somehow if he had only been a better brother and not gone to baseball practice the day she was hit by a car she might be as healthy as everyone else. As he became an adolescent, it became his mission to look out for her, and he thereby became her surrogate parent, teacher, and friend.

He got his first part-time job when he was thirteen, working as a busboy at a greasy spoon restaurant. He hated the work, but since he was underage it was the only job he could find. He remembers making a promise that he would make life better for himself and his sister, that he would never lose his temper, or use drugs as his father did. After graduating from high school, Alex went on to college, which he paid for himself, and worked his way up through various jobs, eventually into management, and then consulting with others about how to run their businesses.

His earliest memory is of being five years old, and walking out on the fire escape of the family apartment. As he looked around, admiring the view, he heard a scream. His mother rushed out, grabbing Alex and sweeping him back into the apartment. She yelled at him and told him how dangerous it was to be on the fire escape. She scolded him and told him to be more careful. He feels confused, and vows to be more careful and not upset her.

As their relational dynamics became clearer, it was possible to disclose the following formulation to the couple regarding their interlocking relationship dynamics. Elizabeth grew up feeling special but cheated. Although she was aware that she could get attention for her specialness, she was also aware of how fleeting it could be. Getting attention was wonderful, but being able to hold on to it was another matter. She measured life and others by how much they could take care of her and notice her, and she became a master at playing roles to attract their attention. As she grew older, she felt her "specialness," i.e., her beauty, youth, and energy, fading. The empty-nest syndrome, with her planned, only child (so he would always feel special) leaving home, was hitting her hard. She felt abandoned by her husband, who worked too many hours. She was soon to be abandoned by her son (he too left her for college some five years earlier, as her first love had, and might eventually move out). She felt lonely and pessimistic. The onset of her current, chronic depression, roughly coincided with her son leaving for college. She seemed to be utilizing depression as a coping device to deal with life, to draw others to her as she had seen modeled by her mother. Although it appeared that she was biologically vulnerable to clinical depression, there was no question that she had learned to use her symptoms to rally support for herself.

Alex grew up believing he had responsibility for everything. In many ways this was an accurate assessment. His conscientiousness helped keep his family intact. Gradually, the line between conscientiousness and control began to blur, and unless he controlled his, and others', life, he sensed a somewhat uneasy, impending doom. His solution was to do more, to work harder, to control more, and to be busier. His only break from such a rigid, tense style was to be ill. Also, through his symptoms of fear of heights and insomnia, he could ask for a break and take time off for himself without having to admit that he was shirking responsibility.

The interlocking dynamics gradually became clear to them. Elizabeth's depression was reframed as a way of asking to be cared for, and her irritability as her "strategy" for keeping their relationship intact. She valued love, the marriage, and family, and wanted them to be happy. She was trying to keep her family together, and to look out for her husband and his health. Alex also was trying to keep his family together, and his working so hard was reframed as being for the same motive that Elizabeth had. In effect, they were told that their symptoms were serving the same purpose, just in different ways. Could they now communicate such desires in more prosocial, constructive ways?

Alex's controlling behavior, and Elizabeth's emotionality, were mutually complementary. She was encouraged to "teach" him to be more passionate, and he was urged to be her consultant on matters of organization. They grasped this way of working, and though they still had characteristic "rough spots," they found they grew more affectionate with each other.

Maintenance and Termination

Elizabeth's depression lifted, and although she could still be somewhat "blue," she found more satisfaction with Alex. Alex was encouraged to go into business for himself, and after some hesitancy, he did. He began to work out of his home, and his consulting business flourished. He gained greater control over his schedule, worked less hours more efficiently, and found more pleasure at home. A brief course of cognitive-behavior therapy for his phobic issues, with his wife as coach and co-therapist, worked very well. Within a short time, he found himself crossing bridges, riding escalators, and flying with virtually no anxiety.

These dynamics were worked on in individual and couple therapy. The road was rocky at times, but after a year and a half, the couple progressed to the point of monthly maintenance sessions. Elizabeth still sees her individual therapist for supportive work. Over the next eighteen months, Alex scheduled three follow-up sessions to review progress and get feedback. Elizabeth and Alex report considerably more satisfaction with their marriage, and little, if any conflict. Alex has learned to be less rigidly controlling, and Elizabeth, although still somewhat "dramatic," feels more connected and valued. Having her husband work out of the home and spend more time with her, she reports, has helped her tremendously.

STRENGTHS AND LIMITATIONS

The main strength of this integrative systemic-psychodynamics approach is that it combines two effective therapeutic approaches in the treatment of a relational pattern that has not proven to be particularly amenable to either the systemic or psychodynamic approaches alone. Its limitation, if any, is likely to be related to the clinician's own level of training and experience in integrating and utilizing both the systemic and psychodynamic approaches. Also, purists attached to either the family systems or the psychodynamic model may balk at the prospects of utilizing such an integrative approach.

BENEFITS FOR THE FAMILY

The short-term benefit of this approach is that it can reduce symptomatic distress and relational impairment effectively and quickly, which most often occurs in the rebalancing subsystem phase of treatment. This can reverse the abiding sense of demoralization that threatens the very viability of a committed relationship. The long-term benefit is that modification of personality dynamics can further stabilize the relationship and reduce the subtle, but real influence of family-of-origin dynamics.

In this particular case, recognizing the impact of personality disorders and psychodynamics made sense of Elizabeth's Axis I clinical depression, which previously was, for all practical purposes, treatment resistant. Focusing on the personality disorder's dynamics helps put Axis I symptoms of depression in a relational context, making them more treatable. Furthermore, this approach helped each partner to understand the other rather than seeing him or her as "crazy." As such, it empowered each partner to make changes in himself or herself and in the relationship, leading to each being happier personally and in the marriage. Finally, the broad family focus made it possible to therapeutically address the triangle with the son, which not only interfered with the progress of couples therapy, but also kept the son "stuck" at home and retarded his individuation and self-differentiation from his family of origin. In short, this approach facilitated the recognition of how family members of those with personality disorders are impacted by the disorder.

INDICATIONS AND CONTRAINDICATIONS

The indications for this approach include:

1. couples in a committed relationship in which one partner exhibits histrionic personality traits or disorder and the other exhibits obsessive-compulsive personality traits or disorder;
2. sufficient distress or impairment to warrant couples therapy;

3. willingness of both partners to attend and be engaged in the therapeutic process; and
4. sufficiently intact object relations.

Contraindications for this approach include:

1. imminent divorce or no desire for reconciliation by one partner;
2. minimal ego functions (e.g., reality testing, impulse control) that preclude or delimit psychodynamically oriented interventions;
3. comorbid borderline personality disorder in one or both partners that unexpectedly and inordinately destabilizes the relationship;
4. acute or chronic psychosis, alcohol or drug abuse or dependence that inordinately destabilizes the relationship; and
5. a history of suicide ideation or gestures in a partner with current high risk for completing suicide.

MANAGEMENT OF TRANSFERENCE ISSUES

Although transference is a common phenomenon when working with personality-disordered individuals in one-to-one psychotherapy, the potential impact of transference in conjoint couples therapy is considerably lessened due to the neutralizing effect of the presence of a third party in conjoint sessions. Since the overall treatment is framed as couples therapy, the lessened intensity of the transference tends to generalize to individual sessions with the respective partners. Transference may be expressed as a tendency to triangulate the therapist or attempts to get the therapist to ally with one partner over the other. For example, Elizabeth sought the approval of the therapist around grasping the concept of indirect communication. Supervision by someone experienced in relational dynamics can be quite helpful in breaking and avoiding such triangulation.

MANAGEMENT OF CRISES
AND ACTING-OUT BEHAVIOR

Because attention-getting strategies, including suicide threats and gestures, are not uncommon in histrionic individuals under considerable stress, a few words on dealing with such acting-out behavior is warranted. Generally speaking, the potential lethality of suicide threats and gestures can be gauged by the extent to which the attention sought is achieved. For instance, a histrionic female who feels unappreciated or lonely, takes an overdose of sleeping medication, and immediately calls her estranged partner has a much lower level of lethality than another person who overdoses and makes no effort to seek attention. In emergency room situations involving histrionic partners, I have been repeatedly impressed with how quickly crises de-escalate when the object of attention can be summoned in person or by phone to talk with the histrionic. Of course, the therapeutic task with such individuals is to find more adaptive ways of dealing with their attention-getting needs.

What about the obsessive partners with regard to acting-out behavior and crisis situations? It is a common perception that individuals who are very controlling, such as the obsessive partner, may either snap or fall apart if the relationship ends, or may become violent when his or her control and security are threatened. In my clinical experience, I have seen obsessive partners deal with their underlying anger in many ways, ranging from angry outbursts to throwing objects, but seldom do they engage in physical violence. It seems that even when these individuals appear to "lose it," they retain sufficient impulse control to regulate types of acting-out behavior that they consider unacceptable and guilt-producing. Given that increasing, cumulative stress is a trigger for their acting-out behavior, the therapeutic challenge is to help these individuals better recognize the nature of the stress response.

INTEGRATION WITH PSYCHIATRIC SERVICES AND ROLE OF MEDICATION

The use of psychiatric services in this approach tends to be limited to psychiatric referral, usually for medication evaluation, treatment, and monitoring. Because of the stated contraindications, the need for inpatient hospitalization is rare. Typically, psychiatric referral for medication evaluation is prompted by troublesome anxiety or depressive symptoms. On occasion, obsessive-compulsive disorder (OCD), which exacerbates ruminative thinking and worry, can slow or derail progress in conjoint or individual sessions (Sperry, 1995b). Although OCD can coexist with obsessive compulsive personality disorder (OCPD), as in Freud's famous case of the Rat Man, the prevalence is about 15 to 18 percent only (Jenike, Baer, and Minichiello, 1990). In such instances, certain classes of antidepressants, including the SSRIs like Prozac, can provide some symptomatic relief. However, these medications reportedly have little or no effect on OCPD itself, and thus psychotherapy is the treatment of choice (Jenike, 1991).

CULTURAL AND GENDER ISSUES

Interestingly, the common stereotypes usually associated with histrionic personality, e.g., flirtatious, bubble-headed females or Don Juan-like and macho males are not borne out in clinical practice or in research studies. Although women may be diagnosed with histrionic personality disorder more than males, "the sex ratio is not significantly different than the sex ratio of females within the respective clinical setting" (American Psychiatric Association, 2000, p. 712, reprinted with permission from the *Diagnostic and Statistical Manual of Mental Disorders,* Fourth Edition, Text Revision, copyright 2000 American Psychiatric Association). Furthermore, cultural norms vary widely regarding emotionality, impressionability, and charm, such that histrionic behavior may be more common in some cultures, among both men and women, than in others. For example, Hispanics tend to be more emotionally expressive than the British (McGoldrick, 1998).

With regard to obsessive-compulsive personality disorder, the disorder appears to be diagnosed about twice as often among men (American Psychiatric Association, 2000). However, certain obsessive traits, such as being hard working, punctual, and attentive to detail are noted as often among professional women as among professional men. Perhaps changing gender roles resulting in women becoming more empowered and having new options for recognition and attention is part of the reason behind the apparent decline in the number of histrionic–obsessive couples noted in the clinical practice today.

Nevertheless, clinicians routinely encounter couples with a histrionic female partner and an obsessive male partner, as in the case involving Elizabeth and Alex. One wonders how much gender roles influence such couple presentations. In Western culture, the female partner is stereotypically more emotional and males are stereotypically more controlled. This is an area that warrants further exploration.

FUTURE DIRECTIONS

This formulation of the integrative psychodynamic-systemic approach to the histrionic-obsessive couple is based currently on clinical experience. To the author's knowledge, no efforts have been made to research this approach by way of clinical trials to establish it as an empirically validated treatment, nor do plans exist to develop a treatment manual version of it. At this point, this approach is more art than science, and its effectiveness and efficacy depends on the skill of the clinician. Addressing these areas would certainly be beneficial in terms of future development of the integrative psychodynamic-systemic approach.

In conclusion, when both partners present for couples therapy with significant psychopathology, particularly personality disorders, systemic couples therapy interventions alone are seldom effective. Instead, a focused, combined approach utilizing individual and conjoint couples sessions is the treatment of choice. Individual sessions need to focus on the interlocking personality disorder dynamics impacting the relationship, whereas couples sessions can focus on rebalancing the relationship while decreasing skill deficits and increasing functional capacity. This approach is consistent with the emerging trend of tailoring individual and couples therapy to client needs and expectations.

REFERENCES

American Psychiatric Association (2000). *Diagnostic and statistical manual of mental disorders,* Fourth edition, Text revision (DSM-IV-TR). Washington, DC: American Psychiatric Association.

Carlson, J. and Sperry, L. (Eds.) (1998). *The disordered couple.* New York: Brunner/Mazel.

Haley, J. (1963). *Strategies of psychotherapy.* New York: Grune and Stratton.

Horowitz, M. (1991). *Hysterical personality style and histrionic personality disorder*. New York: Jason Aronson.

Jenike, M. (1991). Obsessive-compulsive disorder. In B. Beitman and G. Klernman (Eds.), *Integrating pharmacotherapy and psychotherapy* (pp. 183-210). Washington, DC: American Psychiatric Press.

Jenike, M., Baer, L., and Minichiello, W. (1990). *Obsessive-compulsive disorder: Theory and management*, Second edition. Chicago: Year Book Medical Publishers.

McGoldrick, M. (ed.) (1998). *Re-visioning family therapy*. New York: Guilford.

Minuchin, S. and Fishman, C. (1981). *Family therapy techniques*. Cambridge, MA: Harvard University Press.

Sperry, L. (1978). *The together experience: Getting, growing, and staying together in marriage*. San Diego: Beta Books.

Sperry, L. (1995a). *Handbook of diagnosis and treatment of DSM-IV personality disorders*. New York: Brunner/Mazel.

Sperry, L. (1995b). *Psychopharmacology and psychotherapy: Maximizing treatment outcomes*. New York: Brunner/Mazel.

Sperry, L. (1999). *Cognitive behavior therapy of DSM-IV personality disorders*. New York: Brunner/Mazel.

Sperry, L. and Carlson, J. (1991). *Marital therapy: Integrating theory and technique*. Denver: Love Publishing.

Sperry, L. and Maniacci, M. (1998). The histrionic-obsessive couple. In J. Carlson and L. Sperry (Eds.), *The disordered couple* (pp. 187-206). New York: Brunner/Mazel.

Chapter 6

Integrative Marital and Family Treatment of Dependent Personality Disorders

William C. Nichols

INTRODUCTION

Dependent personality disorders (DPDs) are collections of traits that are found in normal people, but which have become accentuated and rigid in some individuals so that they impair their functioning or cause distress. The dysfunctional patterns of behavior and thinking have been present since early adult life and have been recognizable in the affected client for a long time (Morrison, 1995).

Dependent personality disorder has undergone some descriptive alterations in the half-century since the American Psychiatric Association issued its first *Diagnostic and Statistical Manual of Mental Disorders* (American Psychiatric Association, 1952). Historically, dependent personality types were referred to as "passive-dependent" personalities, and were known as "oral characters," who manifested a constant demand for attention, passivity, dependency, a fear of autonomy, a lack of perseverance, dread of decision-making, suggestibility, and such oral behaviors as smoking and drinking (Maxmen and Ward, 1995).

The American Psychiatric Association's first diagnostic and statistical manual (now loosely referred to as DSM-I) included a category of passive-aggressive personality, dependent type. DSM-II essentially ignored it, the closest thing being mention of an inadequate personality (American Psychiatric Association, 1968). In the DSM-III (APA, 1980), the current term of dependent personality disorder was established and described as roughly equivalent to the DSM-I category of passive-aggressive personality, dependent type.

Anxiety and fearfulness and a general desire to be taken care of are considered the hallmarks of dependent personality disorders. Dependent personality disorders are classified in the standard psychiatric nomenclature under cluster C in DSM-IV, along with avoidant, and obsessive-compulsive personality disorders. Specifically, the diagnostic criteria for dependent personality disorders, as adapted from DSM-IV (APA, 1994, pp. 668-669), are as follows:

"A pervasive and excessive need to be taken care of that leads to submissive and clinging behavior and fears of separation" (p. 665, reprinted with permission from the *Diagnostic and Statistical Manual of Mental Disorders,* Fourth Edition, copyright 1994 American Psychiatric Association) that appears by early adulthood and is found in a variety of settings, as indicated by at least five of the following:

- Needs excessive advice and reassurance in making everyday decisions.
- Needs other persons to take responsibility for his or her major life areas.
- Fears loss of support or approval to the extent that he or she has difficulty expressing disagreement with others (this does not include realistic fears of retaliation or retribution).
- Has problems starting projects or doing things on his or her own (due to low self-confidence, rather than low energy or motivation).
- Seeks nurturance or support from others by excessive means, including volunteering to do unpleasant things.
- Has excessive feelings of discomfort or helplessness when alone because of exaggerated fears of being unable to care for self.
- Urgently seeks a replacement relationship to provide care and support when a close relationship is lost.
- Has preoccupation with unrealistic fears of being left to take care of self.

The World Health Organization's *International Statistical Classification of Diseases and Related Health Problems,* Tenth Revision (ICD-10) (1992) requires that a person meet only three of the six criteria it lists to be diagnosed as manifesting a dependent personality disorder. The ICD-10 category also includes asthenic, inadequate, passive, and self-defeating disorders. As adapted, the six ICD-10 criteria for dependent personality disorder are:

- Encouraging or permitting others to make most of his or her important life decisions.
- Subordinating personal needs to the needs of others on whom he or she is dependent and unduly complying with their desires.
- Being unwilling to make reasonable demands on people he or she depends on.
- Possessing exaggerated fears of being unable to care for himself or herself, and feeling uncomfortable or helpless alone.
- Being preoccupied with fears of abandonment by one with whom he or she has a close relationship and thus being left alone.
- Inadequate capacity for making everyday decisions without receiving excessive advice and reassurance from others.

Personality disorders, from reports of testing, appear to be the least reliable diagnoses in the DSM.

Personality disorders generally appear to originate in childhood. When adequate attachment bonds with parents are not formed, low self-esteem and dysfunctional adult interpersonal styles often result (Bowlby, 1977a,b). Dependent personality disorders, as well as some of the other personality disorders, can be viewed as ways of dealing with or expressing an inadequate sense of self and difficulties in forming and maintaining close intimate relations with others (Marshall and Barbaree, 1991). As Lantz (1993) noted, family members transform dependency into intimacy—we tend to become intimate and to feel close to those on whom we are dependent. In general, the characteristics of dependent personalities are effectively recognized when the developing person is at a stage in which he or she is expected to be establishing clear indications of functioning as an emergent adult. There appears to be fairly general agreement that this diagnosis is not applicable until at least age 16 or 17, and perhaps later.

According to Bornstein (1998), mental health professionals, for a century or so, have emphasized the maladaptive and problematic aspects of dependent personality traits. Citing empirical findings, he maintains that dependency is not merely a deficit condition but is also reflective of a number of healthy and adaptive traits and behaviors.

Bornstein has also evolved what he terms a cognitive/interactionist model of interpersonal dependency, which reconceptualizes the etiology and dynamics of dependency in object-relations/interactionist terms. Overprotective, authoritarian parenting, gender role socialization, and cultural attitudes regarding achievement/relatedness are considered the antecedents of dependent personality traits (Bornstein, 1993, 1996, 1997; Bornstein et al., 1996). The perspective that dependency can be associated with active, assertive actions on the part of the dependent person, in certain circumstances, (Bornstein, 1995) is compatible with clinical and social observations.

IMPACT ON THE FAMILY

A considerable amount of the literature on the behaviors and attitudes of persons with dependent personality disorder appears to imply that the disorder is essentially something residing entirely in the client/patient. Unfortunately, the diagnostic categories in the American Psychiatric Association's diagnostic and statistical manuals have been based on an individual orientation. As Reiss (1996) has noted, despite DSM-IV's significant contributions, it "is best regarded as an important base for ongoing clinical research classification" (p. xiii).

The role of family members sometimes seems to be restricted primarily to the client's earlier years and inadequate attention given to current behaviors that may contribute to the ongoing dependency of the client. The individuation issues of the dependent personality (to use Bowen's [1978] term), for example, frequently cut both ways: the clinging child is afraid to let go; and the controlling parent, when a close examination is made, often does not wish to release the dependent child and tacitly encourages the dependency. Clinical observation by the author over several decades supports the idea that collaboration between parent(s) and child, often unconscious, exists in many ongoing dependency relationships. This same "holding on" behavior by parents is seen in other situations in which a client carries other diagnoses (Nichols, 1985), but it seems to be markedly evident in families in which an adult child carries this diagnosis and plays the dependent, non-differentiating role more readily than do other offspring.

Whatever the sources of the dependent personality disorder in an adult child—and indications are that the person may have been punished as a child for being assertive or gregarious—the parents are likely to be faced with difficult choices about how much of the dependency to gratify and how much and what kind of responsibility to place on the offspring. Considerable amounts of patience and wisdom are needed to respond effectively to the dysfunctional behaviors and demands. Sometimes parents agonize over their adult child's (usually a daughter) continuation in a psychologically or abusive marriage, without recognizing that their strong domination of the child during formative years provided powerful "basic training" for living in an abusive, subordinate relationship. Current messages to "get out of that marriage" and "don't put up with it" conflict with the conditioning that prevailed in the messages of the parents in the years of living in the family of origin. Both parents and adult child are bewildered by their inability to make adequate affective connections and effect satisfactory understandings.

In specific terms, DPD persons may frustrate their siblings and parents by their dependency, failure to take responsibility for themselves, their denial of reality, and their use of pressures—such as bribery, cajolery, repeated promises to change, and threats—in an effort to retain relationships, their occasional pessimism, and shifting of blame. Family members may variously regard them as "shiftless," selfish, infantile, manipulative, helpless, parasitical, and so on. Failure to learn the basic skills of independent living may elicit frustration and apprehension for their ability to cope.

Several sets of factors contribute to people's tendency to adopt marital and parental roles based on experiences in their family of origin. Psychologist Walter Toman (1993) has contributed a large and influential amount of research and theory to the effects of family constellations, specifically the impact of one's ordinal and sibling position and roles, on personality and social behavior. His findings indicate that sibling positions have predictable characteristics, including how patterns of dependency and of control and domination are clearly related to where one fits in the family. An oldest sister of brothers, for example, learns early and thoroughly how to be strong and independent and how to readily and cheerfully take care of men. Those who experience such caring learn how to fit in with it and how to relate dependently to those who would be caretakers. With regard to the relationships formed outside the family (including new families formed as adult children leave home and start their own families),

Toman described what he calls the "duplication theorem." This is stated in the proposition that, "other things being equal, new social relationships are more enduring and successful, the more they resemble the earlier and earliest (intrafamilial) social relationships of the persons involved" (Toman, 1993, p. 76).

Another set of experiences that affects how one behaves in his or her own marriage and family relationships is related to the patterns that were observed and experienced in the marital and family relationships in one's family of origin. The "models of relationship" (Skynner, 1976; Nichols, 1988, 1996b; Nichols and Everett, 1986) give powerful impetus to one's conscious and unconscious values and attempts to duplicate patterns exhibited by the significant persons in his or her family of origin.

SETTING

The clients in this case were seen in outpatient treatment in a private practice office in a suburban section of a major metropolitan area, when the author was engaged in clinical practice. Clientele who were served in that setting came primarily from middle-class and upper-class backgrounds and included a significant number of professional and middle management and upper management personnel from businesses, along with a sprinkling of blue-collar workers. Most clients were either self-referred, often making contact on the recommendation of former clients, or were referred by other professionals. Although children were seen in family cases, especially in association with divorce and post-divorce custody situations, the majority of clients were adults, ranging in age from twenty to seventy.

The therapist carries dual credentials, being licensed both as a clinical psychologist and as a marriage and family therapist, and conducted a general practice consisting of approximately 50 percent marital, 40 percent individual, and 10 percent family cases. Although the therapist worked collaboratively with other therapists on occasion, including the two with whom he shared an office suite, he was the only therapist working with the clients described in the following case example.

A strength of this private practice setting was that it permitted the use of appropriate treatment methodology and the use of sufficient time to secure needed change without the structures imposed by artificial limits from bureaucratic requirements of institutions or from managed care restrictions. Decisions regarding time, modality, length of therapy, and related matters were determined by agreement between the therapist and the clients.

TREATMENT MODEL

How to deal with personality disorders? Millon (1999) indicated that a particular approach was needed for each kind of disorder, e.g., behavioral treatment for some, cognitive approaches for others, and psychoanalytic approaches for still others. In an earlier work describing a classification system based on social learning theory, Millon (1981) described four characteristic reinforcement styles: dependent, independent, ambivalent, and detachment; and eight basic personality styles, including *passive-dependent,* a term then used in the DSM. He proposed that individuals must meet three criteria—rigid use of coping behaviors, repeated self-defeating cycles, and questionable stability in stressful situations—to be diagnosed as manifesting personality pathology.

Some therapists and researchers assume treatment regimens should be laid out and strictly followed in terms of the symptoms or disorders manifested by the client/patient. It is agreed here that treatment should be tailored to the specific needs of the case, although not in the sense of using a treatment manual and applying similar interventions with each client who carries a common diagnosis. Rather than assuming that a particular mode of treatment should be applied to all individuals manifesting certain symptoms or meeting the criteria for a given diagnosis, the assumption here is that a variety of factors determine treatment approach and modes of intervention. Therapy, and family therapy in particular, in recent years has begun to recognize that such factors as culture, family context, gender, and ethnicity must be taken into consideration when assessing and treating clients.

The interests and abilities of the therapist shape the therapeutic approach used with clients. The treatment model used with this case was the integrative family therapy approach developed by the author over several decades (Nichols, 1985, 1988, 1989, 1990, 1996a,b, 1998, 1999, 2000, 2001; Nichols and Everett, 1986). This approach permits the use of psychotherapy with individuals as well as the use of conjoint marital and family therapy. The treatment of the individual is done in context, with particular emphasis on the family setting and dynamics that influence the person. Even when a person is interviewed alone, he or she is regarded as a part of a family system, and interventions are made with careful attention to the influence of the family.

This integrative approach is termed *integrative* rather than *integrated* because along with the clear and firm foundations on which it rests, it involves a fluid and dynamic process of learning and interacting with the client, or client system, which one has agreed to join in a therapeutic endeavor. Elements of this approach are in a continuing process of change, and the approach is never completed, never totally finished.

Integrative therapy, as defined here, involves the integration of selected aspects of three major theories: psychodynamic, behavioral, and systems theories. These theories provide coverage for both the "inside" and the "outside" dimensions of human personality, that is, with the individual, intrapsychic functioning of the person and the major factors that impinge on him or her from significant contexts to affect behavior and relationships.

The parts of psychodynamic theory selected for this integrative approach explicitly emphasize not only unconscious processes (and dream processes) but also relatedness. W. R. D. Fairbairn's object-relations theory (Fairbairn, 1952, 1954) and Harry Stack Sullivan's interpersonal theory of personality (Sullivan, 1953a,b, 1954) both provide a two-person psychological model, in contrast to the individual, intrapsychic emphasis of traditional psychoanalytic theory. Their approaches offer some similarities and some important differences.

In developmental terms, they both consider personality development and psychopathology as stemming from the interaction between the environment and the developing person (Slipp, 1984, 1988). Fairbairn (1952, 1954) posits that the human being, rather than being driven by sexual impulses as held in traditional psychoanalytic theory, has an object-seeking ego from the beginning and is driven to form attachments to other persons from the beginning of life, to seek "objects" or relationships rather than to discharge tensions. Sullivan (1953a), in emphasizing the interpersonal, interactive nature of personality, went so far as to say: "Personality is the relatively enduring pattern of recurrent interpersonal situations which characterize a human life" (pp. 110-111). Among the factors emphasized by Sullivan were the importance of communication, where he provided a highly useful explication of communication, language, and symbols, and the role of anxiety as the major disruptive force in interpersonal relations and the most significant factor in the development of serious difficulties in living (Sullivan, 1953a). Sullivan's emphasis on the role and effect of culture and emphasis on communication processes and human development complement the work of Fairbairn.

Fairbairnian object relations, particularly as developed and expanded by Henry V. Dicks and others, provides significant assistance in explaining mate choice and continuation in an intimate relationship, whether healthy or unhealthy (Dicks, 1963, 1967; Willi, 1982, 1992). Selected processes used from psychodynamic theory include projective identification, introjection, projection, and collusion (Nichols and Everett, 1986).

Behavioral theories focus essentially on individual observable behaviors and learning. Problems with both individuals and families are seen as arising primarily from interpersonal problem stimulation and reinforcement in interaction. That is, behaviors by one unit—individual or group—elicit dysfunctional emotions, cognition, and behavioral responses in others. For example, some parents use methods of punishment in an effort to change their child's undesired behaviors, but gain only temporary change (Patterson, 1982). The result is a reciprocal coercive pattern in which the child's return to undesired behaviors results in more coercive behavior by the parents. On a more positive note, reciprocity—the tendency for couples to reward one another at basically the same rate—is a widely used construct in marital therapy (Jacobson and Margolin, 1979; Patterson and Reid, 1970). Used in several forms, e.g., quid pro quo (Lederer and Jackson, 1968), "holistic" contract (Stuart, 1980), and "good faith" contract (Weiss, Hops, and Patterson, 1973), the preference here is for encouraging clients to engage in "volunteering" behaviors in which one partner offers behaviors on behalf of the other without the expectation of immediate benefit or reward (Nichols, 1988, p. 105).

Family systems theory is exceedingly helpful in providing an understanding of how human interaction occurs in a systemic fashion, and in stressing connectedness between and among persons. The major concepts adapted from general system theory (von Bertalanffy, 1968) in addition to the contextual dimension, are organization, subsystems, wholeness, boundaries, hierarchy, open and closed systems, equifinality, feedback, nonsummativity, stability and change, structure, and process (Nichols, 1996b, p. 52). Family system theory not only provides assistance in comprehending and assessing how individuals function in their major contexts but also some of the impact that the context has in shaping the interaction among persons. As noted elsewhere, when systems theory is combined with psychodynamic theory it becomes easier to recognize that the person is not a passive recipient of outside forces, but, as Allport (1955) insisted decades ago, is proactive. This dovetails nicely with Fairbairn's (1954, 1963) concept of an active object-seeking ego from the beginning of life that continues to be proactive in succeeding years. This understanding has important implications for placing expectations on clients to participate in the formation of a therapeutic relationship and alliance, and assuming responsibility for working at changing.

The integrative approach referred to here is more an integration of orientations than of methods as such, as noted elsewhere (Nichols, 2001). The methods include interviews, both individual and, typically, conjoint (marital, and sometimes total family), as indicated by the situation and the dynamics of the clients; genograms (McGoldrick and Gerson, 1985) or background information forms (Nichols, 1988, pp. 108-111) or both; broad questions with "projective" possibilities followed by probes and specific questions (questions focused on selected topics); and therapist observation of client behaviors in the interview.

The case factors that determine the nature and form of the therapeutic interventions used with the client or clients include:

- the presenting complaints of the clients, including the nature and severity of the initial complaints, any symptoms presented at the beginning of the contact with the client, and any problems that emerge in subsequent contacts;
- the present functioning and strengths of the clients, including any background or historical elements that contribute to the current functioning of the client;
- the developmental level of the client and client effectiveness in dealing with appropriate developmental challenges (Nichols, 1996b, pp. 122-298); and

• the therapist's orientation and abilities, including the kind of alliance that one is able to form and maintain with the clients.

The centrality and crucial importance of the therapist-client relationship in securing positive outcomes seems to have been established in psychotherapy. In this integrative therapy approach it is essential to establish and maintain a therapeutic relationship between therapist and clients to form a therapeutic alliance—an agreement to cooperate in a mutual effort to carry out therapeutic tasks and achieve therapeutic goals (Nichols, 2001).

Treatment in this particular case followed an approach in which therapeutic work with one person was combined with conjoint treatment with the marital partner. At the beginning, the husband was not open to the conjoint marital therapy that was so crucial to a successful outcome. It was necessary to give attention to the adequate resolution of some individual issues and to make certain that the requisite conditions for doing conjoint work were present before proceeding with conjoint work.

Assessment and treatment generally go hand-in-hand in therapy. A distinction needs to be made between assessment and diagnosis. The latter refers to the classification of individuals into psychological/psychiatric nosological categories. Assessment, as used here, includes not only the processes, functioning, problems, strengths, needs, and potentialities of a client, but also the functioning and characteristics of the family system. In terms of the ongoing nature of the assessment-treatment relationship, one begins making interventions virtually from the outset of contact with the client(s) and continues making additional assessments as treatment proceeds.

The various levels of assessment include individual (intrapsychic) and interpersonal (systems) elements and the sociocultural settings in which the individual and system are located and function. Where a marriage is part of the therapeutic picture, it is important to give attention to demographic and ethnic considerations, but it is also crucial to retain sight of the individual. In mate selection, the perspective here is that even with proper consideration of demographic, cultural, and ethnic factors, it is imperative to examine internal psychological issues to understand both one's choice of a mate and the marital interaction that follows (Nichols, 1978; Dicks, 1967; Scharff and Scharff, 1989; Willi, 1982, 1984).

Assessments of the object-relations capacities of individuals are made routinely and receive particular attention whenever interpersonal relations play a significant role in the client's problems or object-relations improvement promises to contribute to better personal functioning. Observation of client interaction with his or her spouse and interaction with the therapist; client descriptions of relationships with spouse and others, as well as feelings about them; and general questions, such as "What attracted you to your mate?" and subsequent probing questions and explorations of the expectations one has of the marital partner (Sager, 1976) in interviews provide the therapist with significant indications of the level of object relations at which a client functions. Is a client operating at a need gratification level in which the other person is valued essentially for what he or she can provide or does for the client? That is, is the need primary, and, in the client's view, the other exists only to fulfill the need? Or does the client function at the object-constancy/object-love level in which the other is valued whether or not he or she serves a desired need?

Schema developed by Olson (1988) for use in classifying family studies can be usefully adapted to therapy classification and treatment: individual level (DSM symptoms as symptoms/presenting complaints/problems), marriage (marital problems), parent-child (parent-child problems), family (nuclear family and extended family problems), and community (community and social levels) (Nichols, 2001).

Assessment of a client or client system that presents to the therapist can lead to treatment, to some other kind of assistance, or to no treatment, depending on what the initial assessment suggests regarding the need for change and level of motivation for change permits. Where treatment is indicated, the kinds of techniques selected depend on the factors described previously, including the kind of relationship and therapeutic alliance formed with the clients. Some general guidelines that typically are followed: If a delimited, discrete problem exists, the choice often is straightforward, direct intervention interventions. For such matters as divorce mediation, marital enrichment, and parental training, specific behavioral approaches can be used. When the problems pertain basically to communication difficulties or the need for skill training, behavioral and educational techniques or interventions are primary choices. If the issues are concerned essentially with relationships or attachments between persons, psychodynamically oriented approaches are the primary choice.

Typically, this involves a combination of marital and individual treatment. Complex problems with indications that the difficulties are maintained by systems patterns in the family call for intervention at the family systems level, starting with focusing on the present family system. When multigenerational or transgenerational factors seem to be maintaining problems and symptoms, the initial treatment of choice is family-of-origin work in which the "problem client" is interviewed with his or her family, or with portions of it as indicated by the problems and the situation (Nichols, 1996b, 2001).

When issues are present that constitute a crisis, such as major substance abuse or family violence, the crisis elements need to be dealt with first, as is typical in psychotherapy. After the crisis has subsided, then it is time to shift the focus to systemic factors that affect both the individual's symptomatology and the family's functioning.

CASE EXAMPLE

Ann and Tom Merchant contacted the therapist while in the midst of a marital separation. Ann made the initial telephone call, saying that her husband, Tom, had recently moved out, that they had seen their clergyman, who had recommended that they call the therapist for an appointment, and that Tom had asked that she make the call. She was given an appointment time and asked to have her husband call and confirm that it was workable for him. She agreed. Tom called and left a message that it was an acceptable time, and they were seen a few days later.

They appeared at the office a quarter hour before the appointment time, and each completed a copy of the background information form used by the therapist (see Nichols, 1988, pp. 110-111, for a copy of the form, and pp. 97-124 for an outline of an initial interview process). The background information form indicated that both were twenty-five years old, were gainfully employed (Tom in sales and Ann as manager of a department in a large insurance firm), were physically healthy with no illnesses or medication, had been married two years, along with additional information on the family of origin of each. Ann held a bachelor's degree, whereas Tom had attended college for only a few months, and then had returned home and gone to work for his father.

When they entered the therapist's office from the reception room, they made an impressive picture: both were slender, blonde, fair, fashionably dressed, and generally attractive. The picture was marred only by the tension that was evident in each. Although visibly tense, Ann managed to succinctly and clearly state their problem as she saw it: Tom had moved out recently and was living with a young, divorced mother of a young child, and it was not clear why he had moved out and where things were going, although she wanted him to come home and work on whatever problems that they had. Tom did not have much to say, and glanced at Ann periodically as if he were depending on her to do the talking, and then somewhat belatedly and bewilderedly recognizing that she could not talk for him regarding the relationship with the other woman. In contrast to Ann's clear statement about wishing to continue the marriage, Tom expressed his ambivalence, saying that he did not know what he wanted to do about the situation. In addition, the couple talked about Tom's work situation—he was a salesman for his father's food-processing company. Ann had been pressing him to "get out from under the thumb" of his domineering father, to decide what he wanted to do and to go back to school and get education/training for a career of his own. His father had assigned him the role of salesman and had sent him to assertiveness training to improve his sales skills.

A brief exploration followed of how the couple met (they were introduced by Tom's older sister, who worked with Ann and had thought she would be a good match for Tom), and queries regarding what attracted them to each other (Tom: "She was so confident and knew what she wanted to do, and I felt at home with her from the beginning," and Ann: "He was so kind and easy to get along with, and he was so easy to love").

Separating the pair for brief individual sessions, the therapist formed an even stronger impression of Ann's commitment to Tom and the marriage, forming a tentative conclusion that she would be amenable to any reasonable course of action to work on the situation. Ann possessed good object-relations development and clearly functioned at the level of object constancy in which the other was valued for his own worth and not simply on the basis of whether he met a desired need. She also demonstrated a history of handling responsibility for others and herself quite well, stemming from her ordinal position as the older sister of sisters, and from taking over family tasks and sharing administration following her mother's death.

Tom's dependency characteristics emerged even more clearly when he was seen alone. He could not identify any clear reasons why he was living with the other young woman, but did convey that he did not wish to lose Ann.

The couple's need for help and the positive cast placed on the therapist by the clergy colleague who had referred them were helpful in the establishment of an early relationship of trust and the beginning formation of a therapeutic alliance. When the therapist carefully and succinctly set forth a plan in which Tom would come in alone for two or three sessions in an effort to gain some clarity, both readily agreed after a few questions were answered.

Tom's story as it emerged in the individual interviews was that in the early years he (evidently displaying the charming, winsome traits characteristic of a younger brother of an older sister; Toman, 1993) had been "well taken care of" by his sister, who was four years older than he. There had been no real problems with his parents that he could remember, until the eighth grade when he "began to like girls." This was a turning point with his exceedingly religious parents. Two years later, his high school sweetheart became pregnant, and his father compelled him to break up with her and to pay all the expenses for a costly abortion out of state. Tears rolled down his face as he described what had happened and his feelings. Following the abortion, he began taking drugs and his performance in school deteriorated. Working supportively, the therapist provided interpretations as Tom came to understand the role his guilt at "deserting" his high school sweetheart had played in his current attempt to "rescue" the single young mother with whom he was living.

Meeting with both Tom and Ann, the therapist stated his availability to them when Tom had reached the point in which he could work on the marriage. Clear limits were placed on the treatment arrangements. To put it briefly, both were provided support, and Tom was held responsible for reaching a decision and taking action. Approximately four weeks later, with Ann's reiteration of her love, but her expectations that Tom would begin to work on making his own decisions, Tom returned home. Tom called for an appointment, and the pair returned for conjoint marital work. Fortunately, he was married to a person who was comfortable with being in charge and was able to tolerate his dependency, as long as he showed some indication that he would take steps toward functioning more adequately in his work and personal life.

At the end of the initial assessment, Tom was deemed to meet the criteria for a dependent personality disorder diagnosis on the DSM-IV, Axis II, and an Axis V, general assessment of functioning score of approximately 60. Obviously, changes in the personality disorder would not come as rapidly as changes in the neurotic problems. The neurotic problems were uncomfortable for Tom, being uncharacteristic of the young man who had been a regular church participant for all of his life. "Neurotic individuals are usually uncomfortable with their symptoms, whereas individuals with personality disorders often justify and rationalize their behavior," as Maxmen and Ward (1995) put it (p. 390). Once the focus of treatment moved over to Tom's dependent disorder, the focus was placed on the behavior and not on explanations for it.

The therapeutic work subsequently continued to draw upon a base of extensive clinical observations and research regarding the role of marriage and intimacy in dealing with dependency and other personal problems. Such observations as Lantz's (1993) that family members transform dependency into intimacy and that we tend to become intimate with those on whom we feel dependent, and Valliant's

(1978) report that research into earlier childhood experiences, marriage relationships, and present mental health in men indicate that marriage seems to offer men opportunity to overcome previous adverse or deleterious experiences, for example, offered support for the idea that a strong marriage can help people to continue to develop and mature.

Ann continued to encourage Tom to plan a career of his own and to leave the stressful sales position that he held with his father's company. She offered to take steps in their living arrangements that would enable him to quit working full-time, go to school, and work only part-time. At the same time, the therapist worked with them on dealing with their residual issues from the separation and on helping Tom to acquire some of the skills he needed to improve his confidence in his social relationships. Some role-play within sessions and homework assignments were used. Tom also gained some reassurance about his decision-making ability through some psychometric testing and completion of vocational interest inventories.

In many cases, the client's family of origin would have been invited in for sessions as a family unit (without the children's spouses being present). This was not done in Tom's case. The therapist concluded that the chances were much stronger at that time for progress and healthy change by working primarily with Ann and Tom's relationship than by trying to secure effective change with Tom's family, in which the husband-father continued to dominate and to luxuriate in his use of power in both personal and business spheres. Later, when Tom has put a more solid foundation under himself and his marriage, it might be possible to anticipate positive change for Tom through family-of-origin sessions.

With Tom functioning at a stronger personal and vocational level, and the marriage in satisfactory shape for the couple, treatment was terminated by mutual agreement, using a tapering-of-sessions approach. The last follow-up came three years later in a holiday card from the couple to which a note was appended, indicating that Tom had completed a year-plus of college work and was progressing well in a work-study program aimed at a career in a field that he had chosen for himself while still in therapy, and that both partners were enjoying their roles as parents of a young toddler.

STRENGTHS AND LIMITATIONS

The integration of elements from psychodynamic, systems, and behavioral theories provides the therapist with a much more extensive range of understanding and useful interventions than can be found in a unilateral approach to working with clients. Simultaneously the integration of the various theories increases the therapist's confidence that the same outcomes can be secured from different interventions, that is, that the systems' notion of equifinality actually works in practice (Nichols, 2001). Once again, the emphasis here is on adequate, ongoing assessment both of the client's condition and of the results of interventions made by the therapist, rather than on following a preset, predetermined pattern of treatment once an initial assessment has been made.

The psychodynamic, object-relations, and interpersonal emphases in this approach provide strong support for taking a developmental viewpoint with clients. The Fairbairnian and Sullivanian foci on interpersonal relations and the role of actual, rather than fantasied, events in creating pathology is reinforced by Kohut (1971, 1977). Kohut also holds that human beings continue to require object relations in normal development. This has important implications for understanding and treating adult relationships and comprehending how dependency relationships can be healthy and normal.

This integrative approach provides the therapist with a flexible model that permits, as has been mentioned, the tailoring of interventions not only to the symptomatology exhibited by the clients, but also to their peculiarities. Although this is not unique to integrative therapy, it encourages the therapist to keep in mind the cultural, ethnic, and gender categories or systems from which the client comes as a "natural" feature of ongoing assessment that continually examines context as well as the individual.

Flexibility is also present in the possibilities for selection of treatment plans that can be adapted to the particular needs of the case. No assumption is made that treatment will require three or four years or that clients should be "cured" or their "problems solved" in three of four sessions. Rather, the use of ongoing assessment and continual setting and resetting of goals as treatment moves through various stages permits the achievement of short-term and long-term goals and the use of both simple and complex interventions as the situation dictates and permits.

This integrative approach gives attention to both the "inside" and the "outside" aspects of human personality and functioning. Psychodynamic theory and practice provide the opportunity for understanding what takes place in the psychic functions of an individual, in his or her thinking and feeling. Behavioral theory and practice offer an emphasis on learning as well as a practical way of aiding clients in developing adaptive social skills. Good behavioral therapy and practice, along with family therapy's emphasis on changing the context in which persons live and function, give clients opportunity to undergo corrective emotional experience (Wachtel and McKinney, 1992; Nichols, 2001).

In general, integrative models are not easily or quickly mastered, and the integrative approach described here is no exception to that rule. They are unlike technique-oriented models of therapy, which sometimes can be learned by witnessing demonstrations and following the methods used without mastering the theory on which the model is based. With an integrative approach, the therapist must not only master the theory that guides a particular practice, he or she must also master serveral theories, combine their aspects in a rational and functional fashion, and devise interventions that are consistent with the theoretical framework and effective with clientele. Although this may be viewed by some as a limitation, the richness of opportunities for clinical insight and intervention offered by this integrative perspective more than offset any disadvantages.

BENEFITS FOR THE FAMILY

To the extent that family members are involved in the therapeutic work with the client, either as occasional or ongoing consultants or as clients themselves, they are spared some of the frustrations and outright suspicions and anger that frequently affect family members who are shut out of a family member's treatment. Including family members promotes an awareness and understanding of the nature of the problems and of what is occurring in therapy. Family members can be aided also when they experience "multidirectional partiality" in the therapist's attitudes and behaviors (Boszormenyi-Nagy, 1966; Boszormenyi-Nagy and Krasner, 1986), which helps to quell or at least soften feelings of blame and helplessness that sometimes develop from having a troubled person in the family. Furthermore, when they become anxious as a result of coming directly face-to-face with upsetting issues in the treatment process, family members have the opportunity to deal straightforwardly with both those issues and with their anxiety with the assistance of the therapist. When, as is often the situation in dependent personality disorder cases, the therapist provides assistance in locating appropriate sources of practical help, such as for securing vocational guidance or skill development, the family may not only get immediate relief, but also an increased awareness of what resources and supports are available and how to go about securing such practical help when it is needed in the future.

Similarly, family members may be helped by the "assumption of least pathology" (a concept shared with Pinsof, 1995) in which, as used here, the therapist may first try comparatively simple and straightforward approaches to dealing with problems before assuming that in-depth interventions are indicated. This approach may not only result in discernible changes and gains in some instances in what appears to the family members and clients to be a "sensible or commonsense" fashion, it also tends to contribute to the lessening of anxiety and blaming and to increasing feelings of hope. In general, observation of how the therapist regards the personality-disordered family member and responds to difficulties or averts potential problems associated with the disorder can provide other family members with some reasonable degree of feelings of reassurance, as well as guidance and support for making appropriate responses.

Not all of the changes achieved through therapeutic intervention pertain to the diagnosed person. The kind of involvement of family members in the assessment and treatment process embodied in this integrative approach has a tendency to encourage them in many cases to take some responsibility for making a good-faith effort to at least be neutral toward therapy, if not actively supportive, and in some instances to become committed to seeking change. Just as the diagnosed dependent personality-disordered family member can find guidance and support for dropping some of his or her passivity and taking some responsibility for personal actions and life, other family members can benefit from the therapy enterprise by getting understanding and help toward replacing some of their nonproductive stances with more beneficial attitudes and behaviors. This desire or commitment to change may or may not include securing direct therapeutic assistance for themselves to alter the patterns of troublesome relationships that have existed between themselves and the identified dependent personality-disordered offspring, parent, or partner.

INDICATIONS AND CONTRAINDICATIONS

There are no hard-and-fast rules for choosing to use conjoint family therapy or conjoint marital therapy for the treatment of dependent personality disorder. In fact, one of the most extensive discussions of indications and contraindications for family therapy (Glick et al., 2000) does not refer to dependent personality disorder at all. Therapist orientation and preference, client reactions and preference, and therapist judgment are the major determinants more often than not. There are some differences between using conjoint family therapy and conjoint marital therapy.

Both as a practical matter and as an ethical matter, the indications for using at least marital evaluation are persuasive for the author when one sees an individual client who is married (Nichols, 1988), that is, contact is indicated with the spouse when one sees a married client on an individual basis. For married clients who are diagnosed with dependent personality disorder, marital therapy or a combination of marital and individual therapy provide a preferred approach when the spouse of the identified client shows indications of being willing and able to participate in therapy effectively, according to the clinician's assessment. As noted, dependency and intimacy are intertwined, and involving the spouse has the potential for obtaining change and improvement in the client, and securing change and improvement in the marriage generally helps the client as well. For adult clients who are unmarried, the family of origin may provide the major vehicle for helping the client to begin dealing with the symptomatology, if the parents in particular can be enlisted in therapy or as consultants on the client's behalf (Nichols, 1996b).

Although the preference and bias here are in favor of dealing routinely with the significant contextual settings of the client, it is also recognized that situations exist in which individuals need to be seen without direct family involvement. Contraindications for family therapy include the decision by the family members or the therapist that the risks of having the family involved in therapy outweigh the advantages, that the costs will be greater than the benefits. For example, will the family be hurt by getting together in a designated therapeutic setting? Will working with the family of origin hinder the differentiation of the diagnosed member from the family? This was the situation in Tom's case. The therapist's insistence that all members of the family come to therapy is not necessarily the wisest course to pursue—it may in some instances be more appropriate to listen to the protests of clients, at least until it is possible to examine carefully the dynamics of the situation and do necessary preparatory work to decrease anxiety and build bridges of support. Other contraindications include religious or cultural prejudices against therapy, when the psychopathology in one family member would make family therapy ineffective (e.g., dishonesty, manipulative use of therapy), or when the entire family denies that problems exist (Glick et al., 2000).

Contraindications for both conjoint family therapy and conjoint marital therapy also include lack of education and training specifically in those approaches on the part of the therapist, and the absence of agency or institutional orientation and procedures to deal with family problems (e.g., they possess an individual orientation, and the support staff as well as the professionals lack an orientation to family dynamics and family problems, thus making it difficult or impossible to deliver effective family therapy). Obvious incompatibilities between the therapist and the client's family due to major age ethnicity, racial differences, or gender orientation that either party finds too disturbing or that otherwise would make the process nonproductive also make it unwise to use conjoint family therapy.

MANAGEMENT OF TRANSFERENCE ISSUES

Recognition that persons manifesting a dependent personality disorder have a tendency to attach themselves in a dependent fashion and sometimes make dramatic appeals for the therapist to take responsibility for them appears central to working effectively with these persons. A key element in avoiding taking on a "parental" role for a dependent personality is the therapist's success in walking a relatively clear line between communicating concern and willingness to help and actually taking over for the client. An important strategy is to carefully avoid becoming the client's sole or primary source of dependency gratification. Rather, the clinician seeks to spread the responsibility as appropriately as possible between the therapist and other professionals, authority figures, and individuals and groups that have the potential for providing support for the client, while trying to encourage client desire and efforts to assume increasing amounts of personal responsibility in a step-by-step fashion.

With Tom, the dependent personality in this case, the issues were not merely those of helping him to attach more appropriately and maturely with his spouse while seeking to assume more responsibility for making his own vocational and marital decisions, but also to aid him in diminishing his dependent and subordinate relationship with his father and, at the outset, the short, neurotically based relationship with the young woman with whom he was living at the time of the first therapeutic contact. At the same time, the therapist attempted to stay on the sidelines as an interested helper, continually reinforcing the idea that Tom needed to and could decide for himself what he wished to do, and teaching him some decision-making procedures. The therapist consistently deflected any attempt by Tom to give him credit for Tom's periodic and incremental successes, pointing out where the actions were those of Tom or, in some instances, Tom and Ann.

The kinds of intense transference and dependency issues that arise in individual, depth-oriented psychopathology do not occur in the same ways in marital therapy. Working with present client relationships and not encouraging the development of the kind of dependency that is normative in childhood does not eliminate transference issues in therapy, but it does minimize the occurrence of some of the more infantile reactions that occur in intensive one-to-one therapy.

With dependent personality-disordered clients in particular, it seems essential to stay in the present and not try to make the client dependent. Dream work was used with Tom a few times, when he brought up dreams that had a heavy impact on him. The approach was a contemporary model of interpretation that regards dreams primarily as reflections of one's current life problems and unresolved emotional issues from daily living (Mishne, 1993), rather than solely as concerned with wish fulfillment (Freud, [1900] 1958).

A crucial goal in therapy with dependent personalities is to work toward making extreme dependency ego-dystonic rather than "normal" and ego-syntonic. That is, what seems normal and customary to the client needs to be converted to something that is uncomfortable, a symptom, leading to the client's desire for change. This is one of the more difficult tasks in such therapy, requiring more patience and sensitivity from the therapist than we can sometimes manage. Casting the behaviors into a developmental framework and encouraging whatever desires for maturing that the client possesses can be helpful in moving forward without transference interruptions in the therapy.

MANAGEMENT OF CRISES
AND ACTING-OUT BEHAVIOR

This case opened with what the wife (Ann) characterized as a crisis and what the therapist quickly viewed as an instance of acting out of neurotic conflict stemming from the teenage years of the husband (Tom). Both commonsense and general clinical practice call for the therapist to resolve a crisis before proceeding with therapy in an effort to help deal with problems and to secure change. That was the pattern followed in this case.

Tom's spouse was willing and able to tolerate for a few more weeks his living away from home with another woman and the woman's child. Although the details and dynamics of the situation were not explored to any depth with Ann or interpretations offered to her, she seemed to have a intuitive grasp of the dynamics of Tom's involvement, and could wait because she had hope that he was coming home soon.

When exploring the situation with Tom, the therapist tried to provide him with understanding and sympathy for his struggle as he came to understand the symbolic role that the divorceé had taken as he had unconsciously tried to deal with his guilt over "deserting" his high school sweetheart by "rescuing" the woman and her child from their lonely situation. Tom could express the feeling that he wished to "do what was right," but not harm the young woman in the process. With the support went the firm affirmation that the decision was Tom's and that it was necessary for him to take the desired actions at his own initiative.

Once the initial situation was resolved, no more instances of significant crisis or acting-out behaviors were apparent in the therapy sessions, and no more reports of events or behaviors that could be clearly identified as crises or acting-out behavior were reported by the clients. Tom's dependent behaviors were more likely to manifest in problems and concerns regarding his occupation, where he was able to enlist Ann's interest in responding, usually in terms of urging him to make a vocational choice and go back to school.

This case was different from many involving dependent personality disorders in that the client had his dependency needs spread among several individuals and did not make the kinds of clinging and demanding approaches to the therapist that are often found, particularly in instances in which the therapist or other helping professional does not set up and maintain clear and firm boundaries. In the event that salient attachment figures threaten abandonment or actually leave, the therapist needs to move quickly and decisively to support the client's strengths, to provide skill training in everyday coping, to help the client make attachments with other benign figures, including supportive social groups. If symptoms of depression or strong anxiety emerge in reaction, temporary use of antidepressant medication, such as benzodiazepines (Stone, 1993), could be indicated, although Sperry (1995) warns that the use of anxiolytics should be limited and monitored because of the likelihood of abuse by DPD clients.

INTEGRATION WITH PSYCHIATRIC SERVICES AND ROLE OF MEDICATION

Little evidence indicates that using medication results in long-term benefits in individuals' long-term personality functioning (Perry, 1996). Consequently, treatment with medication is not recommended for clients with dependent, avoidant, histrionic, or narcissistic personality disorders (Frey, 1999), and treatment of DPD is generally based essentially on verbal therapies (Stone 1993). Given both the incidence of comorbidity with Axis I disorders and the lack of effectiveness of medications with personality disorders per se, the appropriate course seems to be to use medication with important symptoms from co-occurring disorders rather than applying them with DPD. DPD clients appear vulnerable to anxiety disorder (Tyrer et al., 1997; Dolan-Sewell, Krueger, and Shea, 2001), phobic disorder, dissociative disorders, and somatoform syndromes (Millon and Davis, 1996; Ekleberry, 2000). Reich and Noyes (1987) found links between Axis I (anxiety disorders) and dependent and avoidant personality disorders in clinic populations. A lower degree of association was found in a community population studied by Maier and associates (1992), who reported that approximately one in ten participants interviewed had more than one personality disorder. (A fairly extensive discussion of connections between psychotherapy and medical/psychiatric services is found in Glick et al., 2000.)

Although it is true that many exceedingly dependent personality-disordered persons may present with myriad somatic or physical complaints—and sometimes with genuine physically based illnesses, this is not always the case. The dramatic cases tend to color the perceptions of medical and mental health personnel who come into contact with them. Who can forget persons who manage to get attention by securing multiple surgical procedures and/or complaining until they obtain ongoing pain medication, and whose ills, real or imaginary, are never sufficiently eased to quiet them? It is not clear why dependent persons select one path or another in which to express their clinging, often demanding, behaviors. It does seem apparent that medication, response to telephone calls between therapy sessions, changing appointments at the client's requests, and similar matters all have a symbolic value for the client—they carry the meaning of reassurance, attention.

Experience with colleagues from medical, psychological, and other professional backgrounds in many years of practice in the Midwest and Southern United States disclosed that professional "burnout" from trying to cope with extreme dependency on the part of clients/patients is not uncommon. Not all such dependent persons carry the dependent personality disorder label, of course, but they, like other clinging and demanding individuals, can bother professionals until they are turned away, avoided, referred on to somebody else, or given placebo pills or "magical" forms of advice. Clinicians who have prescription writing privileges can easily find themselves facing ethical struggles over whether to grant something to clients/patients who perceive that it will help them, when the professional is not certain that it will have the desired effect.

These issues were not part of the picture with Tom. Although he had "medicated" himself with drugs for a period in high school, at the time of treatment he had enough ego-strength and attachment to Ann and her sturdy support that psychiatric services and medication were not indicated. Both spouses saw themselves appropriately as healthy, having had fairly routine physical examinations and being given clean bills of health by physicians. Tom's dependency needs dealt more with vocational/occupational matters, and it was possible to keep his attention demands sufficiently gratified through his contacts with several persons, as indicated earlier, so that the focus in therapy was on developing skills and taking positive, productive actions, and learning to live with some honest kinds of recognition from Ann and a few other persons.

CULTURAL AND GENDER ISSUES

DPD is diagnosed more often in women than in men (Frey, 1999), but this may reflect prejudice on the part of clinicians because of gender biases that expect females to be subservient, meek, mild, and generally amenable to having decisions made for them. On the other hand, cultural expectations for males may cause those manifesting the dependent personality disorder to be scorned and denigrated because they demonstrate dependent needs and thus, according to the cultural stereotype, are not sufficiently "macho" or "manly." These patterns would generally prevail in much of North America, and in many other parts of the world, but they are not universal.

Dependency is regarded differently in different societies and cultures. In some Mediterranean societies, for example, children may stay at home until they are married, even though they do not wed until they are approaching thirty years of age. In others, they do not leave home at all—when they marry, their family may add additional space to the family home and the married adult child and spouse move into the new unit.

Therapists should be adequately acquainted with the patterns commonly found in families from different cultural and ethnic backgrounds to be able to assess accurately and appropriately what is found in clients. What would be considered undesirable, and even pathological and dysfunctional, in North American families may be considered normative and expected in a family from an Asian or other non-North American background. Differentiation, for example, considered highly desirable in one culture, might be viewed quite differently in another. (See McGoldrick, Giordano, and Pearce, 1996, for an excellent collection of articles delineating significant ethnic characteristics and differences.)

The integrative approach described here is implemented with every conscious effort to be as gender fair, culturally aware, and accepting as possible.

FUTURE DIRECTIONS

The tradition that emphasizes the intrapsychic nature of personality disorders has been challenged recently. Specifically, calls have been made for a diagnostic system that includes attention to the relational context of personality. Florence Kaslow's (1996) *Handbook of Relational Diagnosis and Dysfunctional Family Patterns* provides excellent guidance for those attempting to understand relational patterns and their role in family and individual functioning. Although it contains very little on dependent personality disorders, the handbook includes a comprehensive and specific schema-focused diagnosis for personality disorders. Young and Gluhoski (1996) propose that personality pathology be assessed in four areas: core themes, coping styles, emotional disposition, and global level of dysfunction, and offer a series of rating scales for dimensions within each area. An important part of this approach is that rather than being categorical, it is primarily dimensional, with clients being rated on the dimensions on 100-point scales.

Eventually, recognition of the need for relational diagnosis, which emphasizes the role of family and relationship factors in the formation and maintenance of symptoms, may become accepted more generally. From a developmental perspective throughout the family life cycle, the *Handbook of Family Development and Interventions* (Nichols et al., 2000) offers a wealth of diagnostic and treatment information also from a family systems and relational perspective and fits nicely with Kaslow's relational material.

On the other side of the spectrum, Siever and Davis (1991) have proposed a heuristic model that addresses several dimensions of personality disorders from a psychobiological perspective. Siever and Davis hope their model will generate further investigation regarding development and treatment of personality disorders. It is hoped that both these and Bornstein's perspectives will be given the significant amounts of attention that they deserve in the near future.

REFERENCES

Allport, G. W. (1955). *Becoming: Basic considerations for a psychology of personality*. New Haven: Yale University Press.
American Psychiatric Association (1952). *Diagnostic and statistical manual of mental disorders*. Washington, DC: Author.

American Psychiatric Association (1968). *Diagnostic and statistical manual of mental disorders.* (Second edition). Washington, DC: Author.

American Psychiatric Association (1980). *Diagnostic and statistical manual of mental disorders.* (Third edition). Washington, DC: Author.

American Psychiatric Association (1994). *Diagnostic and statistical manual of mental disorders.* (Fourth edition). Washington, DC: Author.

Bornstein, R. F. (1993). *The dependent personality.* New York: Guilford Press.

Bornstein, R. F. (1995). Active dependency. *Journal of Nervous and Mental Disease, 183*(2), 64-77.

Bornstein, R. F. (1996). Beyond orality: Toward an object relations/interactionist reconceptualization of the etiology and dynamics of dependency. *Psychoanalytic Psychology, 17,* 177-203.

Bornstein, R. F. (1997). Dependent personality disorder in the DSM-IV and beyond. *Clinical Psychology: Science and Practice, 4,* 175-187.

Bornstein, R. F. (1998). Depathologizing dependency. *Journal of Nervous and Mental Disorders, 186*(2), 67-73.

Bornstein, R. F., Riggs, J. M., Hill, E. I., and Calabrese, C. (1996). Activity, passivity, self-denigration, and self-promotion: Toward an interactionist model of interpersonal dependency. *Journal of Personality, 64,* 637-673.

Boszormenyi-Nagy, I. (1966). From family therapy to a psychology of relationships: Fictions of the individual and fictions of the family. *Comprehensive Psychiatry, 7,* 408-423.

Boszormenyi-Nagy, I. and Krasner, B. R. (1986). *Between give and take: A clinical guide to contextual therapy.* New York: Brunner/Mazel.

Bowen, M. (1978). *Family therapy in clinical practice.* New York: Jason Aronson.

Bowlby, J. (1977a). The making and breaking of affectional bonds: I. Aetiology and psychopathology in the light of attachment theory. *British Journal of Psychiatry, 130,* 201-210.

Bowlby, J. (1977b). The making and breaking of affectional bonds: II. Some principles of psychotherapy. *British Journal of Psychiatry, 130,* 421-431.

Dicks, H. V. (1963). Object relationship theory and marital studies. *British Journal of Medical Psychology, 36,* 125-129.

Dicks, H. V. (1967). *Marital tensions.* New York: Basic Books.

Dolan-Sewell, R. T., Krueger R. F., and Shea, M. T. (2001). Co-occurrence with syndrome disorders. In W. J. Livesey (Ed.), *Handbook of personality disorders: Theory, research, and treatment* (pp. 84-104). New York: Guilford Press.

Ekleberry, S. C. (2000). Dual diagnosis and the dependent personality disorder. *The dual diagnosis pages.* Retrieved from <http:// www.toad.net/~arcturus/dd/depend.htm>.

Fairbairn, W. R. D. (1952). *Psychoanalytic studies of the personality.* London: Routledge and Kegan Paul.

Fairbairn, W. R. D. (1954). *An object-relations theory of the personality.* New York: Basic Books.

Fairbairn, W. R. D. (1963). Synopsis of an object-relations theory of the personality. *International Journal of Psycho-Analysis, 44,* 224-225.

Freud, S. ([1900] 1958). The interpretation of dreams. In S. Freud, *The standard edition of the complete psychological works of Sigmund Freud* (Volumes 3 and 4). London: Hogarth Press.

Frey, R. J. (1999). Personality disorders. In D. Olendorf, C. Jeryan, and K. Boyden (Eds.), *Gale encyclopedia of medicine.* Farmington Hills, MI: Gale Group.

Glick, I. D., Berman, E. M., Clarkin, J. F., and Rait, D. S. (2000). *Marital and family therapy* (Fourth edition). Washington, DC: American Psychiatric Press.

Jacobson, N. S. and Margolin, G. (1979). *Marital therapy.* New York: Brunner/Mazel.

Kaslow, F. W. (Ed.) (1996). *Handbook of relational diagnosis and dysfunctional family patterns.* New York: John Wiley and Sons.

Kohut, H. (1971). *The analysis of the self.* New York: International Universities Press.

Kohut, H. (1977). *The restoration of the self.* New York: International Universities Press.

Lantz, J. E. (1993). *Existential family therapy: Using the concepts of Viktor Frankl.* Northvale, NJ: Jason Aronson.

Lederer, W. J. and Jackson, D. D. (1968). *The mirages of marriage.* New York: Norton.

Maier, W., Lichtermann, D., Klinger, T., Heun, R., and Hallmayer, J. (1992). Prevalences of personality disorders (DSM-III-R) in the community. *Journal of Personality Disorders, 6,* 187-196.

Marshall, W. I. and Barbaree, H. E. (1991). Personality, impulse control, and adjustment disorders. In M. Hersen and S. M. Turner (Eds.), *Adult psychopathology and diagnosis* (Second edition) (pp. 360-391). New York: Wiley.

Maxmen, J. S. and Ward, N. G. (1995). *Essential psychopathology and its treatment* (Second edition, revised for DSM-IV). New York: Norton.

McGoldrick, M. and Gerson, R. (1985). *Genograms in family assessment.* New York: Norton.

McGoldrick, M., Giordano, J., and Pearce, J. K. (Eds.) (1996). *Ethnicity and family therapy* (Second edition). New York: Guilford Press.

Millon, T. (1981). *Disorders of personality: DSM III, Axis II.* New York: Wiley.

Millon, T. (1999). *Personality-guided therapy.* New York, NY: John Wiley and Sons Inc.

Millon, T. and Davis, R. (1996). An evolutionary theory of personality disorders. In J. F. Clarkin and M. F. Lenzenweger (Eds.), *Major theories of personality disorder* (pp. 221-346). New York: Guilford Press.

Mishne, J. M. (1993). *The evolution and application of clinical theory: Perspectives from four psychologies.* New York: Free Press.

Morrison, J. (1995). *DSM-IV made easy: The clinician's guide to diagnosis.* New York: Guilford Press.

Nichols, W. C. (1978). The marriage relationship. *Family Coordinator, 27,* 185-191.

Nichols, W. C. (1985). A differentiating couple: Some transgenerational issues in marital therapy. In A. S. Gurman (Ed.), *Casebook of marital therapy* (pp. 199-228). New York: Guilford Press.

Nichols, W. C. (1988). *Marital therapy: An integrative approach.* New York: Guilford Press.

Nichols, W. C. (1989). A family systems approach. In C. R. Figley (Ed.), *Treating stress in families* (pp. 67-96). New York: Brunner/Mazel.

Nichols, W. C. (1990). Tear down the fences: Build up the family. In F. W. Kaslow (Ed.), *Voices in family psychology, Volume 1* (pp. 177-191). Newbury Park, CA: Sage Publications.

Nichols, W. C. (1996a). Persons with antisocial and histrionic personality disorders in relationships. In F. Kaslow (Ed.), *Handbook of relational diagnosis and dysfunctional relational patterns* (pp. 287-299). New York: John Wiley and Sons.

Nichols, W. C. (1996b). *Treating persons in families: An integrative framework.* New York: Guilford Press.

Nichols, W. C. (1998). Integrative marital therapy. In F. M. Dattilio (Ed.), *Case studies in couple and family therapy* (pp. 233-256). New York: Guilford Press.

Nichols, W. C. (1999). Integrative family therapy. In A. M. Horne (Ed.), *Family counseling and therapy* (Third edition). (pp. 539-564). Itasca, IL: Peacock Publishing Co.

Nichols, W. C. (2000) Integrative marital therapy. In F. M. Dattilio and L. J. Bevilacqua (Eds.), *Comparative treatments for relationship dysfunction* (pp. 210-228). New York: Springer.

Nichols, W. C. (2001). Integrative family therapy. *Journal of Psychotherapy Integration, 11,* 289-312.

Nichols, W. C. and Everett, C. A. (1986). *Systemic family therapy: An integrative approach.* New York: Guilford Press.

Nichols, W. C., Pace-Nichols, M. A., Becvar, D. S., and Napier, A. Y. (Eds.) (2000). *Handbook of family development and interventions.* New York: Wiley.

Olson, D. H. (1988). Capturing family change: Multi-system level assessment. In L. C. Wynne (Ed.), *The state of the art in family therapy research: Controversies and recommendations* (pp. 75-80). New York: Family Process Press.

Patterson, G. R. (1982). *A social learning approach to family intervention: Volume 3, Coercive family process.* Eugene, OR: Castalia.

Patterson, G. R. and Reid, J. B. (1970). Reciprocity and coercion: Two faces of social systems. In C. Neuringer and J. L. White (Eds.), *Behavior modification in clinical psychology* (pp. 137-177). New York: Appleton-Century-Crofts.

Perry, J. C. (1996). Dependent personality disorder. In G. O. Gabbard and S. G. Atkinson (Eds.), *Synopses of psychiatric disorders* (Second edition) (pp. 351-354). Washington, DC: American Psychiatric Press.

Pinsof, W. M. (1995). *Integrative problem-centered therapy.* New York: Basic Books.

Reich, J. H. and Noyes, R. (1987). A comparison of DSM-III personality disorders in acutely ill panic and depressed patients. *Journal of Anxiety Disorders, 1*, 123-131.

Reiss, D. (1996). Foreword. In F. M. Kaslow (Ed.), *Handbook of relational diagnosis and dysfunctional family patterns* (pp. ix-xv). New York: Wiley.

Sager, C. J. (1976). *Marital therapy and couples contracts.* New York: Brunner/Mazel.

Scharff, D. E. and Scharff, J. S. (1989). *Object relations couples therapy.* Northvale, NJ: Jason Aronson.

Siever, L. J. and Davis, K. L. (1991). A psychobiological perspective on the personality disorders. *American Journal of Psychiatry, 148*, 1647-1658.

Skynner, A. C. R. (1976). *Systems of family and marital psychotherapy.* New York: Brunner/Mazel.

Slipp, S. (1984). *Object relations: A dynamic bridge between individual and family treatment.* New York: Jason Aronson.

Slipp, S. (1988). *The technique and practice of object relations family therapy.* Northvale, NJ: Jason Aronson.

Sperry, L. (1995). *Handbook of diagnosis and treatment of the DSM-IV personality disorders.* New York: Brunner/Mazel.

Stone, M. H. (1993). *Abnormalities of personality: Within and beyond the realm of treatment.* New York: Norton.

Stuart, R. B. (1980). *Helping couples change: A social learning approach to marital therapy.* New York: Guilford Press.

Sullivan, H. S. (1953a). *The interpersonal theory of psychiatry.* New York: Norton.

Sullivan, H. S. (1953b). *Modern conceptions of psychiatry.* New York: Norton

Sullivan, H. S. (1954). *The psychiatric interview.* New York: Norton.

Toman, W. (1993). *Family constellation: Its effects on personality and social behavior* (Fourth edition). New York: Springer.

Tyrer, P., Gunderson, J., Lyons, M., and Tohen, M. (1997). Special feature: Extent of comorbidity between mental status and personality disorders. *Journal of Personality Disorders, 11*, 242-259.

Valliant, G. E. (1978). Natural history of male psychological health, Volume III: Correlates of successful marriage and fatherhood. *American Journal of Psychiatry, 135*, 653-659.

von Bertalanffy, L. (1968). *General system theory.* New York: Braziller.

Wachtel, P. M. and McKinney, M. K. (1992). Cyclical psychodynamics and integrative psychodynamic therapy. In J. C. Cross and M. R. Goldfried (Eds.), *Handbook of psychotherapy integration* (pp. 335-370). New York: Basic Books.

Weiss, R. L., Hops, H., and Patterson, G. R. (1973). A framework for conceptualizing marital conflict: A technology for altering it, some data for evaluating it. In L. A. Hammerlynck, L. C. Handy, and E. J. Marsh (Eds.), *Behavior change: Methodology, concepts, and practice* (pp. 309-342). Champaign, IL: Research Press.

Willi, J. (1982). *Couples in collusion.* New York: Jason Aronson.
Willi, J. (1984). *Dynamics of couples therapy.* New York: Jason Aronson.
Willi, J. (1992). *Growing together, staying together.* Los Angeles: Jeremy P. Tarcher.
World Health Organization (1992). *International statistical classification of diseases and related health problems* (Tenth revision). Geneva: Author.
Young, J. E., and Gluhoski, V. L. (1996). Schema-focused diagnosis for personality disorders. In F. W. Kaslow (Ed.), *Handbook of relational diagnosis and dysfunctional family patterns* (pp. 300-321). New York: Wiley.

Chapter 7

Systemic Treatment
of Borderline Personality Disorder:
An Integrative Approach

Malcolm M. MacFarlane

INTRODUCTION

According to the American Psychiatric Association's (1994) *Diagnostic and Statistical Manual of Mental Disorders,* Fourth Edition (DSM-IV), "The essential feature of Borderline Personality Disorder (BPD) is a pervasive pattern of instability of interpersonal relationships, self-image, and affects, and marked impulsivity that begins by early adulthood and is present in a variety of contexts" (p. 650, reprinted with permission from the *Diagnostic and Statistical Manual of Mental Disorders,* Fourth Edition, copyright 1994 American Psychiatric Association). BPD is categorized in the DSM-IV as part of the cluster B personality disorders marked by erratic, emotional and dramatic presentation. It is this erratic, dramatic, and emotional quality of borderline clients that makes this population at once both fascinating and frustrating for clinicians. Everett et al. (1989) wrote that:

> When mental health professionals discuss their most frustrating and problematic clients, they are usually talking about borderline individuals. Many therapists, particularly those in private practice, have reported to us that they simply will no longer work with borderline clients because of typical case management difficulties and the stress that such cases place on them. (p. 1)

Although our understanding of borderline clients and our ability to treat them effectively has improved since Everett and colleagues' writing, BPD remains a challenging and complex disorder for clinicians to treat.

As Benjamin (1996) notes, "For the BPD, everything that can go wrong has gone wrong. There are disorders in every domain of function: cognition, mood, and behavior" (p. 115). The extent of disturbance is reflected in the American Psychiatric Association's (1994, p. 654) DSM-IV diagnostic criteria. For BPD to be diagnosed, there must be:

> A pervasive pattern of instability of interpersonal relationships, self-image, and affects, and marked impulsivity beginning by early adulthood and present in a variety of contexts, as indicated by five (or more) of the following:
>
> (1) frantic efforts to avoid real or imagined abandonment **Note:** Do not include suicidal or self-mutilating behavior covered in Criterion 5.
> (2) a pattern of unstable and intense interpersonal relationships characterized by alternating between extremes of idealization and devaluation
> (3) identity disturbance: markedly and persistently unstable self-image or sense of self
> (4) impulsivity in at least two areas that are potentially self-damaging (eg. spending, sex, substance abuse, reckless driving, binge eating) **Note:** Do not include suicidal or self-mutilating behavior covered in Criterion 5.
> (5) recurrent suicidal behavior, gestures, or threats, or self-mutilating behavior
> (6) affective instability due to a marked reactivity of mood (eg. intense episodic dysphoria, irritability, or anxiety usually lasting a few hours and only rarely more than a few days)
> (7) chronic feelings of emptiness
> (8) inappropriate, intense anger or difficulty controlling anger (e.g., frequent displays of temper, constant anger, recurrent physical fights)
> (9) transient, stress-related paranoid ideation or severe dissociative symptoms (reprinted with permission from the *Diagnostic and Statistical Manual of Mental Disorders,* Fourth Edition, copyright 1994 American Psychiatric Association)

Glick and Loraas (2001) point out that seven of these nine criteria have obvious and important interpersonal implications. The first criteria, frantic efforts to avoid real or imagined abandonment, is a hallmark characteristic of BPD clients. These abandonment issues often have their roots in an early developmental history of loss, abandonment, or parental neglect (Links and Munroe-Blum, 1990; Links, 1992; Marziali, 1992; Zanarini et al., 1989). Such early experiences result in fears of abandonment that are often played out in transferential interactions with spouses and significant others, including therapists (Benjamin, 1996). When BPDs feel they are likely to be abandoned, they may respond with intense, inappropriate anger (criteria eight) and suicidal or self-destructive behavior (criteria five) that may, at times, be aimed at coercing caretaking behavior on the part of the abandoning individual. At times of stress, they can also experience brief psychotic episodes marked by severe cognitive distortions (criteria nine) (Zanarini, Gunderson, and Frankenburg, 1990). This pattern of interactions and responses to stress understandably has a major impact on family members and significant others, and contributes to the BPD's characteristic pattern of unstable and intense interpersonal relationships (criteria two).

Individuals with BPD also tend to suffer from high rates of comorbid Axis I mood disorders, such as depression and anxiety (criteria six). Zanarini et al., (1998) found that 83 percent of borderlines in their sample suffered from major depressive disorder. The high rate of mood disorders has encouraged some researchers and theoreticians to view BPD as part of the spectrum of affective or mood disorders (Millon, 1992), and to explore biological models of etiology. At this point, some evidence appears to exist for a biological basis in the development of BPD, and the view is that at least some of the BPD client's affective instability may be rooted in disturbances in neurotransmitters in the brain (Coccaro and Siever, 1995). There is also evidence for family transmission of hallmark borderline personality characteristics (Silverman et al., 1991), which suggests the possible presence of a genetic component to BPD. BPD is frequently found in parents and other family members of individuals diagnosed with BPD (van Reekum, Links, and Boiago, 1993). This would also suggest the possibility of a genetic component, but many other factors appear to contribute to the development of BPD, including a history of traumatic events, such as physical and sexual abuse.

A number of researchers have noted a strong link between parental physical and sexual abuse, and the development of BPD (Herman, Perry, and van der Kolk, 1989; Zanarini et al., 1989; Stone, 1990). The frequency of reports of childhood sexual abuse among BPD clients ranges as high as 50 to 70 percent in some studies (Paris, 2001). At this point it seems clear that childhood physical and sexual abuse are often factors contributing to the development of BPD. However, Paris (2001) cautions that it is important to recognize that such abuse does not always lead to the development of BPD, and many individuals diagnosed with BPD do not report a history of traumatic childhood abuse. The relationship between the development of BPD and childhood physical and sexual abuse appears to be a complex one, and a variety of factors, including genetic constitutional factors and other social factors, interact in the development of the disorder.

What does seem clear, is that these developmental, biological, and social experiences often result in an individual who suffers from an unstable self-image or sense of self (criteria three). At times this unstable sense of self leads to chronic feelings of emptiness (criteria seven). In the midst of these feelings of emptiness and lack of sense of self, BPD individuals often engage in destructive acting-out behaviors, such as sexual promiscuity, substance abuse, binge eating, suicide attempts, and so forth (criteria four). These behaviors may represent an attempt to achieve a sense of validation or acceptance by others (by being seen as sexually desirable), or an attempt to escape from intolerable feelings of emptiness or low self-worth (through suicide, substance abuse, binge eating to nurture or "feed" themselves, or impulsive spending to help themselves feel better). Unfortunately, these acting-out episodes often damage significant interpersonal relationships, leaving the BPD individuals feeling even worse about themselves and their life situations.

The presence of a disturbed sense of self has given rise to a variety of individual psychodynamic treatment approaches aimed at addressing this aspect of BPD pathology. The object-relations approach of Otto Kernberg (1967, 1975) has perhaps become the most prominent individual psychodynamic model for working with BPD. Kernberg describes "borderline personality organization" as resulting from a "split" in self and object representations stemming from the infant's inability to reconcile abusive, neglectful, or inconsistent parental responses to his or her needs. This "splitting" is at the core of the BPD individual's alternating idealization and devaluation of both self and others, and the resulting instability of interpersonal relationships.

Although an understanding of the individual psychodynamic processes of the BPD client is crucial to effective treatment, until recently attention has tended to focus primarily on the BPD individual, and the significant interpersonal impact of BPD pathology has been ignored. Where the literature has focused on families of borderline individuals, the focus has often been on ways that family members contribute to the development of BPD, not on the impact of BPD symptoms on the family. Mitton and Links (1996) note that:

> Although certain personality disorders, such as borderline, narcissistic, and antisocial personality disorders, have had broad and extensive coverage in the clinical and research literature, there is little information about the functioning of individuals with these or other personality disorders in close, personal relationships. (p. 196)

They continue:

> For the most part . . . little attention has been paid to assisting the parents, siblings, spouses, children, and other family members of patients with personality disorders in managing their close relationships with the patient or to considering the family's involvement in the ongoing treatment plan. (pp. 196-197)

Given the major impact that BPD symptoms can have on interpersonal relationships with family members and significant others, there appears to be a need for a more integrated systemic approach to understanding and treating this disorder—an approach that places the BPD individual in a family context, and that provides assistance to family members in coping with BPD. Fortunately, an emerging literature is aimed at addressing this need.

IMPACT ON THE FAMILY

One indication of the familial need for information and help in dealing with BPD family members is the recent emergence and popularity of a variety of self-help books dealing with BPD. One of the earliest was Kreisman and Straus's (1989) *I Hate You—Don't Leave Me: Understanding the Borderline Personality.* The authors describe a variety of typical BPD behavior patterns and explore how these patterns impact relationships with significant others and family members. Some of the areas they identify as problematic for family members are: coping with borderline rage, living with borderline mood swings, and handling the borderline's impulsivity. They identify a variety of feelings on the part of family members that are typical, such as feelings of guilt, fear, and anger. They outline a number of methods for communicating with the borderline family member, including their "SET" model. SET stands for support, empathy, and truth, three key ingredients in confronting and communicating with the BPD individual regarding the impact of their behavior.

Another self-help book that outlines the impact of BPD behavior and symptoms on family members is Mason and Kreger's (1998) *Stop Walking on Eggshells: Taking Your Life Back When Someone You Care About Has Borderline Personality Disorder.* A companion workbook was recently released (Kreger and Shirley, 2002). Mason and Kreger also describe a number of characteristic reactions to living with a BPD individual, including: denial, anger, depression, bewilderment, loss of self-esteem, feeling trapped and helpless, withdrawal, feelings of guilt and shame, hypervigilance, and a tendency to become drawn into dysfunctional interactional patterns in a codependent process. They point out that BPD behaviors such as verbal abuse, perceived manipulation, and pathological regressive defenses often shatter trust and intimacy in relationships. The authors offer a variety of strategies for family members to "take back control of their life," including seeking support and validation, setting personal boundaries or limits, and developing improved assertiveness, conflict management, and communication skills.

The recommendations and directions taken by the authors of these self-help materials parallel the findings and directions reported in the academic literature. Gunderson, Berkowitz, and Ruiz-Sancho (1997) report that families and BPD individuals identify communication as a major problem, and that conflict and anger are also major problems, as well as suicidality in the BPD family member. Mitton and Links (1996) indicate that research on families of personality-disordered individuals reports considerable burden on the family unit, difficulty dealing with troublesome symptoms and behaviors, chronic economic problems, and stress. They indicate that families often knew little about their loved one's disorder, and that they felt excluded from the treatment process. Other researchers reported that families felt mystified and exhausted by aspects of their relative's illness. In many respects, this feeling of being left out or ignored by treatment providers is reminiscent of the complaints made by families of individuals with serious mental illnesses, such as schizophrenia and bipolar disorder (Johnson, 2001). The need that families are feeling for support and information is reflected in the emergence of organizations such as the National Education Alliance for Borderline Personality Disorder (NEA-BPD), and conferences such as "Family Perspectives on Borderline Personality Disorder," sponsored by NEA-BPD in New York in October 2002.

The focus of intervention recommended for BPD individuals and their family members tends to vary, but a fairly common emphasis is on a combination of education regarding the illness, building an alliance with the family to use the family's influence in the treatment of the BPD individual, and support for the family in dealing with BPD symptoms and acting-out behavior (Mitton and Links, 1996). Other authors focus on interrupting dysfunctional or problematic family interactional patterns such as excessive criticism, emotional disengagement or enmeshment, or high levels of Expressed Emotion (EE) (Glick et al., 1995; Berkowitz and Gunderson, 2002), and on improving marital and family communication processes (Harman and Waldo, 2001).

A variety of models are emerging for intervening with BPD individuals and their families, but to date little general awareness exists of these models, and many mental health clinicians continue to work with BPD from an individual perspective and ignore both the impact this disorder has on family members and the potential that family members have to aid and assist the therapeutic process. There remains a need for the articulation of more family-focused models for treating BPD. It is hoped that the integrative systemic treatment approach that follows will help further the development of this important area of the personality disorders field.

SETTING

The following treatment model was developed by the author in the course of his work at Ross Memorial Hospital Community Counselling Services. Ross Memorial Hospital is a 200-bed community hospital situated in rural Southern Ontario. Community Counselling Services (CCS) is an off-site, community-based, mental health program serving a mixed rural and urban population in the City of Kawartha Lakes. The service is fully funded through the provincial Ontario Health Insurance Program (OHIP).

Counseling and psychiatric services are provided for individuals age sixteen and older who are identified as experiencing mental health problems. Services provided include individual psychotherapy, psychiatric assessment, psychoeducational and treatment groups, as well as marital and family therapy services when at least one family member has been identified as suffering from a mental health problem.

CCS programs cover a broad range, and include a mental health program, psychiatric services, a clinical case management program, a crisis response program, and a child sexual abuse response program, which is funded separately through the Ministry of Community and Social Services.

The center employs a multidisciplinary team approach. Staff backgrounds include psychiatry, marriage and family therapy, social work, psychology, and psychiatric nursing. Although the treatment approach of individual therapists is influenced by their academic background and training, the center as a whole utilizes a broad-based systems approach. Individual treatment approaches are integrated into this systems framework, and every effort is made to ensure treatment approaches for specific presenting problems reflect current research regarding best practices and therapeutic effectiveness. The following treatment approach for BPD is consistent with this treatment philosophy.

TREATMENT MODEL

The Integrative Systemic Therapy (IST) approach described in this chapter has evolved gradually over a number of years (MacFarlane, 1993, 2001, 2003), and reflects a "best practices" approach to treating personality disorders in general and BPD in particular. This approach integrates elements from a variety of treatment approaches that research has indicated are important to the successful treatment of BPD. Integrative approaches are becoming increasingly common in the family therapy field because they offer greater flexibility, an increased repertoire of interventions, higher treatment efficacy, and greater acceptability among clients (Lebow, 1997). Given the complexity of the issues faced by therapists treating BPD, and the challenges of maintaining a therapeutic relationship with BPD clients, these factors are critically important. Like the treatment model described by Nichols in Chapter 6 of this text, the following approach is described as integrative rather than integrated, since it is intended to be fluid and flexible, allowing clinicians to adapt to individual and family differences in presentation and symptomatology.

A Systemic Approach

The core element of this model is the systemic treatment approach outlined by Tomm (1984a,b, 1987a,b, 1988). This model, which is based on the earlier work of Milan Team members Boscolo and Cecchin, uses a process that Tomm (1984a) calls *interventive interviewing* as its primary method of intervention. Interventive interviewing creates change through a process of circular and reflexive questioning. Reflexive questions are questions that are intended to create shifts in how individuals perceive their personal and family situation, thereby creating changes in the belief system or personal or family "map" that guides their behavior and interpersonal interactions. This process is based on the premise that the "mind is social," and that our realities and world views are socially constructed through our interactions with others and the meanings and conclusions we abstract from life events and weave into personal stories or narratives. From the systemic perspective, individuals with borderline personality disorder are not seen as "being" BPD, they are seen as "acting" or "behaving" in borderline ways. A strength of this perspective is that it is always easier to change an interpersonal process, what we "do," than to change what we "are."

This systemic approach incorporates a *social constructivist perspective,* as outlined by Anderson and Goolishian (1988) and Hoffman (1990), and a *narrative perspective,* as described by White and Epston (1990). From this perspective, the individual's and the family's views of reality are seen as being socially constructed through a process of dialogue or "languaging" with others, and a narrative or "life story" is created to explain events in the individual's or family's life. In creating this narrative, certain events or situations are "abstracted" from day-to-day experiences and incorporated into the client's and the family's belief system or life story to support a particular construction or view of reality. Other events that could support an alternate view or construction of reality are ignored or downplayed. A key intervention technique involves the exploration, through a series of deconstruction questions, of how the BPD individual's self-view and worldview has been constructed through their interactions with family members and significant others. From the constructivist perspective, there is no "right" or "wrong" view of reality. All perspectives are equally valid. As this process of exploration takes place, a variety of alternative interpretations or constructions of reality are explored, and the client and the family are encouraged to revise their "story" or "narrative" to one that provides greater opportunities for positive interaction, personal growth, and family change.

Although a full exploration of the systemic approach is beyond the scope of this chapter, a number of aspects of the approach make it particularly useful in treating borderline personality disorder. The systemic approach views human systems as primarily *evolving systems* rather than as homeostatic ones. This promotes a therapeutic orientation toward BPD clients as being engaged in a process of personal growth, rather than as being fixated or "stuck" at a particular level of development. Therapists who work from this perspective will look for signs of growth and development in the past, and encourage a process of personal growth in the present and future, as opposed to seeing their clients as pathological or permanently damaged.

Another useful aspect of the systemic approach is that it permits the therapist to entertain both linear and circular hypotheses regarding the evolution and meaning of problematic behaviors and interpersonal interactions. This flexibility enables the clinician to incorporate a number of models for understanding and intervening in BPD families, including biomedical models, individual psychodynamic models, and cognitive-behavioral approaches. The systemic approach also encourages both therapist and client to adopt a metaperspective in understanding individual and family dynamics. The development of this metaperspective is helpful to the client in that it helps promote an ability to observe his or her "self" in interaction with others, thereby developing an "observing system" that is analogous to what McCormack in Chapter 3 terms the "depressive-subjective" mode of perceiving and relating. This metaperspective is also helpful to therapists in encouraging them to observe and be aware of their own place in the therapeutic process, and how they are affected by the client's and the family's transference processes.

Finally, a central tenet of the systemic perspective is that clients' symptoms make sense in the context in which they originally occurred. This orientation encourages therapists to explore the source or origins of seemingly "crazy" or "irrational" client behaviors to determine how they originally evolved, and to better understand why they are being played out or enacted in transference interactions in clients' current relationships.

An Interpersonal Approach

Benjamin's (1996) interpersonal approach to understanding and treating personality disorders can provide a bridge between individual psychodynamic approaches and a family systems perspective. Because Benjamin outlines her structural analysis of social behavior (SASB) model in Chapter Two of this text, this approach will not be explored in detail.

In essence, Benjamin's SASB model suggests that interpersonal behaviors may be conceptualized in terms of two intersecting interpersonal dimensions or polarities: an affiliative or love/hate dimension, and an interdependence (enmeshment/differentiation or taking control/giving autonomy) dimension (see Chapter 2, Figure 2.1, for an illustration of these dimensions). Interpersonal positions along these dimensions may be directed at another person (focus on others), may be reactions to another person's (perceived) initiations (focus on self), or may represent the way individuals relate to themselves (introject). Benjamin describes the baseline SASB positions for BPD individuals as being **CONTROL, BLAME, ATTACK, ACTIVE LOVE** (focus on others), <u>TRUST</u> (focus on self), and *SELF-ATTACK, SELF-*

NEGLECT, and *SELF-PROTECT* (introjects). For the BPD individual, his or her

> baseline position is one of friendly dependency on a nurturer, which becomes hostile control if the caregiver or lover fails to deliver enough (and there is never enough). There is a belief that the provider secretly if not overtly likes dependency and neediness, and a vicious introject attacks the self if there are signs of happiness or success. (Benjamin, 1996, p. 124)

This vicious introject accounts for the self-destructive behavioral patterns described in the DSM-IV.

Benjamin outlines pathogenic hypotheses in family of origin dynamics and experiences to account for characteristic interpersonal processes in BPD relationships. Her model helps therapists conceptualize BPD psychodynamics, symptoms, and behaviors in interpersonal terms, and understand typical transference interactions and therapeutic impasses. For BPD, Benjamin (1996) postulates that pathogenic experiences include: (1) a pattern of chaos in the family of origin; (2) a developmental history that includes traumatic abandonment experiences; (3) a pattern of physical or sexual abuse that often leads to an internalization of the abuser and a pattern of self-sabotage; and (4) an experience that misery, sickness, and debilitation draw love and concern. These family of origin experiences give rise to an interpersonal style marked by a morbid fear of abandonment and a wish for protective nurturance.

Benjamin outlines five categories of "correct response" for dealing with personality disorders, including: facilitating collaboration; facilitating pattern recognition; blocking maladaptive patterns; strengthening the will to give up maladaptive patterns; and facilitating new learning. The focus here is on pattern recognition and pattern change, not simply insight. Interventions may be drawn from family therapy, psychodynamic, cognitive-behavioral, and other models, as long as they contribute to one of the five categories of "correct response." Benjamin's interpersonal approach fits well with the integrative framework of this treatment model, and the pattern of interventive interviewing using circular and reflexive questions described earlier provides an excellent tool for achieving this pattern recognition and change.

A Psychodynamic Approach

Because individuals displaying BPD symptoms seem to have deficits in their sense of self, an understanding of psychodynamic principles is essential to successful treatment. A psychodynamic perspective can help therapists understand both the intrapsychic and interpersonal processes that influence or drive a BPD individual's behavior and interpersonal interactions, including transference reactions to significant others and therapists. A psychodynamic approach can also be helpful in understanding the origins of these behaviors in early developmental experiences and family interactions.

Again, a thorough review of psychodynamic theory is beyond the scope of this chapter. McCormack, in Chapter 3, provides an excellent overview of the psychodynamic approach as it applies to personality disorders and couples therapy. A number of other authors, including Koch and Ingram (1985), Slipp (1995), Solomon (1998), and Lachkar (1998) outline integrative systemic/object relations approaches to working with personality disorders and BPD in particular. Lachkar and Solomon both address borderline/narcissistic couples and their interlocking patterns of interaction, a pairing of personality disordered individuals that is frequently found in clinical practice.

Excellent summaries of the basic elements of psychodynamic theory needed by marriage and family therapists can also be found in M. P. Nichols (1987) and W. C. Nichols (1996). There are a number of key psychodynamic concepts with which therapists working with BPD should be familiar. *Splitting* refers to a primitive defense mechanism in which individuals split the good from the bad in other individuals or in themselves, in order to reduce the intrapsychic anxiety and conflict associated with facing the reality of both good and bad being together in the same person. In denying or splitting the bad in themselves, they can avoid anxiety regarding an anticipated abandonment, or punishment, and also avoid triggering their harsh and punishing introjected parent. This splitting is the source of the hallmark BPD alternation between idealization and devaluation.

Introjection refers to the internalization of a significant other, along with the dominant affects associated with that person. For instance, an image of a parent may be introjected, along with the critical affect with which the parent was associated. *Projection* refers to the process of casting out those parts of oneself that are unacceptable, and seeing those parts in other individuals. This is a defense against the anxiety of recognizing parts of oneself that would be unacceptable to a critical parent figure, and which would run the risk of provoking punishment from that figure or from the internalized critical introject. *Projective identification* is the process of externalizing a feeling or attitude, projecting it onto another person, then relating to that other person in a collusive manner so as to encourage them to display the qualities that are being projected onto them. An example would be an angry person projecting his or her anger onto a spouse, then behaving in such a way as to encourage the spouse to be angry, thus confirming the validity of the projection. Finally, *collusion* is the process by which two (or more) individuals or family members participate in a mutual process of projective identification through which their individual projections are confirmed and acted out. Each spouse, consciously, or often unconsciously, participates in this process. From a systemic perspective, this collaborative process would, in most cases, be seen as being a result of evolving systems rather than a deliberate or conscious process.

A Cognitive-Behavioral Approach

Because so much of BPD presentation involves cognitive distortions that affect both self-image and interpersonal perception, cognitive behavioral therapies offer a valuable method of intervention. There are a number of excellent works applying a cognitive-behavioral approach to working with personality disorders, including Sperry (1999) and Beck, Freeman, and Associates (1990). The cognitive aspect of cognitive-behavioral therapy (CBT) focuses on challenging and altering dysfunctional cognitions, automatic thoughts, and core maladaptive schemas. CBT therapists use a variety of techniques to challenge and promote change in erroneous belief systems, including: cost-benefit analysis, behavioral experiments, replacing negative thoughts with more balanced thoughts, direct challenges to dichotomized "either-or" thinking, overgeneralization, magnification, fortune-telling, and so forth. In focusing on core maladaptive schemas for BPD individuals, CBT therapists pay particular attention to characteristic BPD schemas or core belief systems such as feelings of unloveability/defectiveness, fear of abandonment/loss, and issues revolving around dependency/incompetence (Sperry, 1999). In many respects, the schemas or core belief systems CBT therapists focus on parallel the interpersonal "maps"of reality or belief systems that the systemic approach sees as guiding behavior and underlying an individual's constructions of reality. Given this similarity of viewpoints, the CBT approach and the systemic approach are easily integrated, and provide a powerful tool for creating change in BPD perceptions.

CBT therapists also focus specifically on maladaptive behavior patterns, and as with Benjamin's (1996) approach, endeavor to promote pattern recognition and pattern change. To this end, they incorporate a variety of techniques and strategies aimed at altering dysfunctional interpersonal BPD behavioral patterns, including: anger management training, relaxation training, communication skills training, limit setting, and problem-solving training. Confrontation regarding problematic behavioral patterns is a key part of this approach, as well as encouraging the development of more healthy interpersonal skills and behaviors.

A Psychoeducational Approach

Psychoeducational approaches for both individuals and families have proven very effective in treating serious mental illnesses such as schizophrenia and bipolar disorder (Goldstein and Miklowitz, 1995). Recently, some researchers and clinicians have been applying similar psychoeducational approaches to working with BPD (Gunderson, Berkowitz, and Ruiz-Sancho, 1997; Berkowitz and Gunderson, 2002). Using multifamily groups, these authors help BPD individuals and their families to understand and cope with three significant BPD deficits in functioning: affect and impulse dyscontrol, dichotomous thinking, and intolerance for aloneness. A psychoeducational approach can help the BPD individual to recognize ways that these deficits cause problems in their current relationships, and to realize that even though they may have had valid reasons for developing these feelings, perceptions, and behavioral reactions in early experiences, these previous experiences are not necessarily a useful guide to behavior in their present relationships. When BPD individuals learn to recognize their affective and interpersonal patterns, they can begin to choose how they will respond to their feelings, rather than acting out their feelings regardless of the impact on others or the realities of their present situation.

Families are also helped through psychoeducation to recognize triggers to BPD crises and acting-out behaviors, and are helped to interrupt these triggers by reducing family stress levels, improving crisis management skills, and reducing expressed emotion (EE). Berkowitz and Gunderson (2002) outline fifteen guidelines for families of BPD individuals, including: "go slowly"—lower expectations and recognize that change will take time; "keep things cool"—speak calmly, maintain routines, and find time to talk and problem solve when not in crisis; and limit setting, "be direct, but careful"—set clear and consistent limits, don't tolerate abusiveness, tantrums, threats or hitting, but be cautious about using threats and ultimatums that can rupture the relationship with the BPD individual, use them only as a last resort. Although these authors apply their psychoeducational approach in multifamily group settings, the psychoeducational principles they outline can be readily adapted to individual and family therapy sessions in an outpatient setting, and they integrate well with the other elements of this model.

A Psychobiological Approach

As discussed earlier, increasing evidence exists for a biological basis to personality disorders, and in particular, to BPD. There is evidence for family transmission of hallmark borderline personality characteristics (Silverman et al., 1991), which suggests the possible presence of a genetic component to BPD, and BPD is frequently found in parents and other family members of individuals diagnosed with BPD (van Reekum, Links, and Boiago, 1993). Researchers have also found that medication, particularly selective serotonin reuptake Inhibitors (SSRIs) has been associated with global improvement in some patients with BPD (Markovitz, 2001). These findings suggest (but do not prove) that part of the cause of BPD is biological.

These research findings regarding the presence of a biological component to BPD are shared with clients and families as part of the psychoeducational process. When BPD symptoms are seen as being, at least in part, a product of biological or biochemical factors rather than a result of "bad" behavior or "bad" parenting, guilt and blame are often reduced in the family system. Many BPD symptoms, including depression, anxiety, self-destructive behavior, anger outbursts, impulsivity, and cognitive disturbance, respond well to treatment with medication. Families and BPD clients are often encouraged to know that appropriate medication can help to reduce or manage BPD symptoms, and this gives families hope for improvement. It is important, however, that BPD individuals and their families don't use this information regarding biological factors to avoid taking responsibility for managing the illness and dealing with family and relationship problems. Biological factors are only part of the whole picture. BPD is a complex, multidetermined illness, and many aspects of the illness are not biologically based. Both the BPD client and his or her family members can and should be held accountable for making needed interpersonal and behavioral changes to better manage their lives and relationships.

Coccaro and Siever (1995) as well as Siever and Davis (1991) provide a framework for understanding psychobiological underpinnings of BPD and choosing effective pharmacological treatment strategies. They describe several dimensions or domains in which BPD individuals experience deficits that may be biologically determined. These dimensions include: cognitive/perceptual organization, which is possibly associated with dysfunction in the dopamine neurotransmitter systems; impulsivity/aggression, which may be associated with disturbances in the serotonin neurotransmitter systems; affective instability, which may be associated with problems in the norepinephrine or serotonin neurotransmitters; and an anxiety/inhibition dimension, which may also be associated with serotonergic dysfunction. Although research into the psychobiology of BPD and other personality disorders is still in its infancy, the finding that many individuals with BPD symptoms experience marked improvement with appropriate medication makes the incorporation of a psychobiological and pharmacological treatment approach a necessity in an integrated treatment model for BPD.

CASE EXAMPLE

Peter Legere referred himself for counseling for depression following his separation from Susan, his wife of eight years. Peter and Susan had two children, Daniel (four) and Kyle (six). Peter worked as a high school teacher in a nearby city, commuting about an hour to work each day. The couple had just moved to the area from another city to be closer to Susan's parents. Peter indicated that a major precipitating factor in the separation had been his own pattern of acting "crazy" in response to the stress and anxiety of moving, his increased drinking in response to the stress of relocating, his blaming attitude toward Susan for initiating this change, and his own feelings of self-doubt, inadequacy, and fear regarding his ability to function in his new teaching position.

Although Peter's initial presentation was consistent with a simple Axis I diagnosis of reactive depression, as treatment progressed, it soon became clear that in addition to depression, he also suffered from borderline personality disorder and had elements of passive-aggressive personality disorder (PAG) as well. This type of comorbidity of BPD with other personality disorders and Axis I disorders is often typical. One can see the presence of BPD traits in his self-destructive drinking, his pattern of blaming or devaluing Susan for initiating the relocation, and in his identity issues and fears regarding his own inadequacy.

Peter was the youngest of two siblings, with a brother five years older. Peter reported that his brother also suffered from depression, was treated with medications, and was on disability. Peter's parents were of French Canadian background, although they had lived most of their life in English-speaking Ontario, where Peter had grown up. Peter's mother died suddenly of a combination of alcohol and drug overdose when he was thirteen. Peter indicates that his mother was an alcoholic and had a history of depression, and some question arose as to whether she may have committed suicide. Peter was the first to find her after her death. Peter describes his relationship with his mother as alternating between an enmeshed closeness, in which he would listen to her for hours as she complained about her life and his father, and a rejected distance when she was drinking and emotionally unavailable.

Peter's father was described as distant and critical. A high level of conflict existed between Peter's father and mother, and the father seemed to deal with his wife's drinking by avoiding her and absenting himself from the home, leaving Peter behind with his inebriated mother. Peter felt his father was always disappointed in him, and this had a major impact on Peter's self-esteem. Peter said his father would call him "a wimp" if he showed unhappiness, and Peter learned early to hide his vulnerable feelings. Peter remembers his father mocking him regarding a scented soap he used when going out to a party, and this type of undermining had a profound effect on Peter's social confidence. Peter avoided social interactions, and rarely invited friends to his home because his father's temper was very unpredictable. Peter always wanted to please his father, and tried hard to do so, but was rarely successful. Over time, Peter came to accept and internalize his father's view of himself as a failure, but he remained angry at his father for the unfairness of this judgment. Peter did experience a brief period of closeness with his father after his mother's death, but his father soon remarried and Peter did not get along with his stepmother. His father died a few years later when Peter was nineteen.

Peter also reported a history of childhood sexual abuse by an older male. His abuser was a man who ran a store in his community. Peter indicated that this man "was like a second father," providing support and nurturing that he did not get from his own father. When the man began abusing him by fondling, Peter felt betrayed, and experienced a great deal of identity confusion. During his teen years, Peter wondered whether he was a homosexual, and he reported a pattern of drinking in social situations to reduce his anxiety regarding sexual identity issues.

The information regarding Peter's family and early history was elicited through a pattern of systemic circular questioning early in the assessment process. From a psychodynamic perspective, one can see the seeds of many of Peter's personal issues affecting his relationships and interpersonal interactions. Peter introjected his father's critical view of him, leading to feelings of inadequacy, low self-esteem, and a tendency to punish and sabotage himself with self-destructive drinking binges, and suicidal acting-out behavior when he felt criticized or inadequate. Peter had a very ambivalent relationship with authority figures in his life, such as his principal. He desperately wanted their recognition and approval, but at the same time he resented the control they exercised, and would engage them in power struggles in a process of projective identification aimed at asserting his autonomy. His later relationships with partners reflected the pattern of emotional ambivalence in his relationship with his mother. He sought nurturance from his partners, but seemed to choose partners who were often cold, distant, or self-involved, much as his mother was when drinking.

Peter's early experiences also parallel the pathogenic hypotheses described by Benjamin (1996) for the development of BPD, including a pattern of chaos in the family of origin due to his mother's drinking, a developmental history of traumatic abandonment (mother's unavailability when drinking, father's emotional and physical absence, mother's death), a history of physical or sexual abuse, and an experience of emotional closeness with his mother that was associated with supporting her in her misery. As Peter's family history began to unfold, connections were made between his early experiences and his present pattern of relating to others, and he was assisted in making connections through both psychodynamic and psychoeducational interventions.

During the first nine months Peter was in treatment, the focus was largely on adjustment to his marital separation, and on grief/loss issues due to not being able to spend as much time with his children as he would like. Peter was very close with both boys, and was determined that they should not experience the absence of a close relationship with their father that he had to deal with. Peter tended to project his anger at the situation onto his wife Susan, who he saw as cold, distant, and controlling, and considerable conflict existed over custody and access issues. Peter was often confronted regarding ways he escalated situations by his combative approach to Susan, and was encouraged to recognize that his emotional intensity was inappropriate, and was rooted more in his father's abuse of authority than in real failings on Susan's part.

Attention was also devoted to addressing his depression. Peter was referred to a psychiatrist at the center for assessment and medication treatment. Peter's relationship with psychiatrists was also characteristic of many BPD individuals. When he first began meeting with a psychiatrist, he was convinced that this was the first doctor to really understand him and his problems, and he believed that everything would be better once the right medication to treat his problems was found. When medications prescribed by the psychiatrists did not completely remove his depression and negative feelings about himself, Peter would blame the psychiatrists, claiming they were incompetent. This process of alternating idealization and devaluation stems from the primitive intrapsychic defense of splitting that Peter likely developed to deal with his ambivalent feelings toward his inconsistently nurturing and rejecting mother. Peter consulted with a total of four psychiatrists during the time he was seen, making private arrangements to be assessed by "experts" outside the center. During the course of his treatment, Peter was prescribed a variety of medications by these psychiatrists, including oxazepam, clonazepam, and Xanax (for anxiety); and imipramine, trimipramine, Prozac, Paxil, trazodone, Luvox, Zoloft, Wellbutrin, and Celexa (for depression). Peter jumped from one psychiatrist to another and one medication to another, desperately, but unsuccessfully, trying to escape from his feelings.

Medication was an essential component of Peter's treatment. He was most stable on Prozac, and later on a mix of Celexa and Wellbutrin. Given that Peter had a brother who also suffers from depression, and that his mother suffered from depression, there was good reason to believe that he had, in part, a biological basis for his depression. Psychoeducational interventions supported Peter's use of antidepressant medications, but also emphasized the presence of psychodynamic and family-of-origin factors contributing to the development of Peter's BPD. It was often necessary to remind Peter of these psychological factors contributing to his depressed mood and interpersonal problems, and to confront him with the reality that although medications could help, medications alone were not the answer. He would not get better until he started looking at his feelings and maladaptive behavior patterns in a serious way, took responsibility for his issues, and stopped projecting the blame for his interpersonal difficulties onto others. This was a difficult concept for Peter to grasp.

About nine months into his treatment, Peter met and became involved with Marie, a woman he met on a vacation to Quebec. Part of the attraction may have been a similarity of family ethnic backgrounds. Another aspect of the attraction for Peter was that Marie seemed to be giving him lots of emotional "strokes," providing the promise of a partner who would prop up his fragile sense of self-esteem. Peter and Marie were seen in a conjoint therapy session early in their relationship, and it was obvious that Peter's BPD issues would cause problems in the relationship. In the initial session, Marie presented as reserved, independent, and self-possessed, almost to the point of seeming detached. Peter was presenting in this session as needy, negative, and critical of himself, seeking affirmation and sympathy, but inviting criticism through his self-denigrating behavior.

Marie and her nine-year-old daughter moved from Quebec to live with Peter, but it wasn't long before problems surfaced in the relationship. It seemed that Marie was not able to meet the demands Peter placed on her for her time and affection, and she gradually grew resentful, and began to withdraw, much as Peter's father had done. Peter's drinking increased, and he became more depressed. He began to act out in his job at the high school, leading to conflict with his principal. Typically, he failed to take responsibility for his actions, blaming the school administration for a lack of understanding. The situation escalated, with a series of drug and alcohol overdoses over a period of several months that were reminiscent of his mother's behavior, and that led to police intervention and multiple hospitalizations. These overdoses seemed aimed toward coercing Marie into nurturing and rescuing behavior, but actually had the opposite effect of increasing her frustration and alienating her even further.

A number of couples sessions were held with Marie and Peter during this period of crisis, but they tended to be crisis-driven, and Marie was very reluctant to engage in a process of looking at herself or her part in the process. In particular, Marie was not open to discussing Peter's issues regarding his feeling of disconnection with her and her lack of warmth and intimacy. At one point, Peter indicated the couple had not had sexual relations in over a year. Psychoeducational interventions aimed at helping Marie to understand Peter's illness and interrupt the escalating circular interactional pattern of criticism and withdrawal were largely unsuccessful. Marie tended to blame Peter, and saw the entire situation as his fault. This pattern of blame and critisicm triggered Peter's own vicious introject from his critical father, and served to add fuel to his own self-destructive, attention-seeking behaviors. Marie seemed to have some narcissistic personality disorder qualities, and could be quite cold and distant, focusing on her own needs and leaving Peter to struggle with his own feelings of rejection. As discussed earlier, the narcissistic/borderline marriage is not an unusual pattern in personality-disordered couples.

Eventually, the crisis escalated to the point where Peter left work on disability for a year. This began an intensive period of therapeutic work focused on pattern recognition and changing maladaptive patterns. Through a series of systemic questions and CBT interventions, Peter was able to recognize key triggers to his acting-out behavior. Peter identified four major triggers: concern and stress regarding lack of money due to his impulsive spending, which left him feeling like the failure his father had always said he was; issues regarding not feeling valued by authority figures, particularly in his job as a teacher (these issues also stemmed from his relationship with his father); stress and conflict regarding custody and access issues with Susan; and conflict and feelings of being unloved by Marie.

Peter was able to recognize that these issues triggered old schemas or belief systems that portrayed him as being a failure and unlovable, and also old grief and loss issues regarding unmet emotional needs. When these old schemas were triggered, he would find himself catapulted back to an emotional ego state to when he was about age six or seven, feeling unloved or unfairly punished, and he would either relate to others in the present from this six-year-old whiney, attention-seeking, ego state; or he would lash out at others in anger for treating him unfairly and not understanding him. These reactions inevitably led to problems in his current relationships, and resulted in criticism and rejection that further fueled the dysfunctional cyclic interactions.

A variety of interventions were used to help Peter move past these patterns of behavior, and to develop new and more appropriate responses to frustrated needs and conflictual interpersonal relationships in the present. Peter was taught relaxation skills to deal with his anxiety, and help him to self-soothe. Peter was also taught communication and assertiveness skills to help him deal with conflict more appropriately. Cognitive interventions were used to help Peter recognize typical cognitive distortions or errors in thinking, such as fortune-telling (in which he would anticipate rejection or negative responses to his requests), magnification (in which he would take a small error on his part and magnify it to the point where it seemed as though his entire efforts were useless, making himself feel like a failure), mind reading (in which he would believe that others were thinking the worst of him), and black-and-white thinking (in which he would believe that if he couldn't do something the way he wanted to do it, there was no point in doing it at all). Therapy also focused on grieving the lost nurturing that he never had in his childhood, and on recognizing that it is unrealistic to expect others in the present to provide what he missed as a child, and that trying to coerce others to provide what he missed will inevitably lead to problems in his current relationships due to his anger at never feeling loved enough.

A process of systemic questioning was used with Peter to deconstruct messages and belief systems Peter had learned in his family that led to schemas or perceptions of himself as unlovable and unworthy of being loved. As a teacher, Peter had a good knowledge of child development, and a passionate commitment to the children he taught. Peter was able to recognize that he was entitled to be cared for and loved by his parents in an entirely different way than he had been. Eventually, Peter was able to construct a new story or narrative for his life that challenged his negative view of himself based on his father's criticism and his mother's inconsistent affections. In this new story, built on remembered successes drawn out by a series of systemic questions about past events and successes in his life that he had ignored or discounted, Peter was no longer a failure. He was, instead, a person who had the courage and determination to become a successful teacher despite the handicap of parents who had been unable to provide for his emotional needs.

As Peter had an opportunity to grieve past losses and learned to recognize his maladaptive interpersonal patterns and substitute more healthy and adaptive behaviors, his relationships with friends, co-workers, and authority figures improved, his depression lifted, and his pattern of self-destructive acting out declined. Unfortunately, Peter's relationship with Marie did not last. Marie decided to separate, and this was a difficult time for Peter, with a brief period of renewed acting out. However, Peter had made enough progress in recognizing and dealing with his own issues that he was able to re-center himself and move forward with his life.

Peter returned to work, and made a successful reintegration into the workplace. He focused more on the joy he received from teaching and reaching out to his students, and less on the frustrations of school politics and periodic slights he received from other staff at the school that, in the past, had triggered his feelings of worthlessness. Peter was able to trust "the system" enough to begin a process of applying for custody of his two sons, and eventually he and Susan reached an agreement that the boys would come to live with him when the oldest started high school. Peter also met and began a new relationship with a woman who taught at a local elementary school. With an improved awareness of his own issues, this relationship seemed to be moving in a much more positive direction than his relationship with Marie. Peter's therapy concluded about five years after he first began treatment. I still see him from time to time in the community, and he reports that he is stable and that things are going well for him with his new partner and with his sons.

STRENGTHS AND LIMITATIONS

One of the major strengths of the integrative systemic therapy approach is that it combines a variety of treatment models that have proven treatment efficacy, thereby providing clinicians with a tremendous amount of flexibility in intervening in problematic BPD family dynamics. The cognitive-behavioral therapy component of IST is well researched and documented as effective. A number of excellent manuals for CBT are available, including the texts by Sperry (1999) and by Beck, Freeman, and Associates (1990) mentioned earlier, that deal specifically with personality disorders. Solid research evidence exists for the utility and effectiveness of the psychobiological and pharmacological elements of the model. The psychodynamic components of IST have, for many years, been found to be clinically useful in treating personality disorders. Although the clinical utility of Benajamin's interpersonal SASB model is not quite as well researched, it too, is based in sound clinical and empirical findings. The psychoeducational component of the model is only beginning to be researched as applied to treatment of BPD individuals and their families, but the psychoeducational principles on which this model is founded have been demonstrated as effective in a variety of studies of psychoeducational family therapy for schizophrenia and bipolar disorder. The systemic treatment approach that forms the core of this model is also well accepted and had demonstrated its utility and effectiveness in a variety of settings.

One disadvantage of the IST approach is that it is a complex model that requires a high degree of training and clinical skill. Psychodyanmic concepts are complex, and many therapists trained in marriage and family therapy are not well versed in psychodynamic models and interventions. Likewise, CBT is a treatment approach that requires a specific knowledge base and set of skills to apply effectively. Although IST offers a great deal of flexibility, it does require a skilled clinician to blend the various elements of the model into a smooth exploration of therapeutic issues, and to choose and implement the wide range of interventions offered by the model's diverse elements.

Finally, although this approach to psychotherapy for BPD individuals and their families can be applied briefly, it is not a brief therapy model. Benjamin (1996) states that, "The fastest possible reconstruction of a personality disorder will take at least one year, and the normative one two years or more" (p. 89). Even Magnavita (1997), writing about short-term dynamic therapy for personality disorders, notes that short-term therapy of personality disorders may range from twelve to forty sessions, and for treatment refractory groups, up to eighty sessions.

Entrenched personality patterns such as those found in individuals with BPD are not easily amenable to change, and often third-party insurers are reluctant to provide reimbursement for the long-term therapies necessary to establish stable and lasting changes in BPD symptoms. Increasingly, however, research such as that summarized by Gabbard (2000) is documenting the cost savings inherent in effective treatment of personality disorders, even if such treatment is long term. When one considers Peter's situation, with the costs of repeated hospitalizations, response by emergency services, visits to numerous psychiatrists, third-party reimbursement for multiple medications, disability payments for a year off work, and other associated expenses, one can see that psychotherapy that interrupts these costly patterns of acting-out behaviors becomes a bargain, even if it takes a number of years to achieve results.

BENEFITS FOR THE FAMILY

Any treatment that leads to improvement in BPD symptoms and acting-out behavior will inevitably benefit the family of the BPD individual. The IST approach has a number of advantages that make it particularly helpful to family members. The systemic approach is a treatment model that is very respectful of clients. Karl Tomm (1992), in his lectures, outlines a number of ethical positions that therapists can take with families. He insists that respect is the highest ethical posture. The systemic principle of therapeutic neutrality orients practitioners toward a nonblaming approach to families, that is curious about how family members relate to one another, and how families are affected by the BPD member's symptoms. The narrative component of this model, pioneered by White and Epston (1990), is also known for its highly respectful attitude toward clients, and for its active efforts to counter "pathologizing discourses" that may lead families to feel blamed for their loved one's problems.

The psychoeducational component of the IST treatment approach also provides many benefits for BPD families. As with families of individuals with serious mental illnesses, families of BPD individuals often feel mystified and exhausted by aspects of their relative's illness, and feel excluded from the treatment process, or blamed by treatment providers. The psychoeducational perspective adds an inclusive element to the treatment model and actively works to involve families in their loved one's treatment. Therapists are interested in how the BPD individual's behavior affects others in the family, and are active in their efforts to share information that can help family members better understand their loved one's behavior, and improve their skills for helping and coping with their BPD relative.

INDICATIONS AND CONTRAINDICATIONS

The integrative systemic therapy approach is highly flexible and appropriate for many BPD clients and their families. However, the use of conjoint sessions is contraindicated in some situations. Conjoint family therapy would not be indicated in cases in which the BPD client is actively psychotic, but family meetings without the psychotic BPD family member may be quite appropriate to provide family members with information and reassurance. Conjoint sessions also would be inappropriate when relationships with the BPD individual's family of origin are so toxic, conflictual, or blaming that conjoint family sessions would be destructive to the individuals involved or destabilizing to the BPD client. This may be the case when there is an extensive and unacknowledged history of physical, sexual or emotional abuse, or when there are high levels of blaming behavior from family members, or from the BPD individuals themselves. In such cases, it is normally best to proceed with individual therapy for the BPD client.

Depending on the situation and family background, psychoeducational interventions with family members may play a role in reducing conflict and increasing understanding of the BPD client, as well as exploring any role family members may play in interactions with the BPD client. However, if the primary BPD client is uncomfortable with his or her family having any contact or sharing information, or if these psychoeducational family meetings are simply being used by family members to triangle the therapist and deliver negative messages to the BPD client, then psychoeducational sessions may not be possible.

MANAGEMENT OF TRANSFERENCE ISSUES

Clients with BPD are noted for their pattern of engaging therapists in transference reactions, either attempting to coerce the therapist into providing unconditional love and nurturance, or threatening and venting their anger at their therapist for perceived abandonments. It is essential for therapists working with BPD individuals and their families to be familiar with typical BPD transference reactions, and to have well-developed skills for dealing with these transference reactions.

One advantage of an approach that involves the BPD family members directly in the therapy process is that transference reactions are more likely to be played out in front of the therapist with the BPD's significant others than to be enacted between the therapist and the client. When transference interactions between family members occur in the therapy session, the therapist has an opportunity to interrupt dysfunctional relationship patterns, clarify intentions and interpretations, and encourage new and healthier ways of interacting. Furthermore, knowing the family members involved helps the therapist avoid being triangled or drawn into the BPD individual's construction of reality or view of his or her family with all of its distortions. This allows the therapist to maintain a neutral position with regard to other family members and their motivations, to help the BPD client to "reality test" their perceptions, and to be flexible in exploring alternate views of reality that may be more helpful to the BPD client in relating to family members.

When other family members are not available and therapists are working individually with the BPD client, managing transference will involve using psychodynamic principles and interventions to increase the BPD client's awareness of the ways he or she is replaying old family interactional patterns in the relationship with the therapist and with others in his or her life. To do this effectively, the therapist must remain centered emotionally and differentiated from the client's emotional processes. The countertransference reactions that the therapist feels are most likely guides to how others in the BPD individual's interpersonal sphere feel and react to the BPD client. If the therapist can share his or her reactions in a safe and nonblaming way, then the client can benefit from these reflections and become more aware of his or her impact on others and why others react to him or her as they do. The therapist's ability to self-supervise by adopting a meta-perspective or "observing systems" stance in relationship to interactions with the client is a critical skill. Regular supervision is also of critical importance to therapists treating BPD individuals, and can be extremely helpful in maintaining this "observing systems" perspective and managing transference.

MANAGEMENT OF CRISES AND ACTING-OUT BEHAVIOR

BPD clients are also known for their frequency of crises and their tendency toward acting-out behavior. It is not unusual for BPD clients to contact their therapists when experiencing a crisis (often one they had a role in provoking), and to want their therapist to drop everything and see them immediately to "fix" their problem. At times the crisis is one of suicidal feelings, or an actual suicide attempt. The therapist is faced with a dilemma. If they respond, they reinforce acting-out behavior that is often aimed at coercing caretaking by the therapist to prove that the therapist "loves" them. If they don't respond, they will be faced with accusations of callous abandonment by the client, and may be in violation of legal or ethical requirements for failing to respond appropriately to a life-threatening situation.

Being clear with the BPD client about personal and therapeutic boundaries is often a first step in managing crisis behaviors. Clear, firm boundaries accompanied by a warm and caring attitude can provide the BPD client with a safe therapeutic environment to work through old issues. When clients act out, they are enacting old transference reactions with the therapist. When the therapist can stay connected and emotionally available, and at the same time be firm about personal and therapeutic boundaries, BPD clients have an opportunity, perhaps for the first time in their life, to experience a relationship with someone who does not reject them for "bad" behavior. This allows them to begin the process of integrating their "good" and "bad" views of self and other, and to move beyond their primitive defense of splitting and the alternating idealization and devaluation of others that accompanies this defense.

Unfortunately, the reality of the crisis the BPD client presents sometimes requires protective responses from the therapist. These protective responses may at times involve involuntary hospitalization for the client. As Benjamin notes in Chapter 2, crisis response is not therapy, and therapy stops while crisis response is being delivered. Once the client returns to therapy (if they do), then therapy resumes with an examination of the crisis and an exploration of the interpersonal meaning of the caretaking response he or she forced the therapist into taking. It is also made clear to the client that this type of crisis response is not what therapy is about, and that it interferes with the process of therapy, and delays their ultimate recovery. Through this exploration process, the client hopefully begins to develop an increased awareness of his or her maladaptive behavior patterns, and to move toward more adaptive methods of meeting emotional needs and managing interpersonal relationships.

INTEGRATION WITH PSYCHIATRIC SERVICES AND ROLE OF MEDICATION

When BPD clients act out, more is going on for them than just a conscious or unconscious manipulation of the people around them. One of the key aspects of BPD is that BPD individuals are often flooded and overwhelmed with the intensity of their emotions. As McCormack indicates in Chapter 3, the BPD individual experiences emotions in a manner that is characteristic of a much earlier stage of development, in which little separation between their "self" and his or her emotional state exists. The client's fragile sense of "self" is overwhelmed by the intensity of his or her emotions, and he or she is driven to act to seek immediate relief, with little concern for how it is obtained, or how such actions affect others. BPD individuals need assistance in moderating the intensity of their emotional reactions, and appropriate use of medication is one avenue to provide this relief.

As discussed earlier, increasingly solid evidence suggests the presence of a biological component in BPD, and psychopharmacological interventions are therefore a valid and useful tool. Therapists should not hesitate to refer clients to a psychiatrist for medication review, or to dialogue with a client's family physician regarding medication options. Most family physicians will appreciate knowledgeable input from therapists to help them with BPD individuals, who can often be challenging patients. Ideally, the prescribing physician should use a model such as that outlined by Griffith et al. (1991), which emphasizes that medication is only a part of the overall treatment for BPD, and that it is intended as an adjunct to psychotherapy, not as a replacement. Often, if the intensity of the BPD individual's emotional reactions can be reduced, he or she is more able to tolerate and explore his or her feelings in therapy, and self-soothe and moderate his or her behavior in interpersonal relationships, thus facilitating relationship change.

Medications may help manage a number of BPD symptoms, including depression, anxiety, and cognitive distortions. The American Psychiatric Association's (APA) (2001) "Practice Guideline for the Treatment of Patients with Borderline Personality Disorder" uses symptom categories similar to those outlined by Siever and Davis (1991) and Coccaro and Siever (1995), described earlier in this chapter. For treatment of affective dysregulation symptoms, such as mood lability, rejection sensitivity, inappropriate intense anger, depressive "mood crashes," or outbursts of temper, the APA guidelines recommend treatment with SSRI antidepressants. For treatment of impulsive-behavioral dyscontrol symptoms, such as self-mutilation, promiscuous sex, or reckless spending, SSRIs again are the initial choice for treatment. For cognitive-perceptual symptoms, such as suspiciousness, derealization, depersonalization, or hallucinationlike symptoms, the APA recommends low- dose neuroleptics, which may not only improve psychotic symptoms, but also depressed mood, impulsivity, and anger/hostility.

CULTURAL AND GENDER ISSUES

The American Psychiatric Association's (1994) DSM-IV indicates that BPD is diagnosed predominantly (about 75 percent) in females. Swartz et al. (1990) reports similar findings, however Mattia and Zimmerman (2001) note that other studies have found no association between gender and diagnosis of BPD. Some researchers, such as Herman, Perry, and van der Kolk (1989), noting the association between childhood physical, and in particular sexual abuse and BPD, have suggested that the predominance of females among those diagnosed with BPD may be accounted for by the epidemiological findings that females are at two to three times greater risk for sexual abuse than boys. This suggestion should be viewed with caution, however, as it is indicated that sexual abuse is often underreported in males (Hunter, 1990). It is also possible that borderline symptoms in males may be misdiagnosed as conduct disorders, antisocial personality disorder, depression, or other disorders. As Peter's case clearly shows, males too can suffer from BPD, and clinicians need to be alert to the presence of BPD in males, so that they can be accurately diagnosed and receive the help they require.

In terms of cultural issues, the DSM-IV indicates that BPD is not a culture-bound phenomenon, and has been identified in many settings around the world. Caution should be given, however, to cultural factors in making the diagnosis of BPD. Some cultures may display characteristics that parallel BPD symptoms, and it is important not to diagnose individuals with BPD when what they are displaying is in fact normative cultural traits. In Peter's case, for example, he comes from a French-Canadian ethnic background that is similar in many respects to that described by Langelier (1982). Some French Canadians tend to feel that they have been ill treated by the rest of Canada, and can display feelings of anger and entitlement that may appear similar to BPD symptoms. Langelier also notes that many Franco-Americans tend to use defense mechanisms such as denial and displacement, and may blame others for personal inadequacies and failures, and assume a martyred stance. Again, some of these characteristics may apply to French Canadians, and may parallel BPD symptoms. In Peter's case, although cultural factors may have played a small role in his personality presentation, the severity and degree to which his symptoms were displayed across a wide range of situations and interpersonal relationships, including with Marie, who was of French-Canadian background herself, strongly confirms the diagnosis of BPD.

FUTURE DIRECTIONS

In terms of future directions, perhaps the most significant concern is for clinicians working with BPD individuals and their families to incorporate a family-systems perspective into their work. As seen from this chapter, BPD is an illness that has a profound effect on family members. Many family members feel confused and overwhelmed by their loved one's behavior, and are desperately seeking direction and solutions that can help them cope more effectively with BPD symptoms and behaviors. Marriage and family therapists and family psychologists have a great deal to offer BPD families, as well as an important role to play in the treatment of BPD.

In terms of the integrative systemic therapy approach outlined in this chapter, further research into the model's effectiveness in treating BPD and assisting BPD families is clearly needed. Although solid research support exists for many components of the model, the model as a whole is very much in its infancy, and is subject to further validation and development. Indeed, one of the challenges to researching the effectiveness of integrative models such as IST lies in an aspect that is also one of its strengths—flexibility. Integrative models such as IST are often applied differently by different clinicians, thus making it difficult to standardize research designs. Despite this difficulty, research remains possible into many aspects of the model, and perhaps one of the most urgent areas to document is the effect of the approach on improving BPD families' sense of burden and quality of life. If family-oriented intervention models such as IST can help BPD families cope more effectively, relieve their sense of burden, and improve family relationships, they will have demonstrated how much they can offer to BPD individuals and their families.

REFERENCES

American Psychiatric Association (1994). *Diagnostic and statistical manual of mental disorders* (Fourth edition). Washington, DC: American Psychiatric Association.

American Psychiatric Association (2001). "Practice guideline for the treatment of patients with borderline personality disorder." Retrieved August 26, 2002, from <http://www.psych.org/clin_res/borderline.book_1.cfm>.

Anderson, H. and Goolishian, H. A. (1988). Human systems as linguistic systems: Preliminary and evolving ideas about the implications for clinical theory. *Family Process, 27,* 371-393.

Beck, A., Freeman, A., and Associates (1990). *Cognitive therapy of personality disorders.* New York: Guilford Press.

Benjamin, L. S. (1996). *Interpersonal diagnosis and treatment of personality disorders* (Second edition). New York: Guilford Press.

Berkowitz, C. B. and Gunderson, J. G. (2002). Multifamily psychoeducational treatment of borderline personality disorder. In W. R. McFarlane (Ed.), *Multifamily groups in the treatment of severe psychiatric disorders* (pp. 268-290). New York: Guilford Press.

Coccaro, E. F. and Siever, L. J. (1995). The neuropsychopharmacology of personality disorders. In F. E. Bloom and D. J. Kupfer (Eds.), *Psychopharmacology: The fourth generation of progress* (pp. 1567-1579). New York: Raven Press.

Everett, C., Halperin, S., Volgy, S., and Wissler, A. (1989). *Treating the borderline family: A systemic approach.* San Diego: The Psychological Corporation.

Gabbard, G. O. (2000). Psychotherapy of personality disorders. *Journal of Psychotherapy Practice and Research, 9*(1), 1-6.

Glick, I. D., Dulit, R. A., Wachter, E., and Clarkin, J. F. (1995). The family, family therapy, and borderline personality disorder. *Journal of Psychotherapy Practice and Research, 4*(3), 237-246.

Glick, I. D. and Loraas, E. L. (2001). Family treatment of borderline personality disorder. In M. M. MacFarlane (Ed.), *Family therapy and mental health: Innovations in theory and practice* (pp. 135-154). Binghamton, NY: The Haworth Press.

Goldstein, M. J. and Miklowitz, D. J. (1995). The effectiveness of psychoeducational family therapy in the treatment of schizophrenic disorders. *Journal of Marital and Family Therapy, 21,* 361-376.

Griffith, J. L., Griffith, M. E., Meydrech, E., Grantham, D., and Bearden, S. (1991). A model for psychiatric consultation in systemic therapy. *Journal of Marital and Family Therapy, 17,* 291-294.

Gunderson, J. G., Berkowitz, C., and Ruiz-Sancho, A. (1997). Families of borderline patients: A psychoeducational approach. *Bulletin of the Menninger Clinic, 61*(4), 446-457.

Harman, M. J. and Waldo, M. (2001). Family treatment of borderline personality disorder through relationship enhancement therapy. In M. M. MacFarlane (Ed.), *Family therapy and mental health: Innovations in theory and practice* (pp. 215-235). Binghamton, NY: The Haworth Press.

Herman, J. L., Perry, C., and van der Kolk, B. A. (1989). Childhood trauma in borderline personality disorder. *American Journal of Psychiatry, 146*(4), 490-495.

Hoffman, L. (1990). Constructing realities: An art of lenses. *Family Process, 29,* 1-12.

Hunter, M. (1990). *Abused boys: The neglected victims of sexual abuse.* New York: Fawcett Columbine.

Johnson, E. D. (2001). The partnership model: Working with families of people with serious mental illness. In M. M. MacFarlane (Ed.), *Family therapy and mental health: Innovations in theory and practice* (pp. 27-53). Binghamton, NY: The Haworth Press.

Kernberg, O. (1967). Borderline personality organization. *Journal of the American Psychiatric Association, 15,* 641-685.

Kernberg, O. (1975). *Borderline conditions and pathological narcissism.* New York: Jason Aronson.

Koch, A. and Ingram, T. (1985). The treatment of borderline personality disorder within a distressed relationship. *Journal of Marital and Family Therapy, 11*(4), 373-380.

Kreger, R. and Shirley, J. P. (2002). *The stop walking on eggshells workbook: Practical strategies for living with someone who has borderline personality disorder.* Oakland, CA: New Harbinger.

Kreisman, J. J. and Straus, H. (1989). *I hate you—don't leave me: Understanding the borderline personality.* New York: Avon Books.

Lachkar, J. (1998). Narcissistic/borderline couples: A psychodynamic approach to conjoint treatment. In J. Carlson and L. Sperry (Eds.), *The disordered couple* (pp. 259-284). Bristol, PA: Brunner/Mazel.

Langelier, R. (1982). French Canadian families. In M. McGoldrick, J. K. Pearce, and J. Giordano (Eds.), *Ethnicity and family therapy* (pp. 229-246). New York: Guilford Press.

Lebow, J. (1997). The integrative revolution in couple and family therapy. *Family Process, 36,* 1-17.

Links, P. (1992). Family environment and family psychopathology in the etiology of borderline personality disorder. In J. F. Clarkin, E. Marziali, and H. Munroe-Blum (Eds.), *Borderline personality disorder: Clinical and empirical perspectives* (pp. 45-66). New York: Guilford Press.

Links, P. and Munroe-Blum, H. M. (1990). Family environment and borderline personality disorder: Development of etiologic models. In P. S. Links (Ed.), *Family environment and borderline personality disorder* (pp. 3-24). Washington, DC: American Psychiatric Press.

MacFarlane, M. M. (1993). Empowering the client: Toward a systemic, constructivist and narrative treatment approach in Ontario's community mental health centres. In G. Duplessis, M. McCrea, C. Viscoff, and S. Doupe (Eds.), *What works! Innovation in community mental health and addiction treatment programs* (pp. 179-193). Toronto: Canadian Scholar's Press.

MacFarlane, M. M. (2001). Systemic treatment of obsessive-compulsive disorder in a rural community mental health center: An integrative approach. In M. M. MacFarlane (Ed.), *Family therapy and mental health: Innovations in theory and practice* (pp. 155-183). Binghamton, NY: The Haworth Press.

MacFarlane, M. M. (2003). Systemic treatment of depression: An integrative approach. *Journal of Family Psychotherapy, 14*(1), 43-61.

Magnavita, J. J. (1997). *Restructuring personality disorders: A short-term dynamic approach.* New York: Guilford Press.

Markovitz, P. (2001). Pharmacotherapy. In W. J. Livesley (Ed.), *Handbook of personality disorders: Theory, research, and treatment* (pp. 475-493). New York: Guilford Press.

Marziali, E. (1992). The etiology of borderline personality disorder: Developmental factors. In J. F. Clarkin, E. Marziali, and H. Munroe-Blum (Eds.), *Borderline personality disorder: Clinical and empirical perspectives* (pp. 27-44). New York: Guilford Press.

Mason, P. T. and Kreger, R. (1998). *Stop walking on eggshells: Taking your life back when someone you care about has borderline personality disorder.* Oakland, CA: New Harbinger.

Mattia, J. I. and Zimmerman, M. (2001). Epidemiology. In W. J. Livesley (Ed.), *Handbook of personality disorders: Theory, research, and treatment* (pp. 107-123). New York: Guilford Press.

Millon, T. (1992). The borderline construct: Introductory notes on its history, theory, and empirical grounding. In J. F. Clarkin, E. Marziali, and H. Munroe-Blum (Eds.), *Borderline personality disorder: Clinical and empirical perspectives* (pp. 3-23). New York: Guilford Press.

Mitton, M. J. E. and Links, P. S. (1996). Helping the family: A framework for intervention. In P. S. Links (Ed.), *Clinical assessment and management of severe personality disorders* (pp. 195-218). Washington, DC: American Psychiatric Press.

Nichols, M. P. (1987). *The self in the system: Expanding the limits of family psychotherapy.* New York: Brunner/Mazel.

Nichols, W. C. (1996). *Treating people in families: An integrative framework.* New York: Guilford Press.

Paris, J. (2001). Psychosocial adversity. In W. J. Livesley (Ed.), *Handbook of personality disorders: Theory, research, and treatment* (pp. 231-241). New York: Guilford Press.

Siever, L. J. and Davis, K. L. (1991). A psychobiological perspective on the personality disorders. *American Journal of Psychiatry, 148*(12), 1647-1658.

Silverman, J. M., Pinkham, L., Horvath, T. B., Coccaro, E. E., Klar, H., Schear, S., Apter, S., Davidson, M., Mohs, R. C., and Siever, L. J. (1991). Affective and impulsive personality disorder traits in the relatives of patients with borderline personality disorder. *American Journal of Psychiatry, 148*, 1378-1385.

Slipp, S. (1995). Object relations marital therapy of personality disorders. In A. S. Gurman and N. S. Jacobson (Eds.) *Clinical handbook of couple therapy* (pp. 458-470). New York: Guilford Press.

Solomon, M. F. (1998). Treating narcissistic and borderline couples. In J. Carlson and L. Sperry (Eds.), *The disordered couple* (pp. 239-257). Bristol, PA: Brunner/Mazel.

Sperry, L. (1999). *Cognitive behavior therapy of DSM-IV personality disorders: Highly effective interventions for the most common personality disorders.* Philadelphia, PA: Brunner/Mazel.

Stone, M. H. (1990). Abuse and abusiveness in borderline personality. In P. S. Links (Ed.), *Family environment and borderline personality disorder* (pp. 133-148). Washington, DC: American Psychiatric Press.

Swartz, M., Blazer, D., George, L., and Winfield, I. (1990) Estimating the prevalence of borderline personality disorder in the community. *Journal of Personality Disorders, 4*, 257-272.

Tomm, K. (1984a). One perspective on the Milan systemic approach: Part I. Overview of development, theory, and practice. *Journal of Marital and Family Therapy, 10*, 113-125.

Tomm, K. (1984b). One perspective on the Milan systemic approach: Part II. Description of session format, interviewing style, and interventions. *Journal of Marital and Family Therapy, 10*, 253-271.

Tomm, K. (1987a). Interventive interviewing: Part I. Strategizing as a fourth guideline for the therapist. *Family Process, 26*, 3-13.

Tomm, K. (1987b). Interventive interviewing: Part II. Reflexive questioning as a means to enable self-healing. *Family Process, 26*, 167-183.

Tomm, K. (1988). Interventive interviewing: Part III. Intending to ask circular, strategic, or reflexive questions? *Family Process, 27*, 1-15.

Tomm, K. (1992). *Client empowerment through interventive interviewing.* Conference sponsored by Whitby Psychiatric Hospital at Markham, Ontario, Canada, September.

van Reekum, R., Links, P. S., and Boiago, I. (1993). Constitutional factors in borderline personality disorder: Genetics, brain dysfunction, and biological markers. In J. Paris (Ed.), *Borderline personality disorder: Etiology and treatment* (pp. 13-38). Washington, DC: American Psychiatric Press.

White, M. and Epston, D. (1990). *Narrative means to therapeutic ends.* New York: Norton.

Zanarini, M. C., Frankenburg, F. R., Dubo, E. D., Sickel, A. E., Trikha, A., Levin, A., and Reynolds, V. (1998). Axis I comorbidity of borderline personality disorder. *American Journal of Psychiatry, 155*(12), 1733-1739.

Zanarini, M. C., Gunderson, J. G., and Frankenburg, F. R. (1990). Cognitive features of borderline personality disorder. *American Journal of Psychiatry, 147*(1), 57-63.

Zanarini, M.C., Gunderson, J. G., Marino, M. F., Schwartz, E. O., and Frankenburg, F. R. (1989). Childhood experiences of borderline patients. *Comprehensive Psychiatry, 30*(1), 18-25.

Chapter 8

Family Treatment of Passive-Aggressive (Negativistic) Personality Disorder

Jon Carlson
Kimberly A. Melton
Kim Snow

INTRODUCTION

Passive-aggressive personality disorder, more recently referred to as negativistic personality disorder, is listed currently as a personality disorder "not otherwise specified" in an appendix of the fourth edition of the American Psychiatric Association's (APA) *Diagnostic and Statistical Manual of Mental Disorders* (DSM-IV) as well as in the text revision of the DSM-IV (APA, 2000). This disorder is typically characterized as a personality style marked by a pervasive pattern of negativistic and hostile attitudes that are expressed indirectly in passive resistance to demands for adequate performance in both social and occupational functioning (APA, 1994, 2000). This resistance is expressed through procrastination, intentional "forgetting," stubbornness, and inefficiency, particularly in response to tasks assigned by a perceived authority figure.

The term *passive-aggressive personality* originated in a U.S. War Department Technical Bulletin in 1945 (U.S. War Department, 1945). The document acknowledged an "immaturity reaction" exemplified by "passive measures, such as pouting, stubbornness, procrastination, inefficiency, and passive obstructionism." This immaturity reaction represented a passive resistance to the external demands of military life. The term *passive-aggressive* was then used in the Veterans Administration nomenclature of 1949 (U.S. Joint Armed Services, 1949), and subsequently appeared in the first DSM published by the American Psychiatric

Association in 1952. DSM-I listed passive-aggressive personality disorder (PAPD) with three subtypes: passive-dependent, passive-aggressive, and aggressive (APA, 1952). Each of these subtypes was thought to represent manifestations of the same condition, which occurred interchangeably in the same individual.

Diagnostic revisions took place with the publication of DSM-II in 1968, and the passive-dependent or aggressive subtypes were no longer a part of the diagnostic category of PAPD. The DSM-II definition of the disorder identifies a key relational issue that speaks specifically to a "hostility which the individual feels he dare not express openly" (APA, 1968, p. 44). The DSM-II further characterizes the disorder as an "expression of the patient's resentment at failing to find gratification in a relationship with an individual or institution upon which he is overdependent" (APA, 1968, p. 44). (Reprinted with permission from the *Diagnostic and Statistical Manual of Mental Disorders, Second Edition*, copyright 1968 American Psychiatric Association.)

With this revised definition came questions about the reliability of a diagnosis that clearly inferred a hidden motivation (Wetzler and Morey, 1999). Due to problems of reliability and disagreement as to whether PAPD is a pervasive pattern of behavior occurring in a wide range of settings or merely a situational reaction, the DSM-III work group considered removing the disorder. PAPD was included in the DSM-III, however the diagnosis included an exclusion criterion that prevented PAPD from being diagnosed in the presence of any other personality disorder. PAPD was the only personality disorder to have this exclusion criterion (Wetzler and Morey 1999). Furthermore, the DSM-III definition of PAPD was defined narrowly as indirect resistance to external demands as manifested by procrastination, dawdling, stubbornness, intentional inefficiency, and "forgetfulness" (Wetzler and Morey, 1999).

The PAPD exclusion criterion was omitted with the publication of the DSM-III-R (APA, 1987). Moreover, the definition of PAPD included emotional tone, attitudes, interpersonal perception, and interpersonal conflict. The interpretation was expanded to include sulking and unjustifiable protestations, obstructionism, unreasonable criticisms, resentment of suggestions, and inflated appraisal of one's own productivity (Wetzler and Morey, 1999). Despite the DSM-III-R revisions, the diagnostic category was considered unclear and problematic for several reasons. Millon's criticisms of the diagnosis suggested that the disorder had never received widespread clinical acceptance, was defined too narrowly, and was too difficult to differentiate among other personality disorders. To further complicate the diagnosis, some clinicians suggested that the use of passive-aggressive tactics was more of a situational reaction than a stable personality pattern (Wetzler and Morey, 1999).

To address these concerns, the DSM-IV task force decided to include the disorder in the Appendix rather than in the main text. PAPD is listed in the DSM-IV and its text revision (DSM-IV-TR) as passive-aggressive (negativistic) personality disorder. Research criteria for the disorder include

> a pervasive pattern of negativistic attitudes and passive resistance to demands for adequate performance, beginning by early adulthood and present in a variety of contexts, as indicated by four (or more) of the following:
>
> (1)   passively resists fulfilling routine social and occupational tasks
> (2)   complains of being misunderstood and unappreciated by others
> (3)   is sullen and argumentative
> (4)   unreasonably criticizes and scorns authority
> (5)   expresses envy and resentment toward those apparently more fortunate
> (6)   voices exaggerated and persistent complaints of personal misfortune
> (7)   alternates between hostile defiance and contrition. (APA, 2000, p. 791, reprinted with permission from the *Diagnostic and Statistical Manual of Mental Disorders,* Fourth Edition, Text Revision, copyright 2000 American Psychiatric Association)

Despite the long and somewhat complicated history of the disorder and its current place in the DSM-IV-TR, a discussion of passive-aggressive or negativistic personality is warranted. It is our intention to accurately portray this disorder as it exists using current DSM-IV-TR terminology and symptomotology. However, consistent with the various DSM revisions, the conceptualization of this disorder has changed and evolved over time. Therefore, we find it most useful to talk about a spectrum of passive-aggressive negativistic behaviors, which we refer to as a PA (Neg) style.

Family or marital therapy in which one member uses a PA (Neg) style has proven difficult historically (Slavik, Carlson, and Sperry, 1998). However, based on the current conceptualization of the disorder, implications for family dynamics are clear. The family system, often defined by power structures and hierarchies, provides a relational setting in which passive-aggressive strategies might be employed. The husband whose wife demands that he attend her company's holiday luncheon might convincingly "forget" the date and schedule an important business meeting during the same time. In the family dynamic this sort of "forgetting" or passive resistance allows the husband to protest his wife's demands by not attending her company's luncheon without actively refusing her requests. The wife then feels frustrated, but her husband's response to her frustration is, "Honey, I'm so sorry. I can't believe I scheduled that meeting the very same day as your luncheon." Although this example demonstrates one aspect of the PA (Neg) style, all aspects of passive-aggressiveness (negativism) can be inherent in family dynamics.

IMPACT ON THE FAMILY

It is useful to understand the predisposing factors that may contribute to the development of a PA (Neg) style in children and later in adulthood. Commonalities may exist in families in which children learn or develop the use of PA (Neg) strategies. Millon (1981) and Millon and Davis (1996) proposed that extreme contradictory parental attitudes and inconsistent training methods contribute to this development. They suggest that although many children experience these parental incongruities and inconsistencies, the child who develops a PA (Neg) style will have experienced and been impacted by these models with great frequency during the early years of development.

A major impact of this type of family system on the development of a PA (Neg) style in children is a heightened sense of emotionality. This increased reactivity results from the kind of thinking illustrated for us so eloquently by Tom Hanks in the movie *Forrest Gump:* "Life is like a box of chocolates. You never know what you're gonna get." Due to inconsistency and opposition in the family system, the child often becomes confused and bewildered, unable to determine what to expect from his or her environment (Millon, 1981; Millon and Davis, 1996). The same behavior, which pleases one parent at one moment, may displease the other parent or even the same parent at another given moment. The child then finds himself or herself in a double bind, not sure how to behave in a given situation or which behavior, compliance or disobedience, will elicit the desired parental response (Millon, 1981; Millon and Davis 1996). The result is a child who is incapable of influencing his or her environment consistently. Therefore, the child chooses ambivalence in place of more direct behavior.

Millon and Davis further note the presence of conflicting and incompatible communications between parents and children in the development of a PA (Neg) style. These communications send an overtly kind verbal message, which is sabotaged by a covert nonverbal message. The verbal message is "I love you." The nonverbal message is "Get away." This contributes to an "approach-avoidance conflict" (Millon, 1981; Millon and Davis 1996). These messages teach the child to model ambivalence in his or her own thoughts, feelings, and behaviors.

According to Millon (1981), an additional factor present in families, which may serve as a predisposition for the development of passive-aggressiveness in children, is sibling competition. This competition often results in a feeling of resentment toward a younger or more talented sibling that cannot be expressed directly. Millon notes that many individuals exhibiting a PA (Neg) style report having been "dethroned" by a younger sibling. This dethroning causes a sudden change in the family system and specifically impacts the sense of security felt by the child. No longer feeling the joys of the mother's direct attention and affection, the dethroned child feels anger, antipathy, and hostility toward the younger sibling. Moreover, Millon (1981) notes the autonomy/dependency conflict that occurs as a result of the position that the dethroned child finds himself or herself in. The child is told of the rewards of being a big brother (autonomy and independence), whereas the younger (more dependent) sibling is clearly the child being rewarded (receiving mother's affection and attention).

If each of the above factors is present in a family system, the home environment may become a breeding ground for the use of PA (Neg) tactics. Kaslow (1983, p. 136) states, "Passivity can be a powerful and hostile stance; it makes others exceedingly uncomfortable and also forces them into taking the initiative to say or do almost anything to break the uncomfortable silence and/or impasse." Kaslow suggests that this passive behavior often makes the PA individual seem like a victim being overpowered by a demanding other. However, when the circular pattern inherent in family relationships is examined, the PA (Neg) family member can also be seen as a perpetrator (Kaslow, 1983).

When a child uses a style that may be characterized as passive-aggressive or negativistic, the child may use passivity, noncompliance, and nonperformance as a controlling and attention-getting behavior. However, the child (often a teenager) who uses tactics such as complaining of being misunderstood, being sullen and argumentative, and unreasonably criticizing and scorning authority more appropriately falls under the diagnostic category of oppositional defiant disorder (ODD) according to the DSM-IV-TR. Criteria for this disorder include deliberately annoying others; blaming others for one's own mistakes or misbehavior; being touchy or easily annoyed by others, often angry and resentful; and frequently spiteful or vindictive (APA, 2000). Therefore, it is possible that this condition may serve as a precursor to the development of PA (Neg) disorder in adults. No research has supported this hypothesis, since ODD is more commonly thought to be a precursor to antisocial personality disorder in adults.

The impact on the marital system when one partner uses a PA (Neg) style is significant. Despite their interpersonal ambivalence, individuals who use a PA (Neg) style remain strongly interested in relationships (Slavik, Carlson, and Sperry, 1998). However, their ambivalence in thoughts, feelings, and actions create a push-pull pattern in the marital relationship. According to Slavik, Carlson, and Sperry (1998), resistance in the marital relationship occurs in issues of finances, sexual behavior, parenting, trust, communication, and even the purpose of a relationship. Slavik, Carlson, and Sperry (1998) note that, more often than not, the presence of PA (Neg) tactics in the marital dyad leads to an impasse, and decisions are made by the other partner by default. The partner using a PA (Neg) style is ambivalent about his or her wants and needs, leaving the other partner to make judgments for the family (and later criticizing or resenting those judgments).

Millon and Davis (1996) suggest that the difficulties that appear in the marital dyad are similar to those that existed in the PA (Neg)'s parental and sibling relationships. The struggle between independence and dependence is apparent. The PA (Neg) wife seeks closeness from her husband yet rejects his attempts at intimacy. She vacillates between first encouraging and then rejecting her husband's interest and security. The messages she sends are usually unclear and contradictory. He begins to push for more of her time and the intimacy that he feels they need, however his wife resists these attempts at intimacy, and quickly accuses her husband of attacking her by being overly critical and demanding.

Millon and Davis (1996) discuss the interpersonal conduct of the PA (Neg) personality as it might apply to the marital relationship. Their interpersonal strategy is described as "discontented and unpredictable . . . both seductive and rejecting . . . demanding and then dissatisfied" (p. 551). Millon and Davis further characterize this behavior as "an effective weapon not only with an intimidated or pliant partner but with people in general" (p. 551). Millon (1981) suggests that the interpersonal problems of the PA (Neg) are different from that of most personality-disordered individuals. Rather than developing a rigid interpersonal style, individuals demonstrating a PA (Neg) style lack commitment to any particular mode of behaving. Therefore, they are constantly shifting between one action and another, creating confusion and frustration for their partners.

SETTING

If the passive-aggressive client is married and able to maintain moderate relationships in the personal, social, and occupational domains, it is recommended that the therapeutic setting of choice be couples therapy on a weekly basis. The family therapist can work with the couple from an integrative systemic approach. This approach allows both partners to gain insight into how their own behavior feeds into the dysfunctional patterns of interaction that they each perpetuate in their marital relationship, as well as other relationships in the various domains of their lives.

If the passive-aggressive style of behavior impedes the client in his or her ability to hold a job and maintain healthy positive relationships with significant others, individual therapy is also recommended. Again, this would typically be on a weekly basis. The clients in the case study were seen weekly for couples therapy in a private practice setting. The husband was also seen individually to address some of his vocational concerns.

TREATMENT MODEL

Treatment strategies, techniques, and goals vary among different theoretical perspectives. Millon and Davis (1996) suggest that a single model of treatment is not effective for individuals with personality disorders. Instead they suggest that an integrative approach, which incorporates multiple treatment techniques, is most useful with these individuals. We believe that an integrative family system treatment model works best when working with clients exhibiting PA (Neg) behaviors. Other well-known family-systems perspectives that have been used in treating these individuals and their families include a psychodynamic family approach, cognitive-behavioral family approach, and an Adlerian family approach. We will discuss treatment strategies from each of these perspectives, since the integrative family system approach draws from the many techniques employed in these models.

Pyschodynamic Family Approach

An underlying belief consistent with the psychodynamic family therapy approach is a belief in the unconscious, which is outside of the awareness of the individual. This unconscious is strongly impacted by past experiences, which influence present behavior. Therefore, the psychodynamic family therapist is interested in early childhood experiences, particularly with regard to developmental relationships between family members and parental figures. The goal of psychodynamic family therapy is to "free family members of unconscious restrictions so that they'll be able to interact with one another as whole, healthy persons" (Nichols and Schwartz, 2001, p. 213).

Psychodynamic therapists see the use of PA (Neg) tactics as a defensive technique, much like a defense mechanism. A defense mechanism, in Freudian terms, is an unconscious way of coping with anxiety. When overused, these defense mechanisms distort reality and lead to unstable personality adjustment. The PA (Neg) individual has developed the vacillating pattern of relating with others as a means to protect his or her self-esteem or to reduce anxiety (Nichols, 1992). Uncomfortable with his or her own need for dependency and unsure how to satisfy his or her needs, the PA (Neg) family member frustrates others through ambiguity, first wanting closeness then preventing it. The PA (Neg) individual is left feeling angry and resentful, blaming others for relationship difficulties. Nevertheless, the PA (Neg) personality cannot express his or her anger directly for fear that he or she will ultimately be rejected.

Future relationships with perceived authority figures become reminiscent of earlier relationships with caretakers (Millon and Davis, 2000). Therefore, the transference relationship that occurs between individual family members and the therapist becomes a focus of therapy. The role of the therapist in this transference/countertransference relationship is that of a "good enough parent" (Nichols, 1992, p. 239). The therapist demonstrates effective parenting by offering support, encouragement, and nurturing to family members. This role provides a model from which family members can learn how to feel, think, and behave with one another.

The therapeutic strategy used in working with such a family is to provide a context in which family members can appropriately express feelings, especially anger, directly in a supportive and accepting manner. Therapy is initiated by looking at the early experiences of each of the individual family members, since the fate of the individual is interrelated with that of the family as a whole (Nichols and Schwartz, 2001). The psychodynamic therapist is particularly interested in a child's anal stage of development. The anal stage is of interest due to its inherent themes of autonomy versus external control (Millon and Davis, 2000). During this time, children encounter the need for self-control. Parents who are overcontrolling, demanding, and rigid set the stage for the development of an anal-retentive personality. As a result, "the child may react by 'holding back' and refusing to perform, developing stubbornness, stinginess, and concealed anger" (Millon and Davis, 2000, p. 478). This reaction is thought to be the underpinnings of later underperformance in both social and occupational functioning.

Stricker (1983) notes that with a strong therapeutic alliance, the therapist can expect an honest display of vacillation and inconsistent work on behalf of the PA (Neg) client. Stricker (1983) goes on to say that as the client moves closer to accepting his or her hostility, anger, and dependency, he or she will experience anxiety due to fear of recognition. This fear of recognition will likely induce the use of familiar passive aggressive defenses. However, if the client is sufficiently engaged in therapy, rather than terminating treatment, these defenses will act as means of blocking the therapist or therapeutic process. Such attempts can be discussed later in therapy (Stricker, 1983).

Often the PA (Neg) client will attempt to pass responsibility for progress to the therapist. This demonstration of dependency is often accomplished by asking the therapist questions such as, "What should I do?" (Stricker, 1983). The therapist might reflect, "You would like me to make decisions for you?" (Stricker, 1983, p. 15). The preferred result of this sort of dialogue is that the client will come to understand his or her passive dependency on others. The therapist and client would then begin to explore the positives (caring and support) and negatives (anger and resentment) of feeling dependent on others (Stricker, 1983). The therapist helps the client see the connections between earlier dependent relationships and the current transference occurring between the client and the therapist. Thus the psychodynamic family therapist focuses on processes such as working through, interpretation, and gaining insight.

Cognitive Behavior Therapy

Although the psychodynamic family therapist looks to early development, unconscious drives, and caregiver relationships to understand the client's problems, the cognitive-behavioral family therapists seeks to understand the client's problems by looking at the client's thoughts, feelings, and behaviors occurring in the present. The therapist works with the PA (Neg) client to help him or her identify the automatic thoughts that are believed to be at the root of the client's problems. These negative thoughts can be examined and modified.

According to Burns and Epstein (1983, p. 82) the primary goals of cognitive-behavioral therapy with PA (Neg) clients are:

1. teaching clients to identify difficult situations and become aware of their negative feelings;
2. training clients to identify the cognitions or thoughts associated with these negative feelings and difficult situations;

3. helping clients identify the distortions in the automatic thoughts;
4. teaching clients to substitute more rational thoughts in place of their distorted negative thoughts;
5. helping clients recognize their self-defeating assumptions and attitudes and develop a healthier personal value system; and
6. modifying self-defeating behavior patterns and enhance communication skills.

The role of the cognitive behavioral therapist is collaborative in nature. The therapist works with the clients to understand patterns of family interaction that occur as a result of family members' core schemas. Schemas are defined as "cognitive structures or core beliefs through which people filter their perceptions and structure their experience" (Nichols and Schwartz, 2001, p. 529). Underlying beliefs or assumptions govern the relationships among family members. Therefore, distorted assumptions must be restructured to improve the family dynamic.

Just as clients maintain self-schemas filled with personal perceptions through which they view themselves and their world, family members maintain similar "family schemas." Frank Datillio, as cited in Nichols and Schwartz (2001), holds that individuals have schemas relating to both their family of origin and to families in general. Within these schemas are the beliefs about how a family is supposed to interact, roles that members are supposed to maintain, beliefs about why problems exist within the family, and how problems should be dealt with. These schemas impact how family members think, feel, and behave toward one another (Nichols and Schwartz, 2001).

For PA (Neg) clients, cognitions are typically negativistic in nature. Their own beliefs are as contradictory as their behavior. Family members attempting to relate with such an individual often find his or her messages confusing and ambiguous. The cognitive-behavioral family therapist uses techniques such as cognitive mediation in marital interaction developed by Epstein, Schlesinger, and Dryden (Thomas, 1992). This method helps couples examine the meanings they assign to each other's messages and teaches them to clarify beliefs that are held through improved communication skills. Therapists also teach functional and analytical skills related to relationships, and behavioral skills, such as assertiveness training, communication training, problem solving, and conflict management (Thomas, 1992).

Although cognitive-behavior therapists focus on the faulty cognitions and distortions of the PA (Neg) family members, the Adlerian perspective focuses on the purpose of the PA (Neg) behavior and how that behavior fits with the client's worldview.

Adlerian Family Therapy

The Adlerian perspective views individuals who rely on negativistic styles of behavior as being discouraged and pessimistic about their effectiveness in life (Slavik, Carlson, and Sperry, 1998). These individuals tend to choose behaviors that promote and maintain their ambivalent lifestyle convictions rife with binds and such conceptions as "Life is unfair, and unpredictable," and "I am competent/I am incompetent." Thus, although PA (Neg)-style behaviors may leave an individual feeling discouraged, unappreciated, and resentful, they will continue to perpetuate this negativistic behavior because it fits with how such individuals see their world. Adlerian therapy also honors the difference in families of origin and helps each partner to understand how they came to believe their mistaken goals and their private logic/ worldview.

Adlerian-trained therapists view oppositional or passive-aggressive behavior as attention-getting behavior since the covert resistant style may prove more purposeful for the PA (Neg) partner than assertive behavior that could be undermined or dismissed by the opposing partner. For the PA (Neg) couple, the marital relationship becomes the battlefield for these power struggles. Interactions in these relationships are intense, unstable, and manipulative. These negative and covert interactions typically leave both partners feeling ambivalent within the relationship.

The goal of therapy from an Adlerian standpoint involves a cooperative assessment of goals and treatment planning. The Adlerian therapist implements a plan that includes aspects of behavioral, affective, and cognitive interventions to help align the couple toward attaining a common goal of cooperative decision making. This goal of collaboration would in turn help the couple to increase their social interest and the ability to relate to each other in a cooperative and productive manner.

Since power struggles and confrontation are typical ways that the PA (Neg) couple deals with each other, it is extremely important that the goals are aligned. Aligned goals inhibit the typical dysfunctional pattern of resistance and power struggles, and provide the Adlerian therapist a foundation or base from which to work and encourage the client's success. This may be implemented by such strategies as paradoxical intent, humor, limit setting, transparency, and self-monitoring. Psychoeducation plays a large role in how the Adlerian therapist works with a PA (Neg) couple. "Therapy will be psychoeducational about self, the other, and relationships" (Slavik et al., 1998, p. 305).

Integrative Couples Therapy

As stated previously, we feel that an integrative family systems model is the most beneficial approach to working with a couple or family that presents with a PA (Neg) style. An integrative approach provides a comprehensive framework through which to view the complex dynamics inherent in these family systems. Individuals can be understood only by examining the biological, psychological, and social factors that contribute to their development and to the development of their family system. We believe that an integrative family systems perspective does just that. The integrative model that we have chosen to illustrate is integrative couples therapy (Stuart, 2002). We have chosen this approach due to its emphasis on multicultural sensitivity, tailored treatment, and objectivity. We begin by explaining the theoretical assumptions inherent in this approach, the roles of both the therapist and the client, the methods of assessment used, the goals of therapy, and the strategies or tactics used to reach those goals. Furthermore, we discuss how such an approach can be used in working with couples in which one or more members demonstrate the use of a PA (Neg) style.

ICT is crafted from an understanding of affective, behavioral, cognitive, developmental, environmental, family-of-origin, and genetic aspects of the partners' interaction (Stuart, 2002). According to Stuart, no single factor is more significant than the others, however, any one factor may play a more dominant role in a particular client's presenting problem. This approach borrows from many other theories (such as family systems, constuctivism, attachment theory, cognitive behavior, psychoanalytic, and social learning theory) and tailors the therapy for the client or couple.

Created by Richard Stuart in the 1960s, ICT is based on the fundamentals of principled pragmatism, which contend that humans have an inherent capacity for constructive change (Stuart, 2002). All human behaviors are seen as attempts to achieve a sense of personal well-being. A core value in this approach is respect for the decisions that partners make concerning the future of their relationship, regardless of whether they choose to continue or dissolve the marriage.

At the initiation of therapy, the couple is given a series of assessment forms, such as the Couple's Precounseling Inventory (CPI), the Family of Origin (FOO) Inventory, and the Couple Therapy Goal Attainment Scale (GAS), that will assist the therapist to create/tailor an integrative approach that will be most effective with a particular couple and address the multiple factors of their PA (Neg) style. FOO Inventory is frequently used to learn about the developmental experiences that contribute to each partner's internal working models. This sixteen-page form solicits data about family history and other influential relationships in childhood. The REP Grid affords an overview of the criteria that each partner uses for the assessment of self and significant others in the past and the present. The GAS is used to rate the couple's functioning at the current time. All of these tools can be used at regular intervals during the course of treatment to assess how the couple is progressing.

ICT views the therapeutic process as a unique collaboration of the therapist's style and background blending with the culture, history, and presenting problems of the couple. ICT integrates the information gained from the objective assessment tools listed previously with information provided by the couple in the session. Rather than focusing on pathology, ICT focuses on clients' strengths as keys to helping them achieve their goals.

ICT calls for creating a collaborative, nonhierarchical relationship with clients, the therapist being neither an inspired guru nor an obedient servant who follows clients' leads. The ICT therapist's role is to help clients find better means of achieving their goals by mobilizing and building upon their existing strengths (Stuart, 2002). The ICT therapist allows each person to feel heard and understood within the relationship. This is particularly important when dealing with a PA (Neg) couple since neither partner feels very safe and trust is a major issue. The PA (Neg) partner fears being attacked by others and feels very unappreciated and misunderstood in relationships. Typically, the other partner feels sabotaged and undermined, and thus does not trust the PA (Neg) partner. Therapists are called upon to use "leading consciousness" when working with a conflicted couple, which sensitizes them to the partners' potential reactions in every aspect of their intervention (Stuart, 2002, p. 326). This is of extreme importance when dealing with a PA (Neg) couple because they may try to undermine many of the therapeutic interventions in much the same way that they undermine other relationships in their lives. It is critical that the therapist remains aware of the PA (Neg) dynamics that are being enacted and the transference and countertransference issues that will be played out as a result of the PA (Neg) tactics.

This awareness can be facilitated using a structural family therapy technique that incorporates a transactional analysis (TA) method called *noticing*. The therapist and the couple begin to notice actual behavior and transactional patterns within the relationship. It is critical that the therapist assists the couple to become aware of their transactional dynamics without being critical, blaming, and especially without arousing resistance. If the therapist maintains an attitude of friendly curiosity about what is occurring both within the couple relationship and within the therapeutic relationship, the therapist can encourage the clients' own curiosity and ability to notice (Slavik, Carlson, and Sperry, 1992).

Integrative couples therapy (ICT) views the relationship as the primary entity in the therapeutic process. Both partners are seen as equally important to the therapeutic process, but the focus is the interaction and the relationship between the couple. When working with a PA (Neg) couple, it is critical to focus on the relationship, since it has a history of being used as a battleground for resentment, covert hostility, a battle between dependency and individuation issues, and power struggles. A core aspect of the relationship is a feeling of being misunderstood by one's partner. Neither party views the relationship as very safe or secure, yet each partner is still drawn to it. If the couple can learn to work together to make the relationship a safer place, then they (with the therapist's guidance) can gain insight and begin to build a stronger foundation based on cooperation and respect rather than hostility.

A primary therapeutic goal of ICT is to establish a collaborative, nonhierarchical relationship with clients in which "clients are the acknowledged authorities on their goals and the therapist is acknowledged as the authority on the means to achieve them" (Stuart, 2002, p. 326). Establishing a therapeutic rapport and establishing hope with clients early in therapy are seen as crucial to ICT therapy. Again, this is especially pertinent when working with PA (Neg) clients who may view the possibility for change as "hopeless" and tend to view the world very negatively. If the couple can begin to feel that they do indeed have the power to change the negative dynamics, they can begin to feel safe within the relationship.

Another goal of ICT is to help clients enhance their skills in communication and bargaining to build confidence in the likelihood that exchanges will be equitable. Because many PA (Neg) couples often become entrenched in a destructive and negative style of communication, the therapist teaches the couple more effective ways to meet their needs. This is done in a mutually respectful manner in which both partners and the marital relationship are honored. Therapists model direct and clear communication. Tactics, such as the use of paradox by the therapist, are seen as counter to this approach. According to Stuart (2002) the use of paradox models only manipulation and indirectness. Since the PA (Neg) client is prone to this behavior it should not be reinforced. Clients' goals are framed based on the thoughts, feelings, and actions that come most naturally to the couple, with the therapist using the clients' metaphors and language to bring about the desired change. In general, ICT begins with behavior change as a route to promoting insight.

Because of the integrative nature of ICT, many techniques and interventions are used that are tailored to the specific couple that the therapist is working with. This said, certain techniques and interventions are more common to this approach. Frequently used techniques include establishing rapport and hope, building on the clients' strengths, framing goals using the clients' language, clarifying and finding common goals, positive-change- oriented techniques (such as "caring days"), acting "as if," and two-winner negotiation skills (Stuart, 2002).

Although much support exists for the use of integrative approaches in both family and individual therapy, no specific research has been conducted to validate the effectiveness of ICT in working with personality-disordered couples. Stuart (2002) suggests that such definitive tests are not possible, since each clinician develops his or her own personal approach based on the uniqueness of the clients. Clinical use of ICT has shown promise in working with conflicted couples. The sensitivity of the therapist is essential to maintain a safe environment for conflicted couples to reach their goals. It is important to remember, however, that the focus of the ICT model is on positive and healthy attributes of the couple. Therefore, the ICT therapist does not look to the pathological aspects of the "personality-disordered" individual. The therapist defines individuals based on their own unique attributes, values, belief systems, and behaviors.

CASE EXAMPLE

Moira and Walter have been married for nine years. This is the second marriage for Walter. Moira has worked for the same health care company for fifteen years. She currently works as an administration personnel manager and recently went back to school to complete her degree in business administration. Walter works as a car salesman. Although he has been involved in the car industry for twenty years, his career pattern has been sporadic at best, since he tends to move to different car dealerships every two years or so, and vacillates between remaining in the auto industry and wanting to be a golf professional. Walter has a fourteen-year-old son from his previous marriage who visits infrequently, and Moira and Walter have a five-year-old daughter from their union.

Moira initiated the marital counseling because, in her words, "I am fed up with Walter's job insecurity, and the ambivalence and lack of decision making from Walter regarding our marriage and future." Moira complained that Walter is often late with paying the bills, and that he takes so long to do particular household chores that she ends up doing them because it is easier just to do them herself than to keep nagging him or waiting for him to do it. Although Moira's initial call seemed to focus on her complaints about Walter, she indicated that he was willing to come in for marital counseling and that both were committed to working on the marriage.

Moira and Walter arrived separately for the initial session since both were coming from work. Moira entered the therapy session infuriated since Walter was fifteen minutes late for the appointment. She immediately began to chastize Walter and was very argumentative. This guided the theme for the initial session, since Moira's major issue with Walter was his undependable and resentful nature. His major issue with Moira was that she overfunctioned in all domains of her life and always took charge. In his words, Moira was "a perpetual nag." Moira would always find fault with everything that Walter did or attempted to do, and his reaction was one of resistance. Further prompting from the therapist established that this was a common theme for both partners from their families of origin.

Walter came from a Polish family in which his father spent little time with the family and died from alcoholism when Walter was in the third grade. Walter recalled and described his father as distant and always unavailable even when he was home. Walter characterized his mother as a strong woman who raised five children by herself. Walter was the baby of the family, with an older brother and two older sisters, until he was displaced and dethroned by a younger brother. He described his older brother as aloof and very much like his father. His older sisters and his mother catered to Walter until his baby brother came into the picture. Walter talked about his resentment and anger at being replaced as the object of his mother's and sisters' affections by his baby brother, whom he never got along with.

The same year that Walter's brother was born, Walter developed several childhood illnesses. Walter's sickly childhood served as a way for Walter to still receive much of the attention that he craved from his mother. Walter suffered from childhood asthma, frequent migraine headaches, and back pain. He was diagnosed with tension myositis syndrome (TMS) when he was fourteen. Walter's understanding about his medical condition was that his back pain was benign (though painful), and was caused by emotional distress, tension in particular (Sarno, 1991).

Moira grew up in an Irish Catholic household with seven younger siblings. She described her father as "a weak and good for nothing oaf who loved the drink." Moira saw her mother as the glue that held the family together and the one who would try to keep her father on "the straight and narrow." Early in life, Moira found herself as a parentified child trying to help her "ma" with the constant demands of the younger children. Moira describes herself as a devout Catholic. Although she stated that she is clearly unhappy in her marriage, she does not see divorce as an option because "they were married in front of God and true Catholics remain that way."

Psychological assessment determined that Walter had passive-aggressive personality disorder and Moira had features of histrionic personality disorder. Patterns of passive-aggressive or negativistic behavior were apparent in almost all of Walter's interactions with significant relationships (especially with authority figures). Further probing into Walter's history revealed a series of conflicts and strife with intimate and work-related relationships. Walter disclosed that his divorce was initiated by his former wife and followed several tumultuous years of constant battling between the spouses. Walter felt that his former wife, whom he also described as "a nag," was very controlling and demanding. He saw himself as a victim, and although he did acknowledge that his ex-wife described him as unreliable, indecisive, and pessimistic, Walter lacked any insight regarding the role that his behavior might have played in the demise of the relationship.

Further examination of Walter's job instability and fluctuating pattern of direction and employment painted an occupational picture splattered with conflict, covert hostility, impulsivity, and cutoffs. Walter always seemed to have difficulty getting along with others—managers, co-workers, and some customers. He would often arrive at work late and was notorious for not coming into work the day after a confrontation with a manager or co-worker. In Walter's words, his TMS or other physical ailments would flare up and he would be rendered incapacitated for a day or two. Walter's lack of self-confidence and fear of competition always seemed to inhibit Walter from pursuing his dream and ideal occupational choice of being a golf pro. Although the career he had resigned himself to in car sales was also very competitive, Walter would always place himself back in the same negative situation that he dreaded, quitting jobs frequently and impulsively because of the hostility and power struggles that seemed to follow him. This self-destructive pattern of behavior left Walter feeling very victimized, resentful, and unappreciated by others.

During the initial session, it became quite apparent that Moira would talk for the two of them. Even if the therapist asked Walter a direct question, Moira would immediately answer for him as if he was not there and she knew what he was thinking. The therapist commented on this pattern and asked whether this was a typical pattern that occurred within the marital dyad. Walter then became much more verbal and shared that Moira never took the time to listen to him and would assume that she knew what was best for him. Walter admitted retaliating by consenting to go along with her demands and then sabotaging them later, such as agreeing to go to the pharmacy for her, but returning late and forgetting the item that she had sent him to pick up.

As the therapy proceeded, the therapist was able to help the couple recognize ("notice") the familiar patterns of interactions that were dysfunctional to them yet were accepted because of their past history and cultural upbringing. These familial patterns of interactions were also evident in the assessment forms (The FOO and the REP Grid) that Moira and Walter had filled out early in treatment. The therapist pointed out how Moira tended to dominate and "mother" Walter and how his reaction would always be to become stubborn and rigid in his stance. Walter and Moira were able to see how her behavior was very characteristic of "Irish women" who tended to be the backbone of the family and push their men (McGoldrick, 1996), but also how Walter's Polish heritage and personal history revealed a history of domination. Walter illustrated a classic Polish response to feeling dominated or controlled, which was to become stubborn and resist any form of oppression or perceived threats (Folwarski and Marganoff, 1996).

As the therapist educated Moira and Walter on their cultural backgrounds and styles of relating to each other, she also reframed the negative attributes they had assigned to each other in more positive tones. Walter's stubbornness was portrayed as "strong-mindedness and persistence," and Moira's need to control and push Walter was described by the therapist as "her wanting to support her husband and her way of showing how she cared for him." The therapist then asked both Moira and Walter to come up with some other ways that they might be able to demonstrate their caring and persistence that would be more helpful and feel more loving to them as a couple. This was implemented through a technique called "Caring Days" (Stuart, 1980), in which the therapist assigned homework to the couple that reinforced more positive and loving ways that each partner could relate to each other. The therapist asked Moira and Walter, "What do loving things look like for each you?" She then had them list seven to ten specific things that their partner could do that would show that they feel loved and then exchange the lists. This exercise helped the couple focus on positive exchanges rather than the negativistic style that they were accustomed to using with each other.

Not only did this activity allow Moira and Walter to express to each other different ways that they felt loved and appreciated, but it also addressed some cultural and gender assumptions. Moira demonstrated a specifically Irish tendency of not articulating her needs and feelings. She assumed that if she was really loved by Walter, he would know her feelings without having to be told (McGoldrick, 1996). The therapist's subtle questions about the assumed roles of men and women within this family became an important first step in enabling Moira and Walter to change lopsided and dysfunctional gender patterns that were perpetuating some of the negativistic behavior that they had become entrenched in.

The therapist was also sensitive to the fact that both Irish and Polish families do better with homework assignments that can be done in the privacy of their own home. Since the therapist knew that she was also dealing with a couple who have a passive-aggressive style and might "forget" or sabotage the homework to resist authority, she addressed this up front and illustrated how this homework assignment was aligned with their own goals. The therapist also placed Moira and Walter in the role of the experts of their relationship, thus there was no authority for them to undermine and resist. If they were to sabotage the homework, they would ultimately be sabotaging themselves.

Although Walter does not see himself as a traditional Polish Catholic, he does maintain some traditional Polish patriarchal family values that are compatible with Moira's background. Both espouse traditional beliefs surrounding marriage, gender roles, housekeeping, and child care. As with most other domains, Walter has a low profile when it comes to cooperating with the care of their five-year-old daughter, Maureen, and contributes little toward the housework. Although Moira complains frequently about Walter's ambivalence about becoming more involved with Maureen and herself, she "confessed" that she feels that she does a better job than he would if he did become more involved.

The therapist was able to help the couple to see how Moira's tendency to "overfunction" (just as her mother had done) prevents Walter from being able to participate as much as he would if she was not "mothering" him. Walter also concurred that he would like to do more with his daughter without Moira's inference. It was agreed that one evening a week, Walter and Maureen would have some father-daughter time, and Moira could take advantage of this time for herself. Moira was not to take charge and plan the event for them, but rather Walter and Maureen would take the initiative. Through encouragement, psychoeducation, and accentuating their strengths, Moira and Walter learned more favorable and healthy ways of relating to each other.

STRENGTHS AND LIMITATIONS

Integrative couples therapy can be an effective way to assist couples struggling with PA (Neg) style to learn better skills and to have a more meaningful and positive relationship. Literature and research findings emphasize the usefulness and efficacy of couples or family therapy with these clients since family therapy focuses on the complex network of relationships that often sustain this personality style and provides a forum for the clients to see their behavior played out and its impact on themselves and others (Millon, 1981; Millon and Davis, 2000). These factors are among the strengths of this model.

Unfortunately, despite the advantages of ICT and an integrated family systems approach to treating these clients, research reveals that progress in therapy may be limited for a passive-aggressive/ negativistic style client. It is fairly typical for these clients to appear compliant and engaged on the surface, yet they covertly undermine and resist any therapeutic efforts. Many PA (Neg) clients tend to view the therapist as an adversary (someone in authority) rather than as a collaborator (Millon, 1981; Millon and Davis, 2000). Often marriages involving a PA (Neg) style client are made more tolerable through insight, communication, and behavior skills learned through the therapeutic process, but the basic pattern of PA behavior within the marriage is never fully eliminated (Gehrke and Moxom, 1962).

Because so much of the PA (Neg) personality is deeply rooted and unconscious, resistances will impede the effectiveness of most therapeutic procedures. Extensive psychoanalytic therapy focusing on a thorough reconstruction of the personality may be the only means of altering this deeply ingrained pattern of behavior. It is important to note, however, that with current managed care and HMO funding, longer term psychoanalytic work may not be financially viable.

BENEFITS FOR THE FAMILY

Treatment approaches that utilize ICT or other integrative models offer clients and their families many benefits. One major benefit of the ICT model is that it incorporates core aspects that allow couples and family members to feel respected, heard, and hopeful. A number of other elements also help make integrative approaches such as ICT the preferred model of treatment for clients who demonstrate a PA (Neg) style.

First, ICT therapists create relationships with clients and their families based on mutual respect. Couples are part of a team whose goal is to improve the functioning of the family system. ICT therapists provide an environment in which trust is paramount. This allows couples to feel a sense of respect and empowerment. As suggested earlier, individuals who demonstrate a PA (Neg) style often resist demands of authority figures. Therefore, this nonhierarchical therapeutic relationship minimizes resistance and opens the door to progress.

Second, as noted previously, the ICT therapist has in his or her toolbox the best techniques from numerous psychological perspectives. The approach is truly integrative in that therapists employ effective methods from several schools of thought. Therefore, the therapist is open to trying new and different techniques depending on the needs of the client. Clients and families with similar diagnoses often come to therapy with very different presenting problems. Moreover, clients and families vary in their responses to therapy and in their level of comfort with the therapist. The ICT therapist tailors his or her approach, without limitations, to address the needs of these families. The couple views the therapist as responsive to their unique pattern of strengths and weaknesses.

Third, the ICT model is based on a belief in the capacity for change. Change is expected to take place, and the therapist is a guide whose goal is to facilitate change. This process is not dependent on a complete restructuring of the personality. Rather, changes can occur in each session or in each interaction between the couple or the family. The message to the couple or the family is one of hope. Family members internalize this sense of hope and therefore create their own expectations for change.

INDICATIONS AND CONTRAINDICATIONS

Conjoint family therapy is seen as the preferential mode of therapy when dealing with passive-aggressive couples because so much of their negative interaction occurs within the realm of the marital relationship. By having couples work on their relationship together and learn how they are contributing to the negativistic patterns that they find themselves in, the therapist can then assist the couple to learn more effective ways of dealing with each other.

As with all couples therapy, if a situation exists in which a pattern of the power struggles and passive resistance has a history of escalating to violence, both partners would be seen individually until each partner had learned how to de-escalate and manage the conflicts. In these cases, clients would be treated in much the same manner as with domestic violence cases. Once the couple has learned effective coping skills and self-control, then the therapist can begin work on the passive-aggressive style that the couple initially presented.

MANAGEMENT OF TRANSFERENCE ISSUES

Transference plays a critical role in the therapeutic progress when working with PA (Neg) clients. The therapeutic relationship often becomes the "tabula rasa" for negativistic clients to demonstrate the passive-aggressive interactions that they use in all other realms of their lives. Millon and Davis (2000) describe a "seesaw struggle that is often enacted between the patient and the therapist" (p. 574). The PA client will vacillate between pleasing and submissive behavior one session and then resistant and hostile aggression the next. It is also customary for the PA client to want the therapist's affection and then refute the genuineness of the affection once received. Throughout the therapy process, supportive interpersonal techniques can facilitate the client's recognition of the negativistic style and help the client to see the residual effects from the childhood and family of origin.

The roundabout tactics that negativistic clients engage in to display their resentment and hostility can place many obstacles in the way of the therapeutic process. These include, but are not limited to, arriving late, missing appointments, forgetting homework assignments, poor boundaries, anger projection, noncompliance with the treatment planning, and abrupt termination. The therapeutic relationship may be the first relationship that the client has that does not feed into the passive-aggressive types of behaviors and ambivalence that most PA (Neg) clients also feel toward dependent relationships. Through gentle guidance, support, encouragement, and the use of various techniques, the PA client can learn to moderate the negativistic behavior to the point that he or she can engage in reasonably satisfying relationships with others.

Therapist gender may also be significant in terms of transference reactions. In the case of Moira and Walter, for example, who were seeing a female therapist, it is important that the therapist explore the dynamics surrounding the therapist's gender, as well as how each partner views women. Strong women have played predominant roles in both Moira's and Walter's lives. Both clients grew up with strong mothers who held the family together, and fathers who played a lesser role. Since the therapist is also female, she may be depicted by both partners as someone capable (another strong woman) who can hold this family together. Through the assessment process and an understanding of the cultural and familial backgrounds, the therapist has learned that both Moira and Walter have a deep-seated sense of powerlessness and some dependency issues. Caution also needs to be used to ensure that the therapist does not assume too much responsibility and power, in which case she might be viewed as an authority who dispenses instructions that are to be followed. (This is especially significant since Irish and Polish clients are prone to viewing therapy as similar to Catholic confession, in which you tell your sins and then seek forgiveness.) It is therefore paramount that the therapist not fall into the trap of fostering dependency in Walter and Moira, and that she encourages both Moira and Walter to assume responsibility for their past and present behaviors.

MANAGEMENT OF CRISES
AND ACTING-OUT BEHAVIOR

PA (Neg) clients are notorious for a vacillating and inconsistent style of relating to others and seeing the world. Their turbulent feelings, attitudes, and behaviors allow for little internal equilibrium or consistent external gratification. Negativistic clients frequently live in a phenomenological state of unhappiness and generally feel dissatisfied with themselves. Their irritability and impassivity provokes them to behave unpredictably and to appear sullen, restless and obstructive much of the time. Not only do they live in an inner world of chaos and tension but they act out their anger and resentments toward the rest of the world (Millon, 1981; Millon and Davis, 2000).

The therapist has the challenging role of illustrating the effectiveness of treatment to clients who by their negativistic nature are likely to discount or resist any progress that is made. When everything appears to be progressing well in therapy, it is not uncommon for the PA (Neg) client to abruptly discontinue therapy and claim that it is a "waste of time." It is important for the therapist to not become engaged in the passive-aggressive pattern of behavior and either want to "fix" the client or take the termination personally. This pattern of termination is characteristic with the PA (Neg) style of cutoffs and undermining those they see in authority roles.

PA (Neg) clients tend to be very dramatic and typically enter therapy in a highly agitated state, but once the immediate crisis is over, it is not uncommon for them to minimize what was once a major crisis or to terminate treatment. The therapist will have to "go with the flow" and use this as an opportunity to illustrate the passive-aggressive style of resistance rather than giving in to countertransference feelings or reactions. Much of the focus of therapy will be exploring the patterns of resistance and a long and slow pace of therapeutic progression with many ups and downs can be expected.

Therapists must also be cautious about impulsive and vacillating behavior of PA (Neg) clients who may misinterpret some therapeutic directives as rejection. This in turn may result in the PA (Neg) client suddenly feeling guilt-ridden and depressed, and in some circumstances even becoming suicidal. Although suicidal crises are uncommon among PA (Neg) clients, it is important to note that suicide is the ultimate form of passive aggression. When PA (Neg) clients show suicidal signs, they must be taken seriously, and hospitalization needs to be a treatment option. A major focus of therapy is to guide these clients into recognizing and owning the sources and character of their ambivalence, and to reinforce a more consistent approach to life.

INTEGRATION WITH PSYCHIATRIC SERVICES AND ROLE OF MEDICATION

It is common for negativistic clients to present with overlapping Axis I or Axis II disorders, such as depression, anxiety, or other personality disorders. If a client presents with anxiety or depressive features, pharmacological agents, such as benzodiazepines or antidepressant medications (often selective seratonin reuptake inhibitors), may be utilized. Medication should be used as a last resort in treatment, since it is common for these clients to also be resistant or passive-aggressive in their medication compliance.

The use of medication with PA (Neg) clients poses several problems. As mentioned previously, an issue with medication compliance exists. Another consideration is that little evidence exists at present of a biological basis for this disorder. Given this, it seems best to address clients' thoughts and feelings in psychological and social domains rather than resorting to medications that are not supported by either the theoretical or empirical literature.

CULTURAL AND GENDER ISSUES

The increasing diversity of our society will require the therapist to be more culturally competent as they enter the twenty-first century. Race, gender, religion, class, age, sexual orientation, immigration status, and disability are critical identity issues that therapists must take into account to understand clients and their behaviors (McGoldrick, Giordano, and Pearce, 1996, p. 25). Therapists must consider the cultural context in which a behavior evolves as well as have an understanding of what the behavior means for the client. When working with passive-aggressive clients, certain cultural histories may foster this type of behavior more than others. This is evident in Walter's case because he is from a Polish-American heritage, and distance and cutoff seem to be the preferred way that Poles deal with strong emotions. Most Poles do not stay emotionally connected with individuals once tensions rise and they are most likely to remain silent, rather than take an "I" position on difficult or toxic issues. Poles are also notorious for holding grudges. A combination of persistence and stubbornness often operates to prevent dialogue in which both parties in the conflict can be heard (Folwarski and Marganoff, 1996).

As we can see, much of this behavior demonstrates an overlap between culturally learned behavior and passive-aggressive behavior. Thus, it is important that the therapist take into account where this behavior comes from and how deeply ingrained it may be in Walter's family of origin. Being culturally knowledgeable provides the therapist with a framework from which to help Walter to learn more adaptable behaviors. Since Walter's PA (Neg) behavior is adversely impacting all domains of his life, it is evident that much more is going on with Walter's behavior than his cultural indoctrination. Walter has always had problems relating to his family of origin and his extended Polish-American community, as well as fitting in with the norms of the dominant North American culture.

From a culturally sensitive perspective, the therapist is also aware that although Moira and Walter come from divergent cultural backgrounds, some commonalities exist between their histories that need to be taken into consideration. Many Irish and Polish clients tend to regard therapy as something shameful since there is a tendency to keep personal problems private. A resistance is also present to exposing the family to shame that may play a significant factor in the therapeutic alliance. The therapist needs to tread delicately since she can be seen as an "outsider influence" and an accuser, rather than a helper if she is not sensitive to the deep-seated shame that is inherent in this family.

Many Polish have been raised and shaped by powerful cultural messages and concerns regarding bringing shame to the family. The question, "What would the neighbors think?" is a typical Polish concern. Moira's traditional Irish Catholic upbringing also reflected feelings of shame since her family of origin did not look favorably on therapy or airing one's "dirty laundry" in public. According to McGoldrick, Giordano, and Pearce (1996), for Irish Catholics, "Problems are a private matter between themselves, and God" (p. 546). Moira was raised to believe that if you just prayed hard enough and were worthy, God would be merciful. Suffering alone was also seen to be a common way of coping with life's difficulties.

One of the key issues that the therapist has to address with Walter are the complexities of his shame—stemming from his cultural background, his gender, and his personal beliefs. Shame is often viewed as a dominant theme in the experience of many Polish Americans since they are associated with an ethnic group that is considered "dumb" by the larger society (Folwarski and Marganoff, 1996). The daily criticism and scrutiny that Walter continues to reap from his wife is very familiar to Walter since he grew up under the scrutiny of extended family members because of his sickly childhood, which also brought shame upon his family.

A three-generational genogram that the therapist constructed with Walter and Moira revealed that Walter's parents had changed their Polish surname to an Anglicized name before Walter's birth (an example would be changing the name Majewski to the Anglicized "Major"). Walter indicated that his family believed that the name change would help his father in business (since people would remember his name better) and distance the family name from the negative Polish stereotypes (in Walter's words, "They hid their Polishness"). Since Polish Americans tend to change their name more than any other ethnic group, and a negative self-image and cultural image is associated with changing one's surname (Lopata, 1975), the therapist processed the shame and negative feeling that Walter had inherited through his cultural assimilation as a Polish American.

Another cultural piece of knowledge that the therapist had to take into consideration was that neither Moira nor Walter grew up in families in which they expressed their inner emotions. It became quite apparent to the therapist that Moira was extremely articulate yet unable to express her true feelings. She would complain about Walter with a great deal of flair and drama, yet she kept everything on a surface level, describing all of Walter's behaviors, but little of her own feelings and reactions. Although she presented with a great deal of wit and charm, she appeared to struggle when it came to personal reflection and self-examination. Since the therapist already acknowledged what a deep-seated issue "shame" is for both partners, it is paramount that the therapist be culturally sensitive regarding how she approaches the couple's inability to relate to one another on a deeper level. Reframing and focusing on their strengths can be a way that the therapist can help Moira to contain her reactions and become comfortable with her deeper feelings, and Walter can be encouraged to express rather than repress his feelings.

Although cultural elements seem to dominate the clinical picture in this case example, and Walter is the partner who presents as the PA (Neg) individual, therapists must also be aware of the impact of gender roles in our society on the assessment and treatment of PA (Neg) personality disorder. Although little research has dealt with gender differences regarding passive-aggressive personality disorder, Maier and colleagues (1992) have noted that passive-aggressive personality disorder tends to be more frequently diagnosed in females. Given the presence of power differentials between males and females in our society, which feminist writers such as Goldner (1989) have described, it is possible that women sometimes need to resort to the use of passive-aggressive behaviors and interpersonal styles to assert their own individuality and autonomy. The passive-aggressive style may be a way for women to avoid the social stigma and rejection that are often associated with women who are seen as challenging or aggressive in advocating for their own needs and wants. The fact that this disorder may be diagnosed more in women than in men may be an artifact of therapists' immersion in a patriarchal culture, rather than a genuine epidemiological gender difference. Given these considerations, it would be important for therapists to be attuned to these gender implications, and to ensure that women who seem to display passive-aggressive traits are not given a pathologizing individual diagnosis when their behavior instead represents a normal adaptation to societal gender imbalances in power.

FUTURE DIRECTIONS

Further research regarding treatment of passive-aggressive (negativistic) personality disorder is in order. Research is needed to provide information on the reliability and validity of this disorder and on its diagnostic criteria and distinguishing features. Millon and Davis (2000) have proposed several variants of the basic negativistic pattern including the following subtypes: vacillating (borderline features), abrasive (sadistic features), discontented (depressive features), and circuitous (dependent features). Research should explore the clinical utility of these subtypes and the frequency with which they occur in the population. A psychometric study of DSM-IV criteria by Fossati and colleagues (2000) does not support the distinct subtypes proposed by Millon and Davis. However, this study does agree with Millon's (1981) earlier work that proposed that passive resistance should not be deemed the core symptom of PAPD. Both Millon and Davis (1996) and Fossati et al. (2000) suggest that the complaint of being misunderstood in relationships with others should be the core diagnostic criteria.

As noted, research regarding the use of ICT with personality-disordered couples is limited. This is due to the integrative nature of the therapy and the fact that each therapist tends to apply various aspects of the model differently in order to meet the specific needs of the individual couple. Although this presents a challenge to future research, it certainly does not indicate ineffectiveness of the treatment model. Further investigation is also needed regarding the use of pharmacological treatments both alone and in conjunction with therapy.

Future research regarding the effectiveness of treatment models with clients using a PA (Neg) style seems contingent on credence given to this disorder within the DSM nomenclature. Due to the relegation of passive-aggressive (negativistic) personality disorder as a disorder "not otherwise specified" in the DSM-IV-TR, current research regarding a PA (Neg) style and its treatment is somewhat limited.

REFERENCES

American Psychiatric Association (1952). *Diagnostic and statistical manual of mental disorders* (First edition). Washington, DC: American Psychiatric Association.

American Psychiatric Association (1968). *Diagnostic and statistical manual of mental disorders* (Second edition). Washington, DC: American Psychiatric Association.

American Psychiatric Association (1987). *Diagnostic and statistical manual of mental disorders* (Third edition, Text revision). Washington, DC: American Psychiatric Association.

American Psychiatric Association (1994). *Diagnostic and statistical manual of mental disorders* (Fourth edition). Washington, DC: American Psychiatric Association.

American Psychiatric Association (2000). *Diagnostic and statistical manual of mental disorders* (Fourth edition, Text revision). Washington, DC: American Psychiatric Association.

Burns, D.D. and Epstein, N. (1983). Passive-aggressiveness: A cognitive-behavioral approach. In R.D. Parsons and R.J. Wicks (Eds.), *Passive-aggressiveness: Theory and practice* (pp. 72-97). New York: Brunner/Mazel.

Folwarski, J. and Marganoff, P. (1996) Polish families. In M. McGoldrick and P. Marganoff (Eds.), *Ethnicity and family therapy* (Second edition) (pp. 658-672). New York: Guilford Press.

Fossati, A., Maffei, C., Bagnato, M., Donati, D., Donini, M., Fiorilli, M., and No-vella, L. (2000). A psychometric study of DSM-IV passive-aggressive (negativistic) personality disorder criteria. *Journal of Personality Disorders, (14)*1, 72-80.

Gehrke, S. and Moxom, J. (1962). Diagnostic classification and treatment techniques in marriage counseling. *Family Process, 1*(2), 253-264.

Goldner, V. (1989). Generation and gender: Normative and covert hierarchies. In M. McGoldrick, C.M. Anderson, and F. Walsh (Eds.), *Women in families: A framework for family therapy* (pp. 42-60). New York: Norton.

Kaslow, F.W. (1983). Passive-aggressiveness: An intrapsychic, interpersonal, and transactional dynamic in the family system. In R.D. Parsons and R.J. Wicks (Eds.), *Passive-aggressiveness: Theory and practice* (pp. 134-152). New York: Brunner/Mazel.

Lopata, H.Z. (1975). The Polish American family. In C.H. Mindel and R.W. Habenstein (Eds.), *Ethnic families in America: Patterns and variations* (pp. 15-40). New York: Elsevier.

Maier, W., Lichtermann, D., Klinger, T., and Heun, R. (1992). Prevalences of personality disorders (DSM-III-R) in the community. *Journal of Affective Disorders, 53*, 173-181.

McGoldrick, M. (1996). Irish families. In M. McGoldrick, J. Giordano, and J. Pearce (Eds.), *Ethnicity and family therapy* (Second edition) (pp. 544-566). New York: Guilford Press.

McGoldrick, M., Giordano, J., and Pearce, J. (1996). *Ethnicity and family therapy.* (Second edition). New York: Guilford Press.

Millon, T. (1981). *Disorders of personality.* New York: John Wiley and Sons, Inc.

Millon, T. and Davis, R.D. (1996). *Disorders of personality: DSM-IV and beyond.* New York: Wiley Interscience.

Millon, T. and Davis, R. (2000). *Personality disorders in modern life.* New York: John Wiley and Sons, Inc.

Nichols, M.P. (1992). Psychoanalytically oriented family therapy. In M.B. Thomas (Ed.), *An introduction to marital and family therapy: Counseling toward healthier family systems across the lifespan* (pp. 230-257). Upper Saddle River, NJ: Macmillan Publishing Co.

Nichols, M.P. and Schwartz, R.C. (2001). *Family therapy concepts and methods* (Fifth edition). Needham Heights, MA: Allyn and Bacon.

Sarno, J.E. (1991) *Healing back pain: The mind-body connection.* New York: Warner Books.

Slavik, S., Carlson, J., and Sperry, L. (1992). Adlerian marital therapy with the passive-aggressive partner. *The American Journal of Family Therapy, 20*(1), 25-35.

Slavik, S., Carlson, J., and Sperry, L. (1998). The passive-aggressive couple. In J. Carlson and L. Sperry (Eds.), *The disordered couple* (pp. 299-314). Bristol, PA: Brunner/Mazel, Inc.

Stricker, G. (1983). Passive-aggressiveness: A condition especially suited to the psychodynamic appraoch. In R.D. Parsons and R.J. Wicks (Eds.), *Passive-aggressiveness: Theory and practice* (pp. 5-24). New York: Brunner/Mazel.

Stuart, R. (1980). *Helping couples change.* New York: Guilford.

Stuart, R. (2002). Integrative therapy for couples. In J. Carlson and D. Kjos (Eds.), *Theories and strategies of family therapy* (pp. 317-352). Boston, MA: Allyn and Bacon.

Thomas, M.B. (1992). *An introduction to marital and family therapy: Counseling toward healthier family system across the lifespan.* Upper Saddle River, NJ: Macmillan Publishing Co.

U.S. Joint Armed Services (1949). *Nomenclature and methods of recording mental conditions.* U.S. Joint Armed Services.

U.S. War Department (1945). Nomenclature and method of recording diagnoses. *War Department Technical Bulletin.* Medical 203, Washington, DC: Author.

Wetzler, S. and Morey, L.C. (1999). Passive-aggressive personality disorder: The demise of a syndrome. *Psychiatry, 62*(1), 49-59.

Chapter 9

Family Therapy of Avoidant Personality Disorder

Peter D. McLean
Carmen P. McLean

INTRODUCTION

Avoidant personality disorder (APD) is often unrecognized, or misunderstood as mere shyness. Family therapists recognize that focusing treatment exclusively on an individual with APD, without looking at the family system and its influence, is misguided. Evidence suggests that negative behavior interactions between family members are associated with relationship distress, and that members' use of aversive control (nagging, threatening, withdrawing, etc.) is associated with a variety of dysfunctional outcomes for children (Dattilio, 1998). This chapter will look at avoidant personality disorder from an integrative perspective. We will integrate individual perspectives of psychopathology and emotional distress within a systems framework. This approach acknowledges the family's crucial therapeutic role in treating the APD individual. Family members are often co-opted into behaviors that inadvertently reinforce APD symptoms and behaviors. For the child or adult with APD, the family systems perspective views the relationship, cognitions, emotions, and behaviors as exerting a mutual influence on one another, which can maintain dysfunction in the family unit. However, the family can be a key factor in improving the quality of life of the avoidant family member through understanding, encouragement, support, and collaboration in therapeutic tasks.

The cognitive-behavioral therapy (CBT) approach to family therapy has enjoyed renewed attention. Patterson (1971, 1982) applied the concepts of cognitions to family members, and the larger research community quickly expanded these theoretical constructs to family dynamics and interactions. Integrating the empirically supported approaches of CBT with family therapy when working with psychopathology is a natural conclusion for today's therapist. CBT family therapy with a family whose member has APD operates on the premise that the degree of distress or warmth in familial relationships is directly influenced by an interaction of cognitive, behavioral, and affective factors. Specifically, the family therapist will pay particular attention to the "family process" or sequences of behavior and interaction among family members in session, and will listen for expression of thoughts and feelings. Understanding this process, the therapist will then help the family develop skills for better communication and problem solving, and devise "experiments" to test novel behaviors. This approach to skill development, communication enhancement, and hypothesis testing is supported by evidence that families referred for relationship distress exhibit more dysfunctional communication and less constructive problem-solving behavior than do satisfied families (Baucom and Epstein, 1990).

ANXIETY: NORMAL VERSUS PATHOLOGICAL LEVELS

We begin by describing the continuum of social anxiety from normal, to socially phobic, to avoidant personality-disordered groups. Almost everyone reports apprehension, discomfort, and physical symptoms of anxious arousal (e.g., increased heart rate, blushing, sweating) in specific performance situations where they are subject to social scrutiny from important strangers. Public speaking, stage appearances, and social gatherings in which individuals are potentially exposed to competent and compelling others are familiar examples of normal social anxiety. Anxious arousal typically decreases with experience, after one becomes highly practiced at such activities. However, such anxiety is both rational and limited to the situational demands of the task. In contrast, specific social phobia follows the same pattern, but in a more extreme and irrational form. Anxiety symptoms increase, including associated cognitive distortions, which lead to people with specific social phobia avoiding feared situations. People who are unable to urinate in public washrooms (i.e., "shy bladder"), or those who avoid restaurants because they fear being closely observed by others and anticipate their hands shaking noticeably as they eat or drink, illustrate the specificity of these social fears. In comparison to individuals with specific phobia, normally anxious people are less avoidant of their feared social situations and tolerate low levels of anxiety. Unlike those with specific social phobia, normally anxious people do not think of themselves negatively, as they imagine how others perceive them (Roth and Heimberg, 2001). In crossing the boundary from normal social anxiety to specific social phobia, we notice increased subjective and physiological levels of situational fear, increased avoidance of feared social situations, and the presence of cognitive distortions in which attention is focused increasingly on possible threat and irrational beliefs about what others are thinking. These trends increase in magnitude as we move further along the continuum of social anxiety.

Generalized social phobia represents a more pervasive experience of social phobia that goes well beyond specific performance situations to characterize most social situations. Individuals with generalized social phobia demonstrate broadened avoidance patterns that include avoidance of occupations that involve significant social interaction due to fears of disapproval and rejection. Generalized social phobia usually begins in late childhood or early adolescence, and although its severity over time fluctuates considerably, it is uncommon for this subtype of social phobia to remit entirely (Wittchen and Fehm, 2001).

APD occupies the far end of the social anxiety spectrum in terms of both severity and persistence of anxiety, and it is firmly rooted in a broader context of psychopathology. APD is defined by the American Psychiatric Association (APA, 1994, pp. 664-665) in the *Diagnostic and Statistical Manual of Mental Disorders,* Fourth Edition, (DSM-IV) as

> A pervasive pattern of social inhibition, feelings of inadequacy, and hypersensitivity to negative evaluation, beginning by early childhood and present in a variety of contexts, as indicated by four (or more) of the following:
>
> (1) avoids occupational activities that involve significant interpersonal contact, because of fears of criticism, disapproval, or rejection

(2)   is unwilling to get involved with people unless certain of being liked
(3)   shows restraint within intimate relationships because of the fear of being shamed or ridiculed
(4)   is preoccupied with being criticized or rejected in social situations
(5)   is inhibited in new interpersonal situations because of feelings of inadequacy
(6)   views self as socially inept, personally unappealing, or inferior to others
(7)   is unusually reluctant to take personal risks or to engage in any new activities because they may prove embarrassing (reprinted with permission from the *Diagnostic and Statistical Manual of Mental Disorders,* Fourth Edition, copyright 1994 American Psychiatric Associati⟨ ⟩

People with APD use social avoidance as a primary coping mechanism and can be differentiated from schizoid personality disorder, with whom they have historically been confused (Livesley, West, and Tanney, 1985), by their desire for social contact (Alden et al., 2002). Those with APD long for normal social relationships, whereas those with schizoid personality disorder are indifferent, or even disdainful of social relationships. APD prevalence rates are in the 0.05 to 1 percent range (APA, 1994), and it occurs in women as often as men. However, those with a diagnosis of APD account for 10 to 20 percent of clients at mental health outpatient clinics.

A complicating feature for practitioners is the high rate of comorbidity associated with APD. For example, Oldham and colleagues (1995) found a 48 percent co-occurrence rate between APD and any mood disorder. The co-occurrence of APD and dependent personality disorder is also high. In these cases, those with APD develop extreme dependence on family members because they are considered to be relatively familiar and safe. The family members are often conflicted, since they want to encourage social independence in their family member with APD, but at the same time know how painful other social interactions are for their family member. The implications in terms of the family dynamics in which a family member has APD are considerable.

By virtue of being an Axis II disorder, APD is considered to represent a configuration of personality traits that are relatively rigid. Perhaps the most well-researched model of personality in terms of descriptive taxonomy is the five-factor model identified by Costa and McCrae (1992, 1998). Of the five broad domains of personality function identified in this model, neuroticism and extraversion are the largest. Taken together, when neuroticism (i.e., anxiousness) and introversion (polar opposite of extraversion) are present in severe form, as in APD, subtraits of personality become evident, including characteristics of being timid, easily embarrassed, socially avoidant, avoidant of novelty, and poor tolerance for negative emotions (for review, see Alden et al., 2002; Widiger, 2001). In addition to being severe, APD is relatively chronic as well. The six-year test/retest correlations of self-ratings on neuroticism and introversion are 0.83 and 0.82 respectively, and spousal ratings on the same traits are almost as high (Costa and McCrae, 1994). The enduring quality of these personality domains limits the improvement that can be expected in the adjustment of those with APD, particularly in the absence of therapy.

What are the pathways through which APD is formed? Heritability estimates for introversion and anxiousness are approximately 50 percent (Widiger, 2001), which identifies a strong biological influence in APD. The biological contribution to APD represents a vulnerability, which then interacts with social experience from an early age forward. Painful childhood experiences, including childhood physical and sexual abuse, unresolved losses, sustained bullying, and rejection by peers or caretakers could interact with biological vulnerability to shape APD (Roche et al., 1999).

Families with a member having APD have a long time to become used to this disorder and its behavioral manifestations. They frequently assume the family member with APD is just introverted or "nervous" around strangers and other people. Families attempt to persuade and educate their APD member about the advantages of having friends, playing group sports, joining clubs, going to camp, and endless other social activities—all to no avail. They typically set up social occasions involving the member with APD, in the belief that a little exposure to amicable social activities will motivate the family member to first tolerate, then enjoy, and finally to seek out social interactions with nonfamily members. Ultimately, families give up expectations that their family member with APD will ever become socially comfortable. They stop pushing and begin to accommodate, and finally become co-opted into colluding with their family member's social avoidance. Families are almost always torn between the tendency to empathize with their family member distressed by APD and their feelings of resentment produced by the extra burden of caring for and protecting this individual in light of his or her illogical and maddening, social avoidance.

Few studies have examined the psychopathology of ADP. In comparison, much work has been done to understand the nature of social phobia and its antecedents. Since APD is understood to exist on a continuum, from shyness, to social phobia, and finally APD on the most extreme end of social discomfort, investigators have generalized some of the findings from social phobia to APD to provide direction in development of theoretical and treatment models.

The treatment model described for APD in this chapter is based upon the short-term structured treatment for APD developed by Alden (1989) with minor modification. This treatment program was developed for group treatment, but we found it easy to adapt for individual and family treatment as well. It consists of four primary components: psychoeducation about APD, changing beliefs about social evaluation and competence, graduated behavioral exposure, and interpersonal skills training.

Conceptions of family therapy, including psychodynamic, cognitive-behavioral, and family systems approaches, have a lot to offer in the delivery of treatment relevant to APD. Our bias in the recommendations contained in this chapter is to adopt an evidenced-based approach to both understanding and treating APD. To date, this favors a cognitive-behavioral orientation. This said, we are very mindful of the rich contributions made by the other family therapy orientations that have also struggled to understand and influence APD. Most important, we are acutely aware that the success of the cognitive behavioral therapy approach to family therapy of APD depends upon a full awareness of family dynamics and the ability of the therapist to enroll the cooperation of family members to deal constructively with the impact of having a family member with APD and to secure the family's assistance in therapeutic tasks.

An essential question for everyone is, what is reasonable to expect in way of therapeutic response to family therapy for APD? This is a particularly relevant question given the significant biological basis for APD and its designation as a personality disorder, which by definition is relatively intractable. The most empirically based answer to this question comes from Alden's (1989) study. Participants were well screened to ensure they met diagnostic criteria for APD and randomly assigned to one of three CBT component treatments or to a no-treatment control group. All three treated groups demonstrated statistically significant improvements in behavioral and a variety of self-report measures, including social reticence, anxiety symptoms, and satisfaction with social activities. To help interpret these findings, Alden compared the pre- and posttreatment scores on standardized questionnaire measures of self-esteem and social reticence to normative scores. Before treatment, the APD groups were approximately two standard deviations below the normal population comparison on these measures. After treatment, the treated APD participants were one standard deviation below the normal comparison group. In general, this suggests that the ten weekly group sessions of two to two-and-a-half hours' duration are responsible for a 50 percent improvement in APD symptoms. This is a remarkable and encouraging achievement, and it is expected that combining the treatment components into a single protocol, as we do in this chapter, along with the advantages of treatment within a family context, that these results can be replicated by family therapists working in the community and perhaps improved upon. Nonetheless, APD is a condition of pervasive and entrenched social avoidance that represents a daunting treatment challenge, and expectations for change need to be realistic.

IMPACT ON THE FAMILY

The impact on the family of having a member who has APD is quite significant. With time, families typically come to regard APD as an "invisible illness" responsible for their afflicted family member's de facto disability. The exact nature of family impact though, will depend upon how generally available and supportive the family is to the APD member, and how individual members emotionally bond and develop interactive patterns. Certainly the adjustment to one another on the part of both the APD member and the family, is gradual and nondramatic. A primary reason for this slow evolution is that the family member with APD will conceal and deny his or her inner feelings and fears with consummate skill, usually presenting instead as an agreeable, nonoffensive individual who is shy, excessively private, and oversensitive to criticism. In reality, the APD member is easily embarrassed, hypervigilant about social interactions, feels both ashamed and inadequate in social situations that have not been avoided, and "fakes it" as best as possible and in a socially acceptable manner. We estimate that relatively few people with APD and their families realize that the symptom picture represents APD.

The first signs of this disorder frequently start in infancy or early childhood, when social inhibition and fear of strangers and novel situations are developmentally appropriate, and often are not considered to be remarkable. In most children, this early shyness, and other expressions of social apprehension such as avoidance, normally dissipate in later childhood or early adolescence. In APD, these symptoms actually increase during this period. During late adolescence and early adulthood, APD symptoms intensify further, becoming pervasive and rigid. This is fateful, since it is during adolescence and early adulthood that building social relationships becomes key to adjustment and quality of life.

Family Reaction Themes

Empathy

A strong and natural response to newborn children is empathy. All family members join in speculating what the baby is thinking and feeling. Because the infant cannot speak for himself or herself, family members freely anthropomorphize, attributing motives and carefully tracking any hint of discomfort and maturational change. This normal, intense interest, combined with emotional bonding, sets the stage for lifelong understanding and caring. In most families, it is probably fair to say that family members begin to moderate their empathy for their younger members as these individuals demonstrate self-sufficiency and confidence in coping with social expectations skillfully, this seems not to happen in APD individuals. Family members correctly sense continued social discomfort on the part of their APD member and try not to upset or hurt this person. Families with an APD member seem always ready to feel sorry for this member saying, "We know what she feels, others can't" or, "He is a special person, who can't manage in front of others and needs unique understanding."

Exposure

Good parents encourage children to experience systematic and graded exposure to a variety of social situations to develop social competence and self-esteem. Early social inhibition and fear is forgiven, but alert parents have a good sense of what is developmentally appropriate and act accordingly to afford their child exposure to social situations. First identified as shyness on the part of their young family member, families become aware that the overall breadth and depth of social discomfort and avoidance is not healthy, and begin to push for more social exposure, hoping to overcome the obvious fear of social situations outside of the family. Thus starts a power struggle within families to increase social exposure to their APD family member, despite resistance. From our experience, this power struggle never actually stops. It ebbs and flows for approximately four decades. Specifically, family members, both individually and collectively, try and engage their APD family member in all manner of normal social interactions, in the belief that resistance is just shyness that will go away with social practice.

Persuasion

When asked, "Why won't you play with your school friends?" or "Why won't you go to the picnic?" the persistently enquiring family finds that their reluctant family member holds broad-based fears of social disapproval. Individuals with APD quickly learn not to take unnecessary risks by talking too much, or doing anything that might expose them to social scrutiny. They continuously monitor others for any hint of disapproval, while at the same time working hard to ensure that they are absolutely nonoffensive, as agreeable as possible, and are not showing any somatic signs of their discomfort, such as blushing, hand trembling, sweating, or interruptions in vocal fluency. Indelicate, but normal questions in the schoolyard such as, "So why are you wearing a shirt like that?" are terrifying. As family members discern these beliefs and fears, they dutifully seek to explain them as misunderstandings. Family members further and redundantly explain, "How the world works" socially (e.g., "Be nice to others and they'll be nice to you," or "If he does that, just walk away because he is being a jerk. Who cares?") This unending educational program is, of course, doomed. The APD member listens, but is not moved by reassurance, does not argue or typically reveal any information about his or her beliefs, and takes the easiest route to end the conversation without making any social commitments.

Protection

Understandably, and in keeping with the families' inclination to be empathetic toward its APD member, family members seek to shield this individual from social interactions they know she or he won't like, even though they really want their family member to be independent. Over time, they become unaware that they frequently speak for the family member in social interactions, as though the family member is not present, or as if the member is unable to speak for themselves. This is a welcomed and increasingly expected service performed by family members in consideration of their APD member's sensitivities, which is sometimes viewed as overprotective, or odd by non-family members. Family members usually consider this "protection" as a responsibility and divide the task up to ensure "coverage" when their APD family member is socially exposed (e.g., "Watch out for Alex. He's your responsibility!").

Sensitivity to Criticism

Those with APD are extraordinarily overreactive to real or imagined negative evaluation from others and go to abnormal lengths to avoid the risk. The rough and tumble, but normal range schoolyard teasing and verbal insults are perceived as catastrophic and irreversible. Oddly, no "learning curve" is apparent, at least through to the middle adult years, wherein those afflicted with APD begin to relax and finally figure out that others are not monitoring them, do not consider them socially inept, and may even like them. Clearly, the fears and supporting beliefs are irrational and give rise to constant screening of others for possible negative evaluation, and a readiness to rapidly appease or escape if displeasure is detected or assumed. In families, people learn to adjust to this sensitivity in stages. They can see the tears, crying, and emotional pain so easily induced by relatively harmless comments, actions, and nonverbal signs of communication during the early years. Similarly, they learn the futility of subsequent explanations. Parents scold the siblings of the APD member for not being more respectful of the member's sensitivities, and slowly a double standard develops within the family: the normal one for everyone except the APD member, and a special one "where everyone walks on eggshells" so as to avoid hurting the APD member, or being misunderstood. Family members often feel these requirements are unreasonable and involve a lot of work on their part to accommodate the sensitivities of their family member.

Collusion

Families with an APD member become pressured into accommodating and actively participating in social avoidance. The process is insidious and represents the "path of least resistance" at the time. Making excuses for nonappearance at expected events; speaking for the APD member at a family dinner with guests, even though the APD member is present; feigning social adjustment and busy involvement in studies, hobbies, work, or other nonsocial activities to others on behalf of the APD family member; all may become routine and expected responses on the part of all family members.

Resentment

Caught between a sense of duty and protection on the one hand, and a recognition that their accommodation to their APD family member's fears and social avoidance is irrational, irritating, time-consuming, and often embarrassing, family members may develop resentment toward their APD family member. Of course, such feelings do not go undetected by the APD family member and predictable family dynamics result.

SETTING

Our setting is a community mental health center that offers publicly supported (i.e., no client fees) mental health programs. This is one of a number of similar centers within a regional health authority, divided geographically into population-based "catchments areas" of about 55,000 people per center. Our center has fifteen clinical staff, including nine master's level counselors, two psychologists, two social workers, one nurse, one occupational therapist, and one psychiatrist. Programs within our center are based in general upon client age range (i.e., child, adolescent, adult); both broad and specific diagnostic, or functional groupings (e.g., depression, addictions, panic disorder, social skills training); treatment delivery format (i.e., individual, family, or non-family group therapy); and severity of problem (i.e., acute, maintenance/follow-up, and drop in programs).

Approximately one-third of the people living in our catchment area speak English as a second language. The largest ethnic group is Chinese, split between Mandarin and Cantonese languages, followed by East Indian, Malaysian, and Latin American groups. Although we have clients from all of these ethnic groups in our programs, they are underrepresented since, due to funding restrictions, we can only offer treatment in these languages on an individual basis and when a translator from the community is available.

We find that approximately half of our APD referrals come from a popular and long-standing "shyness" group program (i.e., identified as APD upon screening for entrance to the shyness program), and the other half come directly from community practitioners. If family members are available and interested, they are seen in family therapy by one therapist following the treatment protocol described later in this chapter, for approximately ten sessions, spaced weekly. This constitutes the acute treatment phase, which is followed by three or four follow-up sessions over the next six months. Because about a third of our APD clients live alone as adults, we intermittently run APD group treatment programs and often include the APD family member who is also receiving family treatment for APD. There are no firm rules about "doubling up" treatment in this manner, however we have found that it is often practical to do so, since this allows us to maximize exposure to strangers (i.e., other APD group members) and focus on skill development, while dealing with family issues specifically in the concurrent family sessions. We estimate that about half of our APD clients receiving family therapy are also able to attend a concurrent APD group program.

TREATMENT MODEL

Short-Term Structured Treatment for Avoidant Personality Disorder

This treatment protocol focuses on four key components derived from cognitive behavioral therapy (Alden, 1989) that have been demonstrated as effective for APD. It is understood that this treatment can be effective only if it is placed within the context of known principles of family therapy, which address issues of family structure, power, alignments, and boundaries. We expect that readers will be familiar with a variety of family therapy models, and will focus our discussion of the treatment model as it applies specifically to APD, and on outlining the CBT elements of the approach, which may be less familiar to many family therapists.

Understanding of APD and Expectations of Treatment

This is the psychoeducational component of the treatment model. The symptoms of APD are described to the clients, and it is explained that APD is thought to derive from a biological predisposition that is enabled by environmental factors to become a long-standing behavioral pattern (Kagan, Reznick, and Snidman, 1988) that can by eased by treatment. That is, APD is something that a person is largely born with, which may make attachment difficult, and results in intense social apprehension and fear from all except well-known and trusted others, such as family members. The biological component is emphasized since families often assume that APD is the result of a lack of will power or personal resolve. They use their own experience in overcoming social apprehension as a comparative basis to generalize to their APD family member and do not understand the difference. We explain APD in terms of biological individual differences, such as having an "ear for music" or athletic ability. It is further explained that APD is thought to be maintained by both false beliefs about negative social evaluation and personal competence, and social avoidance. The result of social avoidance is an inevitable, poor familiarity with a broad range of social interactions, a relative lack of "social successes," and a corresponding lack of social confidence. Those having APD and their families need consistent assurance that despite its biological roots, therapy and practice can significantly improve this disorder.

Families are directed to the "here and now," in way of time frame, to avoid excessive excursions into the past. Typical problems the APD family member has, or the family has with this person (e.g., expressing disapproval, starting and maintaining conversations with strangers, interpreting verbal silence as personal disdain, job interviews, making "small talk" to others at work or in grocery store lines, not answering the family phone or door, not offering personal opinions within the family) are detailed, consensus is sought, and if achieved, the problems are placed into rank order. A set of treatment goals are generated from this problem list. These goals form the basis of homework assignments, and the roles and expectations of all family members are specified, since these assignments are practiced over the course of therapy.

Cognitive Challenges

Specific fears underlying each client's behavioral avoidance patterns are identified and challenged by generating and evaluating alternative interpretations for each situation. Typically, those with APD strongly hold two particular beliefs: that others are especially looking at them, and that others evaluate them negatively. It is important not to try and talk people with APD out of these beliefs, but instead to consider such conclusions as one of a number of possibilities, and to then go on and find out, through behavioral experiments, which is correct. For example, when do people generally look at others, and why? Task the client with the job of watching people watch others in public places, such as coffee shops, on buses, on the street, or while sitting in shopping malls. They will likely report that most people do briefly watch others, probably out of boredom. Such "experiments" should be used often to weaken the previous, negative conclusion held by the client and replace it with a more normal (i.e., likely) conclusion.

APD clients also often conclude that others view them as "different." In other words, they assume others are "put off" by their appearance, what they say or do, or some combination. When asked to speculate on what others think about their appearance, what they say and what they do, the therapist is struck by the overwhelming pejorative bias, as clients conclude, "They think I look stupid," "See me as a klutz," "Feel sorry for me," "Think I talk weird," or "Figure I can't do anything right." In each instance, it is therapeutically useful to elaborate exactly what the basis is for the assumed conclusion others have made about the client. It allows the therapist to zero in and set up a behavioral experiment. "Oh, so you think that if someone doesn't talk to you soon after they sit beside you on the bus, they have written you off as not worth talking about. Well that is possible, but is it probable? What other reasons might there be for this behavior?" We write each of the client's key faulty assumptions, three to five other possible interpretations and ways of finding out which competing assumption is more likely, on a large, white board.

Families offer an easy opportunity to start this process, because the client can "debrief" family members about what they were thinking with regard to the client. This process is extended to behavioral experiments, first within the family, and then outside the family, to develop a range of alternative and normal interpretations for each worry, as well as reasonable ways of collecting evidence (e.g., "If the person at work you think is bored by you answers with enthusiasm when you ask him how his weekend was, what would this mean?").

Clients are taught to try and ignore symptoms of somatic anxiety they fear others will detect, and to shift their attention instead to prosocial behavior. We help them develop a ready repertoire of socially acceptable "excuses" for each symptom, by asking them and their family members for alternative explanations that might account for the embarrassing symptom. For example, blushing might be passed off as an allergy, and mild sweating as a result of eating food that was too spicy.

Graduated Exposure

An analysis of each client's interpersonal problems, in terms of both themes (e.g., dealing with criticism, making requests of strangers, expressing affection) and associated fear, is undertaken to develop themes of situations, ranked by distress. Families are most helpful in identifying the four or five main themes an APD client typically has. A range of ten to twenty examples, or situations within each theme is generated and then rank-ordered by the anticipated distress it would cause the client to engage in this situation. For convenience, distress is estimated using the subjective units of discomfort scale (SUDS), with "100" representing the "most anxious you have ever been" and "0" as the "most relaxed/laid back you have ever been." Clients systematically expose themselves to these theme hierarchies on a graduated basis, starting with the easiest, after first role-playing the selected scenarios and their various potential outcomes with both therapist and family members. Table 9.1 illustrates a theme hierarchy for meeting strangers socially and stating contrary opinions in conversations and its accompanying SUDS ratings. The rule of thumb is that clients should practice hierarchy items at the same SUDS level (creating equivalent scenarios, as necessary) until they achieve a reduction in SUDS of about 50 percent.

Exposure begins with in-session role-playing with the therapist to model appropriate behavior. Role-playing with family members act-

TABLE 9.1. Abbreviated Theme Hierarchy for Exposure in the Treatment of APD*

Item/Situation	SUDS Rating (%)
Arranging to meet and talk again	95
Taking an opposite point of view "Well, seems to me that there is another way to see it . . ."	90
Exploring another person's opinion "What do you think about . . . ?"	80

Personal inquiries and self-disclosures
    "Do you have any children?"
    "I was born in Quebec, but have lived in Denver for ten years."
	70

Maintaining conversations (e.g., asking follow-up questions)
    "How do you like working for Harrison International?"
    "Do you ever get tired of traveling so much?"
	65

Starting a conversation with an attractive/powerful person	60
Starting a conversation with a "moderate risk" person	45
Starting a conversation with a "low-risk" person (e.g., a kid, someone unattractive, or unthreatening)	20

*Normally this list would be expanded to ten to twenty items.

ing as strangers is next, followed by in vivo homework assignments. An important therapeutic task is to motivate the APD client to engage in these fear-provoking scenarios and ensure that family members are similarly respectful and encouraging (e.g., positive coaching). The overall goal of graduated exposure is to approximate a wide range of developmentally normal social situations to reduce fear and avoidance and foster confidence.

Interpersonal Skills Training

Clients are taught the general steps of how friendships are formed and the specific nature of requisite behavioral skills are identified and practiced, including: listening/attending skills, empathetic sensitivity, appropriate self-disclosure, and respectful assertiveness. Each skill is targeted to situations relevant to the client's life, modeled by the therapists, discussed, and then practiced with family members. Homework assignments are then generated for weekly social tasks in between treatment sessions. Special attention is reserved for issues associated with developing intimate relationships. The nature of intimacy is discussed and a social analysis of how close friends and romantic relationships are developed, in terms of understandings and skills, is made explicit. Three levels of social interaction are practiced in succession.

General assertiveness. The first level, general assertiveness, is intended to cover a range of social interactions, from self-introductions and ways of maintaining conversations, to soliciting information and opinions from others, offering contrary opinions, giving compliments, and dealing with both criticism and anger. Individuals with APD are fearful and passive in novel social situations, and exercising even basic social skills provides them with an important sense of control over social outcomes. We set up a series of tasks as part of the exposure hierarchies described earlier, but also integrate cognitive challenges with these exercises. For example, we ask APD clients to initiate three conversations a day, predict people's reactions, and to reconcile this reaction with their prediction (APD clients inevitably overpredict negative reactions), and introduce themselves at least once per day.

High on most APD clients' exposure hierarchies is coping with criticism and diffusing anger. Again, families provide an ideal "training ground" in which to practice skill development in these areas. For example, in role-playing the APD client will be encouraged to practice a number of constructive and de-escalating statements when confronted with an angry family member (e.g., "What would you like me to do instead?" "That might work. Let me think about it and I will get back to you before dinner. Is that alright with you?"). A number of excellent assertion training manuals are available (e.g., Paterson, 2000) that APD clients may use to augment their clinic appointments.

Forming friendships. Second, the process of forming friendships is addressed. Clients are encouraged to develop a number of acquaintances in different venues and to pursue activities together. This has the effect of taking the attention off the client. The skills of listening, demonstrating empathy, self-disclosure, and asking for favors are modeled, practiced as homework, and then reviewed during the following session. Two very useful means of easing interpersonal angst on the part of APD clients are to help them learn how to show interest in others and how to provide approval. APD clients usually believe (incorrectly) that they need to be clever, humorous, widely informed, and interesting in interpersonal encounters. The idea is to shift attention away from the client to the individual the client is addressing and to leave a positive impression. This can usually be accomplished by showing interest in others and giving compliments, two skills in which APD clients are highly inexperienced and apprehensive.

Starting with family members and then generalizing to acquaintances, APD clients are tasked with showing interest and following up in detail. For example, "How was your day?" could continue with, "What did you do for lunch?" or, "Do you ever get caught up?" In talking about a summer cabin, the client might inquire how the conversation partner found the cabin in the first place, and how difficult it was, what alternatives were under consideration at the time, how naturalistic the setting is, and what adventures have been had. Of course, the process is endless, but with practice clients will discover most people do not mind talking about themselves to an *interested* other party.

We recommend that APD clients develop the habit of giving routine positive feedback to others, with comments such as, "What a good idea," "Good for you," "You sure did a good job on that," and "Thanks for doing that for me." We view giving positive social feedback as one of the single most effective means of social influence, and since it is low risk in terms of being ignored, it is most useful for APD clients. Starting with in-session modeling and role-playing with family members, the client is asked to provide positive feedback to others for a total of five to ten times per day. Caution is required to ensure that the client or family member does not regard this practice as "insincere" or "manipulative." It is explained that the skill involves finding deserving activities or thoughts to comment upon, and that not doing so has the effect of taking the other person for granted and missing an opportunity to enhance the other person's self-esteem (McLean and Woody, 2001).

Developing intimate relationships. Finally, the process of developing intimate relationships is an important issue for most APD clients. If the client is already in an intimate relationship, the therapist may decide to skip this area for skill development. Also, it is not advised to explore or develop this skill area in the presence of parents, and possibly siblings, because of privacy issues. We recommend individual or group sessions (with other APD clients) to fully discuss issues of development of trust and commitment, demonstration of affection, and evaluation of the partner's comfort and willingness to evolve the relationship (i.e., stages and pacing of intimacies).

The four therapeutic tasks discussed earlier are loosely integrated in that they are adjusted to the client's circumstances. We find that the first session is used for the basic understanding of APD and expectations of treatment. In the second session, cognitive challenges are introduced, and in sessions 3-10, all three components are developed simultaneously (cognitive challenges, graduated exposure, and interpersonal skill training). The following case example illustrates how these various elements of the treatment approach are blended and applied in clinical practice.

CASE EXAMPLE

Alex is a twenty-four-year-old single male who lives in a small apartment and is financially supported by his father. He is in his second year at a community college after having worked in a variety of service and warehouse jobs since completing high school at age seventeen. He reports that he neither liked or disliked elementary and high school, and that he had little contact with extracurricular activities, including sports, music, clubs, or summer jobs. When he was ten years old, his parents underwent a hostile divorce and he subsequently lived with his mother and sister until age twenty-two, when he moved into his apartment and his mother remarried.

Self-conscious about his small physical stature, Alex presents as an otherwise pleasant and somewhat socially stiff individual who is easy to engage in casual conversation. It quickly becomes evident that Alex is very keen to please and that he lacks some judgment in excessively pursuing superficial questions and smiling somewhat inappropriately. He has a few former high school friends, but he has seen only one of them in the past year. On that occasion, his friend was with her date and all three went to a movie. He watches a lot of TV and movies, usually eats at local fast food restaurants, averages college grades in the B-C range, and sees his mother and sister about twice a week. When he was referred, he had no club memberships or routine social activities he engaged in and no apparent hobbies aside from watching TV. However, he was able to articulate a good range of goals, even though he wasn't acting on many of them. He was socially isolated and inhibited in new situations, but got along well with his family members, all three of whom lived separately.

Upon exploring Alex's social life, several unusual themes appeared. First, he was excessively preoccupied by others' opinions of him, often asking the interviewer what he thought of something Alex had said to a teacher, fellow student, or "friend" some time earlier. He would recount bus rides, for example, in which the passenger next to him would comment to him in an innocuous, but open-ended way and he would subsequently ruminate about what this stranger really meant and what he himself should have said differently. Second, it was clear that Alex seldom followed through with social opportunities, even though he wanted desperately to have a girlfriend and an active social life. Each time a social situation was discussed, Alex would wonder why the other party did this or that and what he could have or should have done. This speculation eventually had to be interrupted, as it became redundant and predictable. Third, Alex expressed fear of going out into many main streets in his city, and to those movie theaters, malls, or other places, where he may encounter "ethnic gang" members. He felt these people knew a lot about martial arts, were menacing, and might prey on "white guys" if he was alone or with a girlfriend. Alex had no history of abuse or threat from such people, although he watched a lot of TV violence and had witnessed a number of schoolyard fights involving ethnic males.

Alex was not depressed and did not evidence paranoid thinking. We felt that he was significantly underachieving and determined that he met criteria for APD. He agreed to treatment, which involved family therapy with his mother and sister, who was two years his senior, in combination with group treatment with five others who met criteria for APD (three males and two females, ages twenty-two to thirty-seven). Alex's mother and sister seemed well adjusted, were frustrated with their inability to influence him effectively, and were delighted for the treatment opportunity. Given Alex's age and independent living arrangement, we asked his mother and sister whether they would attend family therapy with Alex every other week for a total of five sessions as Alex simultaneously attended ten group therapy sessions for treatment of APD. All agreed.

Early family therapy revealed Alex had a history of "turning people off" because he tended to "interview them" rather than do activities with them. Cognitive distortions also became evident, including: (1) his belief that others "write me off because I'm not buff and tall—they just tolerate me," (2) that the way to be interesting is to ask lots of questions, (3) others routinely monitored him and later discussed and made fun of his "flaws," (4) an assumption that others were critical of him if interpersonal encounters did not turn out the way he predicted (Alex would become resentful or disinterested in further contact in response to this distortion), and (5) that "ethnic-looking" males in the fourteen- to thirty-five-year age range "had it in for him." Subtle forms of avoidance also became clear in that Alex would decline family dinners at his mother's home if guests were to be present, and he also declined to either double date with his sister or "hang out" with her and her friends.

Alex's sister and mother had to be encouraged not to just give Alex reassurance and encouragement regarding his social desires. They have been doing this for almost two decades to no avail. Instead, they were asked to help Alex challenge his faulty assumptions, develop and test alternative interpretations, practice targeted social skill areas for development, and support him in social exposure exercises. As noted earlier, many of these agenda items were also targeted in the APD group Alex was attending. For each of the five cognitive distortions, Alex generated three to five alternative explanations with the help of his sister and mother. This also involved setting up behavioral experiments to find out which of the alternatives were more likely. For example, it would be difficult to verify whether others talk about him privately. Instead, the therapist asked him to survey some of his sister's friends to see how often they did the same to others. Results indicated that this is a common, but innocent pastime that did not detract from their interest in the particular person they discussed.

Behavioral exposure hierarchies were developed for Alex to engage the areas previously avoided due to fear of "ethnic males." All of these areas were considered objectively safe. Exposure also included family dinners with guests, and Alex was tasked with listening, respectfully taking contrary positions, showing interest by asking reasonable questions, and giving positive feedback. Finally, Alex developed a regular social schedule of activities, with an emphasis on sustained, normal, socially shared activities. Initially Alex made little progress with this, but his sister arranged for him to accompany her and some of her friends to social events. This provided an opportunity for "debriefing" in the following treatment session, to rationalize any misconceptions between Alex and his sister regarding the same events. Another exposure hierarchy involved inviting classmates to coffee at his community college and selectively moving this activity to lunches and off-site activities of mutual interest. Alex's social skills training occurred mainly in the APD group sessions and focused on defining and avoiding "emotional smothering" and the development of diplomacy in questioning others socially.

By end of treatment, Alex reported that he had joined a local gym, one college club, sat closer to the front of all his classes, was going out socially at least one evening per week, had met three new "friends" at college, and had repeatedly encountered "ethnic males" with no difficulties. Upon follow-up, three months later, these gains had been maintained. However, although Alex increased his social rate of activity and "hung out" with several girls, he did not yet have a designated girlfriend.

STRENGTHS AND LIMITATIONS

The CBT approach to family therapy for APD offers a number of advantages, but the main ones are its structure, focus on the remediation of deficits, challenge of fears and cognitive distortions, and the enrollment of family members into the therapeutic enterprise in a constructive manner. Given the pervasive and enduring nature of APD, it is easy for both families and therapists to be overwhelmed with the inflexibility of the psychopathology. A strategic focus on specific processes offers hope and relief.

The obvious skill deficits, specific fears, and behavioral avoidance patterns, as well as the clear presence of cognitive distortions (e.g., faulty beliefs), offer clear targets for the structured CBT family therapy approach to the treatment of APD. This approach uses insight, but recognizes that insight is an insufficient condition for a change in APD. Consequently, it also utilizes fear habituation through exposure exercises, and skill development to build a normative repertoire of social skills to increase social effectiveness. It is educational and prosocial in nature, promoting generalization over time. Furthermore, the focus discourages blaming within the family and unnecessary exploration of family dynamics and history, while pooling the insights and willingness of the family to help out in very tangible ways.

Although the CBT family therapy approach to APD has not been evaluated, the CBT approach in general has been studied, with encouraging results. It is safely assumed that adding the advantage of family assistance can only improve this effort. The empirical basis for CBT, in general, derives from an experimental approach to understanding psychopathology and testing treatment components. It draws on a long history of systematic investigation and treatment in the area of social phobia (see McLean and Woody, 2001, pp. 84-129, for review), and since APD is considered to be a more severe extension of social phobia (continuum theory), much of this work can inform the treatment of APD.

There are however, drawbacks that limit this treatment's general utility. First, families may not be available or cooperative, in which case individual or group treatment is the alternative. Also, many therapists are not trained in CBT approaches and may not be confident in attempting to employ CBT techniques, even within a family context. Fortunately, a number of high-quality CBT therapist guideline books are now available that address specific diagnostic problems and promise to make evidence-based treatments readily available to practitioners of all backgrounds. Nevertheless, practitioners not trained in CBT are often uncomfortable in holding clients accountable for agreed changes, particularly when fear is present. CBT practitioners, like athletic coaches, have learned that consistency and strength bring the best results in the face of apprehension and noncompliance, but it is recognized that this is an acquired therapeutic skill. The social support offered by group and family treatments are helpful in overcoming this limitation, as are behavioral experiments. Finally, it is important to establish limited expectations for any treatment of APD. A 30 percent functional improvement in APD is enormous therapeutic success by any measure, which will translate into marked improvement in quality of life for the APD client!

BENEFITS FOR THE FAMILY

Families with an APD member are usually slow to recognize the magnitude of this disorder. When the disorder's scope becomes appreciated, families feel compelled to try and understand its evolution. The most familiar avenues of understanding are to review family history and to compare the APD family member with any siblings. Parents often feel guilty or vaguely responsible for not preventing the development of APD, but tend to become resigned to it by the time their child with APD has moved into early adulthood.

Family therapy for APD can serve to significantly reduce blame and sense of responsibility within families for the plight of their member with APD. Parents tend to be at a loss to account for the development of APD in their son or daughter, and family therapy can provide a welcomed understanding. The explanation of biologically mediated sensitivity, the roles of distorted beliefs and behavioral avoidance, and the delayed acquisition of key social skills is something most families can understand. Furthermore, the explanatory model points the way toward treatment objectives. This allows most families to participate in an acceptable and very tangible way in the treatment requirements of family therapy for APD. It is our impression that the rate of family compliance with treatment for APD is quite high. We speculate that this is because family members can so easily understand and relate to the tasks of family treatment for APD. The relative tangibility of CBT family therapy allows families to improvise upon treatment themes and become quite involved, creative, and enterprising.

Properly educated and motivated by the therapist, families can support and move the therapeutic agenda ahead at a better rate than could reasonably be expected from individual or group therapy alone. They do this by changing family dynamics and focusing on clear and constructive tasks in a collaborative manner. In some ways, it seems that families have pent-up frustration and despair as a result of a history of failed attempts to help their APD member become more socially comfortable, and that consequently they are glad to assist, once they know how to do so. They relate well to the practical nature of this family-therapy approach, to the benefit of the APD member.

Another important benefit of family therapy for APD is that the treatment outcome expectations are specified in terms of a likely range, and are empirically informed. Treatment improvements of 30 percent are usually justified and can be as high as 50 percent. These improvements are realistic and welcomed and help to combat both pessimistic and idealized expectations for treatment outcome.

INDICATIONS AND CONTRAINDICATIONS

To improve treatment outcomes, client and treatment variables need to be matched for compatibility, and we recommend the inclusion and exclusion criteria noted in the following paragraphs. In terms of conjoint family therapy however, we have found substantial additional benefit in having the couple and/or family present in the delivery of CBT family therapy for APD. When a couple is seen in conjoint treatment, they are not seen exclusively as one individual with APD and the other as an unaffected partner, but rather as a dynamic unit whose patterns of reactions are interdependent.

When one partner presents with APD, the other partner has a significant history of adapting to these unique features of personality. Virginia Satir (1967) acknowledged the systemic influence in families, recognizing that therapy would reveal "repetitious, circular, predictable communication patterns, . . . allowing the couple to eventually redefine their relationship" (p. 1). The family practitioner can capitalize on strengths as well as any destructive or counterproductive responses or patterns by family members toward their member with APD. The CBT family therapist relies on the partner or other family members to encourage and sustain client change, with an understanding that family equilibrium may fluctuate. When dealing with a child, adolescent, or adult dependent, we always try and have both parents available, if at all possible. In the case example noted earlier, the client's father lived out of town and was unable to attend.

Indications for CBT Family Therapy for APD

- Willingness of whole family to attend treatment (children ten and under excluded)
- Desire of client for change
- Willingness of client and family to complete home and community assignments
- DSM-IV diagnosis of APD

Contraindications for CBT Therapy for APD

- Schizoid personality disorder (often confused with APD because they seem the same, except schizoid individuals are not upset by their social avoidance)
- Cognitively unable to engage treatment (e.g., psychosis, paranoia, or mental retardation present)
- Primary alcoholism on part of the client
- Marital/family violence
- Clinical depression (should be treated before APD)

MANAGEMENT OF TRANSFERENCE ISSUES

Transference can be defined simply as a set of beliefs, expectations, and emotional responses that a client brings into the client-therapist relationship. Individuals with APD have particular reason to cloud the therapeutic environment with such stereotypic bias. First, there is good reason to suspect that adverse childhood experiences, such as isolation, rejection, and other negative childhood social experiences, may be overrepresented in APD individuals. Meyer and Carver (2000) found that students with APD symptoms acknowledged significantly more negative childhood memories than did students without personality disorders. This would suggest that APD individuals would be more likely to be wary and to project the impact of such experiences onto "other" adults, especially those in a trusting relationship, such as parents and therapists. Second, by definition those with APD are judgmental in the extreme by virtue of their pathological social sensitivity and belief that others judge them as socially incompetent and somewhat despicable. Accordingly, therapists need to anticipate that the APD client will view them as others (i.e., transference recipients). In this case it is safe to assume that APD clients, despite outward congenial appearances, will assume the therapist(s) is critical of them, views them as unfortunate, incompetent, a waste of time, and is simply putting his or her time in, in a half-interested manner. These reactions to both the therapist and family members are likely to be unconscious on the part of the APD family member and are indicative of their earlier unresolved conflicts with negative social encounters.

To manage these biases, therapists first need to be aware that the APD client most certainly harbors a private perception of what others are thinking about him or her, including the therapist. Since therapists (and parents) will be viewed as knowledgeable, powerful, and socially competent, relative to themselves, APD clients will respond by being polite, conflict avoidant, and will strive toward socially appropriate, minimal exposure at all cost.

Given this awareness, therapists can then break down their clients' transference tendencies into their cognitive, affective, and behavioral components. In each case, it is useful to counter the APD client's likely role as a passive recipient in relation to the therapist who is probably cast as the provider of help. Initially, it is important to help clients understand that although their reactions are understandable, other explanations may account for the thoughts and feelings they experience. Issues of transference are inherently biased—projections onto others, stemming from cognitive distortions characterized by exquisite social sensitivity, result in false perceptions of rejection and disdain. To counter these tendencies, the therapist needs to help the client consider the possibility that his or her assumptions may be incorrect, and to figure out a way to test which competing assumption may be right. This leads directly into the cognitive challenging component of treatment, wherein the client is encouraged to examine the full range of possible interpretations pertaining to social encounters and perceptions. From this perspective, transference is considered a natural part of cognitive bias in APD. It is understood that transference, as a perceptual bias, also is applied to family members. This affords ample opportunity for the APD member to be encouraged by the therapist and family members to critically examine and test their automatic assumptions about other people. It specifically asks, "What do you think others think about you in this situation? And why would they? How would you know whether you are right or wrong?" In this manner, conclusions about parental shame and intolerance can be systematically evaluated. CBT family therapy lends itself well to such cognitive challenges.

MANAGEMENT OF CRISES
AND ACTING-OUT BEHAVIOR

By its nature, APD is neither dramatic or given to crises. That said, a therapeutic crisis could emerge when noncompliance develops. Clients are loath to engage in exposure exercises and demonstrate a virtual visceral aversion for social engagements. Therapists need to step back a little with the client and family to reposition the treatment goal and its anticipated benefits. Frequently, repetition of an earlier and less stressful goal is useful in building confidence and organizing a second start. It must be emphasized that treatment gains come slowly and only as a result of sustained effort on several fronts—building confidence through graduated practice and an integrative family approach to problem solving and support.

The second crisis that typically occurs is familial impatience. Family members say they are busy people who do not have the time to spare if their APD member does not make more effort. Therapists can only sympathize, knowing that the fatigued family has borne the brunt of such avoidance for many years. However, the therapist's first step should be to correct the notion that such noncompliance represents indifference rather than fear. A redundant therapeutic task is to reengage the family and client in a structured, goal-directed, and skill-based direction toward hard-won social competence.

INTEGRATION WITH PSYCHIATRIC SERVICES
AND ROLE OF MEDICATION

APD clients rarely require integration with psychiatric services except for medication consultations, or management of comorbid conditions such as depression, which may emerge over the course of treatment. In general, individuals with APD do not act out, are cognitively intact, interpersonally compliant, and do not represent a danger to either themselves or to others. As a result, integration with psychiatric services provides little benefit. Some therapists consider community psychiatric support groups as a possible stepping-stone toward further social integration. In our view, APD individuals are better served by alternative socialization "vehicles," such as volunteering. The difference is that psychiatric support groups can be quite introspective and model poor mental processing of social stimuli (e.g., reacting in an indifferent or angry fashion), whereas volunteer settings can offer more normal social skills, especially gratitude and easy conversation.

Medication can play a significant role with selective APD clients. Those who exhibit somatic hyperarousal in threatening social situations (excessive sweating, agitation), or behavioral inhibition (vocal blocking or being unable to focus and smoothly respond), can benefit from supplemental pharmacological support. This is entirely consistent with an integrated, multidimensional approach to treating APD, featuring family therapy, CBT, and pharmacotherapy.

High-potency benzodiazepines, such as clonazepam, have proven to be effective in treating social phobia, but are not recommended for APD, where the focus of social fear is more generalized due to the risk of substance dependence. However, selective serotonin reuptake inhibitors (SSRIs) can be helpful. Knutson et al. (1998) demonstrated, for example, that negative affectivity declined and social affiliation increased as a function of plasma levels of paroxetine in normal volunteers, during a four-week double-blind study. A number of medications from the SSRI family, such as Celexa, appear to be promising agents that can potentiate psychotherapeutic efforts. However, we are aware of no clinical trials using APD subjects and SSRI interventions to date.

CULTURAL AND GENDER ISSUES

Rates of APD are similar among females and males across cultures. However, expectations about social behavior can influence the interpretation of APD behavior. For example, in male-dominated cultures women are often expected to be nonassertive, socially avoidant, generally compliant, and avoidant of conflict. APD needs to be distinguished from culturally specific conditions. In Japan, *taijin kyofusho* (TKS) is understood to be a fear of interpersonal relations (Stein and Matsunaga, 2001), characterized by the afflicted person's fear of offending others and concerns about their own offensive smell, gaze, or appearance. However, this condition is separate from APD, as there is no fear of embarrassing oneself.

The therapist is wise to ask APD clients and their family members about their view of symptoms and problematic behaviors, as well as their respective opinions about the etiology and optimal treatment for such symptoms and problematic behaviors. In this way, therapists are less likely to make judgments based upon their own cultural values and gender perspectives. A shared view of both the development and treatment of APD symptoms will increase both understanding and compliance. Given the increasing multicultural backgrounds of mainstream clinic populations, and our awareness of lifestyle and socioeconomic strata influences on social behavior and expectations, we need, more than ever, to sensitively and respectfully explore the meaning behind symptoms in APD families to increase effectiveness of treatment.

FUTURE DIRECTIONS

As with other personality disorders, APD has not had the benefit of large-scale clinical trial investigation. This will likely change as the pharmacotherapy industry develops new agents that target social phobia. However, a focus on early detection and intervention of APD offers exciting promise. Social phobia has been found to be a common cause of future psychopathology in young, school-age children, and a number of efforts are underway to train elementary school teachers and counselors to screen their students for social fears and to develop group programs that prevent the full development of social phobia. It is a natural extension to train these same gatekeepers to detect pending APD. Such youngsters will require additional attention, given the relative severity of their symptoms, and early parental involvement would be advisable. In many ways, APD seems to be a cumulative disorder, since adverse social experiences mount and beliefs become rigid. Early intervention to prevent or moderate the course of APD seems to offer the greatest hope.

REFERENCES

Alden, L.E. (1989). Short-term structured treatment of avoidant personality disorder. *Journal of Consulting and Clinical Psychology, 57*, 756-764.

Alden, L.E., Laposa, J.M., Taylor, C.T., and Ryder, A.G. (2002). Avoidant personality disorder: Current status and future directions. *Journal of Personality Disorders, 16*(1), 1-29.

American Psychiatric Association (1994). *Diagnostic and statistical manual of mental disorders* (Fourth edition). Washington, DC: American Psychiatric Association.

Baucom, D.H. and Epstein, N. (1990). *Cognitive-behavioral marital therapy*. New York: Brunner/Mazel.

Costa, P.T. and McCrae, R.R. (1992). *Revised NEO Personality Inventory (NEO-PI-R) and NEO Five-Factor Inventory (NEO-FFI) professional manual*. Odessa, FL: Psychological Assessment Resources.

Costa, P.T. and McCrae, R.R. (1994). Set like plaster? Evidence for the stability of adult personality. In T. Heatherton and J.L. Weinberger (Eds.), *Can personality change?* (pp. 21-40). Washington, DC: American Psychological Association.

Costa, P.T. and McCrae, R.R. (1998). Trait theories of personality. In D.F. Barone, M. Hersen, and V.B. van Hasselt (Eds.), *Advanced personality* (pp. 103-121). New York: Plenum.

Dattilio, F.M. (Ed.) (1998). *Case studies in couple and family therapy.* New York: Guilford Press.

Kagan, J., Reznick, J.S., and Snidman, N. (1988). Biological basis of childhood shyness. *Science, 240,* 167-171.

Knutson, B., Wolkowitz, O.M., Cole, S.W., Chan, T., Moore, E.A., Johnson, R.C., Terpstra, J., Turner, R.A., and Reus, V.I. (1998). Selective alteration of personality and social behavior by serotonergic intervention. *American Journal of Psychiatry, 155,* 373-379.

Livesley, W.J., West, M., and Tanney, A. (1985). Historical comment on the DSM-III schizoid and avoidant personality disorders. *American Journal of Psychiatry, 142,* 1344-1347.

McLean, P.D. and Woody, S.R. (2001). *Anxiety disorders in adults: An evidence-based approach to psychological treatment.* New York: Oxford University Press.

Meyer, B. and Carver, C.S. (2000). Negative childhood accounts, sensitivity, and pessimism: A study of avoidant personality disorder features in college students. *Journal of Personality Disorders, 14,* 233-248.

Oldham, J.M., Skoldol, A.E., Kellman, H.D., Hyler, S.E., Doidge, N., Rosnick, L., and Gallaher, P.E. (1995). Comorbidity of axis I and axis II disorders. *American Journal of Psychiatry, 152*(4), 571-578.

Paterson, R.J. (2000). *The assertiveness workbook.* Oakland, CA: New Harbinger Publications, Inc.

Patterson, G.R. (1971). *Families: Application of social learning to family life.* Champaign, IL: Research Press.

Patterson, G.R. (1982). *Coercive family processes.* Eugene, OR: Castalia.

Roche, D.N., Runtz, M.G., and Hunter, M.A. (1999). Adult attachment: A mediator between child sexual abuse and later psychological adjustment. *Journal of Interpersonal Violence, 14,* 184-207.

Roth, D.A. and Heimberg, R.G. (2001). Cognitive-behavioral models of social anxiety disorder. *The Psychiatric Clinics of North America, 24*(4), 753-771.

Satir, V. (1967). *Conjoint family therapy.* Palo Alto, CA: Science and Behavior Books.

Stein, D.J. and Matsunaga, H. (2001). Cross-cultural aspects of social anxiety disorder. *The Psychiatric Clinics of North America, 24,* 773-782.

Widiger, T.A. (2001). Social anxiety, social phobia, and avoidant personality. In W.R. Crozier and L.E. Alden (Eds.), *International handbook of social anxiety: Concepts, research, and interventions relating to the self and shyness* (pp. 335-356). New York: John Wiley and Sons.

Wittchen, H.U. and Fehm, L. (2001). Epidemiology, patterns of comorbidity, and associated disabilities of social phobia. *The Psychiatric Clinics of North America, 24*(4), 617-641.

Chapter 10

Treating the Borderline Mother: Integrating EMDR with a Family Systems Perspective

Christine Ann Lawson

INTRODUCTION

The enigma of borderline personality disorder (BPD) requires a multidimensional perspective that examines neurological, interpersonal, and family systems dynamics. Because BPD is defined by the American Psychiatric Association (2000) as a pattern of unstable relationships characterized by "extremes of idealization and devaluation" (p. 710, reprinted with permission from the *Diagnostic and Statistical Manual of Mental Disorders*, Fourth Edition, Text Revision, copyright 2000 American Psychiatric Association), psychotherapists should be aware of potential ramifications for mother-child interactions. Borderline "splitting," the inability to integrate positive and negative perceptions, results in intense but contradictory emotional messages that create a "push-pull" interpersonal dynamic. Muller (1992), Teicher (2000), and Schore (1997) suggest that splitting is the result of an undeveloped corpus callosum, a part of the brain that normally develops by the time a child is thirty-six months old. Early experiences with a mother who alternates between extremes of love and hate ("push-pull" interactions) apparently impairs the growth of neural networks responsible for integrating the child's left and right hemispheres (Teicher, 2000; Muller, 1992). Teicher (2000) explains, "Very inconsistent behavior of a parent (for example, sometimes loving, sometimes abusing) might generate an irreconcilable mental image in a young child" (pp. 62-63), thereby preserving the perception of mother as good while creating a negative self-perception.

According to Perry (1999), inconsistent mother-child interactions characterized by neglect, depression, and/or trauma disrupt normal brain development in children. Teicher (2000) found that patients with a history of verbal, physical, sexual abuse, and/or neglect had a significantly smaller corpus callosum (the part of the brain that connects the two hemispheres) than a control group. Neural connections between the hemispheres apparently fail to develop, leaving the individual trapped in the emotional world of a two-year-old child. Like drawing water from separate faucets, emotions are either "hot" or "cold" (positive or negative), depending on the current experience. Unable to temper negative with positive emotions, BPD patients, like toddlers, are flooded with intense emotional states. Many patients describe feeling *disconnected* and experience a desperate need for *connection* with someone who provides emotional stability. Thus, as family systems theorist Murray Bowen (1978b) observed, "borderline schizophrenics" function "only by finding new dependent attachments to other people who will guide and advise them, and from whom they borrow enough self to function" (p. 92).

Research on brain functioning indicates distinct differences between BPD and schizophrenia. Bowen's patients would not meet the current *Diagnostic and Statistical Manual of Mental Disorders* (DSM) criteria for schizophrenia as it is now understood. Schizophrenia is considered to be genetically determined, resulting in misplaced neurons rather than from early emotional experience (Harvard Medical School, 2001). Bowen's comprehensive investigation of patient-family interactions clearly depicts the consequences of splitting in mothers who suffer from borderline pathology. Bowen (1978a) provided the following example of this "push-pull" dynamic (split and contradictory messages):

> A psychotic son was eating a late lunch alone. The mother stopped to help him. She buttered his bread, cut his meat, and poured more milk for him. At the same time she was urging him . . . to become more grown up and to learn to do more for himself. (p. 57)

Schore (1997) explains that a mother's response serves normally as an affect regulator for her infant's developing brain. Borderline mothers, however, cannot regulate their own emotions, and are therefore unable to consistently soothe and comfort their children (Glickhauf-Hughes and Mehlman, 1998). Interactions with their children can be confusing, unpredictable, and volatile. One clinician observed that women who were raised by borderline mothers recreated pathological dynamics with their newborns, and that the baby became "the mother's own ill parent" (Trout, 1991, p. 314).

Although BPD can develop from a variety of circumstances other than being raised by a borderline mother (Zanarini and Frankenburg, 1997), one study found that the most predictive factor determining the development of BPD was an anxious attachment to a mother whose interactions vacillated between "push-pull" and "hot and cold" (Salzman, Salzman, and Wolfson, 1997, p. 76). Bezirganian, Cohen, and Brook (1993) found that BPD can result from being raised by a mother who is unpredictable and inconsistent in her interactions, who manipulates her child through guilt, and uses threats of abandonment as punishment. Understandably, children must defend themselves against anxiety associated with this pathological interaction. From a psychodynamic perspective, separating the perceptions of the "good" and "bad" mother serves as a primary defense mechanism for the child (Kernberg, 1985). As can be seen from the information described earlier, neuropsychological research provides evidence that the process of splitting results in a variety of neurobiological effects, particularly on the structure and function of the corpus callosum (Teicher, 2000). As Kernberg (1985) points out, although this type of defense may reduce anxiety in children, it can also result in borderline personality disorder in adults.

Considering that unstable relationships define BPD, surprisingly little research has been conducted on how borderline mothers interact with their children. The dearth of literature describing interactions between borderlines and their children reflects the difficulty of data collection. Bowen's (1978a) unique observations were derived from an experimental program in which entire families were hospitalized for a period of two years, a study whose cost prohibits replication today. Bowen (1978c) surmised that the "mother projects her own weak self into the child which results in a psychological orientation in which she is completely strong and the child is weak" (p. 8). Bowen's (1978c) staff observed the mothers making statements such as "You are sick," triggering a defensive attack by the child such as "*You* are the one who is sick" (p. 7). If questioned about their perceptions, the mothers became enraged. Bowen identified the mothers' inability to acknowledge their own disordered thinking as a major obstacle complicating treatment.

Fluctuating between desperately wanting help yet rejecting help makes intervention challenging. Borderline splitting creates "push-pull" dynamics that leave therapists, researchers, and family members caught in cycles of feeling "sucked in" and "spit out" (Gunderson and Lyoo, 1997; Lawson, 2000). Danti, Adams, and Morrison (1985) found that borderline mothers were reluctant to participate in their study because they feared discovering that they had damaged their children. Yet these same mothers expressed the belief that their children had indeed been damaged and needed help. Trout (1991) warned that pathological dynamics enacted between borderline mothers and their children can be difficult to observe because the behaviors are often unconscious. Bowen (1978c) suggested that the intensity of the mother's reactions can trigger repression even among mental health professionals:

> It was always a new and surprising experience for the staff to see and feel the intensity of a mother's involvements. There has been an intellectual awareness of this for a long time, but each new observation causes a reaction as if the staff member is experiencing this for the first time. It has the quality of an emotional experience that can be tolerated only for brief periods without re-repression. (p. 6)

Masterson (1976) attributed the etiology of BPD to the unique "push-pull" quality of the mother's interactions, and claimed that the mother of every borderline is borderline herself. Other researchers suggest that even if a small percentage of borderlines were raised by borderline mothers, the need for intervention is justified (Segal, 1990; Weiss et al., 1996). Weiss and colleagues (1996) found that children of borderline mothers had more psychiatric diagnoses, including impulse control disorders and BPD than a control group. Segal (1990) explains that the borderline mother's fluctuations between idealization and devaluation have a decisive impact on a child's developing personality. Unfortunately, perceptual splitting can sometimes make intervention impossible.

Intervention requires a delicate balance of compassion and concern. Although the borderline mother's split perceptions make treatment difficult, intervention is crucial. BPD has a pervasive impact on individual, marital, and family functioning. Life-threatening situations can result from the borderline's impulsivity and/or rage. Raine (1993) found a relationship between BPD and extreme violence in male subjects, yet this author found no studies examining violence by borderline mothers. Abusive borderlines, males as well as females, are not likely to seek treatment, and may rarely be identified within clinical populations. Helping these individuals recognize their disorder requires extreme sensitivity. Eye movement desensitization reprocessing (EMDR), combined with a family systems perspective can enhance the effectiveness of therapeutic intervention and may prevent the intergenerational transmission of BPD.

IMPACT ON THE FAMILY

Kerr and Bowen (1988) observed that patterns of attachment and levels of differentiation can be passed from one generation to the next. Perry (1999) explained that the neurobiological effects of the mother-child attachment affect not only individuals, but the entire family. Although no genetic link has been attributed to BPD, Zanarini and Frankenburg (1997) found that BPD was significantly more prevalent among first-degree relatives of borderlines than among controls. As noted earlier, Weiss and colleagues (1996) found that children of borderline mothers had more psychiatric diagnoses, including BPD, than children of mothers with other personality disorders. These researchers concluded that children of borderline mothers are at risk for developing BPD and should be "followed accordingly" (p. 289). Children of both sexes are at risk for developing BPD.

Studies of the prevalence of BPD among family members of borderlines found an almost equal distribution of males and females in nonclinical samples (Links, Steiner, and Huzley, 1988; Loranger, Oldham, and Tulis, 1982). Although males with BPD are more prevalent than previously thought (van Reekum et al., 1993), they are more likely to be found in prison rather than in clinical populations. In the face of possible abandonment, males are more likely to commit acts of violence such as homicide rather than suicide.

Although the prevalence of BPD females within clinical populations was initially attributed to a high incidence of sexual abuse, researchers are de-emphasizing the importance of a single type of abuse in the development of the disorder (Gunderson and Sabo, 1993; Zanarini and Frankenburg, 1997; Fonagy, Target, and Gergely, 2000; and Links, Steiner, and Huzley, 1988). Therapists are cautioned not to assume a correlation between BPD and childhood sexual abuse since sexual abuse is often accompanied by emotional neglect and/or other forms of abuse (Zanarini and Frankenburg, 1997). Teicher (2000) found that verbal abuse or emotional neglect can also impair brain development, which leads to BPD. Johnson and colleagues (2001) found that children who experienced maternal verbal abuse were more than three times as likely to display borderline and other personality disorders than children who were not verbally abused.

Zanarini and Frankenburg (1997) explain that there are as many ways of *being* borderline as there are ways of *becoming* borderline. Kroll (1988) found that fifty-six different combinations of the DSM criteria fit the description of borderline personality disorder. Consequently, every borderline mother has her own unique cluster of symptoms that impact her functioning. Not all borderline mothers are suicidal, self-mutilate, abuse drugs or alcohol, suffer from eating disorders, or engage in self-destructive behavior. Not all borderlines appear to be angry or depressed initially. Alarming symptoms such as suicidality or self-mutilation attract the therapist's attention, whereas while perceptual splitting is often overlooked.

The borderline mother's attempts to avoid abandonment are a consequence of her need for connectedness with someone who offers emotional stability. The borderline's mood, therefore, typically reflects the status of her relationship with her primary attachment figure, whether that figure is her child, her spouse, a pet, or her therapist. Gunderson (2001) maintains that when the borderline's attachment figure is present and supportive, the borderline feels empty and depressed. When the attachment figure is present but not supportive, the patient feels angry and self-destructive. When the attachment figure is absent, the borderline feels terrified, desperate, paranoid, and may dissociate. If the attachment figure is her own child, however, the borderline mother's fear of abandonment creates separation anxiety in her child. A tragic example was a divorced, borderline mother who was so distraught upon hearing her seven-year-old son announce that he wanted to live with his father that she lost control of their car, which flipped and rolled. Following the accident the young boy changed his mind about wanting to live with his father and developed disabling separation anxiety.

The borderline mother's children may love her as much as they fear her, and may be unable to separate without experiencing survival anxiety (Glickauf-Hughes and Mehlman, 1998; Loranger, Oldham and Tulis, 1982; Shachnow et al., 1997; Silverman et al., 1991; and Zanarini and Frankenburg, 1997). Danti, Adams, and Morrison (1985) observed that children as well as spouses often become borderline mothers' caretakers. Children who receive the borderline mother's positive projections, "all-good" children, may become "parentified" and function as little adults, feeling overly responsible for their mother's well being (Lawson, 2000). Children who receive primarily negative projections, "no-good" children, may develop BPD as a consequence of negative interactions. Children may receive various combinations of positive and negative projections, setting the stage for development of BPD (Lawson, 2000).

Linehan (1993) suggested that reciprocal interactions develop between borderline patients and family members. She explained that parents and children mutually shape and reinforce behavioral interactions, exacerbating "the invalidating and coercive system, leading to more, not fewer, dysfunctional behaviors within the entire system" (p. 58). Kerr and Bowen (1988) observed that emotional dysregulation is learned and can be passed through generations. The father's role in the family, however, may mitigate the effects of the borderline mother's disordered interactions.

Frank and Paris (1981) suggest that the amount of approval a daughter perceives in the relationship with her father may mitigate the effects of being raised by a borderline mother. Frequently, however, fathers participate in what Bowen (1978c) described as "the family projection process," and support the mother's negative projections of a child in order to relieve his own anxiety. Bowen (1978c) observed that fathers tended to be "weak, conforming, and devoted in the relationship to the mother" (p. 13). Triangulation occurs when various family members attempt to avoid becoming the target of the borderline's rage. In the effort to avoid conflict, fathers may collude with their wives or their children, and children may collude with one another, depending on the circumstance.

Although the character structure of men who marry borderline women varies widely, the common denominator is their tendency to avoid conflict. Lachkar (1992) employs theories of self-psychology and object relations to explain the interaction between borderline women who marry narcissistic men. Lachkar (1992) explains that narcissistic fathers withdraw when hurt, whereas borderline mothers react with notorious rage: "The borderline may be destructive in order to stir things up and punish, while the narcissist may be destructive because of preoccupation with self" (p. 82). Both Masterson (1976) and Bowen (1978a) observed that men who marry borderline women generally fail to intervene in the pathological dynamics between their wives and their children. They distance themselves emotionally from the family by immersing themselves in work or other pursuits.

Emotional cutoff may result when borderlines perceive family members as nonsupportive or threatening. The borderline's all-or-nothing perceptions can be observed when a close friend or family member is suddenly perceived as rejecting or critical. The borderline mother may shut out offenders by refusing to acknowledge their existence, or by physically shutting them out of her home. One borderline mother kicked her teenage daughter out of the house, changed the locks on the doors, and threw away her photographs. Emotional cutoff triggers survival anxiety in children because their survival depends on their attachment to their mother.

In cases of divorce, a borderline's efforts to avoid abandonment intensify. Vicious custody battles can ensue when borderline mothers divorce, as each parent can become emotionally self-absorbed. Children with borderline mothers and narcissistic fathers are often used by their parents as little therapists. Lachkar (1992) states that in custody cases children become "sacrificial objects" (p. 78).

Ratey (2001) explains that the brain's job is to ensure the survival of its owner. Children with borderline mothers face an inherent conflict. Their attachment to mother is crucial for survival. Yet, if mother is a threat to survival (either through neglect or abuse), the brain must protect the child from recognizing this deadly paradox. Failing to integrate the contradictory experiences of the "good" with the "bad" mother reduces anxiety because the image of the good mother is preserved at the expense of the child's positive self-image.

SETTING

The setting in which this treatment model can be applied ranges from private practice to intensive outpatient treatment centers. The essential element required of the setting is the therapist's long-term availability so that continuity and consistency is maintained across time. The setting, in fact, may be less important than the continuity of the relationship with the therapist. For example, a therapist who initially treats a hospitalized borderline patient should ideally provide ongoing, long-term outpatient treatment. Although contemporary treatment centers rarely offer this opportunity, borderline patients require consistency, continuity, and long-term treatment.

TREATMENT MODEL

Bowen's family systems theory combined with EMDR provides a flexible treatment model that can be used in any clinical setting. Murray Bowen was a trained psychoanalyst who taught at the Menninger Clinic where he studied "mother-child symbiosis." Bowen recognized a distinctive pattern of alternating cycles of closeness and distance that seemed to repeat throughout generations. Nearly fifty years before technology made it possible to observe actual deficits in brain functioning, Bowen identified a pathological form of separation anxiety that served as a driving force behind this "push-pull" dynamic. Bowen's concepts of triangulation, the family projection process, differentiation, and emotional cutoff describe the functioning of families with borderline mothers so accurately that the brilliance of his observations can only now be fully appreciated. At the time of Bowen's work, the distinction between schizophrenic and borderline patients was not understood. Today, his theory offers a useful framework for understanding the intergenerational transmission of BPD— "a pathological form of attachment driven by anxiety that subverted reason and self-control" (Nichols and Schwartz, 2001, p. 138).

Incorporating EMDR can enhance Bowen's family systems approach. Bowen believed that the therapist should strive to stay out of the patient's emotional system and avoid the transference. Therapists who treat borderline patients, however, find that avoiding the transference is impossible (Gabbard, 2001). The borderline's pattern of relatedness is unavoidably reenacted with the therapist.

Gabbard (2001) claims that no research supports the efficacy of short-term treatment for borderline patients. Borderline mothers, in particular, require long-term treatment to establish a strong therapeutic alliance necessary for tolerating painful self-revelations and incorporating EMDR. Long-term treatment builds new neural networks (Vaughan, 1997) as the result of the new relational experience (Levitan and Kaczmarek, 1991). Social environments are known to increase branching of nerve cells. Rats kept in cages with other rats develop more dendritic branching than rats kept in isolation (Camel, Withers, and Greenough, 1986). Recent research on the neurobiological impact of EMDR indicates that EMDR apparently stimulates growth of neural connections within the corpus callosum, gradually alleviating the process of splitting (Manfield, 1998), an excellent technique for treating BPD.

Gabbard (2001) urges therapists to acknowledge the borderline mother's fear that integrating her positive and negative perceptions will result in the "destruction of all loving aspects by the intense hatred" she feels (p. 54). The therapist's tasks, therefore, are: (1) helping the borderline mother accept the reality that the process of splitting will not change without therapy, and (2) helping her understand that this defense mechanism allowed her to feel safe as a child, but now poses a serious threat to her well-being. Engaging a borderline mother in treatment requires helping her understand that although she is not to blame for her disorder, she *is* fully responsible for the consequences of *not* seeking treatment. She must understand that her intense feelings of love and hate can be safely integrated and therefore mitigated, and that her emotional experience of herself and others can be more balanced.

Engagement in Treatment

Borderline mothers are terrified of discovering that they may have harmed their children. They truly love their children and often bring their children to treatment while refusing help themselves. Therapists who understand the underlying brain dysfunction of BPD can appreciate why borderline mothers cannot "see" their own contradictory behavior. Their single greatest fear is discovering that something is wrong with *them* and that they may lose their children or spouse. Their fear of abandonment drives their behavior at every level. The most threatening statement to make to a borderline mother is that she needs help, to suggest that something is wrong with her, and yet, she must be encouraged to seek treatment. Appealing to her love for her children can reduce her anxiety and increase her motivation. Helping her recognize that her children love, need, but fear for her can provide the motivation for change.

Many borderline mothers come to treatment with full knowledge of their difficulties in relationships. In other cases, however, the *Structured Clinical Interview for DSM-IV Axis II Personality Disorders* (First et al., 1997) or "SCID-II" can help borderlines recognize their disturbed relational patterns. The SCID-II includes 119 questions that can be completed by *both* the borderline mother and her spouse, in order to incorporate the spouse's view of the patient's functioning, and vice versa. Results can be shared during the structured interview and are less likely to trigger defensive reactions if the therapist provides feedback regarding *both* partners.

Borderline mothers may express a preference that their husbands or children be included or excluded from treatment. Respect for the patient's needs and wishes is important, but the therapist ultimately controls the treatment. Limitations imposed by the therapist's schedule, practice setting, and theoretical base must be explained before treatment begins.

Patients who meet *any five* of the nine criteria for BPD listed in the DSM should be told their diagnosis. The diagnosis of BPD should never be withheld from a patient. In any other branch of medicine, failure to inform a patient of a potentially life-threatening disorder, one that seriously impairs perception, judgment, and functioning, would constitute malpractice. Understanding one's diagnosis, the need for treatment, and the possibility for change can be extremely validating if the therapist presents the information in a nonpejorative manner. Gunderson (2001) explains that telling the patient her diagnosis is essential to establishing realistic treatment goals and validates her sense that her suffering is real. Failure to establish a clinically honest relationship with a borderline patient is a setup for failure and violates trust—the basic premise of the therapeutic relationship.

The Bowenian goal of increasing self-differentiation reflects the borderline's need to reduce separation anxiety and abandonment depression. Treatment goals should be tailored to fit each individual patient, reflecting the broad spectrum of levels of functioning. Unrealistic goals can exacerbate the patient's self-hatred by reinforcing feelings of failure and inadequacy.

The therapist's initial focus is on establishing a nonthreatening, emotionally safe environment. The first stage of treatment provides enough time for the therapist to observe and experience relational dynamics and obtain a thorough family history. Bowen used a family diagram to organize relevant information regarding relational patterns (now referred to as a *genogram*) (Kerr and Bown, 1988). Issues regarding separation and individuation, differentiation and fusion, can be indicated on the diagram and discussed with the patient.

Core Issues

Kerr and Bowen (1988) believed that change in a family system can result from change in an individual family member. Differentiation, or individuation, is a process that has a ripple effect on relationships throughout the family, and is the core issue in the treatment of borderline mothers. Individual treatment is a powerful form of intervention because the therapist becomes a primary attachment figure. Issues around separation may be apparent in the first session. Borderline mothers may have difficulty saying good-bye, ending a session, tolerating the therapist's vacations or illnesses, and they may feel easily criticized or rejected. Understanding and interpreting these interactions provides the opportunity for the patient to reflect on her interactions in a nonthreatening environment. *For the borderline mother, separation is the core issue underlying her conflicts with her children, her spouse, other family members, and her therapist.*

Separation anxiety is the single most powerful trigger for impulsive and destructive behaviors. Any issue involving separation can trigger anxiety in borderlines, making mothering a particularly challenging task. Understanding perceptual splitting is essential to identifying triangling behavior and emotional cutoff. Separation anxiety prevents the borderline mother from thinking before acting, and drives her to redirect her need for connectedness to a third party.

Bowen's (1978b) concept of "process questions" encourages patients to reflect on their own feelings and thoughts. Questions such as, "Why do you think you reacted that way?" help borderlines identify triggers that can lead to impulsive or destructive behavior. For example, when a borderline mother complains about feeling victimized by her child, the therapist's reaction, including silence, can reinforce her distorted perception. Process questions encourage patients to reflect on why and how they felt victimized.

Responding to a borderline mother's complaint of victimization by her child should include: (1) empathizing with her feelings, (2) clarifying her role in the interaction, and (3) clarifying the issue underlying her perception—which is always about separation being experienced as rejection or betrayal. If therapists choose option 1 and only empathize with her feelings, they run the risk of enabling her perceptional distortions and increasing the intensity of her negative projections. If therapists choose option 2 only, they run the risk of alienating the borderline mother because she feels criticized. Therefore, the most appropriate response is to choose all three and do them in the order mentioned.

After asking the borderline mother to reflect on her behavior, the therapist could say, "It feels disrespectful when Sara chooses her own hairstyle. You get so angry that you find a way of making her feel what you feel, but then neither one of you feels respected" (an example of Bowen's family projection process). To emphasize the core issue, the therapist might add, "It's hard for you to let Sara *be a separate person* and make her own choices without *feeling rejected.*" The same approach can be used with the mother's relationships with her spouse and other family members. Gabbard (2001) emphasizes the importance of encouraging borderlines to reflect on their role in interactions with others, including interactions with the therapist.

Kerr and Bowen (1988) believed that the therapist should remain a neutral observer rather than participate in the transference. Yet most therapists who treat borderlines find that avoiding the transference is impossible. Gabbard (2001) stresses the importance of the therapist's role as both participant and observer. The therapist allows the transference to develop while reflecting on the patient's perceptions. For example, setting limits often triggers anger and increased demands by the patient, requiring the therapist to point out boundary violations. As the therapist sets limits, the transference fluctuates between idealizing to devaluing perceptions of the therapist. Process questions illuminate these interactions and help the patient recognize the process of splitting.

Containing a borderline's hatred and rage is an essential component of treatment. Therapists must tolerate being loved as well as being hated by the patient, and will experience ambivalent feelings about the patient. Acknowledging and interpreting these feelings is crucial in the "working through" stage of treatment that precedes use of EMDR. This stage can take months or even years, depending upon the patient. A great deal of this work involves gaining an understanding of the patient's trauma history. Patients with dissociative disorders require more containment and structure.

Integrating EMDR

Although EMDR was used initially to treat post-traumatic stress disorder in adult trauma victims, the technique has been found to be equally effective for reprocessing traumatic experiences from childhood. Perry (1999) states, "The memory of trauma is carried not only throughout the lives of individuals by their neurobiology, but also in the lives of families by family myths, childrearing practices and belief systems" (p. 32). Perry (1999) proposes that traumatic experiences such as neglect or abuse significantly alter the developing brain. Prolonged separation or sudden abandonment during childhood can be experienced as a threat to the child's survival. Perry (1999) notes that the brain develops a sensitizing pattern as the result of traumatic experience, altering the brain's alarm system to fire "false alarms" when faced with circumstances that are associated with the original trauma. Any number of false beliefs may be reexperienced, such as "I am in danger," or "I am helpless." The emotional, physical, and neurological reaction to a current *perceived* threat is beyond the individual's conscious control, and is reexperienced as intensely as the original trauma.

Incorporating EMDR with a family systems perspective can significantly enhance the therapeutic experience (Manfield, 1998). By stimulating both hemispheres of the brain, the borderline mother "makes the connection" between the past and the present. Irrational self-beliefs formed in childhood are integrated and transformed by her adult perspective. EMDR activates rapid communication between each hemisphere of the brain as patients process a specific thought, feeling, or experience, creating a more balanced perception by facilitating integration of both positive and negative perspectives. Manfield (1998) states, "Not only does EMDR stimulate interhemispheric communication in people whose brains show abnormal brain lateralization caused by a history of trauma, but some of the changes appear to endure" (p. 5). Van der Kolk (1997) demonstrated that bilateral hemispheric activity persists following termination of EMDR. Rapidly alternating sensory stimulation between right and left hemispheres, whether through auditory, visual, or tactile channels, appears to access a part of the brain not affected by verbal therapy.

Research regarding the effectiveness of EMDR remains controversial (Lipke, 2000). Empirical studies have been plagued by difficulties, such as varying levels of therapist competence, the number of sessions in which EMDR was used, and inappropriate comparisons of patients who have suffered a single traumatic experience with patients who have a history of trauma. Scheck, Schaeffer, and Gillette (1998) randomly assigned sixty female subjects with a history of childhood abuse to two sessions of EMDR versus two sessions of client-centered therapy. These researchers discovered a significant difference between the groups, supporting the efficacy of EMDR. However, other studies provide less convincing results (Jensen, 1994), perhaps due to inconsistent or inappropriate application of the technique (Lipke, 2000).

EMDR provides an opportunity for borderline mothers to develop a more balanced view of themselves and others within the context of a therapeutic relationship. Lipke's (2000) explanation of the goal of EMDR is reminiscent of Bowen's (1978b) family therapy goals, "to encourage the integration of dysfunctional and functional associative networks . . . , thereby changing the dysfunctional network into a functional one" (Lipke, 2000, p. 79).

EMDR should be initiated after a strong working relationship has been established. Traumatic childhood experiences, such as sexual abuse, may be associated with shame and embarrassment, and often create self-beliefs such as "I am bad." Irrational self-beliefs do not necessarily change with insight-oriented therapy, and inevitably must be addressed with EMDR. Borderline patients have layers of negative self-beliefs that must be addressed over time.

During EMDR the therapist is involved minimally as the patient forms new connections and insights. The borderline patient may feel anxious and "disconnected" at first because the technique creates emotional distance. When EMDR works well, the borderline mother experiences herself as more open, more balanced, less fearful, and more "whole." As she gains a more balanced view of herself, the borderline mother recognizes less of a need for her therapist. The relational connection that facilitated her growth is eventually replaced by her own internal connections. The transference then becomes the focus of remaining EMDR sessions.

Termination

EMDR apparently facilitates growth of new neural connections in the corpus callosum, creating a palpable affective shift in the patient. In each case where EMDR worked well among my patients, family members were the first to comment on the change. One husband told his wife, "I don't know how therapy works but I can tell that it's working." The success of any treatment approach, however, varies with each individual.

Termination should be discussed well in advance of the actual event. If the therapist believes that further work is needed, unresolved issues should be specified. Ultimately, however, the decision to terminate remains with the patient, and in some cases, is beyond the control of the therapist. Waldinger and Frank (1989) suggest that the high rate of treatment dropout among borderlines is a function of splitting. The patient's perception of the therapist can shift without warning from good to bad, gratifying to frustrating, accepting to rejecting. The patient may react with retaliatory rejection, aggression, or complete withdrawal. The prudent therapist should contact the patient to explore the reason for a rupture, and express a sincere desire to understand why the patient felt injured. Remaining available for future consultation is important regardless of the reason for termination.

CASE EXAMPLE

Mary is a thirty-seven-year-old Caucasian borderline housewife with two daughters ages six and four. Her husband is employed in sales, and spends a great deal of time away from home. She sought treatment initially for overwhelming anxiety, insomnia, and depression. Mary complained of feelings of emptiness and despair, episodes of intense rage, and had a history of extramarital affairs. She had no history of self-mutilation or suicidal ideation. During the course of treatment her older daughter was diagnosed with a learning disability and her younger daughter was diagnosed with attention deficit hyperactivity disorder (ADHD).

Mary described her mothering as fluctuating between extremes of overindulgence and flat-out rejection of her children. She cycled through periods of immersing her daughters in undivided attention, reading up to seven consecutive books at bedtime, and then screaming obscenities if they begged for more. Her "push-pull" interactions created severe separation anxiety in her children. When dropping her younger daughter off at preschool, the teacher had to literally drag the child out of the car because she could not bear leaving her mother.

Mary was the younger of two children born to a narcissistic father and an overwhelmed and depressed mother. Shortly after Mary's birth, her mother became the primary caregiver for Mary's maternal and paternal grandmothers. Mary recalled accompanying her mother on daily visits to her grandmothers' homes as her mother cared for these aging women. As a child, Mary perceived herself as a burden, and felt emotionally neglected.

Although Mary excelled in school, her parents responded by telling her not to draw attention to herself. Mary's case is an excellent example of how borderline personality disorder can develop from sheer emotional neglect and unintentional shaming of a child's normal emotional needs. She experienced no verbal, physical, or sexual abuse, but grew up idealizing her "allgood," self-sacrificing mother, while viewing herself as undeserving, bad, and shameful.

Mary's mother told her that she had been an overactive, anxious child who was never happy. Mary developed attention-seeking behavior that reinforced her belief that she was "too needy." She had an unrelenting need to be with others and dreaded being alone. Pressured speech made her train of thought difficult to follow, and her high level of anxiety was palpable during the first interview.

I treated Mary for three years before using EMDR to address her feelings of emptiness. During this time we identified numerous issues, such as the reason for her extramarital affairs, unrelenting feelings of rage and despair, and fluctuations in her sense of self. We discussed her diagnosis of BPD, and she eagerly read about the disorder. Although she never experienced suicidal ideation, Mary agreed with the BPD diagnosis. After three years of treatment, Mary gained a great deal of insight and grew in self-awareness, but symptoms of BPD did not abate. I then suggested we try EMDR.

Before EMDR, Mary came to appointments at least twenty minutes early. For three years she brought her own bottled water to sessions, despite the fact that I have a water cooler in my waiting room. Her irrational fear that she could not get what she wants drove her to near panic, particularly when she was not in constant contact with others. When I asked her what issue she most wanted to address through EMDR, she identified this belief that her needs would not be met. Her earliest memory of that belief was when she was two years old, riding in the backseat of the car on a family vacation. She was thirsty and asked her father to stop so that she could get a drink of water. In her memory, she pictured her father angrily telling her no, scolding her, and shaming her for asking him to stop. She felt responsible for her father's annoyance and believed, for the first time in her life, that she would not be allowed to have what she needed.

Mary brought the mental picture to mind with the words, "I can't get what I want." Eye movements are simply one way of stimulating interhemispheric brain activity. Some clients wear headphones with alternating tones rather than watching the therapist's fingers move back and forth across their visual field. Mary chose to wear the headphones as she thought about her memory, her self-belief, and her feelings regarding this early experience. With minimal feedback from the therapist, the client can be instructed to say "stop" when a new awareness, understanding or insight has been discovered. The client reports his or her thoughts, feelings, and perspectives and continues processing his or her "train of thought" until he or she reaches a more realistic and balanced view of himself or herself in relation to the traumatic experience.

Through the process of EMDR, Mary recognized the pervasiveness of her fear that her needs would be more than others could bear. She also realized that, as an adult, she had been more than able to get what she wants—that, in fact, she was obsessed with getting what she wanted. As we proceeded through the sets of EMDR, she began to make more connections between past and present. At the end of the session she said that she felt as though a black tumor in her brain had been smashed. The belief that she could not get what she wanted no longer existed. She could literally see that her frantic efforts to get her needs met were based on childhood feelings of deprivation, and that coming early for sessions simply recreated feelings of frustration. She realized that, as an adult, she had more than she actually needed.

Over the next few weeks I noticed that Mary no longer came early for her sessions, and no longer brought her bottled water. She seemed strangely calm and spoke more slowly. One month after the initial EMDR session, she commented on the changes she noticed in herself: "I feel free now, but sort of overwhelmed at the realization that I can get almost anything I want. There are so many choices. I used to be driven, just driven all day long, and the panic is gone now. I don't need to exhaust myself anymore just to get some rest. At first I missed not feeling negative, you know, not feeling deprived. But now I realize that it never got me what I wanted anyway, so who wants to do that? That part of me is gone. It's like waking up from a dream and realizing that my life didn't need to be as hard as I made it. I'm not even mad at my parents anymore. Of course they couldn't give me what I needed, they never got what they needed from their parents."

Mary then leaned forward and said, "I'd better whisper this in case it doesn't last . . . but I'm happy with my husband. It's like being at a restaurant and you're eating a good meal and someone comes along and offers you a different dish. I feel like saying, 'Uh, no thanks, I'm enjoying this one.'" Mary gained a greater sense of differentiation and individuation that was apparent in her new perception of her self in relation to her husband and children. As Kerr and Bowen (1988) proposed, the process of change "has been called 'defining a self' because visible *action* is taken to which others *respond*" (p. 107, emphasis theirs).

As a result of treatment, Mary developed a more balanced view of herself and others. She recognized that she indulged her children with more attention than they needed to compensate for what she had missed as a child. She identified her tendency to project her fear of rejection onto her children and began to separate her needs from her children's needs. The ability to set limits accompanied the realization that her needs could be met and allowed her to enjoy rather than fear relationships. Prior to treatment, she regressed to feeling and behaving like a deprived and angry child whenever she visited her parents or brother. During the course of treatment she learned to enjoy their visits without losing her sense of self or behaving like the frustrated child she once had been.

Six months after the first EMDR session, Mary confronted a new fear. Although the first EMDR session allowed her to believe that her needs could be met, she was afraid of making the wrong decision. If she continued to benefit from continued EMDR it might mean that she would no longer need therapy. Patients who were emotionally deprived as children may be fearful of losing the connection with their therapist. As a child, Mary felt deserving of her mother's attention only when she was hurt or ill. In the transference she feared not feeling entitled to therapy if she began to feel "too good." Individuating from the therapist becomes the final focus of treatment.

In the second EMDR session, Mary realized that as a child, her life depended on maintaining the attachment to her mother. Yet as an adult she recalled many occasions in which she demonstrated that she was more than capable of taking care of herself even at a young age. She realized that no danger existed in allowing herself to feel good, and that she could decide for herself whether she wanted to continue therapy.

Mary decreased the frequency of her appointments and tapered sessions off to once a month. She is no longer interested in extramarital affairs, nor does she complain about her husband's inadequacies. Her desperate need for constant connectedness with others dissipated slowly as she realized that many of her relationships were not satisfying. Her emotional energy is invested in several activities that allow her to enjoy being alone. Although she enjoys interacting with others, she no longer feels compelled to do so, and is more comfortable setting limits. She recently stated, "I really don't miss feeling like a victim. That part of me is gone."

STRENGTHS AND LIMITATIONS

EMDR integrated with a family systems perspective can have a transformative effect on borderline mothers and their families. The mother's treatment can have a ripple effect throughout the family as she develops the ability to integrate positive and negative perceptions of herself and others. Although Mary's husband was not willing to participate in her treatment or invest in his own therapy, their relationship improved as a result of Mary's growth. Mental health depends on the ability to maintain a balanced perspective, of good and bad, right and wrong, love and hate. Just as neural networks grow with each new experience in life, so too can families. A therapeutic relationship that nourishes the root of a family system strengthens the entire family.

EMDR appears to offer borderline mothers a form of reconstructive surgery for derailed emotional development. One patient explained, "It felt like something in my brain was untangled . . . like correcting a stitch in knitting—we went back and reworked the tangled connections so that now I'm back on track." Traumatic attachment experiences apparently disrupt neurobiological and interpersonal functioning, and leave patients stuck in the past. Although further research is needed to explain how EMDR works, a family systems approach combined with EMDR offers the opportunity for individuals and families to develop more fulfilling connections.

All treatment approaches, however, as with all human beings, have their limitations. Some borderline mothers may be too fearful to commit to the long-term treatment necessary for change. A family systems perspective may be perceived as threatening, especially for patients who see their child as the identified patient (a view that mental health professionals sometimes reinforce). The treatment model proposed requires a great deal of sensitivity on the part of the therapist. The therapist must have the courage to be straightforward about the mother's need for treatment, and the mother must have the courage to change.

Even in the best of circumstances, however, treatment can fail. An unstated assumption necessary for any successful treatment is the patient's capacity to trust and the patient's capacity for hope. A family systems perspective and EMDR cannot transform a patient who has no hope or trust. Some severely traumatized patients survived their childhood by relinquishing hope. They may send their children to treatment because they fail to recognize their own need for help, or because they have given up hope that they can be helped. These mothers deserve compassionate understanding rather than condemnation.

BENEFITS FOR THE FAMILY

Kerr and Bowen (1988) noted a dramatic decrease in the child's symptoms when parents focused on their own need for treatment. In Mary's case, her children's behavior improved as her own anxiety decreased. Because she no longer perceived differing perspectives as threatening, she felt no need to keep secrets from her husband and could tell him what she needed openly. She experienced herself and others as whole individuals, capable of making decisions and accepting the consequences. As her anxiety subsided, the tension in the family dissipated. Her children could be dropped off at school without protest because their anxiety decreased with hers.

The borderline mother no longer creates triangles or enlists allies when she understands that she can ask for what she needs directly and trusts her own perceptions. When perceptions are integrated rather than split, the patient can see "both sides" of conflicts, issues, individuals, and experiences. Although her husband continued to travel, Mary no longer felt resentful about being left alone with the children. She explained that, in many ways, she found it easier because she trusted his commitment to the family.

The benefits of successful treatment of borderline mothers are enormous. The tragic consequences that can result from impulsivity and uncontained emotion affect the entire family. A borderline mother's fear of abandonment can paralyze the family and have tragic consequences. Prior to treatment Mary believed that divorce was inevitable. Although she eventually became convinced that she married the right person, not every patient may come to the same conclusion. Mary's situation was unique in that she lacked any significant history of trauma or abuse, and had many positive life experiences prior to treatment. No therapeutic technique produces the same results for every patient.

INDICATIONS AND CONTRAINDICATIONS

Borderline mothers are best treated in individual therapy because splitting complicates couples and family treatment. However, situations occasionally arise that necessitate including a family member in the treatment process to resolve an immediate crisis or specific issue. Family members can offer an enlightening perspective, and may provide crucial information, such as the extent of the patient's suicidal ideation. Whenever a family member contacts the therapist, however, the patient must be informed.

The most important stage of involving family members is during the assessment process. The therapist may request psychological testing of both partners, and should encourage each party to complete the SCID-II *twice*—from one's own perspective of self as well as how the spouse views the self. Learning how partners perceive each other can be a useful therapeutic tool.

Referring family members to different therapists and obtaining their consent to consult with other treatment providers protects the therapeutic alliance. Splitting can be exacerbated by this arrangement, however, and therapists should be alert to possible triangles, distortions, or emotional cutoffs. Traditional family therapy with borderline patients may be hampered by the borderline mother's need for control, her high level of anxiety, her tendency to fluctuate between idealization and devaluation, and stress-related paranoid ideation. Because borderline mothers project their own disorganized thinking onto others, individual treatment is the preferred approach.

MANAGEMENT OF TRANSFERENCE ISSUES

Gunderson (2001) recommends a team approach to treating borderlines because of the difficulties in managing countertransference. Gutheil (1989) reminds clinicians that borderlines present numerous liability risks, such as increased risk of lawsuits, suicide attempts, and boundary violations. Treatment of borderline mothers is best managed with collegial support of the primary clinician. Clinic settings inherently offer a team approach, but private clinicians can seek consultation through peer supervision.

The therapist's ability to identify splitting, distortions, triangulation, and emotional cutoff is crucial to managing the countertransference. Borderlines often accuse therapists of being cold, rejecting, critical, condescending, or uncaring, and can easily trigger defensive reactions. Bowen (1978c) experienced countertransference problems in his study:

> One of the mothers could speak to a staff person and within minutes relay a distorted version of the staff comment to the daughter who would then act on the distortion. One distortion added to another, involving multiple staff members, could become complicated. (p. 11)

Managing the countertransference requires *compassionate clinical honesty* to help the borderline mother recognize her impact on others. Borderlines who threaten suicide or act out in other destructive ways must be informed of the consequences of their behavior. Gabbard explains (2001) that therapists who react by becoming more giving and empathic actually encourage escalation of the patient's provocations. Gabbard and Wilkinson (1994) describe an interaction with a borderline who announced, *"I feel like hell!"* and spent the entire session berating the therapist for failing to help her. At the end of this grueling hour, the therapist responded with compassionate clinical honesty and said, "Now I feel like hell. I'm concerned. I think you're making me feel the hell in you" (p. 147). After a period of silence the patient softened and acknowledged the accuracy of the therapist's response.

Borderline mothers who divorce during treatment can create intense countertransference dilemmas. Court battles may ensue, and the therapist may be required to recommend whether the patient receives custody of her children. Therapists who have not been honest with the borderline mother regarding her diagnosis and need for treatment may find themselves unprepared for custody battles. Any therapist who believes that the patient's children are in jeopardy is morally, ethically, and legally required to inform the patient and other authorities of such concern. Naturally, such circumstances may lead to the patient's premature termination if the therapist has not been straightforward about these concerns throughout treatment.

Borderlines possess an unparalleled ability to evoke anxiety, guilt, shame, and rage in their therapists. Therapists must find a way of acknowledging these feelings so that the patient becomes aware of how his or her behavior affects others. A borderline mother's impulsivity and lack of emotional control can place her children, and sometimes her therapist, at risk. Borderline mothers magnify the therapist's sense of responsibility because of the risks to their children and the possibility of becoming the target of a vindictive lawsuit.

MANAGEMENT OF CRISES
AND ACTING-OUT BEHAVIOR

Gunderson (2001) advocates a five-step approach to managing crisis situations with borderlines. Safety is the immediate concern. With borderline mothers, the safety of her children must also be considered. When a borderline mother phones expressing suicidal ideation (or homicidal ideation) the therapist must assess the level of risk posed to the patient and others, including her children. If anyone is in imminent danger, the authorities must be notified immediately, regardless of the patient's protests. If the therapist determines that the patient is needing only reassurance (a difficult and potentially dangerous assumption), the patient should be allowed to vent briefly. The therapist should inquire specifically what the patient expects from the therapist. Realistic limitations of the therapist's ability to help should be explained. The therapist may suggest self-soothing techniques, but should also encourage the use of community based emergency services. The patient should not expect to rely on the therapist's availability in crisis situations.

Gunderson (2001) recommends that, following any crisis, therapists ask their patients to reflect on how the situation affected the therapist. Asking "How did you think I would feel when you asked me to . . ." helps the borderline mother recognize the impact of her behavior on others. Following a crisis, the patient should be helped to identify the trigger, which most likely is a perceived threat of abandonment. The extent to which the patient used self-soothing techniques can be explored, and anticipated reactions to future "trigger" events should be discussed.

Therapists treating borderline mothers must not be afraid of confronting the patient with the truth about her impact on others. Gabbard (2001) discusses treatment of a suicidal borderline mother who denied that her death would have much impact on her young son. Gabbard states, "Thus when Mrs. B said that her son would cry for a little while but would eventually get over it, I replied, 'No, that's not actually very likely at all'" (p. 52). Gabbard explained the life-long emotional consequences of parental suicide. Borderline mothers can become so absorbed in the immediacy of their own distress that they fail to perceive the destructiveness of their behavior.

INTEGRATION WITH PSYCHIATRIC SERVICES AND ROLE OF MEDICATION

Borderline patients can benefit from the use of both antidepressants and antianxiety medications. In some cases, antipsychotic medications are required when patients exhibit stress-related paranoid ideation. Gabbard (2001) emphasizes, however, that when treatment is split between two different clinicians, the psychotherapist and the psychopharmacologist, borderline splitting is exacerbated. A lack of communication between the treatment providers can result in distorted and misrepresented information, creating a potentially serious situation. The patient may idealize one treatment provider and denigrate the other. Therefore, a good working relationship should exist between the primary therapist and the psychiatrist prescribing medication.

CULTURAL AND GENDER ISSUES

No conclusive evidence exists to support the assumption that BPD is more common among females than males in nonclinical populations (Simmons, 1992; Carter et al., 1999). Differences in how emotions are expressed between genders in various cultures color how "normal" versus "pathology" are defined. Alarcon and Leetz (1998) point out that different cultures assign different roles to parents and spouses, and what is "normal" may not be necessarily healthy.

Linehan (1993) suggests that BPD results from emotional invalidation and/or denigration. Therefore, BPD may be more prevalent in cultures that devalue and denigrate women. The fear of abandonment, high levels of anxiety, and impulsivity may naturally be higher for women whose survival depends entirely on their husbands. The human brain adapts to the environment in which it is immersed—the cultural environment as well as the family environment. BPD may be more prevalent among both males and females in societies in which women are not allowed to function as whole individuals, and males are permitted to be possessive, controlling, and violent with their wives.

FUTURE DIRECTIONS

BPD can seriously impair perception, judgment, and functioning of individuals, families, communities, and societies. Perceptions that are split between all good and all bad create serious conflicts because a peaceful existence requires the ability to balance positive and negative attributes of others. Bowen's (1978b) studies of parents with a "schizophrenic" child demonstrated the chaotic warlike dynamics that can trigger retaliation: "Their conscious and unconscious mechanisms are so involved in offensive and defensive maneuvers that neither can focus on self in the presence of the other" (p. 97). Future research must be directed at developing methods of intervention that reduce defensiveness.

The borderline mother's fear and distrust of mental health professionals is a major obstacle for researchers. The mothers of Bowen's (1978c) patients used professional opinion to reinforce their view of their *child* as sick: "The term *schizophrenia* was used frequently after it was part of the mother's vocabulary" (p. 7). One patient pleaded, "But doctor, you do not understand how it was between my mother and me. The only way that we could be separated was for me to kill her and if she died, I would die too" (Bowen, 1978c, p. 6). A young child with a borderline mother can neither separate—nor survive—without his or her mother. Future research must be directed at developing effective, *early* intervention with borderline mothers and their children.

Public education regarding the widespread effects of BPD on a child's emotional development is essential. Those who work with young children and witness pathological interactions between parents and children must learn the indicators of BPD. The alarming trend of medicating young children who demonstrate behavior problems without assessing the mental health of their parents could well be perpetuating BPD. Without a family systems perspective and early intervention, the transmission of BPD is simply a matter of time.

REFERENCES

Alarcon, R. D. and Leetz, K. L. (1998). Cultural intersections in the psychotherapy of borderline personality disorder. *American Journal of Psychotherapy, 52*(2), 176-190.

American Psychiatric Association (2000). *Diagnostic and statistical manual of mental disorders* (Fourth edition, Revised text). Washington, DC: American Psychiatric Association.

Bezirganian, S., Cohen, P., and Brook, J. (1993). The impact of mother-child interaction on the development of borderline personality disorder. *American Journal of Psychiatry, 150*(12), 1836-1842.

Bowen, M. (1978a). A family concept of schizophrenia. In M. Bowen (Ed.), *Family therapy and clinical practice* (pp. 45-69). New York: Jason Aronson. Reprinted from Don D. Jackson (ed.), *The etiology of schizophrenia* (pp. 346-370). New York: Basic Books.

Bowen, M. (1978b). Out-patient family psychotherapy. In M. Bowen (Ed.), *Family therapy and clinical practice* (pp. 91-99). New York: Jason Aronson. (Reprinted from *Proceedings of the twenty-fourth annual meeting of the Medical Society of Saint Elizabeth's Hospital.* Washington, DC: Saint Elizabeth's Hospital, 1961.)

Bowen, M. (1978c). Treatment of family groups with a schizophrenic member. In Bowen (Ed.). *Family therapy and clinical practice* (pp. 3-15). New York: Jason Aronson. (Originally presented at the sessions on *Current familial studies at the annual meeting of the American Orthopsychiatric Association,* Chicago, March 8, 1957).

Camel, J. E., Withers, G. S., and Greenough, W. T. (1986). Persistence of visual cortex dendritic alterations induced by postweaning exposure to a "superenriched" environment in rats. *Behavioral Neuroscience, 100,* 810-813.

Carter, J. D., Joyce, P. R., Mulder, R. T., Sullivan, P. F., and Luty, S. E. (1999). Gender differences in the frequency of personality disorders in depressed outpatients. *Journal of Personality Disorders, 13*(1), 67-74.

Danti, J., Adams, C., and Morrison, T. (1985). Children of mothers with borderline personality disorder: A multimodal clinical study. *Psychotherapy, 22*(1), 28-35.

First, M. B., Gibbon, M., Spitzer, R., Williams, J., and Benjamin, L. (1997). *Structured clinical interview for DSM-IV axis II personality disorders (SCID-II).* Washington, DC: American Psychiatric Association.

Fonagy, P., Target, M., and Gergely, G. (2000). Attachment and borderline personality disorder: A theory and some evidence. *The Psychiatric Clinics of North America, 23*(1), 103-122.

Frank, H. and Paris, J. (1981). Recollections of family experience in borderline patients. *Archives of General Psychiatry, 38,* 1031-1034.

Gabbard, G. (2001). Psychodynamic psychotherapy of borderline personality disorder: A contemporary approach. *Bulletin of the Menninger Clinic, 65*(1), 41-57.

Gabbard, G. and Wilkinson, S. (1994). *Management of countertransference with borderline patients.* Northvale, NJ: Jason Aronson.

Glickauf-Hughes, C. and Mehlman, E. (1998). Non-borderline patients with mothers who manifest borderline pathology. *British Journal of Psychotherapy, 14*(3), 294-302.

Gunderson, J. G. (2001). *Borderline personality disorder: A clinical guide.* Washington, DC: American Psychiatric Publishing.

Gunderson, J. and Lyoo, I. K. (1997). Family problems and relationships for adults with borderline personality disorder. *Harvard Review of Psychiatry, 4*(5), 272-278.

Gunderson, J. G. and Sabo, A. N. (1993). The phenomenological and conceptual interface between borderline personality disorder and PTSD. *American Journal of Psychiatry, 150*(12), 1906-1907.

Gutheil, T. G. (1989). Borderline personality disorder, boundary violations, and patient-therapist sex: Medicolegal pitfalls. *American Journal of Psychiatry, 146* (5), 597-602.

Harvard Medical School (2001). How schizophrenia develops: New evidence and new ideas. *The Harvard Mental Health Letter 17*(8), 1-4.

Jensen, J. A. (1994). An investigation of eye movement desensitization reprocessing (EMD/R) as a treatment for posttraumatic stress disorder (PTSD) symptoms of Vietnam combat veterans. *Behavior Therapy, 25,* 311-325.

Johnson, J. G., Cohen, P., Smailes, E. M., Skodol, A. E., Brown, J., and Oldham, J. M. (2001). Childhood verbal abuse and risk for personality disorders during adolescence and early adulthood. *Comprehensive Psychiatry, 42*(1), 16-23.

Kernberg, O. (1985). *Borderline conditions and pathological narcissism.* Northvale, NJ: Jason Aronson.

Kerr, M. and Bowen, M. (1988). *Family evaluation: An approach based on Bowen theory.* New York: Norton.

Kroll, J. (1988). *The challenge of the borderline patient.* New York: Norton.

Lachkar, J. (1992). *The narcissistic/borderline couple: A psychodynamic perspective on marital treatment.* New York: Brunner/Mazel.

Lawson, C. (2000). *Understanding the borderline mother: Helping her children transcend the intense, unpredictable, and volatile relationship.* Northvale, NJ: Jason Aronson.

Levitan, J. B. and Kaczmarek, L. K. (1991). *The neuron.* New York: Oxford University Press.

Linehan, M. (1993). *Cognitive-behavioral treatment of borderline personality disorder.* New York: Guilford.

Links, P., Steiner, M., and Huzley, G. (1988). The occurrence of borderline personality disorder in the families of borderline patients. *Journal of Personality Disorders, 2*(1), 14-20.

Lipke, H. (2000). *EMDR and psychotherapy integration: Theoretical and clinical suggestions with focus on traumatic stress.* Boca Raton, FL: CRC Press.

Loranger, A., Oldham, J., and Tulis, E. (1982). Familial transmission of DSM-III borderline personality disorder. *Archives of General Psychiatry, 39,* 795-799.

Manfield, P. (1998). EMDR terms and procedures. In P. Manfield (Ed.), *Extending EMDR: A casebook of innovative applications.* New York: Norton.

Masterson, J. F. (1976). *Psychotherapy of the borderline adult: A developmental approach.* New York: Brunner/Mazel.

Muller, R. (1992). Is there a neural basis for borderline splitting? *Comprehensive Psychiatry, 33*(2), 92-104.

Nichols, M. and Schwartz, R. (2001). *Family therapy concepts and methods* (Fifth Edition). Boston: Allyn and Bacon.

Perry, F. (1999). The memories of states: How the brain stores and retrieves traumatic experience. In J. M. Goodwin and R. Attias (Eds.), *Splintered reflections: Images of the body in trauma* (pp. 9-38). New York: Basic Books.

Raine, A. (1993). Features of borderline personality and violence. *Journal of Clinical Psychology, 49*(2), 277-281.

Ratey, J. (2001). *A user's guide to the brain: Perception, attention, and the four theaters of the brain.* New York: Random House.

Salzman, J. P., Salzman, C., and Wolfson, A. N. (1997). Relationship of childhood abuse and maternal attachment to the development of borderline personality disorder. In M. C. Zanarini (Ed.), *Role of sexual abuse in the etiology of borderline personality disorder* (pp. 71-91). Washington, DC: American Psychiatric Press.

Scheck, M. M., Schaeffer, J. A., and Gillette, C. (1998). Brief psychological intervention with traumatized young women: The efficacy of eye movement desensitization and reprocessing. *Journal of Traumatic Stress, 11,* 25-44.

Schore, A. (1997). Early organization of the nonlinear right brain and development of a predisposition to psychiatric disorders. *Development and Psychopathology, 9,* 595-631.

Segal, B. (1990). Interpersonal disorder in borderline patients. In P. S. Links (Ed.), *Family environment and borderline personality disorder* (pp. 25-40). Washington, DC: American Psychiatric Press.

Shachnow, J., Clarkin, J., DiPalma, C., Thurston, F., Hull, J., and Shearin, E. (1997). Biparental psychopathology and borderline personality disorder. *Psychiatry, 60,* 171-181.

Silverman, J., Pinkham, L., Horvath, T., Cocaro, E., Klar, H., Schear, S., Apter, S., Davidson, M., Mohs, R., and Siever, L. (1991). Affective and impulsive personality disorder traits in the relatives of patients with borderline personality disorder. *American Journal of Psychiatry, 148*(10), 1378-1385.

Simmons, D. (1992). Gender issues and borderline personality disorder: Why do females dominate the diagnosis? *Archives of Psychiatric Nursing, 6*(4), 219-223.

Teicher, M. (2000). Wounds that time won't heal: The neurobiology of child abuse. *Cerebrum: The Dana Forum on Brain Science, 2*(4), 50-67.

Trout, M. (1991). Perinatal depression in four women reared by borderline mothers. *Pre- and Peri-Natal Psychology, 5*(4), 297-325.

van der Kolk, B. (1997). The psychobiology of posttraumatic stress disorder. *Journal of Clinical Psychology, 58*(9), 16-24.

van Reekum, R., Conway, C., Gansler, D. White, R., and Bachman, D. (1993). Neuro-behavioral study of borderline personality disorder. *Journal of Psychiatric Neuroscience 18*(3), 121-129.

Vaughan, S. (1997). *The talking cure: Why traditional talking therapy offers a better chance for long-term relief than any drug.* New York: Henry Holt.

Waldinger, R. J. and Frank, A. F. (1989). Clinicians' experiences in combining medication and psychotherapy in the treatment of borderline patients. *Hospital and Community Psychiatry, 40,* 712-718.

Weiss, M., Zelkowitz, P., Feldman, R., Vogel, J., Heyman, M., and Paris, J. (1996). Psychopathology in offspring of mothers with borderline personality disorder: A pilot study. *Canadian Journal of Psychiatry, 41,* 285-291.

Zanarini, M. C. and Frankenburg, F. (1997). Pathways to the development of borderline personality disorder. *Journal of Personality Disorders, 11*(1), 93-104.

Chapter 11

Relationship Enhancement Family Therapy with Narcissistic Personality Disorder

Marsha J. Harman
Michael Waldo

INTRODUCTION

According to Greek mythology, Narcissis was a young man who rebuffed the love of the nymph Echo. Other nymphs prayed that the gods would punish Narcissus for his arrogance and cruelty. The punishment decreed was for Narcissus to fall in love with himself, which happened when he saw his reflection in a pool of water. He died beside the pool, having languished from starvation or excessive self-love that could never be consummated (Hamilton, 1942). Thus, narcissistic personality disorder (NPD) was patterned after the mythic figure.

Narcissistic personality disorder was first identified by the American Psychiatric Association (1980) in the *Diagnostic and Statistical Manual of Mental Disorders,* Third Edition (DSM-III), and continues in the fourth edition's text revision (DSM-IV-TR, American Psychiatric Association, 2000). The essential features include a pervasive pattern of grandiosity, need for admiration, and lack of empathy that is present in a variety of contexts and begins by early adulthood. NPD is clustered with other personality disorders that could be described as erratic, emotional, and dramatic, and include antisocial, borderline, and histrionic personality disorders. Although these latter personality disorders could be described as callous, needy, and flirtatious, respectively, NPD is identified by its characteristic grandiosity.

Individuals with NPD tend to display a relatively stable self-image and tend not to be self-destructive, impulsive, or concerned about abandonment issues as would an individual with borderline personality disorder (BPD). They take excessive pride in achievements, but tend to shun emotional displays, and, in fact, have contempt for others' sensitivity, such as that displayed by an individual with histrionic personality disorder. Although individuals with NPD and those with antisocial personality disorder may both be determined, superficial, exploitative, and lack empathy, those with NPD tend not to be impulsive, aggressive, deceitful, or have a history of conduct problems. Those with NPD tend toward perfectionism and believe their performance is superior to that of others. They are inclined to be suspicious and withdrawn only if they fear that their imperfections or flaws may be revealed. It is estimated that approximately 2 to 16 percent of the clinical population, and less than 1 percent of the general population, qualify as NPD, and of those diagnosed with NPD, approximately 50 to 75 percent are men (American Psychiatric Association, 2000). To be diagnosed according to the DSM-IV (American Psychiatric Association, 1994, p. 661), the individual should meet five of nine criteria, including:

(1) has a grandiose sense of self-importance (e.g., exaggerates achievements and talents, expects to be recognized as superior without commensurate achievements)

(2) is preoccupied with fantasies of unlimited success, power, brilliance, beauty, or ideal love

(3) believes that he or she is "special" and unique and can only be understood by, or should associate with, other special or high status people (or institutions)

(4) requires excessive admiration

(5) has a sense of entitlement, i.e., unreasonable expectations of especially favorable treatment or automatic compliance with his or her expectations

(6) is interpersonally exploitative, i.e., takes advantage of others to achieve his or her own ends

(7) lacks empathy: is unwilling to recognize or identify with the feelings and needs of others

(8) is often envious of others or believes that others are envious of him or her

(9)   shows arrogant, haughty behaviors or attitudes (reprinted
with permission from the *Diagnostic and Statistical Manual of Mental Disorders,* Fourth Edition, copyright 1994
American Psychiatric Association)

In the early twentieth century Ernest Jones (1913) wrote about
"The God Complex," a description of what is now known as NPD.
Freud wrote about narcissism in 1914. Major works on NPD done in
the 1970s included extensions of psychoanalytic theory, such as
Kohut's (1971, 1977) self psychology, and Kernberg's (1970, 1974,
1975) object-relations theory.

Kohut (1971) founded the self psychology movement that provides the primary basis for contemporary psychoanalysis. The major
concept is the self—the core of the personality. Inherited characteristics interact with the environment to establish the coherent and enduring
personality. Internalization of experiences with others, or selfobjects,
gradually forms the unified self and the display of predictable and enduring patterns (Moore and Fine, 1990). Kohut differentiates between healthy narcissism, which is a strong, ambitious, cohesive self
striving toward full realization of the personality, and pathological
narcissism, which is a vulnerable, unstable self attempting to bolster
self-esteem. He described personality disorders as disorders of the
self (Kohut, 1977). Three fundamental needs work together to help
an infant identify with the parents/caregivers, and then individuate
from them to emerge as the cohesive individual self:

1. *Twinship,* or alter ego: the parent/caregiver provides likeness/
   sameness experiences that allow the child to feel a sense of be-
   longing. Failure may create a deficiency in these areas.
2. *Idealization:* the parent/caregiver is deserving of admiration
   and idealization, which allows the child to develop values and
   ideals including abilities of self-soothing, regulation of urges,
   and devotion to ideals. Failure contributes to inability for self-
   soothing, self-regulation, and excitement.
3. *Mirroring:* the parent/caregiver consistently reflects pride in the
   infant's accomplishments, and the child develops the self-asser-
   tive ambitions that allow for self-esteem regulation, utilization

of physical and mental activities, and pursuit of goals and purposes. Failure to do so contributes to a lack of self-esteem, feelings of emptiness and despair, and feelings of meaninglessness and purposelessness in life. (Ornstein and Kay, 1990)

Object-relations theory describes the separation and individuation process of the first two years of life (Mahler, Pine, and Bergman, 1975) and how poor differentiation in early primary relationships will affect subsequent relationships (Kernberg, 1974, 1975). Kernberg described individuals with NPD as appearing socially adept but actually having serious distortions in their interpersonal relationships that mimic those between infant and parent/caregiver present in the first years of life. Such individuals are intensely ambitious with grandiose fantasies, but possess feelings of inferiority, emptiness, and boredom, and are dependent on external admiration and praise. They continually seek gratification and ways to prove themselves brilliant and powerful. Yet their love relationships are flawed. They tend to exploit others to reach their goals. When feeling vulnerable, they suffer from chronic uncertainty and intense envy.

Within the last century the concept of NPD has evolved to the current DSM-IV-TR diagnostic criteria. Diagnosis of NPD is based largely on subjective clinical judgment using the DSM. However, some research regarding objective measures of NPD has been conducted. Lachar (1974) found that individuals with only superficial relationships score low on the social introversion scale of the Minnesota Mulitphasic Personality Inventory (MMPI). Raskin and Novacek (1991) found that individuals who are interpersonally exploitative will have an elevated psychopathic deviate scale. On MMPI-2 profiles, Meyer and Deitsch (1996) found the psychopathic deviate—hypomania (4-9) profile common among individuals with NPD. Shafer (1954) found Rorschach responses with an ornate or flashy quality focusing on fancy food, exotic clothing, jewelry, or perfume may also be indicative of NPD. Bellak's (1993) research with the Thematic Apperception Test (TAT) found that NPD may be indicated when stories are void of meaningful content, have a cute ending, or generally avoid essential features of stimuli that may potentially induce anxiety.

IMPACT ON THE FAMILY

A number of therapists have conducted family therapy with couples in which at least one individual has been diagnosed with NPD. Each emphasizes the long-term nature of the therapy if it is to be effective.

When both members of a relationship are diagnosed with NPD, the couple tends to be vulnerable, easily injured and enraged, and blaming of each other (Kalogjera et al., 1998). The individuals tend to have extreme difficulty with real or imagined rejections and slights. As the self feels more vulnerable, the relationship suffers from de-idealization and fragmentation.

Solomon (1998) maintains that marriage brings out infantile feelings as bonds of baby and parent/caretaker are recreated. Defense mechanisms, particularly regression, allow couples with narcissistic and borderline disorders to use blame to vent the infantile rage and spitefulness that emerged during their first two years of life (Solomon, 1989). Demands and a sense of entitlement permeate marriages between partners with NPD because expectations are rarely satisfied. The couple may even collude or subconsciously hide their emotional problems from themselves and others so that destructive forces are kept at bay. Thus the relationship does not change and adapt but relies on defensive strategies to maintain the status quo (Lansky, 1981, 1993).

The core issue in narcissistic and borderline defenses is the lack of boundaries (Solomon, 1998) that are typically developed in the first months and years of life, when the child becomes aware of self and others and self with others (Mahler, Pine, and Bergman, 1975). Individuals with NPD use rationalization to explain personal deficits, defeats, or irresponsible behavior. They may exploit partners to gain advantage, treat the partner as an object to bolster self-esteem, and use feelings for impression management, yet they are so needy that they are unable to accept the caring they do receive. They respond to criticism with feelings of humiliation and rage, although they may mask these feelings with an aura of cool indifference. However, when emotional stability is jarred, verbal or physical aggression may result. Once calmer, the partners with NPD may act as if the incidents never occurred, refuse to discuss them, and expect that equilibrium will return (Solomon, 1998).

Lachkar (1984, 1985, 1986, 1992, 1998) has written extensively, and sometimes with humorous overtones, about the dance in which narcissistic/borderline couples engage. She maintains that individuals with NPD and BPD seek each other as intimate partners so that the dance of attacking BPD and retreating NPD is sustained. The partner with NPD then becomes guilt-ridden and eventually returns to the relationship when the partner with BPD promises to change if the partner with NPD will not leave. Lachkar explains that the individual with NPD is the entitlement lover who cannot imagine the needs of the partner. Individuals with NPD are threatened by the dependency needs of partners with BPD, and prefer partners who affirm their positive attributes. Their emotional lives are shallow, and they believe the world owes them something, yet they are frequently unable to achieve long-term goals and dreams. Their superegos are harsh and punitive, and they use the defense mechanisms of projection and withdrawal when feelings of shame, guilt, and grandiosity emerge.

Several authors have used fairy-tale characters as metaphors for the individual with NPD. Quadrio (1982) likened the individual with NPD to Peter Pan, who may be unfaithful, have difficulty expressing feelings, substitute sex for intimacy, and use distance in a passive-aggressive defense, particularly when angered. However, once people suffering from NPD have abandoned their partners, they will feel extreme separation anxiety and return home. Anxiety may be the event that brings the individual with NPD to therapy.

Kurtz (1996) equated the individual with NPD to Cinderella. Marshall and Larimer (1995) describe the Cinderella syndrome as the expectation that an inadequate investment of one's time or resources will result in an unrealistically large payoff. Kurtz maintained that partners with NPD frequently display a lack of empathy, narcissistic anxiety and rage, projective identification, and cognitive distortions. If both partners have NPD, each begins to view themselves as victims and their partners as inattentive and critical, so that Cinderella begins to view her prince as a frog and he, in turn, views her as a nag.

McWilliams and Lependorf (1990) emphasized the aspects of the grandiose self that appeared to be without need and without sin. In their view, individuals with NPD are reluctant to take responsibility for their choices. They tend to display judgmental, devaluing attitudes. Rather than brag, they simply drop information during a conversation to elicit admiration. Rather than apologize, they may engage in various behaviors: *undoing* such as sending flowers or preparing the partner's favorite meal; appealing to the partner to consider the *good intentions* meant instead of what resulted; *explaining* and excusing the behavior rather than asking for forgiveness; *recrimination* in the form of statements such as,"I can't believe I did that!" or "I'm a lousy person. You shouldn't even bother with me" because these elicit sympathy and may cause a partner to want to relieve the offender's guilt; and/or *deflecting blame* so that the offender may actually blame the partner with statements such as, "You made me do it." Individuals with NPD also display an inability to genuinely thank others or appropriately acknowledge a contribution.

Living with an individual with NPD may force family members to endure dysfunctional circular interactions that are never resolved. To keep the peace, the family member may have to put aside personal needs and desires. Since the family member with NPD alternates between anxiety and rage, or insecurity and withdrawal, other family members dare not express any criticism or any dependency unless they are willing to tolerate disequilibrium in the relationship.

SETTING

We have used relationship enhancement (RE) therapy to work with couples and families primarily in private practice and in university counseling centers. We have used it as single therapists and as co-therapists, with heterosexual and homosexual couples, and with families consisting of parents and children.

The case example that follows was conducted in a private practice office. The office was furnished with gliders and sofas arranged so that the partners could sit across from each other with the therapist seated in view and able to observe both individuals. Clients are self-referred or referred by physicians or friends. Couples, as well as individuals and families, are seen for therapy. The therapists are trained in counseling psychology. The therapist presented in the case study describes herself as following humanistic/existential theory and employing some cognitive behavioral interventions. The therapists also are full-time faculty members of universities, so clients are usually seen in the evenings or on weekends. Evenings appear to be ideal for couples and families to schedule conjoint sessions. Couples often pay for their own therapy since health maintenance organizations (HMOs) frequently do not pay for family therapy or marriage counseling.

TREATMENT MODEL

Bernard Guerney (1977, 1981, 1987) developed relationship enhancement therapy as an educational skills approach to help individuals, couples, and families to improve their interpersonal interactions. Clients learn to express their deepest emotions and gain insight into their own as well as others' concerns. Clients also learn to listen in ways that may have been previously unfamiliar when discussing conflicts. Guerney maintains that nine specific skills may be developed: self-expression, empathic responding, discussion/negotiation, problem/conflict resolution, self-changing, helping others change, generalization, facilitation of appropriate communication, and maintenance. In our experience with using RE, self-expression, empathic responding, and discussion/negotiation are the skills primarily developed.

RE family therapy combines psychodynamic, humanistic, behavioral, and interpersonal perspectives to form a set of skills to be developed by the couple. The skills provide a structure in and out of therapy for the couple to discuss important issues without resorting to ineffective interaction patterns. Research has demonstrated the effectiveness of RE with premarital couples (Ridley et al., 1982), married couples (Brock and Joanning, 1983; Granvold, 1983; Jessee and Guerney, 1981), and sexual dysfunction (Harman, Waldo, and Johnson, 1994, 1998).

RE family therapy has also been successful with couples in which one partner suffered from BPD (Harman and Waldo, 2001; Waldo and Harman, 1993, 1998). We believe that RE may also address many ways in which NPD symptoms are expressed in relationships. Since RE emphasizes empathic communication and listening skills, and avoidance of generalized statements about another's character, it can help interrupt dysfunctional interactions. The structured role changes in RE from expresser to listener, and the need to attend carefully to the partner's feelings prior to paraphrasing them, may also assist in overcoming narcissistic qualities. Snyder (1994) found relationship enhancement family therapy to be helpful with narcissistically vulnerable clients, as well as in recovering erotic intimacy in primary relationships (Snyder, 2000).

The RE approach represents an effective blend of both the expressive and supportive treatment approaches recommended by Horwitz and his colleagues (1996). The strong communication focus of RE can assist clients with NPD to express their fears, wishes, and conflicts in a supportive environment, so that they can feel heard and understood by their partners. At the same time, the highly structured approach and modeling of appropriate communication skills help in correcting narcissistic and attacking interactions. Support is provided for clients with NPD to develop more healthy and adaptive communication, relationship, and problem-solving skills. Therapist coaching can also help clients with NPD understand their partner's feelings and views more accurately, thereby interrupting shallow or negative interpretations and reducing tendencies toward idealization and devaluation (splitting).

Personal characteristics of the individuals determine whether RE family therapy is appropriate. In the initial couples counseling sessions, it is important to observe communication patterns as well as gather historical information about the individuals and couples. Knowledge of the catalyst for the decision to come for therapy is also helpful. As therapists, we usually work with couples who are verbal and have at least average intelligence. A prerequisite for suggesting the use of RE family therapy and the inherent skills training is that both individuals commit to developing more effective communication. There are times when individual therapy is appropriate with one or both of the partners depending on various factors that may interfere with progress. Certainly, individual therapy with the client who is suffering from NPD will be appropriate to work on issues of inferiority and anger. Conjoint therapy is most appropriate for working on relationship issues and developing new communication patterns.

When unskilled couples talk about difficulties they are having, one of the skills that is frequently used least is empathic listening. Empathic listening (Rogers, 1961) and responding involves one partner restating what the other partner says to ensure not only that communication is clear, but also to understand the message from the expresser's point of view. Rather than using empathic listening and responding, most partners form their forthcoming response without clarifying their partners' message. Another difficulty arises when partners present their perspectives, but neglect to make it clear that they are relating their perceptions as opposed to proclaiming reality. Gottman and DeClaire (2001) refer to the use of subjective "I" statements in self-expression as a soft start so as not to arouse defensiveness in listeners. For example, "You are so irresponsible!" is more likely to arouse defensiveness in the person hearing it than would, "I thought you had said you'd be home at six o'clock." Coaching couples to use subjective self-expression can increase the degree to which they demonstrate ownership of their thoughts and feelings.

The two major roles in RE therapy are: (1) expresser and (2) listener. The partners alternate between the roles.

Expresser

Expressers include five features when introducing issues about which they are concerned. These features are:

1. State the problem from a subjective position (e.g., "It seems to me . . ."; "From my point of view . . .").
2. Convey the feelings/emotions associated with the problem.
3. Provide specific examples of events/behaviors related to the problem, but avoid generalized statements, particularly about the partner's character (e.g., "I thought you said you would check the tires, but when I went out, I had a flat," rather than, "You are so thoughtless and irresponsible").
4. Make a request of the partner.
5. Tell the partner what it would mean for the relationship if the request could be fulfilled.

Listener

The listener lays aside whatever thoughts/emotions arise around this issue and concentrates solely on the expresser's statements, realizing that the listener will eventually be the expresser and share another view of the issue. The listener attempts to understand the situation from the expresser's point of view by sharing brief paraphrases of what the expresser asserts. The paraphrasing is to demonstrate that the listener understands what the expresser is verbalizing, and the expresser confirms the listener's comprehension or corrects mistaken impressions. Roles are reversed once the expresser has included the five characteristics in the message and confirms being heard and understood. Thus, the listener becomes the expresser, and the former expresser becomes the current listener.

Therapist/Coach

The therapist/coach's tasks include explaining, demonstrating, coaching expression and listening, and negotiating role changes. It is preferable in the initial interactions to encourage the listener to show understanding after short explanations by the expresser. This assists the listener to practice paraphrasing with shorter pieces of information before attempting to paraphrase longer messages. It is also reinforcing to the listener, who is affirmed for accurately paraphrasing the expresser's message. Another task of the therapist/coach is to reinforce progress in the skills. Positive phrases, such as "Terrific work," "Good job," and "Beautiful," give positive feedback so that the individuals are aware of their progress. Such reinforcement may be particularly important to clients with NPD. It is also important to address inappropriate body language, such as arms crossed over the chest or sarcastic tone of voice. Listeners may exhibit these inappropriate behaviors if they have a difficult time laying aside personal thoughts and feelings in order to empathically listen to the expresser. When this happens, it is important to gain the cooperation of the listener through the therapist's empathic response to the listener and assurance that roles will reverse eventually. It is important for the listener and expresser to remain in their respective roles and to address each other rather than addressing the therapist/coach.

After RE therapy has been explained, but before the first skills-training session begins, we ask each partner to accomplish two important tasks: (1) determine what the individual loves about the partner, and (2) make a list of problems ranked from low level to highly volatile. We have found that it is important for partners to ascertain what they love about the mate before they arrive for the first skills-training session, because it can be antitherapeutic if one partner is perceived as struggling to think of positive qualities about the other. Low-level problems are addressed first during skills training. Highly volatile problems are addressed later after skills have been taught.

Solomon (1998) maintains that successful therapy and loving, intimate relationships such as marriage offer reparative interpersonal experiences. Therapy allows the developmental process that was thwarted in childhood to reassert itself. RE family therapy creates an atmosphere within the marital relationship that encourages further development in areas that may have been stalled by earlier experiences.

CASE EXAMPLE

Claire and Mark came to therapy after Mark discovered that Claire was having an affair with one of her colleagues. Although not previously diagnosed, Claire met the criteria for NPD. She dressed either provocatively or sloppily when she attended therapy. She was an attorney who worked on high profile cases in the corporate world. She made it clear that she had come to therapy only because Mark was overreacting to this situation. She indicated that it was not an ongoing affair. The explanation for the affair was that it just happened because she and Mark had varying schedules that did not mesh. She said she wanted to save the marriage, but that she was not going to tolerate Mark's continual harping about her indiscretion. She felt the affair was understandable and Mark just needed to get over it. She had been attracted to Mark because he was a professor at the university where she had obtained her undergraduate degree. She loved being associated with an intelligent, successful man.

Mark was a full professor of chemistry at a regional university. He admitted that he was drawn to Claire because she exhibited what he referred to as raw sexuality, and he was flattered when she approached him. He usually kept his attention focused on his chemistry research and teaching. He knew she dressed provocatively and did not like it, but Claire became enraged if he asked that she dress more conservatively. He had met her colleagues, including the man with whom Claire was having the affair. He did not believe he had very much in common with them.

MARK: It seems to me that there is a double standard in our relationship. You made it abundantly clear to me that you expected me to be faithful but you feel free to have an affair with the judge. You told me if I ever cheated on you, you would cut my balls off and take everything, but you're the one who cheated.

THERAPIST: What feelings come up for you, Mark?

MARK: I feel betrayed, so hurt, and so angry that I ache.

THERAPIST: Okay, Mark. You're doing great. Claire, can you show understanding to this much?

CLAIRE: You are very angry with me because I had an affair after threatening you that you'd better never cheat on me.

THERAPIST: Is that it, Mark? Does she have it?

MARK: [Nods] Yeah, I guess that's it.

THERAPIST: Perfect, Claire. [To Mark] What is your request of Claire? How would you like it to be, and what would that say about your relationship?

MARK: Well, I'd like for you to hold yourself to the same standard that you hold me, and that we could recommit to each other. I want us to work on the relationship and spend time together rather than doing stuff separately. If you could do that, it would mean that you respected me and respected our relationship, that you were committed to me and to us.

THERAPIST: Okay. Claire, can you summarize what you are hearing?

CLAIRE: You'd like for me to practice what I preach and commit to you anew. That would mean I respected you and the relationship.

THERAPIST: Does she have it, Mark?

MARK: Yes, that's it.

THERAPIST: You both are doing this beautifully. Are we ready to switch? Okay. Mark, you're going to be the listener now and put aside anything you think or want to say, and simply try to understand Claire's point of view, not that you agree with it, but that you understand it. And, Claire, you're going to start with subjective language and talk about a specific example.

CLAIRE: It seems to me that you are overreacting to all of this. I did have the affair with Judge Greene. I didn't mean to hurt you, but it just happened. I'm with these people most of the day. We have lunch and drinks after work. It just happened. I have always been proud to be your wife, and I do respect you. But I do enjoy being around the other attorneys and judges, and that includes Judge Greene. I love talking with all of them about corporate legal issues and their ramifications. I do not relate at all to your stuffy professor friends. I never have, and I resent the fact that you expect me to change. You know . . .

THERAPIST: It seems to me . . .

CLAIRE: It seems to me that you know you would not want to be in on the discussions I have with my co-workers, and I sure as hell don't want to be with your friends. I can spend some time with you, but not all my free time.

THERAPIST: Good job, Claire. Let's let Mark summarize.

MARK: You think I am overreacting to your affair. You don't want to give up your friends, and you hate my friends. You want to work on the relationship to some extent, but you don't want to change very much about the way things are.

THERAPIST: Super, Mark. Does he have it so far, Claire?

CLAIRE: When I hear him say that, I guess it sounds like I don't want to work on the relationship very much.

THERAPIST: Is that what you mean?

CLAIRE: [Quiet for several seconds, obviously thinking.] Mark, when I married you, it was the greatest achievement of my life. I was so proud to be with you.

You were so supportive when I wanted to go to law school. You couldn't have been more supportive. But now I have a new career. Somehow I get energy from being with my new colleagues. I was so flattered when Judge Greene came on to me. I couldn't believe it. You and I were distant. It just happened so quickly . . .

THERAPIST: Terrific, Claire. Let's summarize.

MARK: You saw our marriage as a great achievement, but now you are moving on to newer achievements. The affair happened because we were distant and you felt flattered by Judge Greene's attention.

THERAPIST: Does he have it, Claire?

CLAIRE: Yes, but he sounds angry when he says it.

THERAPIST: Mark, it did sound like you were judgmental and angry when you summarized. Would it be possible for you to summarize while you were trying to view it from Claire's point of view without the judgmental tone? I know this is hard.

MARK: I'll try, but it is hard. [After a few seconds] You feel good about yourself when you achieve. Our marriage was an achievement for you, but you need more achievements to feel good. We have some communication problems so that opened up an opportunity for you to be flattered by Judge Greene's attention.

THERAPIST: What about now, Claire? Do you feel understood?

CLAIRE: Yes. I think he does understand.

THERAPIST: Mark, terrific work. Both of you are working hard at this and doing a fantastic job.

STRENGTHS AND LIMITATIONS

As the example displays, RE family therapy may help an individual with NPD to increase ego-strength through improved communication skills. Empathy may also be developed as the individual uses active listening and empathic responses with a partner. When using RE family therapy, the individual with NPD is allowed to express personal perspectives without being interrupted and attacked, and may experience the other partner listening rather than protesting. As systemic theory recommends, the familiar interaction pattern is interrupted and replaced by a structure in which each partner is affirmed, even though the two may not agree.

RE family therapy may assist partners with NPD to gain ego-strength and develop a more stable identity. These changes may reduce their need to overidealize or devalue their partners. Less frequent attack-and-withdrawal episodes that are replaced by more productive interchanges and problem negotiations may begin to change the narrative of the couple's ongoing history. However, these changes are not usually produced in one or even a few sessions when one or both of the partners suffer from a personality disorder. As stated previously, all research associated with NPD therapy indicates the long-term nature of the therapy. For cognitive shifts and ego-strength to be solidified, a number of intense, successful sessions would be necessary.

Therapists who prefer systemic, humanistic, or experiential theoretical orientations may find RE family therapy useful. The skills training involves both explanation, modeling, and skills practice so that retention and enduring use are more likely. Although the exact structure may not be used when the couple is no longer in therapy, the use of subjective expression, specific examples, identifying underlying emotions, and empathic listening frequently continues. Less dependence on the therapist's coaching and mediation will be achieved as the couple develops confidence in their ability to negotiate and maintain their relationship. Other relationships in the individuals' lives may also be enhanced as skills in interpersonal communication are upgraded.

RE family therapy may be combined with individual therapy as well as psychotropic medication if appropriate. Individuals with NPD will frequently benefit from individual therapy and may also benefit from psychotropic medication if their depressive or anxious symptoms warrant it. In addition, when couples have neglected seeking help until destructive interactions have made each individual so defensive that revenge or flight are the underlying objectives for one or both partners, it may be difficult to have the partner embrace RE family therapy. One partner may come to therapy simply to appease the other with no authentic plan to work on the relationship. Again, RE family therapy is of benefit to those who desire that the relationship survive and prosper, and are willing to make themselves vulnerable.

BENEFITS FOR THE FAMILY

RE family therapy may assist families when various members have symptoms of personality disorders. However, the approach may be helpful regardless of whether family members have been diagnosed with a disorder. Since RE family therapy focuses primarily on the relationship and interactions between family members, the diagnosis is not the fundamental heart of the matter. The major benefit of RE family therapy is that it is effective with most relationships as long as the participants are verbal with a vocabulary extensive enough to communicate intelligently, and are committed to the process.

A fundamental advantage of RE family therapy is the interruption of the repetitive, circular interactions that are taxing, infuriating, and noxious for all parties. If children are involved in the relationship, it can be helpful to ask couples what they think they are teaching their children about relationships, and whether what they are modeling for their offspring is healthy. Most often, the partners will agree that they are modeling a poor relationship. This insight may provide incentive for the couple to change their attitudes and decide that improved interactions are imperative if they are to remain together.

The modeling and skills practice allow for new interactions even though they may seem staged until the skills become more comfortable and spontaneous. Yet the rehearsal and the resulting experiences of being understood, understanding others, and negotiating compromises can be therapeutic and healing, especially with the therapist's coaching. Such rehearsals would be harder to accomplish at home without the encouragement of the coach. For example, the mother of one family in therapy recently commented after her two daughters had practiced the skills regarding a low-level problem that this would have never happened at home. She insisted that they would have been shouting at each other and one would have stormed upstairs rather than coming to an understanding .

With the added complication of a family member with a personality disorder, the interactions that are repetitive and destructive become spontaneous so that little thinking or listening take place other than to determine the most outrageous and hurtful comment that could follow in the interchange. RE family therapy interrupts that cycle and replaces it with healthier communication skills.

INDICATIONS AND CONTRAINDICATIONS

We use RE family therapy with couples and families unless contraindicated. However, couples who desire to come for only one or two sessions will not benefit from this therapy. Likewise, the extent of an individual's intellectual impairment can preclude RE family therapy if the person is unable to enter into the process with the ability to show understanding to others' messages.

Psychotic individuals are not appropriate for RE family therapy during the length of the psychosis. If medication is able to ameliorate the psychosis, and cognitive and emotional stability has returned to the individual, then this therapy may be appropriate. Still, in these instances the other partner is likely to require assistance in coping with a mate diagnosed with a severe mental illness. Nonetheless, for the interpersonal interactions between the two, RE family therapy may be the most appropriate intervention.

With couples in which one partner is diagnosed with NPD, RE family therapy is the preferred intervention, because in addition to teaching communication skills, ego-building features take place. For individuals with NPD, RE family therapy encourages ego-strength, self-stability, and boundary differentiation. Thus, each individual, as well as the couple relationship, is affected.

MANAGEMENT OF TRANSFERENCE ISSUES

Although object-relations theory would encourage transference with the therapist, transference issues are actually minimized with RE family therapy. The RE approach uses the therapist as a coach. If any transference occurs, the individuals may view the therapist as a nurturing parent, since the coaching requires teaching and encouragement. With many of the erratic and emotional personality disorders, the early relationship with the parent/object was flawed and abusive. If the individual experiences the therapist/coach as nurturing, then therapy may prove corrective in some measure in the objects-relations area.

If some negative transference does occur with the therapist, active listening and empathic responses on the part of the therapist would be in order. Again, such client-centered responses could prove corrective in the developmental process. Nonetheless, transference issues with the therapist are not encouraged in RE family therapy, but can be used for curative measures if they do transpire.

Individuals with NPD frequently enjoy being the center of attention but are sensitive to criticism. In the RE approach, each partner is reinforced for both listening and expressing, so that it becomes a positive experience to express concerns appropriately and to listen effectively. Each partner, then, can be successful in both skills. Confrontation in this technique is minimal, but any criticism and subsequent defensiveness should be approached with the endeavor to strengthen fragile egos.

MANAGEMENT OF CRISES AND ACTING-OUT BEHAVIOR

Unfortunately, when individuals are distressed they may behave erratically on occasion. Under those circumstances, therapists would determine whether the crisis pertains to the individual personally or to the couple's interaction. If it pertains to the couple, then RE family therapy would be useful to work through the issues. If the crisis pertains to the individual, then it may be necessary to see the person individually or refer him or her to a physician.

Frequently, individuals with NPD or their partners, particularly if the partner suffers from BPD, can become depressed and suicidal when defense systems begin to crumble. The therapist familiar with personality-disordered individuals will always want to be scanning the interactions for possible defensive reactions, and attempt to treat them immediately. RE family therapy would encourage each partner to become more individuated and secure, and, thus, have less need for unhealthy defense patterns. Until that growth occurs, clear guidelines articulated by the therapist to the family as to how suicidal threats will be addressed and options to deal with depressive symptoms that are healthy rather than destructive should be available. Normalizing depressive symptoms that may occur and even helping the individuals to anticipate these reactions would be important.

When a couple is so entrenched in destructive behaviors that they cannot or will not be coached in the RE skills, then a decision must be made about how to continue. With one couple who could make no progress, they were informed that the therapist could be of little help to them and were referred. Another couple who made little progress continued in individual therapy until they could attempt the RE skills and be successful.

INTEGRATION WITH PSYCHIATRIC SERVICES AND ROLE OF MEDICATION

Depending on the biological need, psychotropic medication may be necessary. An individual's genetic predisposition to an Axis I disorder as well as other various factors contribute to the delicate balance of an individual's brain chemistry. Frequently, an individual's descriptive report of symptoms determines whether a referral to a physician is in order. On occasion, clients have already been diagnosed with an Axis I disorder, and are taking prescription psychotropic medication. Otherwise, clients whom the therapist believes should be evaluated for psychotropic medication are referred to their primary care physician for depressive symptoms or a psychiatrist if bipolar disorder symptoms are identified. Psychiatric specialists are not plentiful in our area, so an initial consultation with a psychiatrist may take as long as two to six months to accomplish. Research recommends psychotropic medication with psychotherapy as the most beneficial therapeutic combination (Beck, 1985; Frank, Karp, and Rush, 1993).

Until they are stable and capable of coherent thought, psychotic individuals would be inappropriate for RE family therapy. Likewise, individuals plagued with depressive and/or suicidal symptoms may not be able to reap the variety of benefits offered by RE family therapy. For example, one partner of a couple seeking therapy was determined to be suffering from depressive symptoms that interfered with the RE family therapy experience. Although the partner faithfully attempted the tasks, little progress was made. Finally, the therapist suggested to the client resistant to medication intervention that she simply experiment with the medication for a month if her physician agreed. Within three weeks, there had been a positive response to a specific serotonin reuptake inhibitor (SSRI), as evidenced by the client conceding, "As I was driving home the other day, I had a rational thought." Progress in RE family therapy became evident once she felt less depressed and was able to focus on issues other than escaping the intense emotional difficulties with defensive reactions

Some research suggests that medication can assist individuals with personality disorders toward increased adjustment (Kellner, 1986; Klein, 1989). Clients with NPD may suffer from depressive symptoms and may be less able to focus on therapeutic issues until the symptoms are ameliorated. Thus RE family therapy combined with psychotropic medication may result in better biological functioning and psychological adjustment for the partner with NPD.

CULTURAL AND GENDER ISSUES

Since communication is a basic skill across all cultures, RE family therapy is appropriate for most cultures. However, some cultures subscribe to very defined and rigid gender roles. For example, cultures described as more patriarchal may view the thoughts or feelings of the female partner as inconsequential. Although such a stance is challenging, the RE family therapist can frequently encourage active listening and empathic responding as a way to improve the relationship.

For example, even a male partner who believes that women are to be submissive, but has come for therapy because his marriage is in trouble, might be willing to listen and attempt to understand his wife's dissatisfaction in order to save the marriage. Likewise, his wife may begin to understand the consequences he perceives if his marriage does not follow the hierarchical norm for his culture. The application of the RE family therapy approach may contribute to the development of a more egalitarian relationship that is satisfying to both partners.

Harman and Waldo (2001) previously noted that many clients, particularly female clients, have experienced abuse. From the object-relations perspective, these women may be stuck in developmental limbo when it comes to relationships. In fact, they tend to re-create relationships similar to those experienced in earlier developmental periods when they marry or become romantically involved. As in earlier periods, these clients have had little opportunity to have their thoughts, feelings, and experiences validated. In addition, women in the world, particularly those from some traditional cultures, tend to have their views minimized or discounted by men who are more privileged or powerful.

Since RE family therapy emphasizes respectful listening and validation of others' communicated messages, previously abused or discounted individuals may experience a positive therapeutic effect. The structured nature of RE family therapy encourages both partners to fully express their viewpoints and allows both genders to speak and be heard. If gender inequalities are communicated, the therapist can remain nonjudgmental and assist the couple to explore the feelings and thoughts associated with such inequalities. The burden is placed on the couple to explore their issues, be heard and understood by each other, and determine what actions would be necessary for mutual satisfaction. If one partner remains rigid and makes demands rather than requests, then RE family therapy may help the conflicting issues emerge, but may not be successful in a positive resolution. Individual sessions or other approaches may be necessary until both partners are able to hear and respond to the expressions and requests of the other. Typically, however, a negotiated middle ground that uses characteristics of solution-focused therapy (O'Hanlon and Weiner-Davis, 1989) may transcend the impasse.

FUTURE DIRECTIONS

Although this case study indicates some success in using RE family therapy with couples in which one partner has been diagnosed with NPD, research with this diagnosis and this modality is lacking. Case studies indicate that RE family therapy can be effective for couples in which one partner suffers from NPD or even BPD, but to date no controlled research studies of RE family therapy as a treatment for such couples and their families have been conducted.

A wealth of research reports successful intervention with RE family therapy, but research with various cultures and families of homogeneous as well as heterogeneous ethnic origins is still needed. Likewise, few studies have been conducted on using RE family therapy with varying sexual orientations and alternative committed relationships—an increasing variant in today's society. Yet increased numbers of couples in committed homosexual relationships are seeking family counseling to improve interaction and communication, as well as preserve the relationship in times of crisis. Some research has been reported on using RE family therapy with mothers and daughters, but studies with various parent-child associations and sibling relationships that appear in original nuclear families and blended families is lacking.

The current therapists have found that RE family therapy is invaluable in assisting individuals with personality disorders to continue development in the areas of differentiation and boundaries with self-others. Improved communication skills allow individuals to experience increasingly successful interpersonal relationships inside and outside the family. Still, more specific research to document this as an outcome of RE family therapy is needed.

REFERENCES

American Psychiatric Association (1980). *Diagnostic and statistical manual of mental disorders*, Third edition. Washington, DC: American Psychiatric Association.

American Psychiatric Association (2000). *Diagnostic and statistical manual of mental disorders*, Fourth edition, Text revision. Washington, DC: American Psychiatric Association.

Beck, A. T. (1985). Is behavior therapy on course? *Behavioral Psychotherapy, 13*, 83-84.

Bellak, J. (1993). *The T. A. T., C. A. T., and S. A. T. in clinical use*, Sixth edition. Orlando, FL: Grune and Stratton.

Brock, G. W. and Joanning, H. (1983). A comparison of the relationship enhancement program and the Minnesota couples communication program. *Journal of Marital and Family Therapy, 9*, 413-421.

Frank, E., Karp, J. F., and Rush, A. (1993). Efficacy of treatment for major depression. *Psychopharmacology Bulletin, 29*, 457-475.

Freud, S. ([1914] 1971). On narcissism: An introduction. In S. Frued. *The standard edition of the complete pyschological works of Sigmund Freud* (Volume 14) (pp. 67-102). London: Hogarth Press.

Gottman, J. M. and DeClaire, J. (2001). *The relationship cure*. New York: Crown.

Granvold, D. K. (1983). Structured separation for marital treatment and decision-making. *Journal of Marital and Family Therapy, 9*, 403-412.

Guerney, B. G. Jr. (1977). *Relationship enhancement: Skill-training programs for therapy, problem prevention, and enrichment*. San Francisco: Jossey-Bass.

Guerney, B. G. Jr. (1981). Marital and family relationship enhancement therapy. *The Relationship, 7*, 9-11.

Guerney, B. G. Jr. (1987). *Relationship enhancement marital/family therapists' manual*. Silver Spring, MD: Ideals.

Hamilton, E. (1942). *Mythology*. Boston, MA: Little, Brown & Company.

Harman, M. J. and Waldo, M. (2001). Family treatement of borderline personality disorder through relationship enhancement therapy. In M. M. MacFarlane (Ed.), *Family therapy and mental health: Innovations in theory and practice* (pp. 215-232). Binghamton, NY: The Haworth Press, Inc.

Harman, M. J., Waldo, M., and Johnson, J. A. (1994). Relationship enhancement therapy: A case study for treatment of vaginismus. *The Family Journal, 2*(2), 122-128.

Harman, M. J., Waldo, M., and Johnson, J. A. (1998). The sexually dysfunctional couple: Vaginismus and relationship enhancement therapy. In J. Carson and L. Sperry (Eds.), *The disordered couple* (pp. 83-95). Bristol, PA: Brunner/Mazel.

Horwitz, L., Gabbard, G. O., Allen, J. G., Frieswyk, S. H., Colson, D. B., Newsom, G. E., and Coyne, L. (1996). *Borderline personality disorder: Tailoring the psychotherapy to the patient.* Washington, DC: American Psychiatric Press.

Jessee, R. E. and Guerney, B. G. Jr. (1981). A comparison of gestalt and relationship enhancement treatments with married couples. *American Journal of Family Therapy, 9,* 31-41.

Jones, E. (1913). The God complex: The belief that one is God, and the resulting character traits. In E. Jones (Ed.), *Essays in applied psychoanalysis,* Volume 2 (pp. 244-265). London: Hogarth Press, 1951.

Kalogjera, I. J., Jacobson, G R., Hoffman, G. K., Hoffman, P., Raffe, I. H., White, H. C., and Leonard-White, A. (1998). The narcissistic couple. In J. Carson and L. Sperry (Eds.), *The disordered couple* (pp. 207-238). Bristol, PA: Brunner/Mazel.

Kellner, R. (1986). Personality disorders. *Psychotherapy and Psychosomatics, 46*(1-2), 58-66.

Kernberg, O. (1970). Factors in the psychoanalytic treatment of narcissistic personalities. *Journal of the American Psychoanalytic Association, 18,* 51-85.

Kernberg, O. (1974). Further contributions to the treatment of narcissistic personalities. *International Journal of Psycho-Analysis, 55,* 215-240.

Kernberg, O. (1975). *Borderline conditions and pathological narcissism.* New York: Jason Aronson.

Klein, R. (1989). Pharmacotherapy of the borderline personality disorder. In J. F. Masterson and R. Klein (Eds.), *Psychotherapy of the disorders of the self: The Masterson approach* (pp. 365-394). New York: Brunner-Routledge.

Kohut, H. (1971). *The analysis of self.* New York: International University Press.

Kohut, H. (1977). *The restoration of the self.* New York: International University Press.

Kurtz, R. R. (1996). The Cinderella syndrome revisited: Intrapsychic and interpersonal dysfunction and marital conflict. *Journal of Psychological Practice, 2*(3), 13-21.

Lachar, D. (1974). *The MMPI: Clinical assessment and automated interpretation.* Los Angeles: Wester Psychological Services.

Lachkar, J. (1984). Narcissistic/borderline couples: A psychoanalytic perspective to family therapy. *International Journal of Family Psychiatry, 5,* 169-189.

Lachkar, J. (1985). Narcissistic/borderline couples: Theoretical implications for treatment. *Dynamic Psychotherapy, 3,* 109-127.

Lachkar, J. (1986). Narcissistic/borderline couples: Implications for mediation. *Conciliation Courts Review, 24,* 31-43.

Lachkar, J. (1992). *The narcissistic/borderline couple: A psychoanalytic perspective to marital conflict.* New York: Brunner/Mazel.

Lachkar, J. (1998). Narcissistic/borderline couples: A psychodynamic approach to conjoint treatment. In J. Carson and L. Sperry (Eds.), *The disordered couple* (pp. 259-284). Bristol, PA: Brunner/Mazel.

Lansky, M. (1981). Treatment of the narcissistically vulnerable marriage. In M. Lansky (Ed.), *Family therapy and major psychopathology* (pp. 163-183). New York: Grune and Stratton.

Lansky, M. (1993). Family genesis of aggression. *Psychiatric Annals, 23*(9), 494-499.

Mahler, M. S., Pine, F., and Bergman, A. (1975). *The psychological birth of the human infant: Symbiosis and individuation.* New York: Basic Books.

Marshall, M. J. and Larimer, D. M. (1995). The Cinderella syndrome. *Journal of Psychological Practice, 1*, 67-71.

McWilliams, N. and Lependorf, S. (1990). Narcissistic pathology of everyday life: The denial of remorse and gratitude. *Contemporary Psychoanalysis, 25*, 430-451.

Meyer, R. G. and Deitsch, S. E. (1996). *The clinician's handbook: Integrated diagnostic, assessment, and intervention in adult and adolescent psychopathology,* Fourth edition. Boston: Allyn and Bacon.

Moore, B. E. and Fine, B. D. (1990). *Psychoanalytic terms and concepts.* New Haven: The American Psychoanalytic Association and Yale University Press.

O'Hanlon, W. and Weiner-Davis, M. (1989). *In search of solutions: A new direction in psychotherapy.* New York: Norton.

Ornstein, P. H. and Kay, J. (1990). Development of psychoanalytic self psychology: A historical conceptual overview. In A. Tasman, S. J. Goldfinger, and C. A. Kaufmann (Eds.), *Review of psychiatry,* Volume 9 (pp. 303-322). Washington, DC: American Psychiatric Press.

Quadrio, C. (1982). The Peter Pan and Wendy syndrome: A marital dynamic. *Australian and New Zealand Journal of Psychiatry, 16*, 23-28.

Raskin, R. and Novacek, J. (1991). Narcissism and the use of fantasy. *Journal of Clinical Psychology, 47*, 490-499.

Ridley, C. A., Jorgensen, S. R., Morgan, A. C., and Avery, A. W. (1982). Relationship enhancement with premarital couples: An enhancement of effects on relationship quality. *American Journal of Family Therapy, 10*, 41-48.

Rogers, C. R. (1961). *On becoming a person: A therapist's view of psychotherapy.* Boston: Houghton Mifflin.

Shafer, R. (1954). *Psychoanalytic interpretation in Rorschach testing.* New York: International Universities Press.

Snyder, M. (1994). Couple therapy with narcissistically vulnerable clients: Using the relationship enhancement model. *Family Journal: Counseling and Therapy for Couples and Families, 2*, 27-35.

Snyder, M. (2000). The loss and recovery of erotic intimacy in primary relationships: Narrative therapy and relationship enhancement therapy. *Family Journal: Counseling and Therapy for Couples and Families, 8*, 37-46.

Solomon, M. F. (1989). *Narcissism and intimacy: Love and marriage in an age of confusion.* New York: Norton.

Solomon, M. F. (1998). Treating narcissistic and borderline couples. In J. Carson and L. Sperry (Eds.), *The disordered couple* (pp. 239-257). Bristol, PA: Brunner/Mazel.

Waldo, M. and Harman, M. J. (1993). Relationship enhancement therapy with borderline personality. *The Family Journal, 1,* 25-30.

Waldo, M. and Harman, M. J. (1998). Borderline personality disorder and relationship enhancement marital therapy. In J. Carlson and L. Sperry (Eds.), *The disordered couple* (pp. 285-297). Bristol, PA: Brunner/Mazel.

Chapter 12

Couples Therapy with a Paranoid Personality-Disordered Client

Paul S. Links
Michelle Stockwell

INTRODUCTION

Paranoid personality disorder falls within the odd-eccentric cluster of personality disorders as described in the *Diagnostic and Statistical Manual of Mental Disorders,* Fourth Edition (DSM-IV) (American Psychiatric Association, 1994), and the diagnosis has appeared in each version of the DSM (Fulton and Winokur, 1993). These individuals are characterized by being socially isolated and feeling alienated from others. In this respect, individuals with paranoid personality disorder, or the other personality disorders in the odd cluster, rarely present for couples or family therapy. Torgersen, Kringlen, and Cramer, (2001) completed the most thorough community prevalence survey of personality disorders in Oslo, Norway, and found that paranoid personality disorder was the second most common personality disorder after avoidant personality disorder. From their survey, the weighted prevalence of paranoid personality disorder was 2.4 percent. However, this prevalence is considerably higher than prevalence estimates that include results from American studies. Weissman (1993) concluded that paranoid personality disorder might be found in 0.4 to 1.8 percent of the general population. Regardless, this diagnosis is relatively common in inpatient psychiatric hospital settings, where it is estimated that 10 to 30 percent of patients meet criteria for paranoid personality disorder. In outpatient settings, it is estimated that approximately 10 percent of outpatients meet this diagnosis.

Paranoid personality disorder was found to be equally common in men and women, and the diagnosis was not related to any particular period of adulthood (Torgersen, Kringlen, and Cramer, 2001). Respondents with a high school education or less were more likely to be diagnosed with paranoid personality disorder than those with post-secondary education (Torgersen, Kringlen, and Cramer, 2001). Individuals who are living without a partner were more likely to be diagnosed with paranoid personality disorder compared to those in an intimate relationship (Torgersen, Kringlen, and Cramer, 2001). Cultural and community characteristics might well be important risk factors that alter the prevalence of paranoid personality disorder. As discussed, Scandinavians and Northern Europeans appear to have higher community prevalence rates of paranoid personality disorder than North American communities. Living in a crowded urban center compared to the outskirts of the city was related to being diagnosed with paranoid personality disorder (Torgersen, Kringlen, and Cramer, 2001). The anomie or isolation of the crowded inner city or the experience of being a new immigrant in a foreign culture might increase the risk for the development of paranoid features in vulnerable individuals.

Although paranoid personality disorder is classified as a personality disorder, increasing attention is given to its relationship to Axis I disorders. Some writers have considered paranoid personality disorder to be part of a paranoid spectrum that ranges from paranoid personality disorder through delusion disorder to paranoid schizophrenia (Sperry, 1995). Researchers have suggested that a familial/genetic relationship exists between paranoid personality disorder and schizophrenia and paranoid psychotic disorders (Siever and Davis, 1991). Studies examining the prevalence of paranoid personality disorder in the families of patients diagnosed with schizophrenia versus matched controls have found mixed results. However, most of these studies have confirmed an increased prevalence of schizotypal personality disorder in the relatives of patients with schizophrenia (Asarnow et al., 2001). Fulton and Winokur (1993) examined family members of patients with paranoid and schizoid personality disorders and failed to find differences in either paranoid or schizoid traits among the respective family members. Follow-up studies are needed to clarify whether patients with paranoid personality disorder might deteriorate to the point where psychotic disorders are manifest as part of the natural history of this disorder. Fulton and Winokur (1993) assembled a cohort of seventeen previously hospitalized subjects with a discharge diagnosis of paranoid personality disorder, but were able to obtain follow-up information on only seven (41 percent) of the subjects at a mean of 7.3 months. The authors found that all seven patients were stable from discharge, and no rehospitalizations were reported.

This suspected association to Axis I or clinical disorders is of relevance to the marital therapist. First, these individuals, perhaps because of their temperamental difficulties, can deteriorate under stress. Under stress, the individual with paranoid personality disorder may progress from paranoid ideation to frank delusions. In addition, clinical disorders can coexist with this personality disorder. Later in this chapter, we present a case example of the relevance of the clinical disorder to the management of these patients. Resolution of the clinical disorder can lead to improvement in their relationship functioning.

This chapter reviews the relationship characteristics of this disorder, discusses assessment issues, outlines a treatment approach and highlights a case example of marital intervention with a spouse who had paranoid personality disorder, and reviews some of the particular management issues that might arise during the treatment of a spouse with paranoid personality disorder.

IMPACT ON THE FAMILY

Individuals with paranoid personality disorder are characterized as being distrustful, secretive, and argumentative, and can be authoritarian in their relationships. Sperry (1995) states that these individuals often perceive situations correctly, but their judgment and interpretation of the situations are impaired. In a relationship, the individual with paranoid personality disorder may demonstrate considerable jealously and anger. These affective responses can place great strain on the nonparanoid spouse, who may be characterized as being rather passive in contrast to the controlling and dominating spouse with paranoid personality disorder (Harbir, 1981).

Paranoid personality disorder features make it difficult for these individuals to have relationships. They can often be isolated and very distrustful of everyone. However, they may have the ability to form a relationship, and in our experience these relationships can be highly interdependent. Once establishing some trust, paranoid individuals show an enmeshed attachment style. These patients are known to become highly dependent in a therapeutic relationship. Compared to those without the disorder, patients with paranoid personality disorder are at increased risk to demonstrate dependent personality disorder or dependent traits (Skodol, Gallaher, and Oldham, 1996). Part of their nature of interacting demonstrates covert or overt controlling behaviors, and these behaviors may be an important part of what they use to maintain the relationship. They may have had a parental figure who was hypercritical, and with whom, in spite of the constant criticism, they show a strong identification. They attempt to deal with a world that they expect to be hypercritical by being defensive in return. Beneath their defensive stance, they may desire to be understood, but have a strong conviction that this will never happen. As a result, they feel isolated and alienated.

Individuals with paranoid personality disorder often demonstrate skill deficits in the way they process their environment. They tend to have dichotomous thinking and selective attention to environmental stimuli, and they overgeneralize from one interaction to all interactions.

SETTING

Patients with paranoid personality disorder are likely to be referred to us when their relationship is threatened and the marriage is in crisis. Our clinical setting is an office-based practice specializing in couples and family therapy. We work closely with community family physicians in a middle-class suburban area. We are married and most often work as a co-therapy team. This was true of the case example provided in this chapter. Our unique working relationship was important to the assessment and engagement of the couple presented in our case example. Given that we are a married couple, we are open about our bias toward marriage and the importance of this formal commitment. The couple in the example found this very reassuring and supportive of their own goals. Having two therapists present was also important in preventing distortions and misperceptions from developing. In a later section, we will discuss how the transference relationship might be diffused in couples therapy compared to individual therapy.

TREATMENT MODEL

Patients with paranoid personality disorder rarely present for couples therapy. We illustrate our model and intervention principles with a case example that is a synthesis of a few cases drawn from our practice. Our model of therapy in the case to be presented was informed by the concepts of psychodynamic theory and self-psychology, in particular. However, our interventions are not limited to modifying defenses and encouraging insight. We see therapy progressing through a series of stages integrating psychodynamic and cognitive-behavioral strategies.

INITIAL ASSESSMENT

Our assessment process begins with a history-taking session with the couple and ourselves. We then complete an individual assessment with each of the spouses, and allow them to choose who they want to see for this single session. The couple is informed that no secrets will be kept and that everything discussed during the individual sessions will be used for the purposes of our couples assessment. Our assessment is completed by a feedback session with the couple when we present our formulation of the problems and outline an approach to treatment. We ask at the completion of this session for the couple's agreement and verbal commitment to a treatment contract.

Paranoid patients' style during the assessment interview is to attack before being attacked. Spouses with paranoid personality disorder will demonstrate cognitive distortions, and their misperceptions of interpersonal interactions will be uncovered by reviewing the history of their significant relationships. Paranoid patients will tend to project, which can be easily detected, and will be confirmed by input from their partner. Paranoid patients tend to be distrustful of the therapist, so the therapist should maintain a professional demeanor and not demonstrate any familiarity with the couple. In addition, the therapist should be very predictable, since unexpected situations or responses may increase the paranoia and drive these patients out of therapy.

As stated previously, attention has to be given to whether a coexisting Axis I disorder is present when seeing a patient with paranoid personality disorder. Some of the more common Axis I disorders that may coexist include delusion disorder, schizophrenia or schizophreniform psychosis, major depression, obsessive-compulsive disorder, and agoraphobia (American Psychiatric Association, 1994). The recognition of these disorders is important because treatment of the coexisting disorder will be crucial. Although not an example of couples therapy, the following case illustrates the need for an accurate assessment and appropriate treatment.

Mr. A had seen Dr. Links for an individual assessment during a psychiatric inpatient admission. He had been charged with attempted murder of his spouse. Mr. A gave a history of an individual with a paranoid personality disorder who had always expressed some jealousy toward his wife's interactions with other men. She became at risk when the patient became depressed and his jealousy developed into frank delusions. The patient developed an elaborate delusional system about his wife's infidelity. Acting on his false beliefs, and fearing that his wife's "lover" wanted him exterminated, he made an attempt on her life. With appropriate treatment of his psychotic depression, the patient's paranoid delusions resolved, and his paranoid character returned to its baseline level.

Patients with paranoid personality disorder may have features of other personality disorders, including narcissistic, borderline, avoidant, dependent, or schizotypal personality disorders. The assessment can focus on attempting to highlight the relationship features and the defensive style of projection in particular. The optimal diagnostic criterion to look for when assessing the spouse with possible paranoid personality disorder is that the patient "suspects, without sufficient basis, that others are exploiting, harming, or deceiving him or her" (reprinted with permission from p. 637 of the *Diagnostic and Statistical Manual of Mental Disorders,* Fourth Edition, copyright 1994 American Psychiatric Association). If this single characteristic is present, then the therapist can have more certainty of the diagnosis and can try to confirm the other DSM characteristics of paranoid personality disorder as the assessment is completed (Allnutt and Links, 1996).

A Psychodynamic Orientation

When severe individual personality pathology is found in one of the spouses presenting for couples therapy, psychodynamic theory can powerfully explain the current crisis. Early formulations of paranoid conditions stressed libidinal or aggressive drives (Aronson, 1989). However, more recently, theorists have understood that paranoid conditions arise from the activation of pathological narcissism (Garfield and Havens, 1991). Kohut (1971) revised our understanding of the developmental role of narcissism, and narcissism was seen as subserving the development and operation of the self. The self was made secure by the "strands of narcissism" that connect to the internal psychic operations. Kohut (1971) viewed a paranoid perspective as emerging from a fragmentation of self. An individual made vulnerable by empathic failures during early development might obtain a sense of equilibrium by the "mastery and control" of self-objects. The self-object describes the role that other persons perform in order that the patient can maintain psychological integrity. However, the other persons are not regarded as separate individuals, but as objects to gratify these needs of the self (Gabbard, 1990). The paranoid patient is in crisis when the control of others, such as a spouse, to sustain self-security is no longer possible or perceived as possible (Aronson, 1989). Garfield and Havens (1991) pointed out that the central issue for the paranoid patient is a mistrust of self. Accordingly, the paranoid patient rejects the painful, victimizing part of himself or herself and projects these aspects externally. For the paranoid individual, the self is experienced as weak, deficient, and vulnerable. Therefore, when the paranoid patient relinquishes his or her paranoid stance, severe depression might ensue (Aronson, 1989).

Stages of Treatment

Our therapy model conceptualizes four steps:

1. Assessment of the individual personalities and their pathologies;
2. Stabilization of the crisis by helping the couple to reestablish and express their commitment to the relationship;
3. Reworking aspects of their mutual projective identifications, and having the spouses own some of the defended-against emotion; and

4. Utilizing cognitive-behavioral or other strategies to lessen the couple's personal vulnerabilities. In the following case, for example, the wife is supported to be more assertive and set limits on her husband's behavior. With the husband feeling more supported, he is able to accept the need for antidepressant medication.

With a disorder of this severity, the first task in determining the appropriateness of couples therapy is to rule out delusional symptoms. Gunderson, Links, and Reich (1991) and Millon (1996) consider paranoid personality disorder to be among the most severe of the character disorders. We reported research data that indicated that paranoid personality traits in previously hospitalized psychiatric patients were significant predictors of the level of personality psychopathology, including dependent, histrionic, and passive-aggressive traits reported seven to ten years later (Links, Heslegrave, and van Reekum, 1998). These data are felt to underscore the severity and poor prognosis associated with this disorder. It is sometimes very difficult to establish a treatment alliance because of the nature and severity of the pathology. In such cases, couples therapy is contraindicated. Salzman (1980) suggested that the therapist has to be very benign and present himself or herself as the "friendly helper." Early interventions have to be well timed and occur after some sense of safety has been established for the patient.

To stabilize the presenting crisis, the therapist can identify the pattern of withdrawal and passivity in the nonparanoid spouse. Typically, as stress increases, the paranoid spouse becomes hypercritical, argumentative, and drives away the nonparanoid spouse. In response, the nonparanoid spouse becomes less communicative, and more secretive, and this aggravates the spousal dynamic. Early interventions can be aimed at trying to break this cycle. Attempts can be made to foster areas where some acknowledgment and validation of each other's feelings exists. This validation can often strengthen the attachment bond. With strengthening of the attachment bond, the couple may feel safer and more able to tackle long-standing issues.

Individuals with paranoid personality disorder need help first to feel safe, and then steps may be needed to decrease the level of stress that is aggravating their cognitive distortions. With the establishment of some stability in the relationship, attention can be turned to deficits in skills. Patients with paranoid personality disorder may benefit from empathy training to improve their ability to place themselves in their partner's shoes. Attempts can be made to decrease their reliance on dichotomous thinking and their readiness to react defensively to any assertion. Some assertiveness communication training can be helpful, and this is likely to be of benefit to both the paranoid and nonparanoid spouse.

CASE EXAMPLE

Mr. and Mrs. B were in their late forties when they presented because of Mr. B's fears that his wife was being unfaithful. The crisis had occurred at an out-of-town business convention, when the wife had been approached by another man for a dance at a gala reception. This single act led the paranoid spouse, Mr. B, to reinterpret a number of different incidents during their trip. His anger amplified, as did his verbal abuse. Some weeks later, Mr. B decided that his wife was not to be trusted, and he threatened separation. However, his distress increased even further when his wife felt that she was ready to consider separation. He suggested that they seek marital counseling.

The couple had a long history of tension and arguing, but in spite of this they had a very stable marriage of more than twenty years. Mr. B had a long history of being degrading, irritable, and argumentative toward his wife, and in the community he was characterized as a very difficult person. However, the couple denied a history of physical violence. Mr. B's verbal abuse and denigrating behavior alternated with episodes of extreme generosity. He would often express his caring and affection for his wife through his generosity, his gift giving, and his attentiveness.

The couple described significant marital problems in the past, however, this coincided with a period when Mr. B was depressed and underwent treatment for depression. He responded well, and the marriage seemed to settle. Both spouses had come from troubled backgrounds. Mr. B had suffered physical and emotional abuse at the hands of his father. However, he strongly identified with his father, had taken up a business career, and opened his own business in a closely related field. Mrs. B had also had a difficult childhood. She had to take on parental responsibilities from a young age, and had always been a self-sacrificing and dutiful person.

The couple had always been very dependent on each other. They engaged in few activities separately. They owned their own business—the wife working under her husband's supervision. They had obtained some significant financial success with their business, yet Mr. B always felt that the "wolves were at the door." He was particularly fearful of government intervention that would destroy his business more so than that of his competitors.

The couple had one son who was in his early twenties and lived in a nearby community. Mrs. B was quite close to her son, and was very dedicated to him. Mr. B had also been close to his son, and being very career oriented he was preoccupied with his son's success. In the past couple of years, conflict had increased between Mr. B and his son. The son had chosen a related career path, but had refused offers to enter the family business. At the time they presented, the father-son relationship was characterized by significant stress, and Mr. B had refused for many months to communicate with his son. Mrs. B continued to see her son, but avoided any reference to him when speaking with her husband.

The therapists' first step after hearing the history was to try to reestablish some sense of safety and security. We acknowledged that the couple had been under stress from a number of fronts, including business stress and the difficulties with their son. As we relabeled the crisis, Mrs. B felt less irritable and became less withdrawn. Her more acknowledging approach to her husband increased his sense of security. He began to accept that his wife experienced many of the same stresses that he experienced. He was particularly gratified when the couple was able to share their perceptions about the business. Mr. B was surprised to hear that she also recognized the external threats, and that they shared many of the same views about the threats. As a result of their increased stability and feelings of safety, the couple made some significant gains at demonstrating more generosity and closeness. This improvement, in fact, was a reflection of a cycle they had gone through many times. However, it did resolve the presenting crisis.

With more stability, and with Mr. B feeling less alienated, Mrs. B was able to confront her husband about some of his behaviors. He felt most able to listen with regard to the situation at work. Mrs. B confronted him with his irritability and his degradation of her at work. He was able to see how this could be humiliating, and also understood how it may scare off customers. As a result, Mr. B resolved to make some change in his attitudes and behaviors at work.

Over this period of time, Mr. B was able to acknowledge that he had symptoms of depression. With increased trust, we were able to get him to consider the need for another trial of antidepressants, which he pursued with his family doctor. In addition, Mr. and Mrs. B began to look at ways of decreasing their life stress. They felt pessimistic about major changes in their work life, but they were able to take on more leisure activities. Despite the couple's progress and their feeling of greater mutual safety, they were still somewhat guarded with the therapists. We clearly perceived that certain areas were "off limits," which the couple refused to explore in therapy. One such area was the unresolved conflict with the son.

The couple continued to cycle through periods of crisis but they were able to return to their comfort and stability. Fewer threats of possible separation were made, and, in general, the intensity of their crises was less. Mrs. B was able to be more assertive with her husband and limit his abuse at work. She also was more able to accept his kindness and generosity. The couple eventually terminated therapy feeling that no more gains could be made.

Some years later, Mrs. B returned asking for some individual help. Things had markedly deteriorated over the past several months. Her husband had suffered a stroke, and had some residual brain damage. His ability to ambulate was restricted, and he was physically more dependent on his wife. In addition, Mrs. B had experienced increased anger and irritability, which partly seemed related to the loss of his mental function. The stroke coincided with the revelation that Mr. B had been having a long-standing affair with a neighbor. Mrs. B learned about this affair at the time of his illness. Apparently, it had been ongoing for years without her knowledge.

Mrs. B presented feeling unable to approach her husband. She felt angry and humiliated by the revelation of the affair. She particularly felt the humiliation that her friends and neighbors had known about this long before she did. However, she remained committed to the marriage. This commitment partly originated from her desire to try to salvage the family, and she had renewed attempts at drawing the son back into the family as the father's health deteriorated. Mrs. B was given acknowledgment for her anger as an appropriate and understandable response. She was given permission to care for herself and ask for others to assist her in her caregiving role. She was able, with this support, to carry on in the marriage.

In our case example of Mr. and Mrs. B, the husband has a deflated self-esteem and sense of security because of a growing distance between himself and his son. He experiences a loss of control because he fears for his business operation due to the external threats from government regulators. Of course, part of husband's vulnerability arises from his biological propensity for bouts of clinical depression. In spite of all this, he can maintain himself until he perceives the loss of his central self-object relationship. He misperceives his wife's friendliness during a social event at a business convention as a sexual advance to another man. Although the wife is typically controlled and victimized by her husband's verbal abuse, she asserts herself against his irrational accusations. The husband's paranoia intensifies. Threatened by the loss of his marriage, the husband accepts the need for therapy.

Mrs. B is a woman who understands self-sacrifice. She typically accepts her husband's emotional abuse in return for the security he provides. He is an excellent provider for the family, and periodically expresses his adoration for his wife. However, Mrs. B is also bound by her sense of powerlessness and vulnerability, which she projects onto her husband. Their mutual projective identifications provide the dependency and security to cement their marriage (Middelberg, 2001).

This couple never progressed in therapy to the stage of examining their mutual projective identifications. We experienced Mr. B as controlling the level of exploration, particularly when we touched on issues related to his estranged son. We felt Mrs. B was content to avoid confronting the issue because she was afraid of losing her contact with her son. Mr. B, in our formulation, saw his son as betraying him by working in a related field, but refusing to join the family business. Not only did Mr. B experience betrayal, but he perceived his son as a potential competitor, perhaps "one of the wolves at the door." To deal with his emotional turmoil, Mr. B chose to avoid all contact with his son. We decided to honor the couple's unspoken compromise. However, in retrospect, some of the resistance was related to Mr. B's secret affair. No doubt, he controlled the therapy to avoid exposure about his infidelity. Instead, he manifested a projection of infidelity toward his wife. We hypothesize that given the severity of his paranoid character pathology, a limited therapy contract was realistic and deeper psychological changes to his character defenses and self-objects were probably not possible.

STRENGTHS AND LIMITATIONS

Our model was informed by psychodynamic theory, and although a rich history supports these constructs, no empirical evidence validates our psychodynamic understanding of paranoid personality disorder. In addition, despite meta-analytic reviews confirming the benefits of marital and family therapy in severe mental illness, including schizophrenia and affective disorders (Pinsoff and Wynne, 1995; Prince and Jacobson, 1995), no research studies have examined the benefits of marital and family therapy with the families of individuals diagnosed as having paranoid personality disorder. Therefore, our model awaits confirmation based on empirical investigation.

Our model incorporates strategies from both insight-oriented approaches and cognitive behavioral therapies. Some readers might consider this integration as a limitation of our model. However, we have adopted an "integrated psychotherapy" approach in our work with personality-disordered clients, and this approach has been considered by Winston and Winston (2001) to offer clients "maximum therapeutic benefit from psychotherapy" (p. 382). In integrated psychotherapy, the therapist selectively uses interventions from different conceptual models to maximize the therapeutic benefits rather than rely on one model alone (Winston and Winston, 2001). The psychotherapeutic model is chosen based on the patient's position on the psychotherapy continuum: a continuum that characterizes a patient based on their level of psychopathology, level of impairments, adaptive capacity, self-concept, and ability to relate to others (Winston and Winston, 2001).

BENEFITS FOR THE FAMILY

Psychoeducational interventions with the family members of individuals with schizophrenia and major affective disorder have been shown to improve the course of these disorders. These approaches are being adapted for the families of patients with borderline personality disorder and are currently being studied (Ruiz-Sancho, Smith, and Gunderson, 2001). Family interventions typically are composed of two elements: (1) education regarding the identified patient's disorder, and (2) application of problem-solving strategies to difficulties that arise in the day-to-day life of the family. These elements can be of value to the family members of individuals with paranoid personality disorder.

Our case example demonstrates some of these elements. The spouse is often the recipient of angry projections, and typically he or she identifies with an aspect of the projected anger, thus accepting some of the self-blame and feelings of personal inadequacy. Our intervention strengthened the spouse's reality testing and allowed her to be appropriately assertive with her husband. The spouse's stance ended her withdrawal, which was serving only to aggravate the crisis. Because of the significant risk of comorbid depression in the identified patient, the couple was educated about this likelihood, and was encouraged to seek appropriate treatment. Mrs. B was able to maintain a role in monitoring her husband's symptoms and encouraging compliance with medication and appointments. The intervention stabilized the marital crisis and improved Mrs. B's sense of well-being.

INDICATIONS AND CONTRAINDICATIONS

Couple therapy is indicated for patients with paranoid personality disorder who are involved in a significant attachment relationship. By definition, an attachment relationship should have the primary function of providing comfort and security to the individuals, and the individuals should perceive that the relationship was intended to have an indefinite existence into the future. As with any psychotherapy, the participants must be motivated, demonstrate some ability to tolerate anxiety, and express a willingness to be open and honest. For individuals with personality pathology, Paris (1996) suggested that the person's history of adequate work performance is a good indicator of the individual's ability to benefit from psychotherapy. We have adopted this criterion when we decide on couples therapy with individuals with severe personality disturbances.

Couples therapy is contraindicated when any one of the following three problems are identified. First, if the couple has a history of spousal violence, particularly if it is recent and escalating, then couple therapy is not indicated. Although Tweed and Dutton (1998) characterized abusive men as likely to have antisocial or borderline personality profiles, spouses with paranoid personality disorder may be at particular risk for physical violence toward their partners. Jealousy is easily aroused in paranoid individuals, and they are likely to appraise their spouses' actions as threatening or malevolent. In order to assert their power and control, paranoid spouses threaten or are violent toward their spouse.

In our case example, we carefully inquired about physical violence during both the couples and individual sessions. In spite of there being no physical violence, a verbally and emotionally abusive relationship existed. When assessing a couple with a history of abuse, Goldner (1998) cautions against an "all-or-nothing" response to the application of couple therapy in these situations. In this case, we chose to proceed with couples therapy because the wife was not felt to be at risk of physical violence, the couple was strongly committed to the marriage, and, over the first few sessions, the husband demonstrated a willingness to accept some personal responsibility for his behaviors. Concerns about safety must be addressed during the individual assessment session, and safety must be the first priority. If the risk of violence is real and immediate, we would assist the wife to develop a safety plan, and put her in contact with an assaulted women's helpline or a women's shelter. If, from the assessment of the perpetrator, the risk of violence was more likely than not to occur, a duty to warn would exist, and the police and/or the victim would be notified of the risk.

Third-party involvement is the second contraindication to therapy, and must end if couples are to proceed with couples therapy. Secrets, if known to exist, cannot be allowed if the couple is to work effectively in therapy. Finally, because comorbid disorders are a frequent complication of severe personality disorders, such as paranoid personality disorder, their treatment may take precedence over couples therapy. Severe depression that impairs day-to-day functioning or frank psychosis will have to be treated before couples therapy is indicated.

MANAGEMENT OF TRANSFERENCE ISSUES

To establish a working alliance with a paranoid patient, the therapist must create and maintain a safe interpersonal distance with the patient. The patient's need to regulate his or her interpersonal distance in the marriage is often the underlying conflict that explains the couple's presentation. Middleberg (2001) labels this pattern of interactions as "couple dances." The mutual projective identifications unconsciously protect the spouses from their deep conflict over the need and fear of intimacy. As in our case example, the paranoid spouse is feeling exceptionally vulnerable. He then projects his "badness" or unworthiness onto his spouse. His wife identifies with the lack of self-worth and withdraws her caring and attention. The distance, once created, stimulates separation anxiety in the paranoid spouse. He now becomes open to accepting help and agrees to see a marital therapist. The couples therapist has the distinct advantage of working with the conflicts around intimacy "once removed." In individual therapy, the conflicts with intimacy may be projected onto the therapist, and the potential for a negative transference is very real. In couples therapy, the "bad" self is already split off and projected onto the spouse. This allows the couples therapist to work on these issues in the relationship, and most likely a positive transference will be allowed to develop. In individual therapy with narcissistically vulnerable patients, transference interpretations may be very antitherapeutic. The patient may experience the transference interpretation as "repeating the behavior of a self-centered primary object, always demanding to be the centre of the patient's attention" (Jimenez, 1993, p. 488). Couples therapy might offer the advantage of exploring the conflicts with the patient's disturbed self by working with the mutual projective identifications manifesting in the couple's crisis.

In spite of this, the therapist still must attend to maintaining a safe distance in the therapeutic relationship. With the paranoid patient, the therapist must maintain a professional demeanor and avoid familiarity. The therapist must be very consistent and predictable. Often with paranoid patients, the therapist experiences the patient's need to maintain a safe distance and underestimates the patient's dependence on the therapist. The therapist must be mindful of the extreme dependency when work toward termination is beginning.

MANAGEMENT OF CRISES
AND ACTING-OUT BEHAVIOR

Patients with paranoid personality disorder because of their primitive defensive styles can manifest acting-out behaviors. The acting out may present as either self- or other-directed violent behavior. The patients' projections might intensify to the point that these patients lose touch with reality. The risk of violence could develop because paranoid patients perceive themselves at risk and act out in a psychotic effort to protect themselves. For instance, delusional individuals, such as Mr. A, may attack their spouse because they believe their spouse is conspiring with a lover to harm them. In a delusional state, patients may attack their spouse, believing they are justified in doing so to protect themselves.

The paranoid spouse might be acutely suicidal when the relationship is at risk of disruption. The disruption of the relationship may be real or perceived. Nevertheless, the patient might become acutely suicidal. The therapist must monitor the patient for the risk of suicide and assess him or her for the standard indicators of risk (Bongar, 2002). Some risk factors for an acute risk of suicidal behavior that might be particularly relevant for the paranoid spouse include increased intake of alcohol, access to a means of suicide (e.g., availability of firearms), marked agitation and global insomnia, and the expression of unendurable emotional pain. Many of these risk factors may be modifiable, such as contracting with the patient to avoid alcohol, having the police remove a gun from the home, and seeking medication for treatment of insomnia or agitation. However, if the therapist feels an acute risk of suicide exists and no immediate reduction of the risk is possible, admission to a hospital must be considered. As in every situation involving patients at risk, supervision or consultation with a trusted colleague should be obtained and documented.

Under duress, the paranoid patient can become litigious. The best defense against a threatened legal action will be the therapist's careful documentation in the patient's clinical record. If the therapist has concerns about the case, a formal consultation with a trusted colleague or ongoing peer consultation may be helpful in managing legal, ethical, transferential, or countertransferential issues.

INTEGRATION WITH PSYCHIATRIC SERVICES AND ROLE OF MEDICATION

Given the risk of comorbid Axis I disorders, the patient with paranoid personality disorder is likely to be involved with other treating professionals. The couples therapist must request permission to have ongoing communication with the patient's other care providers. As in our case example, the couples therapist may initiate the referral for the assessment and treatment of the comorbid disorder. Therapists must be knowledgeable and familiar with the psychiatric services in the community if they are engaged in therapy with patients with severe personality pathology.

The therapist should be aware that paranoid personality disorder might be complicated by the development of a severe Axis I disorder, such as a psychotic depression. Although treatable, a psychotic depression typically requires the use of both an antipsychotic and an antidepressant. For example, the combination of olanzapine, a novel antipsychotic, and an antidepressant has been found to be effective for psychotic depression (Rothschild et al., 1999). Patients with psychotic depression take longer to show a response to therapy and if a response to medication is not demonstrated, then ECT is a reasonable and accepted treatment option. To facilitate the patient's recovery, the couple therapist must remain well informed about the recommended treatment for the comorbid Axis I problems.

CULTURAL AND GENDER ISSUES

Little is known about how cultural and gender issues might impact patients with paranoid personality disorder. Research suggests that paranoid personality disorder is equally common in men and women (Torgersen, Kringlen, and Cramer, 2001). In men, the need to control within their relationships may be expressed by violence or threats of violence. One woman that we assessed with paranoid personality disorder manifested her controlling behavior in relationships in a different way. To control her therapists, this patient repeatedly made complaints to various regulatory bodies about each and every counselor she encountered. Paranoid personality disorder is apparently more common among patients that are poorly educated or illiterate (Torgersen, Kringlen, and Cramer, 2001). The therapist has to keep in mind that the patient may be suspicious because of a lack of comprehension. Strategies and reading material must be presented at a level that is appropriate to the patient's capabilities. Asking in a direct and respectful way about the patient's reading and writing ability might prevent some later difficulties that may be labeled as noncompliance.

Differences between the therapist's and the couple's cultural background might lead to guardedness in therapy. If the therapist has little familiarity with the couple's cultural beliefs, he or she can suggest referral to a therapist from the same cultural community or ask the couple to educate the therapist about the differences as the therapy proceeds. Newly arrived immigrants may be at some increased risk to experience paranoid symptoms as they acculturate to a new country with differing gender roles and a new language.

FUTURE DIRECTIONS

The indications and value of couples and family interventions for individuals with severe personality disorders is only beginning to be recognized (Links and Stockwell, 2001, 2002). Although clinicians have long observed the healing aspects of intimate relationships (Lewis, 1998, 2000), these observations have not been translated into empirically proven interventions. However, for patients with paranoid personality disorder who are in intimate relationships, couples interventions might offer efficient and effective ways of intervening to resolve an interpersonal crisis. With further therapy, underlying personality pathology can be addressed and changed. This chapter is presented to raise awareness of couples therapy in the face of severe personality pathology and to encourage further research into its applications with these patients.

In summary, patients with paranoid personality disorder are infrequently seen in couples therapy. However, when seen, their strong attachment needs can often allow them to engage in therapy. The couples therapist must attend to the possibility of coexisting clinical disorders. These disorders must receive treatment. In the face of restabilization of their attachment relationship, paranoid individuals may be able to work on their skill deficits.

REFERENCES

Allnutt, S. and Links, P. S. (1996). Diagnosing specific personality disorders and the optimal criteria. In P. S. Links (Ed.), *Clinical Assessment and Management of Severe Personality Disorders* (pp. 21-47). Washington, DC: American Psychiatric Press, Inc.

American Psychiatric Association (1994). *Diagnostic and Statistical Manual of Mental Disorders*, Fourth Edition. Washington, DC: American Psychiatric Association.

Aronson, T. A. (1989). Paranoia and narcissism in psychoanalytic theory: Contributions of self psychology to the theory and therapy of the paranoid disorders. *Psychoanalytic Review, 76*, 329-351.

Asarnow, R. F., Nuechterlein, K. H., Fogelson, D., Subotnik, K. L., Payne, D. A., Russell, A. T., Asamen, J., Kuppinger, H., and Kendler K. S. (2001). Schizophrenia and schizophrenia-spectrum personality disorders in the first-degree relatives of children with schizophrenia: The UCLA Family Study. *Archives of General Psychiatry, 58*, 581-588.

Bongar, B. (2002). *The Suicidal Patient: Clinical and Legal Standards of Care*, Second Edition. Washington, DC: American Psychological Association.

Fulton, M. and Winokur, G. (1993). A comparative study of paranoid and schizoid personality disorders. *American Journal of Psychiatry, 150*, 1363-1367.

Gabbard, G. O. (1990). *Psychodynamic Psychiatry in Clinical Practice*. Washington, DC: American Psychiatric Press, Inc.

Garfield, D. and Havens, L. (1991). Paranoid phenomena and pathological narcissism. *American Journal of Psychotherapy, 45*(2), 160-172.

Goldner, V. (1998). The treatment of violence and vicitimization in intimate relationships. *Family Process, 37*, 263-286.

Gunderson, J. G., Links, P. S., and Reich, J. H. (1991). Competing models of personality disorder. *Journal of Personality Disorders, 5*, 60-68.

Harbir, H. (1981). Family therapy with personality disorders. In J. Lion (Ed.), *Personality Disorders: Diagnosis and Management*, Second Edition. Baltimore: Williams and Wilkins.

Jimenez, J. P. (1993). A fundamental dilemma of psychoanalytic technique: Reflections on the analysis of a perverse paranoid patient. *International Journal of Psychoanalysis, 74*, 487-504.

Kohut, H. (1971). *The Analysis of the Self*. New York: International Universities Press.

Lewis, J. M. (1998). For better or worse: Interpersonal relationships and individual outcome. *American Journal of Psychiatry, 155*, 582-589.

Lewis, J. M. (2000). Repairing the bond in important relationships: A dynamic for personality maturation. *American Journal of Psychiatry, 157*, 1375-1378.

Links. P. S., Heslegrave, R., and van Reekum, R. (1998). Prospective follow-up study of borderline personality disorder: Prognosis, prediction of outcome and Axis II comorbidity. *Canadian Journal of Psychiatry, 43,* 265-270.

Links, P. S. and Stockwell, M. (2001). Is couple therapy indicated for borderline personality disorder? *American Journal of Psychotherapy, 55,* 491-506.

Links, P. S. and Stockwell, M. (2002). The role of couple therapy in the treatment of narcissistic personality disorder. *American Journal of Psychotherapy, 56*(4), 522-538.

Middelberg, C.V. (2001). Projective identification in common couple dances. *Journal of Marital and Family Therapy, 27,* 341-352.

Millon, T. (1996). *Disorders of Personality: DSM-IV and Beyond,* Second Edition. New York: John Wiley and Sons, Inc.

Paris, J. (1996). *Social Factors in Personality Disorders: A Biopsychosocial Approach to Etiology and Treatment.* Cambridge: Cambridge University Press.

Pinsoff, W. and Wynne, L. (1995). The efficacy of marital and family therapy: Overview and conclusions. *Journal of Marital and Family Therapy, 21,* 585-616.

Prince. S. and Jacobson, N. (1995). A review and evaluation of marital and family therapy for affective disorders. *Journal of Marital and Family Therapy, 21,* 377-402.

Rothschild. A. J., Bates, K. S., Boehringer, K. L., and Syed, A. (1999). Olanzapine response in psychotic depression. *Journal of Clinical Psychiatry, 60,* 116-118.

Ruiz-Sancho. A. M., Smith, G. W., and Gunderson, J. G. (2001). Psychoeducational approaches. In W. J. Livesley (Ed.), *Handbook of Personality Disorders: Theory, Research, and Treatment* (pp. 460-474). New York: The Guilford Press.

Salzman. L. (1980). *Treatment of the Obsessive Personality.* New York: Jason Aronson.

Siever, L. J. and Davis, K. L. (1991). A psychobiological perspective on the personality disorders. *American Journal of Psychiatry, 148,* 1647-1658.

Skodol, A. E., Gallaher, P. E., and Oldham, J. M. (1996). Excessive dependency and depression: Is the relationship specific? *The Journal of Nervous and Mental Disorders, 184,* 165-171.

Sperry, L. (1995). *Handbook of Diagnosis and Treatment of the DSM-IV Personality Disorders.* New York: Brunner/Mazel.

Torgersen, S., Kringlen, E., and Cramer, V. (2001). The prevalence of personality disorders in a community sample. *Archives of General Psychiatry, 58,* 590-596.

Tweed, R. G. and Dutton, D. G. (1998). A comparison of impulsive and instrumental subgroups of batterers. *Violence and Victims, 13,* 217-230.

Weissman, M. M. (1993). The epidemiology of personality disorders: A 1990 update. *Journal of Personality Disorders, 7*(Supplement), 44-62.

Winston, A. and Winston, B. (2001). Toward an integrated brief psychotherapy. *Journal of Psychiatric Practice, 7,* 377-390.

Name Index

Subject Index

CPSIA information can be obtained at www.ICGtesting.com
Printed in the USA
LVOW101243070912

297548LV00009B/4/P